TUMULTUOUS TIMES IN AMERICA'S GAME

TUMULTUOUS TIMES IN AMERICA'S GAME

From Jackie Robinson's Breakthrough to the War over Free Agency

Bryan Soderholm-Difatte

ROWMAN & LITTLEFIELD
Lanham • Boulder • New York • London

Published by Rowman & Littlefield
An imprint of The Rowman & Littlefield Publishing Group, Inc.
4501 Forbes Boulevard, Suite 200, Lanham, Maryland 20706
www.rowman.com

6 Tinworth Street, London SE11 5AL

British Library Cataloguing in Publication Information Available

Library of Congress Cataloging-in-Publication Data

Name: Soderholm-Difatte, Bryan, author.
Title: Tumultuous times in America's game : from Jackie Robinson's breakthrough to the war over free agency / Bryan Soderholm-DiFatte.
Description: Lanham : Rowman & Littlefield, [2019] | Includes bibliographical references and index.
Identifiers: LCCN 2018056384 (print) | LCCN 2019002635 (ebook) | ISBN 9781538127360 (electronic) | ISBN 9781538127353 (cloth : alk. paper)
Subjects: LCSH: Major League Baseball (Organization)—History. | Baseball—United States—History.
Classification: LCC GV863.A1 (ebook) | LCC GV863.A1 S6887 2019 (print) | DDC 796.357/64—dc23
LC record available at https://lccn.loc.gov/2018056384

∞ ™ The paper used in this publication meets the minimum requirements of American National Standard for Information Sciences Permanence of Paper for Printed Library Materials, ANSI/NISO Z39.48-1992.

Printed in the United States of America

To my dad, Nicholas Difatte (1928–2018),
whose love of the game, particularly its history,
was a profound influence on my life.

CONTENTS

PREFACE

When baseball returned to peacetime normality in 1946 after World War II ended, the American League had developed a well-deserved reputation as being superior to the National League by virtually any measure since the current two-league structure of Major League Baseball came into being with its unilateral declaration of major-league status as a start-up in 1901 and the NL's acceptance of the rival league as an equal in Organized Baseball's 1903 National Agreement. While it is true the NL pennant-winner won four of the first six World Series, the American League has dominated the World Series in every decade since. The AL champion beat out its NL counterpart in eight of the 10 World Series between 1910 and 1919, which includes the Chicago White Sox conspiring with gamblers to deliberately lose the 1919 Series. The American League then went 16–10 in the next 26 World Series through the end of World War II, including four in a row from 1927 to 1930 and five straight from 1935 to 1939. As if the American League's 26–16 dominance in World Series play—with a 140–102 record in games—wasn't enough, the AL won eight of the 12 All-Star Games that became an annual midsummer ritual in 1933 (although wartime contingencies precluded its being played in 1945).

The National League's New York Giants and Chicago Cubs fielded consistently good teams most of those years, and the St. Louis Cardinals had since 1926, but the American League could boast of dynasties. The 1910–1914 Philadelphia Athletics won four pennants and three World Series. The Boston Red Sox won four pennants and World Series between 1912 and 1918. Even the 1916–1920 White Sox were arguably a dynasty, despite their 1919 "Black Sox" disgrace. The Athletics won three straight pennants from 1929 to 1931, each with more than 100 wins. And, of course, beginning in 1921, there was the New York Yankees' "forever" dynasty, winners of six pennants and three Fall Classics before that decade ended, another five pennants in the 1930s—all culminating in World Series triumphs—and three more pennants and two World Championships by the time the war came to an end in 1945. The only National League club that could beg for consideration among the best teams in baseball after the turn of the century were the 1906–1910 Cubs, whose achievement of four pennants and two World Series championships in five years is downgraded by some for being in the Deadball Era.

And the American League had by far the superior players in every decade. The NL could brag about Honus Wagner, Christy Mathewson, and Three-Finger Brown in the first decade; the AL could counter with Napoleon Lajoie, Ty Cobb, George Davis, Elmer Flick, Jimmy Collins, Ed Walsh, Addie Joss, Eddie Plank, and Rube Waddell. While Cobb, Tris Speaker, Shoeless Joe Jackson, Eddie Collins, Home Run Baker, George Sisler, Walter Johnson, and a young pitcher named Babe Ruth—all in their prime—dominated the AL landscape in the next decade, the NL's only players of comparable stature were pitchers Mathewson, nearing the end of his career, and Grover Cleveland Alexander. In the 1920s, Ruth became the greatest player ever; Cobb, Speaker, Collins, Sisler, and Johnson continued to shine; and the likes of Lou Gehrig, Al Simmons, Mickey Cochrane, and Lefty Grove made the AL scene. Rogers Hornsby and Frankie Frisch were their most prominent contemporaries in the National League. Ruth, Gehrig, Grove, Jimmie Foxx, Hank Greenberg, Charlie Gehringer, Joe Cronin, and Joe DiMaggio dominated the 1930s for the American League; the NL's best included Dizzy Dean, Carl Hubbell, Mel Ott, and Arky Vaughan.

That, of course, is not a comprehensive list of the most prominent players in either league, but at a time when players—especially elite players—rarely changed leagues, many more of the best players starred in the junior circuit. Indeed, of the 30 position players to average 6 wins above replacement over one or more five-year periods, 20 were American Leaguers. (Wins above replacement is an advanced metric that measures a player's value relative to what a player called up from the highest level of the minor leagues would contribute to his team; 6 wins above replacement is the middle of the range for an all-star level of performance.) Eight of the 20 AL position players averaged 6 wins above replacement for 10 years or longer, compared to just three of the NL's 10.

But even as Americans celebrated a hard-fought and costly world war in Europe and the Pacific in defense of freedom and democratic ideals, and the major leagues looked forward to baseball as usual with the return of many star players who lost prime years of their careers serving their country in wartime, the balance of power between the American and National Leagues was about to change. The Yankees would remain a dominant team—they were, after all, the "forever" dynasty—but in short order the National League would become the league with all-around better players, with more compelling players, with more excitement, that aroused more fan interest, and that would no longer be a lapdog to American League teams in either All-Star Games or the World Series. This change came because, on October 23, 1945, the Brooklyn Dodgers announced they had taken the controversial, because it was unprecedented, step of signing a black man to play for their top minor-league farm team the next year, with the full intention that he would soon be wearing a Dodgers uniform and taking the field on major-league diamonds in the National League. His name was Jackie Robinson.

Meanwhile, as activist labor unions were flexing their muscles in postwar America, the balance of power between team owners and major-league players was about to head down a path that would shake the foundations of the game and lead ultimately to the biggest crisis in Major League Baseball since the Black Sox scandal. Its name was free agency.

Part I

Baseball's Integration and Expansionist Imperative

Jackie Robinson stealing home. Black trailblazers like Robinson brought an aggressiveness on the basepath rarely seen since the Deadball Era, which helped to define the National League—whose teams were more open to integration than the American League—as the more exciting of the two major leagues. © *Photofest*.

I

BASEBALL'S POSTWAR LANDSCAPE

The "Race Question" and "Player Relationships"

Jackie Robinson's outstanding minor-league season in Montreal for Brooklyn's top Triple-A farm club presented a fundamental challenge to the way Major League Baseball had always been—which was segregated. Although—as various baseball owners and longtime (former) commissioner Kenesaw Mountain Landis, who fashioned himself the moral authority of the game based on his actions to close the sordid chapter of the Black Sox scandal, liked to say—there was no specific prohibition against black players in Major League Baseball. Not that it needed to be that way. It just was. It was the embodiment of the 1896 US Supreme Court decision in *Plessy v. Ferguson* that established the doctrine of "separate but equal," which allowed for discriminating between white Americans and minorities—especially black minorities—when it came to all manner of public accommodations and public policies. Institutionalized segregation was justified on those legal grounds, premised on the concept of voluntary consent of individuals to associate—or not associate—with whomever they wished. As far as the major leagues were concerned, black ballplayers had their own "separate but equal" major leagues—the Negro Leagues—notwithstanding the fallback racial canard that inherently inferior black American ballplayers were in any event not likely to succeed in Major League Baseball.

Branch Rickey knew that was bunk. And Jackie Robinson, in the first postwar year of 1946, was proving that was bunk at the highest level of minor-league baseball. He led the International League in batting, with a .349 average. His .468 on-base percentage was the best in the league. He tied for the league lead in runs scored, with 113, despite playing in 25 fewer games than the co-leader. He swiped 40 bases in 55 attempts. He struck out just 27 times in 444 at bats. His team—the Montreal Royals— finished first by 18½ games and went on to win the minor-league Little World Series. He was their best player and was voted the International League's Most Valuable Player. Jackie Robinson was, in short, an outstanding ballplayer in every way. And he was a dynamic player with a flair for the dramatic when ballgames were on the line. Particularly troubling to major-league owners was the exponential increase in attendance he brought into ballparks around the league to see him play—crowds that included unprecedented numbers of black patrons coming to watch minor-league baseball. Importantly, the same year Robinson was excelling in Triple-A, Negro League catcher Roy Campanella and right-hander Don Newcombe were playing for Brooklyn's Class-B affiliate in Nashua, New Hampshire.

In late August 1946 a Major League Steering Committee, under the direction of the two league presidents, delivered a report to both the owners and Commissioner A. B. "Happy" Chandler, a US Senator from Kentucky named to the position after Landis died in November 1944, that identified the "Race Question" as one of the most pressing problems baseball was facing "in the most critical period in all its history," or so it said in the foreword. Emphasizing the negative in an undoubted effort to try to head off Rickey's clear intention of promoting Robinson to the major leagues the next year and Campanella and Newcombe in the years following, its discussion of the racial issue centered on "methods to protect Baseball from charges that it is fostering unfair discrimination against the Negro by reason of his race and color." Unlike for other "Problems" addressed in the MacPhail Report, as it was called (after Yankees team president Larry MacPhail, the committee chairman who took the lead in vetting and drafting its conclusions), no specific recommendations were made regarding what to do about baseball's Race Question. The committee instead went "on record" that the "overall problem" affected every major-league franchise and needed to be resolved in a way "compatible with good business judgment and the principles of good sportsmanship."

The MacPhail Report's analysis of what it called "facts" stated unequivocally that allowing black players into the major leagues "could conceivably threaten the value" of franchises located in cities with large black populations and deprive them of revenues from renting out their stadiums to Negro League clubs with star players. In a nod to the segregationist "separate but equal" philosophy, the commissioner and the owners were told that the Negro Leagues, the major league equivalent for black players, would be destroyed if their best players left to play in the majors, leaving the vast majority of "professional Negro players" with no league of their own and no hope of ever playing in the big leagues. While proclaiming this was "not racial discrimination," MacPhail's report also unambiguously asserted there were very few Negro League players that had "the technique, the coordination, the competitive attitude, and the discipline" to play in the major leagues.

Any hopes Rickey's fellow franchise executives had that Jackie Robinson would prove to be a one-off who failed to measure up to the exacting standards required to play in the major leagues were dashed by Robinson's excellent rookie season. Playing out of position at first base because Eddie Stanky was the Dodgers' second baseman, Robinson got off to a slow start, hitting just .225 in the Dodgers' 11 games in April, but finished the season with a .297 batting average and led the league with 29 steals. There was absolutely no denying he belonged in the major leagues and could play with the best in baseball. All of this Jackie Robinson accomplished while being thrown at by pitchers and spiked by baserunners, having to endure without retaliation—or even answering back—all manner of verbal abuse, most notoriously from Philadelphia Phillies manager Ben Chapman, a Southerner who did not hide either his prejudice or hostility about having to share a major-league playing field with a black man. And right behind Robinson were Campanella, now in Montreal, and Newcombe, who put in another outstanding season in Nashua.

Three other black players followed Robinson to the major leagues in 1947. If their experience had been the benchmark instead of Robinson's, there might have been no blacks on major-league rosters the next year and quite possibly for many years after that. Larry Doby was signed by Cleveland's maverick owner Bill Veeck on July 2, immediately brought to the majors without minor-league preparation, got into his first game as a pinch hitter three days later (he struck out), and started at first base the day after that. It was the only game he started all year. In 29 games, Doby had just 33 plate appearances—24 as a pinch hitter—with only 5 hits. His riding the bench was recognition by Veeck that despite his having been a star in the Negro Leagues, the 23-year-old probably should have had a year of acclimatization in the high minor leagues the way Robinson had. If not for Robinson's excellence, had Veeck even decided to bring a black man to the majors without the Rickey-Robinson precedent in Brooklyn, Doby would most likely have spent the 1948 season in Triple-A—if, that is, he wasn't cut.

Being cut is exactly what happened to the two other blacks who played Major League Baseball in 1947—the Kansas City Monarchs' Hank Thompson and Willard Brown, both signed by the St. Louis Browns in July, less than three weeks after the Indians signed Doby. Like Doby, both went directly from the Negro Leagues to their new major-league club. Unlike Doby, both were used mostly in the starting lineup. In contrast to Robinson, however, Thompson and Brown had the support of neither their manager nor most of their teammates. While the abuse Robinson was forced to endure without fighting back helped rally even ambivalent Dodgers teammates behind him, Thompson and Brown were sent back to the Monarchs five weeks after they signed. A left-handed batter, Thompson was platooned at second base, starting 18 games against only right-handers. He hit .256, but rode a modest five-game hitting-streak and batted .333 in the nine games he played before he was sent back to the Monarchs. Brown started 18 of the 21 games he played for the Browns. His best day was in his fifth big-league game, when he went 4-for-5 against the Yankees in New York. Otherwise, Brown struggled at the plate and hit just .179 with one home run—a two-run pinch-hit shot off Tigers ace Hal Newhouser that won the game for the Browns just 10 days before he and Thompson were sent down.

The Browns' signing of Willard Brown, a longtime Negro League star, and the young Thompson, still at the very beginning of his professional career, was cynical to the core. Their status as the worst team in baseball contributed to a dramatic drop in attendance from the four previous years when the Browns benefited both from unexpectedly winning the franchise's first-ever pennant in 1944—mostly because many core players on the American League's principal contenders were serving in the military—and the major-league-wide surge in attendance in 1946 that accompanied the return to normalcy in a country that had endured a decade and a half of the Great Depression and World War II. It surely didn't help that they shared the same city—and even the same ballpark—with the defending 1946 World Series–champion St. Louis Cardinals. In the most Southern of big-league cities, team executives figured that Brown and Thompson's talent might give the Browns both a competitive and attendance boost, including drawing from St. Louis's large black community, but the Browns were mostly on the road during the five weeks Brown and Thompson were on their roster. Although their winning percentage improved, the last-place Browns fell further behind in the standings. Including three doubleheaders, the Browns averaged slightly more than 3,000 fans per date in their 19 home games when the two black players were on the club. That was actually less than the Browns' average attendance of 4,162 for the year.

Concluding that Thompson and Brown did not bring value enough to shake the problems that came with having black players on the team, Browns general manager Bill DeWitt released them, saying they had received a fair trial but had "failed to reach major league standards." This was precisely the sentiment that most in Major League Baseball—from players to front office executives to franchise owners—were inclined to believe about black players and were not displeased to see seemingly validated, notwithstanding what Jackie Robinson was accomplishing back east, east of the East River, in Ebbets Field. It didn't matter that Brown and Thompson were treated with contempt and hostility by their teammates, or that manager Muddy Ruel did nothing to rein in that treatment and support his black players. Had they, and not Robinson or Doby, been the first blacks to play in the major leagues, and Rickey (unlikely) and Veeck (perhaps) been intimidated by their "failure," it likely would have been years before another black was given the opportunity.

* * *

The Race Question thrust upon Major League Baseball because of Branch Rickey's signing Jackie Robinson and assigning him to play the 1946 season in Montreal—one step below Brooklyn on Organized Baseball's ladder—was just one fraught issue the game's owners had to contend with in the first postwar year. The second, equally if not more threatening to franchise owners, was more immediate and had to be dealt with early in the 1946 season: the most credible movement since the Players' League in 1890 to organize major leaguers into a union for collective bargaining with the owners on the terms, conditions, and benefits of their employment. If in the spring of 1946 the owners knew they had a one-year grace period in which to either derail Rickey's plan to bring a black player to Brooklyn or come to terms with it, they had no such luxury when it came to the fast-track organization of a major-league players' union. It was either kill it before it came to fruition or deal with the consequences.

The courting of star players the likes of Vern Stephens, Stan Musial, Ted Williams, and Phil Rizzuto in the early months of 1946—with promises of significantly higher pay than they were making in the majors by Jorge Pascual, one of the wealthiest men in Mexico and president of the Mexican League—was a wake-up call for Major League Baseball. With the Great Depression not yet a distant memory and with hundreds of thousands of soldiers returning to the workforce and the country transitioning to an expansive peacetime economy, American workers were increasingly assertive in wanting better and more prosperous lives. Major-league players were no different. When the war ended and dozens of established major-league veterans who had been serving their country in wartime returned to baseball, dozens of others who had filled in for them during the war years were wondering about their major-league futures.

Many of the wartime veterans, having lost two or three years of their baseball prime in the armed forces, chafed under the thumb of owners, almost all tightwads when it came to salaries. With most players signed to annual contracts and all contracts containing a provision known as the reserve clause that bound players to their teams even after their annual contracts expired, team executives had the leverage at any point in negotiations with every player to lay down their final offer for a new annual contract and say, "Take it or leave it—and if you leave it, you still can only play for us, you are not a free agent." Pascual, wanting the Mexican League to become a south-of-the-border rival to the major leagues, at least as far as the quality of players was concerned, moved swiftly to take advantage of this dynamic.

Williams, one of baseball's best-paid players despite only four years in the big leagues and the last three in the navy, turned down Pascual's money. Musial, whose salary was hardly commensurate with his accomplishments, was tempted but declined. Rizzuto agreed to go to Mexico, then changed his mind. Stephens signed up, went to Mexico, was dismayed by the conditions there and feared for his safety (including from Pascual's security men protecting him), and surreptitiously left the country to return to the Browns. In his first, most consequential action as commissioner, Chandler warned that any player jumping to the Mexican League would be banned from the major leagues for five years. For those like Stephens who misguidedly took the plunge, returning before Opening Day would be sufficient to avoid that severe penalty. The threat deterred many players who were considering the Mexican League. The most prominent who went to Mexico anyway were Dodgers catcher Mickey Owen, second baseman Lou Klein and superb lefty Max Lanier of the Cardinals, and Giants bullpen ace Ace Adams. It turned out to be a miserable mistake for those who went. The playing conditions were terrible. Life in Mexico was fundamentally different from life in the United States. And whatever Pascual's personal wealth, the Mexican League was not sufficiently capitalized to follow through for more than a year or two on the salary promises made to American major leaguers.

Major League Baseball acted quickly and decisively to skirt a Mexican League disaster, but the underlying factors that attracted players to Pascual's blandishments and promises, at least enough to listen to them, did not go away. Labor unions in industries across the country were flexing their muscles over wages, employment benefits, and better working conditions at a moment of leverage—many union-organized strikes caused significant disruption in a wide range of industries, some critically important to national security—because the American economy needed their productivity to fuel and sustain the promise of growth and unprecedented global economic superiority. It was a propitious moment for Boston attorney Robert Murphy, whose expertise included labor law, to step in and organize a players' union. He called it the American Baseball Guild.

It was not the first time that major-league players tried to unionize in order to confront the owners with a united front, rather than individually, when it came to grievances (particularly over the reserve clause) and salary considerations. As early as 1885 there was the Brotherhood of Professional Base-Ball Players, whose efforts the owners high-handedly dismissed. There were two occasions in the last decade of the nineteenth century, however, when the owners overplayed their hand. The first was in 1889, when National League owners imposed a salary cap on individual players that was well below fair market value for baseball's best players. That was the final straw for New York Giants shortstop John Montgomery Ward, a well-educated man with a law degree who was instrumental in founding the players' union. When his efforts at negotiation over the reserve clause got nowhere, Ward acted with alacrity to acquire investors and organize a union-run Players' League in 1890. It was a success in that nearly two-thirds of the National League's players, including most of the best in baseball, jumped their clubs to join Players' League franchises, nearly all of which were in NL cities. It was doomed to fail, as it did after just one season, because it could not sustain financial solvency. Although they suffered at the gate in 1890, National League owners were simply better capitalized.

The next time, 10 years later, ended badly for the National League, but also did not in the end enable players to escape the restrictions of the reserve clause. At precisely the moment National League owners were again taking an obstinate stance on player salaries and contractual rights, Byron Bancroft Johnson was in the process of organizing the American League, which he presumptively declared a "major" league. Johnson made it known that player grievances would not be ignored and dismissed in his new league. NL owners made the mistake of presuming the American League, like the Players' League, lacked sustainability. Underestimating the resolve of the players—this time organized in the fledgling Players Protective Association, formed in June 1900—National League owners stuck to their hard line in negotiations. A large number of players, including many of the best in baseball, jumped their reserve-clause contracts and defected to the new league in 1901 and 1902, helping to make the AL a smashing success. By 1903 the National League was ready to admit defeat, sued for peace, and recognized the American League as a fellow (as opposed to rival) major league. The modern two-league structure of Major League Baseball was now official. Part of the settlement, however, was that the two leagues would henceforth respect the player contracts of the other league, and that the player-hated reserve clause would remain in effect as indispensable to the competitive integrity of the game. For the players, it was back to square one.

A decade later the major leagues faced a serious, even existential threat when a federal court in Chicago agreed to hear a case brought by the upstart Federal League in 1914 challenging the legality of the reserve clause. Working from Ban Johnson's playbook, the Federal League targeted major-league players to give the new league major-league credibility. With an eye toward a reasonable and defensible legal position, however, the Federals took the tack of honoring the sanctity of existing multi-year contracts, which clubs had been offering to their best players, and went after only those players whose contracts technically expired with the end of the season. Faced with the strong possibility that the Federal League argument would prevail in the Progressive Era politics and jurisprudence of the time, major-league owners tried to short-circuit both the upstart league and its federal case by co-opting the latest players union— the Baseball Players' Fraternity—that had come into existence two years earlier. To minimize player defections, they agreed to negotiate about grievances and guaranteed that, even in the event the Federal League failed, they would honor the higher-value multiyear contracts that were given star players to keep them from jumping to the new league. The Federal League did fail, after two years. It was soon back to business as usual—just the way the owners wanted it.

Now that the Federal League was history, owners once again gave little ground on player grievances, reduced the salaries of player contracts they considered exorbitant once the contract terms expired, and clung to the necessity of the reserve clause. In 1918 the Baseball Players' Fraternity folded. There were no credible efforts to unionize players again until Robert Murphy announced the formation of the American Baseball Guild in April 1946, on Opening Day of baseball's first postwar season. That a surprising number of players, representing more than half the major-league teams, reportedly supported Murphy's union was a troubling development for team owners, particularly at a time of such union-led labor ferment across the country.

Murphy then both underplayed and overplayed his hand. Rather than trying to organize the players on all or most of the clubs that had expressed interest in his guild to press for a collective bargaining agreement with the owners, Murphy focused instead on just one team—the Pittsburgh Pirates, who had finished a noncompetitive fourth in the last war year and was off to desultory start in 1946. After Pirates executives refused to negotiate his agenda for recognition of the guild and improved conditions for the players, Murphy threatened that Pirates players would hold a strike vote before their home game on June 7. With the backing of the league president and the commissioner, the Pirates' front office called Murphy's bluff.

Murphy was not bluffing, but he also did not have the votes he thought he had, despite widespread pro-guild sentiment among Pirates players, because they were not prepared to risk their careers by going on strike. Three of Pittsburgh's most accomplished veterans had serious misgivings about a strike. Right-hander Rip Sewell was vocal in his adamant opposition to the very idea of a players' union. Third baseman/outfielder Bob Elliott, the team's highest-paid player, did not believe a strike was the way to achieve the guild's goals. Catcher Al Lopez was unhappy that Murphy's strategy was for all the burden of standing up to ownership falling on their club alone. Murphy was barred from the clubhouse during the players' deliberations, and though a majority of the team voted in favor of a strike, they were four votes shy of the two-thirds required to refuse taking the field. The Pirates won that day before nearly 17,000 of their home fans, many of whom, belonging to unions themselves, nonetheless booed their team.

Although this latest effort to effort to unionize major-league players had been dealt a fatal blow, the owners took note of how close Murphy had come. The MacPhail Report presented later that season included a section titled "Player Relationships" that focused on "methods to prevent outsiders from being successful in attempts to organize players into unions or guilds for purposes of collective bargaining," which it called "our most pressing problem." Murphy likely would have been successful, the report stated, had he first tried to organize players in the minor leagues—the pipeline for Major League Baseball. The recommendations for dealing with the problem, which also referenced the need "to protect ourselves against raids on players from the outside"—a reference to Jorge Pascual's very recent effort to recruit major leaguers for the Mexican League—were already in train. After Murphy's gambit failed in the Pirates' clubhouse election, the owners wasted little time in disarming the threat of player unionization by co-opting some of the key issues raised by his American Baseball Guild. That summer the owners met with player representatives from each of the teams to discuss reforms. The Major League Steering Committee was relieved to report to the owners that player representatives were willing "to cooperate in defending baseball against attacks upon the reserve clause." *That* was the most important thing.

In return for that concession, negotiations with the player representatives resulted in the owners agreeing to, among other benefits, a weekly stipend for players' spring training expenses, the establishment of a players' pension fund, a minimum major-league salary, and a limit to how much a player's salary could be cut from the previous year. Rather than recognizing that, in the absence of the scare thrown into them by a skilled labor relations negotiator like Murphy, the owners would not have agreed to those provisions—particularly concerning the pension fund, which many owners feared could seriously undermine their financial bottom line—major-league players were not inclined to press their luck by organizing a truly independent labor union.

* * *

The crisis of baseball's owners having to deal with a players union with real clout was averted. For now—and for two decades, as it turned out. Not so the Race Question. Rickey promoted Robinson in 1947, and the Indians and Browns joined the Dodgers with black players on their major-league rosters in July. Following Jackie Robinson's indisputably outstanding rookie years, Brooklyn and Cleveland were the only clubs that began the 1948 season with an integrated roster. Brooklyn made way for Robinson to play second base, his natural position, by trading Eddie Stanky. Roy Campanella, also on the Opening Day roster, was sent back to Triple-A for more seasoning and recalled at the beginning of July to become the Dodgers' everyday catcher after hitting .325 there. Don Newcombe spent all of 1948 in Montreal and was terrific at the Triple-A level, making a strong case for pitching in Ebbets Field the next year. For the Indians, Larry Doby was in the Opening Day lineup, and in July, Veeck signed a Negro League pitching legend, the ageless Satchel Paige. The Browns of St. Louis were back in the camp of franchises justifying their opposition to integration.

An unfair argument can perhaps be made, given their 10-game lead with seven games left on the schedule, that the 1947 Dodgers would have won the pennant even without Robinson's rookie contributions. The 1948 Indians, however, most certainly would not have won the American League pennant without Doby and Paige. Cleveland finished the season tied with the Boston Red Sox for the best record in the American League, requiring the AL's first-ever playoff to settle the outcome. Doby had an exceptional September as the Indians spent most of the month trying to catch the Red Sox and Yankees in a tight three-team race, leading the club with a .375 batting average and .466 on-base percentage. He finished the year batting .301. On a staff that featured Bob Feller, Bob Lemon, and outstanding rookie Gene Bearden, the 41-year-old Paige was 5–0 in August with a team-best 1.51 earned-run average in five starts and three relief appearances as the Indians kept up with their fellow contenders. He pitched Cleveland into first place with a shutout on August 13 in his second big-league start, threw another shutout a week later, and finished the year with a 6–1 record and 2.48 ERA. The Dodgers, meanwhile, stumbled through the first three months, falling out of contention early and finishing third. Robinson was even better his second year than his first, and Campanella had a strong rookie season of his own.

It didn't matter that with black players as core regulars playing extremely well, Brooklyn in 1947 and Cleveland in 1948 had won pennants, and the Indians the World Series. They were still the only clubs that began the 1949 season with black players on their roster—Robinson and Campanella in Brooklyn, and Doby, Paige, and rookie outfielder Minnie Minoso in Cleveland. Around the same time in May that Minoso was sent to the Indians' Triple-A affiliate in San Diego for more seasoning, the Dodgers called up Newcombe from Montreal. The big right-hander threw a shutout in his first start and, completing 19 of his 31 starts, finished with a 17–8 record to win NL Rookie of the Year honors. Robinson, leading the league with a .342 batting average, was voted the NL's Most Valuable Player. Campanella had a breakout season. The Dodgers won the pennant by a single game, with Newcombe pitching a shutout to put his team on top with just two games to go. They couldn't have done it without them.

The other major-league teams were still on the sidelines. Only Boston's Braves and New York's Giants and Yankees began the 1949 season with any black players on their minor-league affiliates—two for the Giants, and one each for the Braves and Yankees. In July the Giants promoted Monte Irvin, one of the all-time greats in Negro League baseball, and Hank Thompson, despite his having "failed" with the Browns two years earlier, to become one of only three clubs to play the season with an integrated lineup. Thompson was immediately made the Giants' second baseman; Irvin was mostly a reserve. The next year, four teams began the season with black players on their rosters and in their Opening Day lineups—Brooklyn with Newcombe as their starting pitcher, Robinson, and Campanella; Cleveland with Doby; the Giants with Thompson, now playing third, and Irvin soon to assume a starting role; and the Braves with 33-year-old former Negro League star Sam Jethroe in center field. In the fourth year of the Jackie Robinson era, none of the 12 other major-league clubs put a black player on their roster at any time in 1950, and only six had black players in their farm systems.

It was apparent by now there was no going back to segregated major-league baseball, with the Major Leagues for whites and the Negro

Leagues for blacks. But there was still great resistance among a majority of owners to the idea of integrating their teams. Clubhouse chemistry, perhaps more appropriately called "clubhouse culture," was a consideration. There remained widespread hostility among white players to the idea of having black teammates, much of that because most white players had grown up in a segregated society where there was very little, if any, interaction between white and black people on the basis of equality between the races. It wasn't until July 1948, after all, that the United States military was finally integrated by President Harry S. Truman's executive order; black servicemen had served in black-only units, commanded by white officers, when America fought in World War II. And in most other endeavors at this point in postwar America—in neighborhoods, jobs, even in public education—segregation of the races remained the norm, separate and (supposedly) equal. Consistent with the MacPhail Report's assertion that "political and social-minded drum-beaters" were trying "to force major league clubs to sign Negro players," most teams took the position they would not be pressured into integration.

Now that the color barrier had been broken, there was widespread acknowledgment that black players with exceptional talent could not be denied. Giving starting positions to black players of more average major-league ability, on the other hand, was an entirely different matter. From their perspective, the excellence of Robinson, Doby, Campanella, and Newcombe to compete with the very best players in baseball might be undeniable, but they were more the exception than the rule. This perspective ignored the fact that most white major-league players were not up to the talent and skill level of baseball's black superstar trailblazers. Resistance to integration was strongest among those most concerned that black players with average major-league ability would beat out white players of comparable ability for starting positions on major-league teams. Those concerned were not just white players feeling threatened about having to compete with black players for their jobs, but also team executives worried about alienating their teams' overwhelmingly white fan base. Most owners and executives probably understood that ultimately such a development was inevitable, but they were in no rush to get there. Their fallback position on integration was that they would be willing to sign, develop, and promote black players with Jackie Robinson's kind of talent. They would not, however, sign and promote black players who might have more average major-league skills and ability just for the sake of integrating their dugouts.

2

THE YANKEES' DYNASTIC MOMENTUM
RETURNS

Three teams that turned out to be on different trajectories entered the final weekend of the 1948 season with a shot at the American League pennant. Having to protect a one-game lead, the first-place Cleveland Indians were playing their last two games against the Detroit Tigers, who were treading .500 waters. Tied for second and playing each other at Fenway Park were the New York Yankees and Boston Red Sox. If Cleveland lost both games, a series split at Fenway could result in a three-way tie at the top. Although the Yankees were the defending World Series champions, they were still trying to find their postwar mojo. Joe DiMaggio, back from the war, was still their best player—and one of the best in baseball—but older and more prone to ailments. Shortstop Phil Rizzuto, an emerging star when he was drafted in 1943, was not playing at the same level since his return. The Yankees had spent just a single day on top so far in 1948, after beating Boston at Yankee Stadium a week before to put them in a three-way tie for first.

The Red Sox, meanwhile, had seemed poised to dominate the American League for the foreseeable future when Ted Williams, Johnny Pesky, Bobby Doerr, Dom DiMaggio, and Tex Hughson returned from the war and swamped the rest of the league, including the seemingly tired and old Yankees, to win the 1946 pennant. But 1947 was their turn to have a lackluster season, which carried over into 1948 despite the addition of slugging shortstop Vern Stephens to bolster their already formidable offense and Ellis Kinder to strengthen their pitching staff, both acquired (separately) from the Browns. Since trailing by 11 games in early June, however, Boston had by far the best record in the majors and once again looked like a dynasty rising.

The season-ending Red Sox–Yankees showdown was all the more dramatic for Boston being managed by the great former Yankees manager Joe McCarthy. Part of the postwar landscape for Major League Baseball was the sense that old-school managers like McCarthy and longtime National League manager Bill McKechnie could no longer relate to "modern" players whose perspectives were broadened by wartime in America and overseas and by the rapid social and economic changes taking place in society at large. McKechnie was let go by Cincinnati at the end of the 1946 season. McCarthy resigned from the Yankees early in the 1946 season, citing poor health, in spite of his success managing Yankees forever dynasty 2.0 (after Miller Huggins's 1.0 version) to eight pennants and seven World Series titles in 15 years between 1931 and 1945. There could be no disputing his success as a manager, however, and the Red Sox were quick to offer him the top step of the Fenway dugout after their desultory 1947 defense of their 1946 runaway pennant.

On Saturday, the Red Sox eliminated the Yankees, and the Indians beat the Tigers to maintain their one-game lead. Boston won again on Sunday, while Cleveland ace Bob Feller was knocked out in the third, losing to Detroit ace Hal Newhouser. The scene shifted to Fenway Park for a one-game playoff to decide the pennant. The Indians went with rookie southpaw Gene Bearden, despite Fenway Park's short left field being considered a major liability for lefties. A navy wartime casualty—his ship was sunk in a torpedo attack in the Pacific, leaving him with a metal plate to repair a huge gash in his skull and a damaged knee that required a metal brace when he pitched—Bearden already had 19 wins and was pitching with the typical three days' rest between starts.

Boston's best pitcher, Mel Parnell, 15–8 for the season and winner of 12 of his last 14 decisions as a starting pitcher, was also available on three days of rest. Although he too was a southpaw, Parnell had been very effective at Fenway, with an 8–3 record and excellent 2.21 earned-run average. In a decision controversial at the time that has been much debated since, McCarthy decided instead to go with seldom-used right-hander Denny Galehouse, a 36-year-old journeyman with a career losing record who had made just nine starts since mid-June. It turned out to be a losing choice. Galehouse didn't make it out of the fourth inning—didn't get even get one out that inning—while Bearden pitched the Indians to the pennant with a complete-game 8–3 victory. For Cleveland, their 1948 pennant became the foundation for their becoming one of baseball's best teams into the mid-1950s. For Boston, their playoff loss proved to be a pivot away from their presumed dynasty predestination. For New York, much would depend on what happened the next year.

What happened in 1949 was McCarthy's last stand, which sealed the fate for a Red Sox dynasty that never was and helped pave the way for the Yankees to become the next decade's indisputable team to beat in the American League (much to Cleveland's frustration). Once again the pennant was up for grabs on the last day of the season. This time Boston was in New York, tied with the Yankees for first place with 153 games down and just one to go. The Red Sox didn't get there without first having to overcome a 12-game deficit after losing to the Yankees in an Independence Day doubleheader, their eighth consecutive loss at the time. On September 26, with the two teams tied for first, the visiting Red Sox scored four runs in the eighth inning to come from behind to beat the Yankees and take sole possession of first place. It was the first time all season the Yankees were not at the top of the standings. The Red Sox were back at Yankee Stadium five days later for two games to close out the season, up one and needing to win just one.

The Yankees overcame an early 4–0 deficit on Saturday to eke out a 5–4 win and claim a share of first place. Game 154 began as a pitcher's duel between Boston's Ellis Kinder, who had beaten the Yankees a week earlier for his 23rd win and pitched every other day since then in relief, and the Yankees' hard-throwing Vic Raschi, also a 20-game winner. A critical moment came when it was Kinder's turn to bat with one out in the eighth. Only one run had been scored the entire game, and it belonged to the Yankees. With the Red Sox down to their last five outs, McCarthy chose to pinch hit for Kinder. Boston did not score. McCarthy's next decision, arguably as controversial as his Galehouse choice the previous year, was to call on 25-game winner Mel Parnell for the eighth inning—controversial because Parnell had started the day before against the Yankees and didn't make it out of the fifth inning. He was tired. Tommy Henrich greeted him with a home run, Yogi Berra singled, and Parnell's day was done after two batters. In yet another controversial decision, McCarthy brought in Tex Hughson, twice a 20-game winner for Boston but now a pale shadow of the pitcher he had been. Used mostly in relief with an earned-run average over 5.00 when he walked out of the bullpen, Hughson was arguably McCarthy's least reliable pitcher. The Yankees scored three more runs to take a 5–0 lead. Boston scored three in the ninth, but it was game and pennant to New York.

* * *

If the Yankees' forever dynasty had stalled when they were wiped out by the Red Sox in 1946 and eliminated in Boston on the last weekend of the 1948 season, their dramatic victories in the last two games of the 1949 season and their subsequent five-game dismantling of the Brooklyn Dodgers in the World Series proved not only a corrective but the start of the franchise's most dominant run of success—14 pennants in 16 years between 1949 and 1964, the first 10 of those pennants in 12 years under the guidance of one Mr. Charles Dillon Stengel, best known as Casey. Joe McCarthy, widely considered—at the time and since—to be the greatest of all managers (or at least in a virtual tie with John McGraw) based on his Yankees résumé, was 62 in 1949. Stengel was just four years younger when he took charge of the Yankees that year. Given his nine-year résumé managing bad National League clubs, only one of which he led to a barely winning record, baseball pundits were left scratching their heads as to why such a storied franchise as the New York Yankees would hire *him*.

Those last two days on the 1949 schedule might have ended the Stengel era before it even began had the Yankees not beaten the Red Sox to win the pennant after having been on top all season until the final week. Stengel's managerial skills and judgment would have been questioned, as would the reasons why the Yankees squandered their season-long advantage. Instead, it was the beginning of a record-setting five consecutive pennants and five consecutive World Series triumphs. For the first four of those pennants, the Yankees had to fend off tough September challenges. None were won until the final week of the season. But they proved themselves as resilient and relentless as any of the great Yankees teams in the past, perhaps even more so because they so often played with the pennant at stake in the final month. The only time they kept up the McCarthy-era tradition of overwhelming the rest of the league in their pennant-winning seasons was 1953, when they were first in the standings every day after just their eighth game on their way to winning the pennant by 8½ games.

The five-and-five-in-five championship years marked the end of Joe DiMaggio's era and the beginning of Mickey Mantle's. DiMaggio was not as great as he had been after three years away during World War II, but he was also 31 when he returned to baseball. He was merely excellent. In 1947 DiMaggio beat out Triple Crown–winner Ted Williams for the Most Valuable Player Award by a single vote, even though Williams, whose relationship with baseball writers was always antagonistic, was the superior player in every way except defense. DiMaggio's best postwar year, leading the league with 39 homers and the majors with 155 runs batted in, was 1948. It was the 1949 season, however, that shaped DiMaggio's legacy nearly as much as his 56-game hitting streak. Sidelined for the first 10 weeks with a bone spur in his heel that just wouldn't heal, he got out of bed one day in late June, felt no pain, and torched Red Sox pitching for 5 hits, 4 of them homers, in 11 at-bats to drive in 9 runs as the Yankees swept the series at Fenway Park. That was the start of an eight-game Boston losing streak that seemed to doom them for the year. It was as dramatic a return to action by a ballplayer as ever there has been.

By 1951 DiMaggio was physically worn out. Rising in his stead was a 19-year-old from Oklahoma named Mickey Mantle. DiMaggio was cool toward his heir apparent as the Yankees' top star. Their last interaction on the playing field came in Game Two of the 1951 World Series. They converged on a fly ball to right-center hit by one Willie Mays, who was, like Mantle, a rookie. Deferring to the great DiMaggio to make the catch, Mantle pulled up short on the play, wrenched his knee stepping on a drain in the outfield grass at Yankee Stadium, and went down in a heap. It was only his 98th game as a Yankee, and he would never be the same. Which isn't to say that he wouldn't become one of baseball's all-time greats. Joe DiMaggio announced his retirement in December, and Mantle took over in center field in 1952. Almost immediately, he was one of the best players in baseball.

The cornerstone players for all of the five-and-five-in-five years were catcher Yogi Berra, outstanding defensive shortstop Phil Rizzuto, and a trio of pitchers—hard-throwing righties Allie Reynolds and Vic Raschi and lefty craftsman Eddie Lopat—Stengel inherited when he took over in 1949. Berra averaged 26 homers, had two 100-RBI seasons, and batted .294 between 1949 and 1953. Stengel's decision in 1949 to move Rizzuto to the top of the batting order instead of mostly in the bottom third, where previous Yankees manager Bucky Harris had him, may have rejuvenated the agile, diminutive shortstop's career. Rizzuto finished second to Ted Williams for MVP in 1949 and won the award in 1950 when he scored

125 runs and batted .324. Lopat struck out only 11 percent of the batters he faced, but twice led the league in fewest runners allowed per innings pitched. Raschi won 21 games three straight years from 1949 to 1951. One of baseball's stingiest starting pitchers in giving up hits, Reynolds doubled as Stengel's go-to reliever to save victories from 1951 to 1953.

* * *

After Boston's hopes for a pennant were crushed in 1949, the Cleveland Indians became the Yankees' principal competition through the first half of the 1950s. The Indians had been down this road before. Between their first pennant and World Series championship in 1920 and their second of each in 1948, they had consistently good teams and might have captured a few pennants were it not for the curse of having to compete against the Almighty Forever Dynasty Yankees. If it wasn't Huggins's Yankees or McCarthy's Yankees, it had to be Stengel's Yankees.

Cleveland's noteworthy holdovers in the 1950s from the 1948 team that won it all were outfielders Larry Doby and Dale Mitchell and pitching aces Bob Lemon and Bob Feller. Although Feller led the league with a 22–8 record in 1951, his career was already on the decline and he was progressively being moved to the back end of the starting staff behind Lemon, 1949 trade acquisition Early Wynn, and Mike Garcia, the 1949 league leader in ERA as a rookie. All were right-handers. The infield had turned over. Gone were second baseman Joe Gordon, shortstop and manager Lou Boudreau, and third baseman Ken Keltner. All three drove in more than 100 runs in 1948; Gordon and Keltner were second and third in home runs, and Boudreau had probably the greatest single season ever by a player-manager—batting .355 with an overall player value of 10.4 wins above replacement, the best of any player in the American League; winning every first-place vote in the MVP balloting except for two that went to DiMaggio; and managing his team through a season-long three-team pennant race, a playoff victory for the pennant, and the World Series triumph. Replacing Gordon at second base was the Mexican-born Bobby Avila, good defensively and an able number-two hitter. The slugger Al Rosen—the league leader in home runs with 37 in 1950, his rookie year—displaced Keltner at third. Boudreau was let go after the 1950 season. Replacing Boudreau at shortstop proved much more difficult than replacing him as manager.

Al Lopez, a longtime National League catcher in the 1930 and 1940s, took command of the Indians in 1951 and began a managerial career whose defining characteristic seemed to be his teams always finishing second to Stengel's Yankees. After falling just short of the Yankees in 1951 and '52, Cleveland, like every other American League club, was swamped by the 1953 Yankees. Stengel's 1954 team was even better, winning 103 games, the most since McCarthy's 1942 Yankees won the same number. It was in fact the only year any Yankee team managed by Stengel reached the 100-win threshold. But it was not enough. The Indians outdid the Yankees with 111 victories, breaking the AL record of 110 set by the immortal 1927 Ruth and Gehrig Yankees—still considered by many to be baseball's greatest team ever. Doby led the league in homers (32) and RBIs (126); Avila won the batting title (.341); Rosen hit 24 homers and drove in 102 runs; Lemon and Wynn both won 23; and Garcia, with 19 wins, led the league in earned-run average (2.64). Then it was back to Stengel's Yankees on top and Lopez's clubs—the Indians and, later, the White Sox after he left Cleveland in 1957—finishing second.

The Yankees had to win another close pennant race in 1955, making Stengel a perfect 5–0 in pennant races not won till the final week of the season. Berra hit 27 home runs to win his second MVP Award in two years, and his third in five. Leading the league with 18 wins, Whitey Ford solidified his role as the Yankees' ace since returning in 1953 from two years of military service during the Korean War. And Mantle, already an elite player, soared into undeniable superstar status, leading the league with 37 homers.

Thanks to the emergence of Mickey Mantle, Superstar, the Yankees rediscovered their traditional domineering ways and won the next three American League pennants in runaways, giving them four in a row from 1955 to 1958. Mantle was the best player in the American League, based on the WAR metric, each of those years with an average annual player value of 10.8 wins above replacement per 650 plate appearances. He was the best player in all of Major League Baseball in 1955, 1956, and 1957; in 1958, National Leaguers Willie Mays and Ernie Banks were the only major leaguers with a higher player value. And yet Casey Stengel was frustrated that his star player wasn't somehow better. And still, Mickey Mantle played in the shadow of the legacy of the Yankee Clipper, Joltin' Joe DiMaggio.

If ever there was a year Mantle should have come out from the shadow of the revered DiMaggio, it was 1956. He was hitting .400 as late as June

8. With the Yankees unchallenged in the pennant race by the end of August, September's drama was not whether Mantle would win the Triple Crown but whether he would break Babe Ruth's single-season-record 60 home runs. The odds looked good, and given the year he was having it would have been foolish to bet against him. Ruth had 43 homers in 127 games going into September 1927; Mantle had 47 in 129 at the end of August 1956. The Babe reached 60 by hitting 17 in September; the Mick needed 14 to break the record. But sooner or later, the best baseball player on the planet was bound to hit a wall, and Mantle did at the beginning of September. With just 5 hits and no home runs in 33 at-bats in the first 10 games of the month, Mantle fell behind Ruth's pace. He finished with 52 homers, 130 RBIs, and a .353 batting average—all three figures the best in the major leagues. Of baseball's 10 previous Triple Crown winners since the advent in 1901 of two major leagues, only four had led both leagues in home runs, runs batted in, and batting average.

* * *

Before Mickey Mantle became *Mickey Mantle*, the Yankees in their first seven years under Stengel were not definitively a better team than their principal pennant race rivals. A fair argument can be made that the Red Sox in 1949 and 1950 and the Indians from 1951 to 1955 should have had the edge on Stengel's Yankees, at least as far as their core regulars were concerned. The 1950 Red Sox seemed out of the running when Joe McCarthy stepped down as their manager in mid-June after 9 losses in 10 games left them 9½ games back. Under new manager Steve O'Neill, they had the best record in the American League the rest of the way. But it wasn't good enough to catch the Yankees. It didn't help that Ted Williams, reputedly an indifferent outfielder at best, was lost for two months after breaking his elbow when he crashed into the scoreboard while making an outstanding catch in the All-Star Game. Williams had 28 homers and 97 RBIs in 89 games.

Boston's strength was a formidable offense that began with Dom Di-Maggio, Joe's younger brother, at the top of the order, followed by John-ny Pesky, Ted Williams, Vern Stephens, and Bobby Doerr. The Red Sox led the league in scoring by a wide margin in 1949 and '50, and again in 1951. Their .302 batting average in 1950 was the last time any major-league team collectively hit .300. In 1949 Williams and Stephens were first and second in the league in home runs, with 43 and 39, and tied for the most RBIs in the majors with 159. The next year Stephens and rookie first baseman Walt Dropo both drove in 144 runs, leading the majors. Based on pitching WAR, Mel Parnell was the league's best pitcher in 1949 and the third best in 1950.

Boston fans could have been forgiven for believing the Red Sox should have won more than the single pennant they did in 1946 in the six postwar years before Ted Williams, for the second time in his career, had to give up baseball to serve his country in a time of war. Since returning from World War II, Williams's hitting dominance was as close to Babe Ruth as anyone's had ever been. Between then and 1952, when he was called into action as a Marine Corps Reserve officer to fly combat missions in the Korean War, Williams hit 196 home runs, had 746 runs batted in, and batted .340 with an on-base percentage of .485. In those same six years, before his retirement at the end of the 1951 season, Joe DiMaggio had more modest figures, with 142 homers, 607 RBIs, a .304 batting average, and a .392 on-base average. Williams's player value during those six years was 49.4 wins above replacement, overwhelming DiMaggio's 29.4.

Regardless of numbers indicating he was the far better player, which included the four years they were fellow major leaguers before they both went off to war in 1943, Williams was never able to eclipse DiMaggio in the consensus estimation of baseball experts. Part of that was the perception that DiMaggio was the more complete ballplayer, especially given his excellent defense and Williams's indifference to fielding. There was also DiMaggio's indisputable leadership on teams that consistently went to the World Series; Williams played on just one. Both had their signature season in 1941—DiMaggio with his 56-game hitting streak, Williams with his .406 batting average. Both were aloof with the baseball media and the public, but Williams was antagonistically aloof, while DiMaggio's was more a polite reserve.

By the time Williams returned from Korea in August 1953, the Red Sox were a middle-of-the-pack team, where they would remain for the rest of his career. The other core players on the 1949–1950 club had all retired, were near the end of their careers, or had moved on. Williams in left teamed with Jimmy Piersall in center and Jackie Jensen in right to give the Red Sox an offensively productive outfield for the remainder of the decade. Piersall was a talented player whose career was done in by probable bipolar disorder. Jensen led the league in RBIs three times between 1955 and 1959. Williams won back-to-back batting titles in 1957

(.388, exactly five hits short of .400) and 1958. He turned 40 in August 1958. Playing with frequent days off in 1960, mostly when a southpaw started against the Red Sox, Ted Williams hit the 521st home run of his career in the eighth inning of Boston's last home game that year. It was his last major-league plate appearance. He went out in inimical Ted Williams style: He did not tip his cap.

* * *

The excellence of their high-profile pitching staff was what most distinguished the early-to-mid-1950s Indians. Bob Lemon, Early Wynn, and Mike Garcia combined for fourteen 20-win seasons—seven for Lemon between 1948 and 1956, five for Wynn from 1951 to 1956, and two for Garcia in 1951 and '52. But Cleveland also had a formidable offense. Powered by Larry Doby, Al Rosen, and former Negro League star Luke Easter, Cleveland led the American League in home runs five consecutive years from 1950 to 1954. In 1953 Rosen was one hit shy of the batting title and the Triple Crown.

Easter was already 34 years old when he began the 1950 season as Cleveland's first baseman. He and Doby were the only two black players on an American League team that year. His age working against him, as was true for many Negro League veterans, and a broken foot from a pitched ball early in the 1953 season spelled the beginning of the very quick end to Easter's career. Not particularly agile on defense to begin with, Easter's slow recovery from the injury cost him his job the next year. The Indians, however, remained at the forefront of American League clubs when it came to integration: Harry Simpson, signed in 1949, was promoted to Cleveland in 1951 and was their regular right fielder in 1952 before being sent back to the minors the following year, and Al Smith, signed in 1948, was the Indians' left fielder when they won the 1954 pennant.

Age was a primary culprit in Cleveland's fade, which began in 1956, just as the Yankees were rediscovering their dominance. Five of their core position players were 30 or older, as were pitchers Wynn, Lemon, and Garcia. Doby, in his early 30s, had been traded to the White Sox, in part so that Cleveland could resolve their longstanding problem at shortstop since Boudreau's heyday by acquiring Chico Carrasquel in the deal. Carrasquel, however, had just turned 30 and would play only two more years as a regular. Vic Wertz, whom Cleveland acquired to replace Easter as their first baseman in 1954, had his best home run–hitting year with

32—a very distant second to Mantle—but he was also in his 30s. The 32-year-old Rosen retired at the end of the season, done in by a bad back that undermined both his power and his defense.

The Indians did have some young blood that boded well for the future, provided the front office was successful in building around them. Herb Score, a lefty, had a sensational rookie season in 1955 with a 16–10 record and 245 strikeouts in 227⅓ innings, which made him the first qualifying pitcher in major-league history to strike out more than a batter an inning. He did it again in 1956, with 263 Ks in 249⅓ innings, joining Lemon and Wynn with 20 wins. In 1956 the Indians promoted outfielder Rocky Colavito, who had hit 68 home runs the two previous years in Triple-A. Neither player became the foundation for the rebuild of a consistently competitive club in the American League. Score was smashed in the face in his fifth start of the 1957 season on a line drive up the middle by the Yankees' Gil McDougald that all but ended a brilliant career in the making, and the Indians traded Colavito just after the 1959 season despite his league-leading 42 homers.

* * *

For their part, the Stengel-era Yankees always had quality pitching and a dangerous offense. His five-and-five-in-five club and the Mantle-powered team that won four pennants in a row from 1955 to 1958 were always first or second in both scoring and fewest runs allowed, which made them competitive in any context. What set the Yankees apart from first the Red Sox and then the Indians, however, was much greater depth, especially position players on the bench, and a manager who was extraordinarily deft in playing his hand.

In a departure from their championship seasons during the McCarthy years, when virtually all of the Yankees' core players were signed and developed in the club's top-notch farm system, the front office made a series of astute deals, often cash transactions, in the late 1940s and throughout the 1950s to bolster their pennant chances. Pitchers Allie Reynolds, picked up from Cleveland in 1947, and Eddie Lopat, traded by the White Sox in 1948, were two of the first acquisitions without whom it is unlikely the Yankees would have won five pennants in a row. Late in the 1949 season the Yankees traded for Giants veteran slugger Johnny Mize to pinch hit and occasionally play first base. Mize was an indispensable role player for the Yankees the next four years. The same was true of veteran outfielder Enos Slaughter, whose late-season acquisition in 1956 bolstered the Yankees' outfield depth the next three years. Pitchers Bob Turley and Don Larsen, obtained in a massive multiplayer trade from the seventh-place Orioles after the 1954 season, were both important contributors to the Yankees' success throughout the rest of the decade. Larsen threw a perfect game in the 1956 World Series, and Turley was the secondary ace of the Yankee staff behind Whitey Ford most of the rest of the decade. Turley's best year was 1958, when he led American League pitchers with a 21–7 record, after which he pitched a shutout to win Game Five of the World Series, saved Game Six, and pitched 6⅔ innings in relief to win Game Seven.

Stengel, meanwhile, was a master of manipulation when it came to his position regulars. While Mantle, Berra, McDougald (whose versatility allowed Stengel to use him anywhere he was needed in the infield), and Rizzuto (until he was slowed down by age in 1954) were assured a spot in the lineup every game, their manager was famous for platooning at several positions in his starting lineup. Stengel's platooning, however, was not necessarily a strict lefty-righty trade-off such as he had in the outfield with Gene Woodling (a left-handed batter) and Hank Bauer (right-handed) during the five-and-five-in-five years. Like McDougald, virtually all the infielders other than first basemen on Stengel's roster could play any number of positions. Nor was Stengel afraid to pinch-hit for a starting position player—but never for Mantle or Berra, and rarely for McDougald—even early in a game, requiring their replacement in the field, to take advantage of scoring opportunities at whatever moments he considered critical to the game's outcome.

Stengel's constant juggling of his lineup, platooning of players, and frequent position player substitutions, not to mention his appearance and quirky, often rambling, expositions on the game of baseball, contributed to his persona as the wizened "Ole Perfessor." He had an Einsteinian air about him of creative genius, perhaps even a magician. Everything he did seemed to work, even though many Yankees players were discomfited by not having clearly defined roles or a set place in the batting order. By the late 1950s, however, the Yankees front office was wanting to move beyond the controlled chaos of the Stengel years. They decided in 1958 that the contract Stengel had just signed to manage through the 1960 season would be his last. It was hard to argue with his success, so Stengel's age ultimately was the card they played to cash him out. Or, as Casey said when the Yankees unceremoniously thanked him for his service after his team won the 1960 pennant but not the World Series, "I'll never make the mistake of being 70 again."

3

BROOKLYN'S GLORIOUS DECADE OF BASEBALL

It wasn't until just before World War II that the Brooklyn Dodgers went from being mostly a running joke in the National League—because they played poorly and their character actors included the likes of Casey Stengel as both a player and a manager—to a consistently competitive club to be taken seriously. Naming Leo Durocher as manager in 1939 was a start. The Dodgers won 100 games and the penant in 1941 and won 104 in 1942, only to lose out to the 106-win St. Louis Cardinals. One of the teams most hurt by core players being drafted into the war, the Dodgers rebounded in 1946 after three desultory war seasons to take on the Cardinals in an epic pennant race that ended with both clubs sporting the same record at the end of 154 games. St. Louis won the playoff, but the Dodgers now had the Cardinals' old secret weapon.

That weapon—perhaps not so secret—was Branch Rickey, who left St. Louis to come to Brooklyn in 1943. Initially constrained by wartime, including reduced operating budgets and so many young baseball-playing prospects serving their country, Rickey moved with alacrity as soon as he could to emphasize player development and expand the Dodgers' scouting network and minor-league system. This was hardly surprising from the man whose legacy so far was creating the concept of the farm system in the 1920s when he was running baseball operations for the Cardinals. His insight made St. Louis a perennial National League power and was eventually picked up by every other franchise. Rickey's foresight, however, gave the Cardinals a head start they were able to exploit for nine pennants in 21 years through 1946. He endeavored to do the same for Brooklyn. And moreover, beginning with Jackie Robinson, young Dodgers prospects would include black ballplayers.

It was a formula that, on one level at least, made the Brooklyn Dodgers the most successful club in National League history, at least at the time. No prior National League club—and none afterward until the Cincinnati Reds of Pete Rose, Johnny Bench, and Joe Morgan in the 1970s—had finished first six times in ten years, as the Dodgers did in the 10 years of Jackie Robinson's career. And they just missed out on two other pennants, both in dramatic, even agonizing fashion on the last day of the season. The big blemish on their record was that, for their six pennants won, they prevailed in only one World Series. Of course, it wasn't their fault that all six of the World Series they played were against . . . those damn Yankees, to borrow from the 1955 Tony Award–winning musical. They were able to stay a pennant contender for so long by maintaining continuity among their core players and bringing up high-quality reinforcements when needed from their farm system, most of whom, among core position players, were black.

* * *

First baseman Gil Hodges, Jackie Robinson—a first baseman his rookie season, at second base the next five years, and alternating between third base and left field his final four years—Pee Wee Reese at shortstop, Carl Furillo in right field, Duke Snider in center, Roy Campanella behind the plate, and pitchers Don Newcombe and Carl Erskine were the core of the team that Brooklyn sportswriter Roger Kahn dubbed "The Boys of Summer." All played on the Dodgers' pennant-winning teams in 1949, 1952 and '53, and 1955 and '56. Reese, whose rookie year was 1940, Furillo, a rookie in 1946, and Robinson also played on the 1947 pennant-winning Dodgers. That team was in transition between the prewar Dodgers that came back to battle St. Louis for the 1946 pennant and the Brooklyn juggernaut that would be most identified with the Jackie Robinson era. The core players on the 1947 Dodgers included oft-injured outfielder Pete Reiser; right fielder Dixie Walker, a terrific hitter perhaps best known for his outspoken opposition in spring training to playing with a black man; and ace reliever Hugh Casey, whose drinking buddy relationship with Ernest Hemingway did not go unnoticed.

Snider, Hodges, and Campanella were the power bats for the team that led the National League in scoring six times between 1949 and 1956 and in home runs seven straight years beginning in 1949. Hodges topped 30 home runs six times, including 40 in 1951 and 42 in 1954, and had seven consecutive seasons driving in more than 100 runs. Campanella had five seasons with 30 homers and was the league MVP in 1951, '53, and '55—three years in which he also drove in 100 runs and batted .300. Yogi Berra had also won three MVP Awards by 1955, pitting the two in a debate as to not only which one was the better all-around catcher but whether either had a claim to being the best catcher in major-league history.

Campy vs. Yogi was not the only hot debate in New York. Another concerned the city's trio of exceptional center fielders—the Yankees' Mickey Mantle, the Giants' Willie Mays, and Brooklyn's Duke Snider. The Duke was rarely thought to be better than either Mantle or Mays but was an offensive force, hitting over 40 homers five years in a row from 1953 to 1957, leading the league in scoring three times, knocking in more than 100 runs six times, and five times hitting over .300 when the Dodgers played in Brooklyn. In the late 1940s and early 1950s there was also debate about whether the best shortstop in New York was the Dodgers' Reese, the Yankees' Phil Rizzuto, or the Giants' Alvin Dark. Unlike his Yankees counterpart, Reese returned from three years of wartime service in 1946 as though he had never been away. A deft defensive shortstop and productive whether batting first or second, Reese was indisputably one of baseball's most valuable players, playing at an All-Star-level of performance based on wins above replacement virtually every year between 1946 and 1954.

Furillo was equally consistent, if not as good a ballplayer. Renowned for the strength and accuracy of his throws—he had 121 outfield assists from 1948 to 1956—Furillo batted over .300 six times, hit .344 in 1953 to lead the majors, and had five seasons in which he drove in more than 90 runs. Third base and left field, both of which Robinson played between 1953 and 1956, were positions of weakness or unsettled from year to year when the Boys of Summer ruled. Billy Cox, known much more for his glove and his grit than for his bat, started the majority of games at third between 1949 and 1953 but played more than 120 games just once. Left field was a revolving door of players often platooned by Dodgers managers.

Once he had his racially fraught first season behind him and had moved to his natural position at second base, Jackie Robinson from 1948

Duke Snider hit 188 of his 407 career home runs between 1952 and 1956, helping to power the Brooklyn Dodgers to four pennants in five years. © *Photofest.*

to 1952 was nothing less than exceptional. His .323 five-year batting average included a batting title. He hit 80 homers and drove in 453 runs. He struck out in less than 5 percent of his 3,243 plate appearances and got on base 42 percent of the time. Whenever he got on base, Robinson was a threat to cause mayhem, stealing 120 and scoring 539 runs. Robinson's player value of 8.2 wins above replacement per 650 plate appearances was the best of any major leaguer during those five years. Starting 73 games in left and 43 at third base in 1953, Robinson had another outstanding year. From 1949 to 1953, his rolling average five-year player value per 650 plate appearances was 8.7 wins above replacement. By now he was in his mid-30s and beginning the last phase of his career. More prone to injury, more outspoken and critical—including about his more limited playing time and new manager Walt Alston, who took charge in 1954—Jackie Robinson found his final years in baseball to be frustrating ones that belied the extraordinary role he played in the integration of Major League Baseball.

Like the late 1940s and early 1950s Red Sox playing in hitter-friendly Fenway Park, the 1950s Dodgers, playing in hitter-friendly Ebbets Field, were extolled as an offensive powerhouse whose principal weakness was pitching. As with the Red Sox, that characterization was a bit misleading. Brooklyn was among the NL's top three teams in earned-run average each of their pennant-winning seasons. Don Newcombe and southpaw Preacher Roe, a core starter for the 1949–1951 Dodgers, were two of the best pitchers in the National League. Coming to Brooklyn in 1948 in the deal that sent Dixie Walker to Pittsburgh to accommodate his opposition to playing with Robinson, Roe had a 93–37 record in his next seven years with the Dodgers. In 1951 he had two 10-game winning streaks on his way to a superb 22–3 season, by the end of which the toll on his pitching arm sidelined him for the games where the Dodgers needed him most.

The physically imposing, hard-throwing Newcombe was the workhorse of the Brooklyn staff. Like teammates Robinson and Campanella before him, Newcombe in his 1949 rookie season had to grapple with being one of the Dodgers' trailblazing black players—and the first to be given a prominent role not only as a starting pitcher but as a front-of-rotation ace. After a very successful three years to begin his career—in which he went 56–28 and completed 75 of his 102 starts, proving wrong the canard some were peddling that the abilities of black athletes played well for position players but not pitchers—Newcombe had to put his career on hold for two years in his prime when he was drafted into the army in 1952 during the Korean War. His record the three years after he returned—1954 to 1956—was 56–20.

The one area where the Dodgers did not have continuity during the Jackie Robinson era was the top step of the Ebbets Field dugout. Leo

Durocher—the manager who in spring training 1947 famously headed off a rebellion by Dodgers opposed to the very idea of a black teammate by telling them Jackie Robinson was going to make the team, he was going to make the team better, and the front office would be happy to send anyone who didn't like it elsewhere—was suspended that year because of a celebrity lifestyle and associations with gamblers that Commissioner Chandler considered detrimental to the best interests of baseball. Rickey replaced him with Burt Shotton, with whom he had a long personal and professional relationship. Durocher was back in 1948, then fired in mid-summer and replaced again by Shotton, who in turn was replaced by Charlie Dressen in 1951 because Walter O'Malley, the Dodgers' new owner, had the mind-set to break from all things Rickey following an acrimonious parting of ways between them. Dressen's insistence on being rewarded with a multiyear contract for managing the Dodgers to back-to-back pennants in 1952 and '53 led to his replacement in 1954 by Walt Alston. O'Malley believed in one-year contracts.

* * *

The Dodgers fought down-to-the-last-game pennant races three years in a row from 1949 to 1951 against the St. Louis Cardinals, Philadelphia Phillies, and New York Giants. Carried by the offense of outfielders Stan Musial and Enos "Country" Slaughter, the all-around play of second baseman Red Schoendienst, the excellent defense of shortstop Marty Marion, and the pitching of Harry Brecheen and Howie Pollet, the 1949 Cardinals were a veteran team seeking a return to glory after finishing second in the two years since they won the 1946 World Series and four pennants in five years. The 1950 Phillies, nicknamed the "Whiz Kids" for what they accomplished as the youngest team in the majors, carried the burden of a franchise whose last pennant, back in 1915, was the *only* pennant in franchise history. The 1951 Giants, managed by Durocher, were determined to restore the luster of a historically successful franchise that had not won a pennant since 1937 and been mostly a second-division club in the 1940s, but whose 13 pennants since 1901 were still the most by a National League club.

'Twas 1949, and St. Louis, after being in front nearly all of August and September, went into the final day of the season trailing Brooklyn by a game. The Cardinals needed a win in Chicago and a Dodgers loss in Philadelphia to force a playoff for the pennant. The Cardinals did their part, with Pollet winning his 20th, but the Dodgers beat the Phillies in the

10th inning on RBI-singles by Snider and seldom-used outfielder Luis Olmo, one of the players whose five-year ban for jumping to the Mexican League had been lifted in June. The difference in the pennant race was ultimately that while Musial slugged 36 homers, had 123 RBIs, and batted .338, he was only the second-best player in Major League Baseball—by popular reckoning as well as the later-developed wins above replacement metric. The best was Jackie Robinson, whose .342 batting average led the league, as did his 37 stolen bases. Robinson also drove in 124 runs.

In 1950 the Dodgers were once again playing from behind in September. This time, however, with 137 games down and just 17 to go in mid-September, they were 9 games out of the running and in third place. The Phillies were in first place with a 7½-game lead. Their cast included two future Hall of Famers—center fielder Richie Ashburn and right-hander Robin Roberts, both 23 years old and in their third year; a dangerous cleanup hitter in 25-year-old Del Ennis, the Phillies' resident veteran in his fifth big-league season; a scrappy 23-year-old second-year shortstop named Granny Hamner; and 21-year-old southpaw Curt Simmons. Their oldest player of consequence was 33-year-old relief ace Jim Konstanty.

Then the Dodgers got hot, winning 12 of 15, and the Whiz Kids cold, losing 7 of 9. The Phillies were handicapped by the loss of Simmons, who had 17 wins when his National Guard unit was activated as US forces were getting hammered defending South Korea from the North, which had invaded in June. By the time the Phillies showed up in Brooklyn for the final two games on the schedule, their lead was down to two games. Needing to win both to force a playoff for the pennant, the Dodgers won on Saturday to set up a duel of aces—Roberts, 19–11, against Newcombe, 19–10—for the Sunday finale. In the bottom of the ninth, with the score tied, 1–1, seldom-used outfielder Cal Abrams, starting for only the seventh time all year, began the inning with a walk. He went to second on a single by Reese. On Snider's single to center, Abrams charged hard around third base, intent on scoring the game-winning run that would have left the teams with identical records after 154 games, even though there were no outs and it would be close. Ashburn raced in to field the hit and made a perfect throw to nab Abrams at the plate. Roberts escaped the inning unscathed. Not so Newcombe in the 10th. After a pair of singles to start the inning, Dick Sisler—son of the great George Sisler—hit the most consequential home run of his modest big-league career off Big Newk to send Philadelphia to the 1950 World Series. The victory also made Roberts the first Phillies pitcher since Grover Cleveland Alexander in 1917 to win 20 games.

Neither the Cardinals nor the Phillies contested another pennant race until the 1960s. Operating on shoestring budgets, the Cardinals dropped out of contention as their best players from the late 1940s, with the exception of Musial, faded from the scene. Musial won batting titles in 1950, '51, '52, and '57 to give him a total of seven. Since being called up in September 1941, Musial did not have a single season in which he batted less than .310 until he hit just .254 in 1959, his 19th big-league season, at the age of 38. The vast farm system Rickey had built before leaving St. Louis in 1943 was no longer producing the high-quality players to either promote or trade for talent that had been an earmark of the Rickey era. One whom it did produce was right-hander Larry Jackson, one of the National League's best pitchers from the late 1950s to the mid-1960s, including after he was traded to the Cubs in 1963.

Whatever the promises of youth, the 1950 Whiz Kids proved to be one-year wonders, returning quickly to mediocrity, and by 1958 to their historical place as the doormat of the National League. The Phillies finished up the preexpansion eight-team modern history of the National League with four consecutive eighth-place endings. Richie Ashburn, however, led the league in hits three times and in walks and on-base percentage three times, won batting titles in 1955 and 1958, and batted over .300 eight times. Del Ennis remained the Phillies' principal power threat until he was traded after the 1956 season, having that year surpassed Chuck Klein's team record for career home runs. In 11 years with the Phillies (1946–1956), Ennis drove in more than 100 runs six times and hit 259 homers—still third best on the Phillies' all-time list.

Even as the Phillies struggled through the 1950s, Robin Roberts pitched with a durability, precision, and excellence that hearkened back to the workhorse pitchers of the Deadball Era. He went 12 consecutive years, from 1949 to 1960, with at least 31 starts and more than 225 innings pitched. His 20–11 record in 1950 was the first of six consecutive 20-win seasons—the most since Lefty Grove's seven in a row from 1927 to 1933—during which he won 64 percent of his decisions, with a 138–78 record, and completed nearly 70 percent of his 232 starts. Roberts was the major-league leader in games started all six of those years, averaging 39 a season; in innings pitched five times, with more than 300 innings every year; and led or was tied for the major-league lead in wins and complete games four straight years from 1952 to 1955. No National League pitcher has since matched Roberts' 28 wins for the fourth-place Phillies in 1952, and only Denny McLain's 31 in 1968 has exceeded that total. From his rookie season in 1948 until he was let go after the Phillies concluded from his abysmal 1–10 record in 1961 that he couldn't throw "his fastball past his Aunt Matilda," Robin Roberts won 234 games for Philadelphia. He pitched five more years, falling 14 wins short of 300.

Both teams handicapped themselves by being slow to integrate despite the obvious success the Dodgers and the 1950s Giants were having with black players. Until St. Louis beer baron August Anheuser Busch bought the franchise in 1953, the Cardinals front office was adamantly opposed to integration, insisting they could not afford to alienate the team's fan base in what was then the major leagues' southernmost city. New owner Busch, however, was committed to signing black players for the Cardinals, if for no other reason than that a competitive St. Louis franchise, playing in Busch Stadium, as Sportsman's Park was renamed, would be good for his primary business—selling beer, and black Americans drank Budweiser the same as white Americans. The Cardinals signed their first black player in 1953 and integrated at the major-league level the next. The Phillies were the very last major-league team to sign a black player for their minor-league system, in 1955, and the last bastion of segregation in the National League before finally putting black players on their major-league roster in 1957.

* * *

What happened between the Dodgers and Giants in 1951, and how it all ended, is one of baseball's greatest stories ever told—"The Miracle of Coogan's Bluff," a reference to the rocky outcropping overlooking the Polo Grounds. The key plot points are that the Brooklyn Dodgers held a 13½-game lead over the second-place Giants after winning the first of two games in their August 11 doubleheader against the Braves; that with 106 games done and just 48 to go, there was no way the Dodgers—as dominant as they had been so far—could possibly not win the pennant; that the Giants stormed back from that deficit to end the regular season with the exact same record as the Dodgers, forcing a three-game playoff for the pennant; that they split the first two games, bringing it all down to a 157th game at the Polo Grounds; that the Dodgers held a 4–1 lead when their starter and ace Don Newcombe took the mound needing just three outs to seal the pennant; that he gave up a run and left the game with the tying runs on base and Bobby Thomson coming to bat; that Dressen brought in Ralph Branca to save the game; and that Thomson lined a game-winning, pennant-winning three-run homer into the lower left-field stands to complete arguably the greatest pennant race comeback in history. That the Giants lost the World Series to the Yankees is beside the point; that there even was a World Series is usually left unmentioned in the tale.

Directing the Miracle of Coogan's Bluff was Leo Durocher, who in July 1948 went from managing in the borough of Brooklyn to managing in Manhattan within days thanks to a deal arranged by Branch Rickey with the Giants after deciding he had had enough of Durocher in Ebbets Field. Durocher inherited an offensive powerhouse at the Polo Grounds. The year before, the Giants set a new record for home runs with 221, led by first baseman Johnny Mize, with 51. They were undermined, however, by the majors' second-worst team ERA, even though rookie right-hander Larry Jansen staked his claim to the future with an outstanding 21–5 record.

By 1950 Durocher had rebuilt the Giants more to his liking. New York's aging veteran sluggers, Mize included, were gone. The team's new identity was defined largely by brash middle-infielders Eddie Stanky and Alvin Dark, picked up from the Boston Braves to play second base and shortstop, and a pair of black players—Hank Thompson and former Negro League star Monte Irvin—brought up together the previous July. The compelling 1950 tale of the Phillies' Whiz Kids and the Dodgers' late-September surge obscured the fact that after July 4, it was the Giants that had the National League's best record for the rest of the season. Durocher's decision in late July to move Sal Maglie from the bullpen into a starting role was a major factor for their second-half success. One of the players whose five-year ban from the major leagues for playing in the Mexican League in 1946 was shortened to time banished, Maglie was 13–1 after becoming a regular starter. He finished the season with 18 wins, second to Jansen's 19.

Durocher, Jansen, Maglie, and Irvin were featured stars, but the marquee poster boys of the Miracle were younger slugger Bobby Thomson, who already had 99 career homers, and a 20-year-old black kid brought up in May named Mays—Willie Mays. Jansen and Maglie both won 23. Monte Irvin, playing his first season as a regular, finished with 24 home runs, 121 RBIs, and a .312 batting average, and probably was the NL player most deserving of the 1951 MVP Award because he was at his best in the final two months when the Giants caught up to the Dodgers. Thomson's narrative arc went from being a four-year regular in the Giants' outfield, to struggling so badly the first two months that Durocher resorted to platooning him, to replacing the badly injured Hank Thompson at third base in July and making the most of his opportunity to play every day again by demolishing opposing pitching the rest of the way, to his myth-making showdown with Ralph Branca. A more sentimental narrative thread was Durocher's careful nurturing of Mays despite only one hit in his first 26 at-bats, which happened to be a home run off Braves ace Warren Spahn. Thanks to Leo, Willie ended up Rookie of the Year.

Appearing in a prominent, though uncredited, role was Herman Franks. For most of the first half of the season, Durocher was in the dugout and Franks in the third base coach's box. Then, in mid-July, Durocher took over coaching at third, and Franks was . . . where exactly? If he was in the dugout, he was hiding (if anybody bothered even looking for him). Nobody seemed to have asked, "Where's Herman Franks?" They should have, because of an unexpected plot twist.

The twist nobody saw coming in the Miracle of Coogan's Bluff, famously brought to light by Joshua Prager in the *Wall Street Journal* in 2001 and in fascinating detail in his 2006 book *The Echoing Green*, was that Durocher turned out to be a spymaster. Always on the make for a competitive edge, beginning on July 20 with his second-place Giants 7½ games behind the Dodgers, Durocher installed the uncredited Franks behind a powerful telescope in the center-field clubhouse at the Polo Grounds to spy on opposing catchers' signs and relay them through an electrical buzzer system to the Giants' bullpen in deep right field. From there, they were flashed to Giants hitters in their turn at bat. While players and coaches on the field and in the dugout routinely try to pick off the opposing team's signs, the use of spies with binoculars or telescopes beyond the field of play—such as hiding in scoreboards or sitting in the bleachers—was considered out of bounds. Not that it was unheard of. Just three years before, the Cleveland Indians may have benefited during the September stretch of 1948's three-team AL pennant chase from using a naval gunsight Bob Feller brought back from his time in the Pacific during World War II to steal signs from beyond the outfield fence.

The implication of Prager's revelation is that Thomson may not have hit his dramatic pennant-winning homer off Branca if not for Durocher's spy operation—and moreover, that the Giants probably would not even have forced a playoff for the pennant were it not for Franks as their center-field spy. An analysis of the Giants' batting stats at home and away and before and after "Operation Spyglass" was in place suggests their home-field advantage was marginal. But if Spyglass affected the outcome of any one game before the 154-game schedule ran out, its effect was indeed profound; just one fewer Giants win and the Dodgers would have won the pennant without the need for a playoff. Moreover, the Giants' advantage was only at the Polo Grounds. Although they won a remarkable 23 of the 28 home games that remained after Spyglass began, they actually played 10 more games in other teams' ballparks where they did not have that advantage. That included 18 of their final 21 games of the season, when they were rapidly running out of time to catch the Dodgers. If they were going to win, they were going to have to do so with an excellent road record. They did.

Individually among their core regulars, first baseman Whitey Lockman and right fielder Don Mueller might have—*might have*—benefited from knowing the pitch, because both of them hit far more home runs at home than away after Franks took his place behind the scope. In a two-game series against Brooklyn at the Polo Grounds in the beginning of September, Giants batters clobbered Dodgers pitching for 19 runs to win both games, including seven home runs—five by the light-hitting Mueller and two by Thomson, one of which came off Branca. Mueller, who hit only 65 home runs in his 11-year career, became only the fifth player in major-league history to hit five homers in consecutive games. Not even Babe Ruth did that. While Irvin hit well at home both before and after, he tore up opposing pitchers in *their* home ballparks—possibly the single greatest difference in the pennant race. So did Bobby Thomson. While his after batting averages were nearly identical at home (.356) and away (.357), Thomson was a far more potent power-hitter on the road, belting 13 homers and driving in 34 runs, compared to 3 home runs and 18 RBIs at the Polo Grounds notwithstanding his *possibly* knowing what pitches were coming from Durocher's Operation Spyglass.

The playoff game that ended in the Thomson-Branca showdown was Brooklyn manager Charlie Dressen's worst day at the office. Dressen had three consequential decisions to make in the ninth inning, which began with his team leading, 4–1. First was deciding whether to continue with Newcombe, his ace with a 20–9 record, knowing that Big Newk was about to pitch his 32nd inning in eight days during which he had faced 123 batters. Exactly a week before, his 19th win over the Braves kept the Dodgers' rapidly diminishing lead at one, with 150 games down and four (on the schedule) to go. Three days after that, with the Dodgers and Giants tied for first, he shut out Philadelphia on only two days' rest to keep Brooklyn in a first-place tie as New York also won. The next day— the last scheduled game of the season—he pitched 5⅔ innings of shutout ball in relief from the 8th to the 13th inning in a game the Dodgers had to win because the Giants had already won theirs. Brooklyn did win, in 14 innings. And here Newcombe had pitched brilliantly through eight innings allowing just four hits, two by Thomson, whose sacrifice fly in the seventh drove in the Giants' only run of the game. Preacher Roe might have been an obvious choice to pitch the ninth, having thrown only 1⅓ innings in the last week, but appears not to have been considered, either because of a sore arm or because he had given up eight runs in his last 9⅔ innings. Regardless of how tired his ace was, Dressen made his decision when he let Newcombe bat for himself in the top half of the ninth.

That decision proved mistaken as Newcombe gave up a pair of singles and an RBI-double to put the tying runs in scoring position, bringing up Bobby Thomson, the would-be winning run. It was clear Newk could go no further. With Ralph Branca and Carl Erskine both warming up in the bullpen, Dressen's second consequential decision was to call upon Branca to face Thomson despite his bad pitching down the stretch as the Giants closed in on the collapsing Dodgers. Since the beginning of September, Branca had lost 6 of his 7 starts; pitched twice in relief, giving up runs both times; and surrendered 30 runs on 47 hits and 20 walks in 41 innings. Nine of those hits were home runs, including two by the man he was now asked to get out—Thomson—one a fourth-inning two-run blast in Ebbets Field two days before that proved to be the difference in the first game of the playoff.

Whether or not Thomson knew what pitch was coming, Dressen's decision backfired. But Dressen really had no other choice. His bullpen was a shambles. Relief ace Clyde King came down with a sore arm in August, probably from overuse, just as the Giants were beginning their surge to the top. There were no other relievers Dressen felt comfortable using. Erskine, mostly a starter since July, had been having control problems in recent games. Indeed, the narrative about how Dressen decided against Erskine pitching to Thomson with the pennant at stake because he bounced a curve while warming up in the bullpen makes sense—and not to Dressen's detriment. Given that Erskine had walked 8 batters in his last 12⅓ innings, two of which were in relief, getting word that he was having command problems in the bullpen probably did cause his manager to turn instead to Branca.

Dressen's biggest mistake, however, may have been pitching to Thomson at all in that situation, especially with first base open and one out. Next up was the rookie Willie Mays, by all accounts scared to death it might all come down to him. And behind him was another rookie—seldom-used catcher Ray Noble, in the game because Durocher had pinch-hit earlier for his starting catcher. Thomson was hot—he was batting .457 with 6 home runs in the last 23 games; Mays was not—just 3 for his last 32 at-bats with 10 strikeouts; and Noble had only 141 career at-bats with just 33 hits. Conventional wisdom at the time was never to put the winning run on base, which an intentional walk to Thomson would have done to load the bases. Rather than defy that wisdom, Dressen bowed to it. And Bobby Thomson made history.

* * *

Following that debacle, 1952 was the year the Dodgers began promoting black players of more average major-league ability than star players Robinson, Campanella, and Newcombe to fill positions of weakness. In 1952 it was Joe Black, to fill the glaring need for a top-tier reliever made evident by what had just happened the previous year; in 1953 Jim Gilliam was called up to replace Robinson at second base when the 34-year-old began alternating between left field and third base; in 1954 it was Sandy Amoros, to platoon in left field. By 1956 the Dodgers already had Charlie Neal and John Roseboro lined up for the projected near-term need to replace Reese, entering his late 30s, and Campanella, now in his mid-30s.

New York City's two National League rivals both played the 1952 and '53 seasons without one of their top players when Newcombe and Mays were drafted for military service during the Korean War. Brooklyn won the pennant both years. In 1952 the Dodgers went into first place for good on the first day of June, led comfortably for most of the summer, and finished 4½ games up on the second-place Giants. Black was Rookie of the Year, with a 14–3 record and 15 saves in 54 relief appearances. Dressen started him twice at the end of the season, auditioning him for the role of 1950s Phillies ace reliever Jim Konstanty starting the first game of the World Series for Philadelphia. Black pitched a shutout in his first major-league start, lost his second, and started three games against the Yankees in the World Series. Konstanty in 1950 lost his Game One start to the Yankees, 1–0; Black won his, 4–2, but lost his next two starts. The 1953 Dodgers broke away from the rest of the league by winning 48 of the 62 games they played in July and August, finishing with 105 victories—still the most in franchise history. Gilliam was Rookie of the Year, Robinson flourished playing two different positions, and Erskine's 20–6 record was the best in the league. The Giants fell to fifth place with a losing record.

Newcombe and Mays were both back from the army in 1954. Dressen was not. It was understandable that he resented owner O'Malley for not giving him the multiyear year contract he thought he deserved for managing Brooklyn to two pennants in his three years at the helm. On the other hand, it would have been understandable had O'Malley not wanted him back after Dressen could not keep his team from blowing the entirety of a 13½-game lead in less than two months, as happened in 1951. Durocher was still managing the Giants on a multiyear contract. Newcombe had a poor season in his return to baseball, with a mediocre 9–8 record and 4.55 earned-run average. Willie Mays, on the other hand, became an instant superstar, with 41 homers, 110 runs batted in, and a league-leading .345 batting average. The Giants also fortified their pitching staff by trading Thomson to the Braves, now in Milwaukee, for southpaw Johnny Antonelli, one of the National League's best pitchers over the next six years.

Sparked by the excellence of the Say Hey Kid, Antonelli's league-leading 21–7 record and 2.30 ERA, and Maglie's regrouping at the age of 37 to go 14–6, the 1954 Giants prevailed by five games over the Dodgers. They were decided underdogs going into the World Series, however, because their opponent—the Cleveland Indians—had won 111 games, the most by any team since the 116-win 1906 Cubs. But Willie Mays made perhaps the most iconic catch in baseball history with his long run, back-to-the-infield over-the-shoulder catch of Vic Wertz's mighty drive to deepest center field at the Polo Grounds to stymie a Cleveland rally with the score tied in the 8th inning of Game One. In the 10th, with two runners on, pinch-hitter Dusty Rhodes hit a game-ending homer that just barely cleared the short right-field wall near the foul pole to give the Giants the win. Another pinch-hit homer by Rhodes the next day tied the score at 1–1 in a game the Giants went on to win. As they had in 1951, Durocher's 1954 team proved to be Giant spoilers by knocking off the Indians in a World Series sweep.

* * *

On the afternoon of May 5, 1955, the Dodgers beat the Cardinals at home, 4–3, to win their 18th of 20 games so far that season. Their lead was already 7½ games. That evening, across the East River, in what might have been an answer to Brooklyn fans that their longtime lament of "Wait 'til next year" was about to end, the musical *Damn Yankees* opened on Broadway. Six days later the Dodgers' 11-game winning streak came to an end. Their record was now 22–3. Their lead was 9½ games. They led by 12½ in mid-July, by 15½ in mid-August, and won the pennant by a comfortable 13½ games. Newcombe was back in form, with an outstanding 20–5 record. Always a dangerous hitter for a pitcher, Big Newk channeled his inner Babe Ruth, clubbing 7 home runs and driving in 23 runs in 117 at-bats while batting .359. Twice he hit two homers in a game.

The Brooklyn Dodgers and New York Yankees had vastly different postseason histories as they squared off for the 1955 World Series. The Yankees had been to 20 World Series and won 16 of them. The Dodgers had not won any of their seven World Series appearances, the last five of which were all against the Yankees. And their October history was particularly vexed because it always seemed that some odd event did them in. In 1920, against Cleveland, Brooklyn suffered the ignominy of surrendering the first grand slam in World Series history and being at the wrong end of the only unassisted triple play in World Series history—in the same game. And in their series losses against the Yankees, in 1941 there was Mickey Owen's passed ball on strike three that would have ended Game Four and tied the series at two games apiece, allowing the Yankees a from-the-grave opportunity to win the game; in 1947 Al Gionfriddo's robbery of a Joe DiMaggio drive that caused the normally unflustered Yankee Clipper to kick the dirt and Cookie Lavagetto's two-out last-of-the-ninth double that not only broke up Bill Bevens's no-hitter but turned him into the losing pitcher were the series highlights, but the Dodgers lost anyway; in 1949 it was Tommy Henrich's bottom-of-the-ninth homer that beat Newcombe, 1–0, in the opening game; in 1952 Yankee second baseman Billy Martin made a charging knee-high catch close to the mound with the bases loaded in the seventh inning in Game Seven, on a popup everyone else in the Yankee infield lost in the sun, to save the series; and darned if that same Billy the Kid didn't slap a single up the middle in the bottom of the ninth to win Game Six and the 1953 series for the Yankees.

Now it's 1955, and perhaps reserve outfielder Sandy Amoros, most often platooned in left field, or 22-year-old lefty Johnny Podres, just 9–10 for the season, cut a deal with the devil, as did the fictional Joe Boyd-become-Joe Hardy in *Damn Yankees*. Podres beat the Yankees twice, including a masterful shutout in Game Seven that was saved in the sixth inning by a great catch by Amoros at the left-field fence after a long run that not only robbed Yogi Berra of a game-tying double but turned it into a double play; Gil McDougald, the runner on first, was so certain Berra's drive would be a hit and so determined to score the tying run that he failed to consider that Amoros might actually run it down. Or it might have been manager Walt Alston who made the deal with the devil, because he had just then put Amoros into the game. Or it could have been the baseball gods in heaven saying, "This is Brooklyn's 'next year.'"

Brooklyn won again in 1956. This time, however, they played from behind two challengers for nearly the entire season. Milwaukee's Braves were not only persistent but a very good ballclub, and Cincinnati's Reds were unexpectedly competitive. Perhaps because they had finally won a World Series, the Dodgers much of the time seemed almost disinterested in the pennant race proceedings. They did not spend a single day in first place between May 20 and September 11. They quite likely were fortunate to end the season playing nine games against two losing clubs—Pittsburgh and Philadelphia—of which they won five. Starting the final weekend trailing the Braves by a game, they swept their three-game series at home with the Pirates, while Milwaukee lost two of three in St. Louis. Don Newcombe's victory on the last day of the season was the pennant clincher for Brooklyn. It was also his 27th win against 7 losses. Newk was at his best in nine starts in July and August, allowing just 53 base runners, 42 on hits, and 11 runs in 79 innings, including three consecutive shutouts, one against the Braves. His only loss was 1–0 to the Giants on a Willie Mays home run.

The mid-May acquisition of former Giants nemesis Sal Maglie probably made the difference for Brooklyn in the pennant race. While the Braves had Lew Burdette and Bob Buhl to provide quality depth behind Warren Spahn in their starting rotation, the Dodgers had no such talent

behind Newcombe. Maglie, whose 23–11 career record against the Dodgers as a Giant made him no friends in Brooklyn, was 38, thought to be at
the end of his career, and pitching sparingly for Cleveland. Shutting out
the Braves in his second start for the Dodgers in early June, Maglie was a
mainstay in the rotation the rest of the way, with a 13–5 record. His last
two starts in the regular season were a no-hitter against the Phillies that
kept Brooklyn half a game behind Milwaukee on the day Spahn won his
20th, and a complete-game victory against the Pirates that pushed the
Dodgers ahead of the Braves with 152 games down and two to go as
Spahn lost his 11th. Maglie's next start was the opening game of the 1956
World Series—a complete-game 6–3 victory against the Yankees in
which he whiffed 10. Five days later Maglie was even better, holding the
Yankees to 2 runs on 5 hits in 8 innings. That was the day Don Larsen
pitched his perfect game.

* * *

After 10 years playing for the Brooklyn Dodgers, his only major-
league team, Jackie Robinson announced his retirement in December
1956 after the Dodgers traded him to their archrivals in New York, the
Giants. More than a courageous trailblazer for blacks in Major League
Baseball, Robinson became one of the earliest icons of the civil rights
movement. But not for stirring oratory; nor for fighting back against
discrimination in public transportation, schools, and housing; nor for
standing in the front line against armed white mobs and local police with
truncheons, fire hoses, and attack dogs. Not for registering blacks to vote
and demanding that the 14th and 15th Amendments be honored as their
framers intended. Those were all more important than baseball, and
America's black citizens involved in them had much more at stake in
lives, freedom, and livelihood. Instead, Robinson beat them—those who
would have continued to deny black players the opportunity and the right
to play in the major leagues—at their own game.

4

RELOCATION (BRAVES), RELOCATION (BROWNS), RELOCATION (ATHLETICS)

For 50 years, from 1903 to 1952, not only had the eight National League and eight American League franchises remained the same and stayed in place, but the 16 major-league teams played in just 10 American cities. Five—New York, Chicago, Philadelphia, St. Louis, and Boston—had franchises in both leagues; New York was home to two NL clubs and the Yankees. For both leagues, having a franchise in the largest US cities was a priority, but except for New York and Chicago—the country's two most populous cities in the first half of the 20th century—two teams competing in the same city resulted in attendance inequities even though league schedules ensured that both teams were rarely at home at the same time. Typically, in any given season the hometown team that was more competitive drew the lion's share of the citizens who paid to see major-league games. In Philadelphia, St. Louis, and Boston, one or the other club—and sometimes both at the same time—spent many years in the second-division wilderness of their leagues, negatively affecting attendance to the point where they were often in serious financial straits. By midcentury, with some rumblings even in the 1930s, this dynamic called into question whether those three two-franchise cities in particular could really support two major-league clubs.

The one-city, two-franchise sustainability problem was most acute in Boston and St. Louis. Both cities lagged far behind New York and Chicago in population growth; while the number of people living in New York (7.9 million) and Chicago (3.6 million) more than doubled between 1900 and 1950, St. Louis's population increased by just 51 percent, to 857,000, and Boston's by only 43 percent, to 801,000. Both cities had dropped in the ranks of the country's most populous to 8th from 4th for St. Louis and 10th from 5th for Boston. The only major-league cities with a smaller population base were Pittsburgh and Cincinnati; Washington ranked 9th, between St. Louis and Boston. One team in each city was clearly the underdog when it came to drawing fans to their ballpark, and those clubs spent the first half of the century making names for themselves as among the three worst franchises in the major leagues. In St. Louis it was the Browns; in Boston it was the Braves.

* * *

The glory days of National League baseball in Boston were in the nineteenth century, when the Braves, then known as the Beaneaters, won four pennants in seven years between 1892 and 1898 with one of the best ballclubs baseball had yet seen. From 1901 until the end of World War II, the NL franchise won just one pennant and one World Series, by the 1914 "Miracle" Braves, famous for surging from last place in late July 1914 to win the pennant by 10½ games and sweeping the far-better Philadelphia Athletics in the World Series. Soon thereafter, Boston's Braves plunged into decades of mostly horrid baseball, just five times with a winning record in the 29 years from 1917 to 1945. The Red Sox were the far more successful and favored team in Boston, despite not winning a pennant between 1918, when Babe Ruth still played for them, and 1946, when Ted Williams was the star of their show. Even in the 1920s, when the Red Sox were at their worst, they drew more fans into Fenway Park to watch their last-place club than the Braves attracted to Braves Field to watch their club try to stay out of last place, which they were occasionally successful in doing.

The end of the war was a turning point for both Boston clubs. The Red Sox dominated the American League and went to the World Series. Meanwhile, the three local construction contractors known as the Little Steam Shovels, who bought the Braves in 1944, succeeded in recruiting Billy Southworth, whose Cardinals won three straight pennants and two World Series between 1942 and 1944, to take over as manager in 1946 and turn their team into a winner. Within three years, Southworth did exactly that. Right fielder Tommy Holmes, the league leader in hits and home runs in 1945 and second in batting average and runs batted in, was the only star player Southworth inherited from prior management. And returning to Boston from wartime military service were right-hander Johnny Sain and lefty Warren Spahn, neither of whom played any meaningful role in their inaugural 1942 season before being drafted. In 1946 Sain had the first of three consecutive (and four in five years) 20-win seasons; Spahn excelled after being called up in mid-June; and the Braves finished as high as fourth for the first time in 12 years.

The 1947 trade acquisition of third baseman Bob Elliott and the pairing of rookie shortstop Alvin Dark with traded-for second baseman Eddie Stanky in the infield and at the top of the order in 1948 were the final pieces Southworth needed to manage the Braves to their first pennant in 34 years. The foundation for the Braves' trip to the World Series, however, was "Spahn and Sain and pray for rain." Beginning the final month with a half-game lead over Brooklyn, Southworth relied heavily on that maxim as the Braves won 16 of their first 19 games in September to take command of the pennant race. Spahn started five games and had four complete-game victories, including three in eight days. Sain pitched six complete-game victories in six starts in the first 21 days of September, three times on two days of rest. Sain and Spahn were the winning pitchers in the only two games the Braves beat the Indians in the 1948 World Series. There may have been prayers, but there was no rain in either Boston or Cleveland. There were not even travel days; the six-game series was played in six days.

The Braves' time at the top was short-lived. Brooklyn's Dodgers were a better ballclub that got even better when Don Newcombe joined their pitching staff in 1949. Southworth's Hall of Fame managerial career, meanwhile, was coming to a less-than-elegant end in Boston. Southworth's hard-driving approach to managing took a wrong turn after winning the 1948 pennant, at least as far as his players were concerned. His discipline seemed petty and arbitrary, and his game decisions less than astute. He also resumed his battle with the bottle, a problem that had stymied his career in the 1930s before he overcame alcoholism and guided the Cardinals to greatness in the 1940s. The 1949 Braves were out of the running by the end of July, and two weeks later Southworth took a leave of absence to recover his health. Their franchise at a crossroads in 1950, the Braves' trio of owners opted to return Southworth as manager, because he still had three years left on his expensive contract, and get rid of his two most vociferous critics in the clubhouse by trading Dark and Stanky—their highly esteemed double-play combination—to the Giants.

That didn't help. Southworth remained alienated from his players, finally resigning as manager in June 1951. The Giants would not have won their Miracle of Coogan's Bluff pennant without Stanky and Dark.

By now it was also obvious that the Braves' position in Boston was unsustainable. The Red Sox were the powerhouse, fan-favored team in Boston. The Braves were able to hold their own in attendance with the Red Sox the first four years after World War II, when fans flocked to major-league ballparks everywhere, averaging more than 1 million fans. By 1949 the attendance gap between the two clubs widened to more than 500,000 in favor of Fenway Park as the Red Sox fought for the pennant till the last day of the season while the Braves were a noncompetitive fourth. In 1950, the gap was nearly 1 million. The next year the Braves' attendance was below 500,000 for the first time since 1945, and in 1952 the 281,300 fans who paid to watch the seventh-place Braves were by far the fewest in the majors. Having consolidated control of the franchise from his fellow Steam Shovels and concluding that staying in Boston was a money-losing proposition, majority owner Lou Perini stunned the base-ball world during spring training in 1953 by announcing the Braves would be moving permanently to Milwaukee that very season.

With a larger population than Cincinnati and a brand-new major-league-sized ballpark funded by the city, Milwaukee was angling for a franchise to call its own. Moreover, the fact that the Braves' top minor-league franchise played there gave them territorial rights to Milwaukee. For the first time since 1903, the geographic map of the major leagues included a new city. The Braves brought with them seven-year veteran Warren Spahn, one of baseball's best pitchers, and 21-year-old slugging third baseman Eddie Mathews, a superstar in the making. Already with four 20-win seasons, Spahn was the only core regular from the 1948 pennant-winning Boston Braves still on the club in a meaningful role when the franchise moved to Milwaukee. Bob Elliott, the Braves' best position player in 1948, was traded in 1952 to make room for Mathews. Spahn's 122 wins since his rookie year in 1946 were the most won by any *Boston* Braves pitcher in the twentieth century. Only Kid Nichols with 329 and Vic Willis with 151 had more franchise victories than Spahn, and nearly all Nichols's and 62 of Willis's were with the great Boston teams of the 1890s.

Perini was spectacularly right in believing that the Braves' fortunes would turn around with a change of address. The new *Milwaukee* Braves rose from seventh place and 89 losses the previous year in Boston to 92 wins—the most since the 1914 Miracle Braves—and second place in 1953. In each of their first six years in Milwaukee, the Braves led the major leagues in attendance. Attracting fans regionally from across the upper Midwest, the Braves in just their second season in Milwaukee became the first National League club to attract 2 million fans, which they did every year from 1954 to 1957.

By the mid-fifties, the Braves had emerged as a formidable long-term threat to the Dodgers' annual pennant drive thanks to the Steam Shovels' investment in a productive farm system, astute trades, and Perini's willingness to sign and promote black players to the major-league club. Coming up through their minor-league affiliates, besides Mathews, were catcher Del Crandall, shortstop Johnny Logan, and right-hander Bob Buhl. Acquired in trades were right-hander Lew Burdette, in a summer 1951 deal that sent Johnny Sain to the Yankees, and slugging first baseman Joe Adcock from the Reds in 1953. The Braves had integrated their roster in 1950 with center fielder Sam Jethroe. After a poor 1952 season in which he was handicapped by vision problems, Jethroe did not accompany the team to Milwaukee. His place in center field and at the top of the order was taken by another black player, Bill Bruton. Promoted from the Braves' top minor-league affiliate in Milwaukee, Bruton didn't have to change cities. In 1954 the Braves brought up a superb prospect named Hank Aaron, also African American. And waiting in the wings were black minor-league prospects outfielder Wes Covington, infielder Felix Mantilla, and southpaw Juan Pizarro. Mantilla and Pizarro were both Puerto Rican.

Although swamped by the Brooklyn juggernaut of 1955, Milwaukee was considered one of the best teams in baseball going into 1956, certain to give the Dodgers a run for their money. But the Braves sputtered in the first half of June. Milwaukee's Braves were supposed to be better than that, so manager Charlie Grimm paid the price for his club's lackluster performance. Although Leo Durocher, let go by the Giants in 1955, was said to be available, Perini went with Fred Haney, whom he had hired to be Grimm's "first lieutenant" (as *Sports Illustrated* put it) despite three dispiriting last-place seasons managing a very bad Pittsburgh club. No sooner did Haney take over than the Braves got hot. They won their first 11 games under Haney, reclaiming first place, and 32 of the first 42 he was their manager. That was a pace the Braves could not sustain. Enduring a five-game losing streak in early September and a mediocre 14–13 record for the final month were not helpful in a three-team pennant race that was not decided in favor of the Dodgers until the final day of the season. The Braves finished one game back. Aaron broke into elite-player ranks with his league-leading .328 batting average. Adcock hit 38 homers and Mathews had 37. Spahn won 20, Burdette 19, and Buhl 18.

After six consecutive National League pennants won by New York teams—four by Brooklyn's Dodgers and two by Manhattan's Giants—the first-place flag finally went to another city when Milwaukee won decisively by eight-game margins in both 1957 and 1958. In quite possibly the best World Series pitching performance since Christy Mathewson's three shutouts in 1905, Lew Burdette threw three complete-game victories in the 1957 series, allowing just two runs in the second game and throwing shutouts in Games Five and Seven to take down the Yankees. In the 1958 series, a rematch of the previous year, the Braves became just the second team in World Series history, after the 1925 Senators, to blow a three-games-to-one lead.

Milwaukee's chance to secure a dynasty fell flat in 1959. After leading for much of the first half of the season, the Braves spent most of the second half trying to catch the Dodgers and Giants, both now in California. After 154 games, they and the Dodgers had identical records, forcing the NL's third best-of-three playoff in 14 years to decide the pennant. The Braves lost in two games, both by one run. On the verge of forcing a third game, the Braves squandered a three-run lead in the ninth and lost the game—and the pennant—two innings later on a two-out throwing error by Mantilla, playing shortstop because Johnny Logan had been injured earlier in the game. Fred Haney resigned as manager.

Hank Aaron and Eddie Mathews were writing their tickets to Cooperstown in the years from 1956 to 1959. Aaron won two batting titles, batted .333, hit 139 home runs, and drove in 442 runs. Mathews hit 146 homers, had 380 RBIs, and in 1959 led the league with 46 home runs while batting second in his manager's lineup—a very unconventional spot for a power hitter at the time—rather than his customary third or fourth in previous years. Spahn, Burdette, and Buhl (although injured for much of 1957) gave the Braves the most formidable starting threesome in baseball. It should not go unmentioned that the 1956–1959 Braves got significant contributions from four black players—center fielder Bruton; Covington, a left-handed batter platooned in the outfield; utility infielder

Mantilla; and southpaw Pizarro, a spot-starter—who were more average or even marginal major leaguers than was typical for black players in key roles on their teams at the time.

Ironically, the Braves might have won all four years if not for the curious case of the Dodgers' mysterious spell on Warren Spahn—a 20-game winner all four years, only one of whose 84 victories came against the Dodgers. Spahn had such a poor track record against the Dodgers from 1949 to 1953, at 6–17 with a 4.15 earned-run average, that he did not start a single game against them in 1954 and 1955, just one in 1956 (it went badly), and none in 1957. After two relatively good starts against now-LA in 1958 (a win and a loss), Spahn's Dodgers demons returned with a vengeance in 1959. They scored 17 earned runs off him in 25⅓ innings, beating him in all three of his starts and twice more in relief during the 154-game schedule. Called in as a reliever in the ninth inning in the 156th game—the second playoff game for the pennant—Spahn gave up the tying run that sent the game into extra innings.

* * *

The Braves' move from Boston to Milwaukee in 1953 opened the gate for two other losing, financially struggling franchises in two-team cities to go elsewhere for a more profitable and, hopefully, competitively successful future. In 1954 the American League's last-place Browns left St. Louis to the Cardinals by moving east to Baltimore—not west, which would have been more logical in terms of expanding the major leagues' geography across the continent—where they became the Orioles. And in 1955 the Athletics, who fell to the bottom of the AL standings in 1954 as the Browns-turned-Orioles finished seventh, left Philadelphia to the Phillies by moving to Kansas City. In three years, the major leagues had gone from five two-franchise cities to just two—New York and Chicago, the two largest cities in the country.

At midcentury, the Browns and the Athletics were two of the worst teams in baseball. For the St. Louis Browns, that was nothing new. They were arguably the major leagues' worst franchise in the first half of the century. In 49 years since replacing the Milwaukee Brewers—an original American League franchise—in 1902, the Browns had only 11 seasons with a winning record. Their only pennant in 1944 was a year when the American League's best teams were crippled because many of their best players were serving in the armed forces. After baseball's best returned from the war in 1946, the Browns were swamped by superior teams, reverted to their losing ways, and never again had a winning record in St. Louis.

St. Louis had been a Cardinals town since the Redbirds began winning pennants with regularity in 1926. The only year since then that the Browns, who owned the ballpark that both teams called home, outdrew the Cardinals was the year they at long last won the pennant. As the Browns quickly returned to losing following their losing trip to the World Series in 1944, the Cardinals remained one of the best teams in baseball. They drew more than 1 million fans every year from 1946 to 1951, while the Browns saw their attendance settle below 300,000. In each of their last eight years in St. Louis, from 1946 to 1953, fewer fans came to Browns home games than to see any of the 15 other major-league teams—and 1953 was the Braves' last in Boston. It didn't help that after trading star shortstop Vern Stephens to the Red Sox in 1948, the Browns had no prominent everyday player to showcase for their fans. Right-hander Ned Garver was their best player thereafter, a top-tier pitcher in the American League toiling for a bottom-dwelling club. In 1951, his only winning season in St. Louis, Garver amazingly won 20 while losing just 12 for the last-place Browns, who were 32–90 in games that he did not get the decision. Without Garver, the Browns' 5.18 earned-run average for the season was 5.49.

When he bought the franchise in July 1951, former Cleveland owner Bill Veeck knew the Browns were on borrowed time in St. Louis, unless he could do something about it. One of his first acts to encourage the good citizens of St. Louis to come see the Browns, who typically played before scattered thousands at home, was to sign the incomparable Negro League legend Satchel Paige, now 44 (if not older), as a relief pitcher. Ever the showman, Veeck tried stunts, like sending up the 3-foot-7 Eddie Gaedel with a legitimate contract to pinch-hit for the leadoff batter in the home first. Gaedel walked and was immediately replaced by a pinch-runner, and his contract was voided by Major League Baseball. Veeck tried gimmicks like allowing fans in the stands to make managerial decisions at various points in the game with "yes" or "no" placards to questions such as, "Should the Browns sacrifice here?" None of it worked. And when wealthy beer baron August Anheuser Busch bought the Cardinals in February 1953 and stated he was prepared to build a new stadium for his team, Veeck knew the Browns had to leave town.

His original preference of Milwaukee—the city from whence the Browns originally came back in 1902, and the city where he had made a name for himself as owner of a minor-league franchise—was a nonstarter because the Braves owned the territorial rights and moved there themselves. But Baltimore beckoned. A city with a long and distinguished baseball history dating back to the 1890s but without a major-league team since 1902, Baltimore, like Milwaukee, already had a new stadium built with public money to entice a big-league franchise. His fellow owners, however, twice vetoed Veeck's Baltimore plan, motivated in large part by pique at Veeck personally. Once Baltimore's civic leaders understood the animosity the league's owners had for Veeck, they put together a consortium of investors to buy the St. Louis Browns. And once Veeck sold them the franchise, AL owners voted in favor of the Browns' move to Baltimore in 1954, where they took the honorable name of the great National League Baltimore Orioles of the 1890s.

The move to a new city (and name change) did not pay the dramatic immediate dividends that the Braves' move to Milwaukee did. The Orioles drew more than 1 million fans their first year in Baltimore, good for just fifth in league attendance. They finished seventh once again. They did not break the 1 million threshold again until three years later, in 1957, and not again until three years after that. In their first six years in Baltimore, the Orioles were always in the bottom half of the league in attendance, as well as the bottom half of the AL standings. Not until 1960 were the Orioles a competitive ballclub, unexpectedly competing with the Yankees for the pennant and coming in second; they were third that year in attendance.

* * *

Philadelphia's Athletics had a different history. They had nine pennants on their historical ledger but also finished last 17 times. (The Browns, by contrast, ended in the basement just eight times despite their multitude of losing seasons.) The franchise—owned, operated, and managed by Connie Mack—fielded two of the greatest teams in history: the 1910–1914 Athletics, which won four pennants and three World Series in five years, and the 1929–1931 team that put together three consecutive pennants, winning more than 100 games each year, and two World Series championships. As an owner concerned with his bottom line, Mack broke up both dynasties for economic reasons. The result the first time was seven straight terrible seasons at the absolute bottom of the standings before he began rebuilding for his second dynasty. Not so the second time.

The ravages of the Depression prevented, or perhaps excused, Mack from investing anew in his franchise. In 12 years from 1935 to 1946, the Athletics finished dead last nine times, and next to last twice. Running the franchise as a family small business that he wished to pass on to his heirs, Mack refused to sell to people who had the financial resources to turn the Athletics' fortunes around, or even invite deep-pocketed investors to buy a stake in his team. As owner, Connie Mack also refused to step down as manager despite the fact that he was already 68 years old when Philadelphia's Athletics won their last pennant in 1931. Nineteen years later, he was pushing 90. One of baseball's great managers in the first third of the century, Mack had become an anachronism—less astute, often disinterested, and unable to relate to players young enough to be his great-grandsons.

In 1948, however, it looked for much of the summer that the Athletics might—just *might*—give the old man a grand finale. On August 3, half of the American League, including the Athletics, were tied for first. Nine days later, they were actually atop the standings by half a game—the latest any Athletics team had been in first place since 1931. Aside from the fact that the Athletics really did not measure up to the far-superior Yankees, Red Sox, and Indians, their record at this point in the season was deceptive because 62 percent of their games, of which they'd won two-thirds, had been against the four teams that ended the season at the bottom of the standings. With 54 percent of their remaining games against New York, Boston, and Cleveland, it did not figure that Mack's men would be competing for the pennant much longer. And indeed the Athletics won only six of the 25 games they played against the real contenders from mid-August till the end of the season. By the end of the first week of September, the Athletics were 9½ games behind and out of it. The next year, with largely the same team, the Athletics played more according to their talent, ending up fifth before collapsing to the bottom of the heap in 1950 with only 52 wins.

Almost 88, Connie Mack finally retired as manager. But the Athletics were still a Mack family–owned small business—one whose sparse finances made it untenable to stay in Philadelphia. It was not as though the third-largest city in the country, whose population of 2 million was twice as large as Boston and St. Louis combined, could not support two major league teams. But the times had changed. A team that remained persistently noncompetitive, showed no ability or commitment to improving that state of affairs, and played in a ballpark that first opened in 1909 and was shared by the other ballclub in town was bound to fail for lack of fan support. If the script followed what happened in Boston and St. Louis, the team to fail in Philadelphia should have been the Phillies, who had spent most of the previous half century as one of baseball's worst teams, while the Athletics, despite some atrocious seasons themselves, also embodied a distinguished and great history.

But as Mack's franchise went deeper in debt and came close to insolvency, losing all the while, the Phillies were ascendant in the City of Brotherly Love. True, they had a winning record in only 12 of the previous 50 years and had won only two pennants in their entire history, but their second was recent, in 1950. Moving forward, that Phillies team, collectively called the Whiz Kids, was young and dynamic, with compelling stars like Robin Roberts and Richie Ashburn—a stark contrast to the Athletics, whose starting position regulars were consistently the oldest in the majors. It didn't help that Mack traded away top prospects like George Kell in 1946 and Nellie Fox in 1950, both of whom blossomed into Hall of Fame players for their new clubs, and first baseman Ferris Fain right after he won a second consecutive batting title in 1952. Even when they finished fourth in 1952, thanks to Fain's hitting prowess, outfielder Gus Zernial's 29 homers, and an extraordinary 24–7 record by crafty 5-foot-6 lefty Bobby Shantz that earned him MVP honors, the Athletics were only seventh in the league in attendance, drawing 128,000 fewer fans to Connie Mack Stadium than the Phillies, who also finished fourth. The next year, the Athletics' attendance dropped by more than half as they plummeted to seventh place.

The Mack family business was in desperate straits and needed a bailout. Selling was their only option. Contrary to the preferences of soon-to-turn-92 family patriarch Connie Mack, the franchise was sold to Chicago businessman Arnold Johnson, who was quite clear about his intention to move the team to Kansas City. The intervention of the Yankees' Del Webb and Dan Topping, with whom Johnson had close business dealings, sealed the deal with their fellow American League owners. Kansas City authorities, meanwhile, funded a renovation and expansion of the city's minor-league stadium to make it suitable for major-league baseball. The Athletics in their new home rose from last place to sixth in 1955.

Drawing 1.4 million fans, they were second to the Yankees in attendance. That turned out to be their high point in both the standings and attendance in the 13 years the Athletics were in Kansas City before they relocated to Oakland in 1968. It didn't help that their owner's close ties to the Yankees' owners made the Kansas City Athletics seem more like a major-league farm club for the best team in baseball than an independent major-league club in its own right.

5

INTEGRATION'S INCREMENTAL
PROGRESS

By Opening Day on April 17, 1956, exactly nine years and two days after Jackie Robinson made his big-league debut in 1947, it was accepted there was no going back on integration in Major League Baseball. Branch Rickey had required Robinson in his first few seasons to take with equanimity all manner of racially inflected abuse heaped on him by white fans and opponents alike, no matter how vicious, because that's what was needed for him to stay in the game—and not be forced out by being cast as an out-of-control hot-headed n-word—so he could prove he belonged with the very best in previously all-white Major League Baseball. Jackie Robinson did exactly that. Thanks to his forbearance and excellence, the "Great Experiment"—to use historian Jules Tygiel's phrase—unleashed by Rickey was a success. But it was still only a qualified success to the extent that 10 years into the Jackie Robinson era there were still few black players on major-league rosters. Moreover, most black players who had been core regulars on their teams over the course of multiple seasons were elite players—specifically, Robinson, Larry Doby, Roy Campanella, Don Newcombe, Monte Irvin, Minnie Minoso, and just in the last three years, Willie Mays, Hank Aaron, and Ernie Banks—demonstrating they were every bit as good as the best white players.

Black players of more average major-league ability were still at a disadvantage competing with white players of comparable talent for starting roles. Those who won starting positions in any given season had much less margin for error when it came to keeping their job for the long term. Managers and coaches, all of whom were white, had less patience with nonelite black players when they were sidelined by injuries, endured slumps, or were deficient in one aspect of their game or another, and were quicker to conclude that someone else would do better than they did when white players of comparable ability had the same difficulties. Black players also had to be more mindful of the tenor of their clubhouse interactions, lest they be misinterpreted as being a problem personality. The Giants' Hank Thompson, the Dodgers' Jim Gilliam, the Braves' Bill Bruton, and the Indians' Al Smith were the rare exceptions of black players who were more typical of average-ability major leaguers being secure in their starting roles until their overall skills began to diminish with age or chronic injuries and someone better came along. All four played for franchises that were the earliest to be serious about integrating black players capable of playing at the major-league level.

Resistance might have been futile—there was no going back in time—but resistance there was in the American League outside of a handful of clubs. While outstanding black players were making the National League the more exciting league, the AL had just two enduring black stars of its own during the breadth of Jackie Robinson's career—Larry Doby, who had just been traded to the White Sox after eight years playing center field for Cleveland, and Chicago outfielder Minnie Minoso. Just three AL clubs started the 1956 season with as many as two black players on their rosters, including the White Sox with four and Kansas City with three. Two other American League teams began the season with just one black player on their rosters, including the Yankees, which meant that three AL teams—Boston, Detroit, and Washington—had no black players on their Opening Day roster. All told, there were 10 black players on American League Opening Day rosters, six of whom started in their team's first game of the year.

In the National League, by contrast, Jackie Robinson was one of 29 black players on the Opening Day rosters of seven of the eight teams. Only the Philadelphia Phillies had still not integrated their roster. Fourteen black players were in National League Opening Day starting lineups, five of them on the Brooklyn Dodgers, including Robinson, who batted sixth and played third base. With seven players, the Cincinnati Reds had more black players on their roster than any other major-league team at the beginning of the 1956 schedule. The most talked about were right-hander Brooks Lawrence, acquired from St. Louis over the winter, and highly touted rookie outfielder Frank Robinson. After being such a bust in 1955 that he finished the season in the minor leagues, questions about Lawrence focused on whether he could recapture what he had going for him in his impressive 15–6 debut with the Cardinals in 1954. Questions about Robinson focused on whether he would really be as good as he gave every indication of being.

* * *

It turned out the answer to both questions was a resounding yes, and thanks to them the Reds—called the Redlegs since 1954, just so there would be no confusing where the Cincinnati baseball team stood with regard to the great issues of the day in the midst of seemingly perpetual Soviet-American crises in these dark days of the Cold War, not to mention the "Red menace" narrative promoted by the likes of Senator Joe McCarthy—were in their first pennant race since winning the World Series in 1940. Cincinnati had not even had a winning record since the World War II year of 1944. The Reds' most noteworthy players in the postwar years were tall, lean Ewell Blackwell, whose whiplike side-armed delivery caused nearly every right-handed batter to bail in the interest of self-preservation, and first baseman Ted Kluszewski, a left-handed slugger. The promise of greatness that Blackwell's second-year 22–8 record and league-leading 193 strikeouts in 1947 seemed to portend was quickly undone by shoulder and other health miseries that forced him out of the game in 1953. Big Klu entered 1956 off three consecutive 40-home run seasons in which his total of 136 exceeded the mere 109 times he struck out while batting .319.

The unexpectedly competitive Reds began the month of August two games behind the Braves and one ahead of the Dodgers—the two preseason picks to battle it out for the top of the NL standings—in large measure because of the emergence of Brooks Lawrence as the undisputed ace of an otherwise unremarkable starting rotation. Winning his first 13 decisions, Lawrence had run his record to 15–2 and was on pace to easily win 20 games. Lawrence, however, had also pitched 151⅔ innings, just seven fewer than he threw in his 1954 rookie season, and there were two months to go. He pitched terribly in August, losing all six of his starts. His only victory was in relief. His earned-run average for the month was 5.89, bringing it close to 4.00 from 3.32, where it stood at the end of July.

Cincinnati nonetheless managed to win 17 of 30 games in August to enter the final month alive in the pennant chase, 3½ games behind Milwaukee and one behind Brooklyn. The reason was the Reds' onslaught of 50 home runs for the month, 11 of which were by Frank Robinson. On the last day of August, Robinson crashed his 35th homer in the bottom of the ninth to tie the game and set the stage for a comeback win by his team. It was Cincinnati's 191st of the year in 129 games. Paling in comparison to the three-team race for the pennant, and quite likely given little thought, was the fact that Robinson was ahead of Wally Berger's pace when he hit 38 for the Boston Braves in 1930 to set the rookie home run record, and that the Reds were ahead of the 1947 Giants' pace when they hit 221 to set the major-league team record. With a full month to go, it seemed a good bet both records would be broken.

Frank Robinson did not set a new rookie record for home runs. Nor did the Cincinnati Reds set a new team record for homers. Brooks Lawrence did not make it to 20 wins. And Cincinnati never got closer than 1½ games in the final month, ending in third place with 91 wins, two games behind Brooklyn and one behind Milwaukee. Robinson hit his 38th home run on September 11 to equal Berger's mark, but had just 13 hits—none of them home runs—in the 16 games that ended the season. The Reds tied the Giants' 1947 record for homers with one game left but did not get so much as an extra-base hit in the season finale, despite winning, 4–2, in a meaningless game; they had been eliminated the day before. Robinson was unanimously voted the NL's Rookie of the Year. He was the seventh black player to win the award, whose first winner was Jackie Robinson in 1947. All seven were National Leaguers.

After the fact, there were insinuations that the Reds might not have won the pennant because manager Birdie Tebbetts did not want Brooks Lawrence, a black man, to win 20 games. This was supposedly the reason why Lawrence, who won his 19th on September 15 with 13 games left on the schedule, did not get another start even though he was Cincinnati's best pitcher. In fact, he started just three of the Reds' 26 games in the entire final month.

There were two narrative arcs at play behind that insidious insinuation, both of which had merit at a time when Major League Baseball was still grappling with integration. The first was racial prejudice, a hangover from when the major leagues were whites-only, at a time when, notwithstanding the 1954 Supreme Court decision striking down "separate but equal" in *Brown v Board of Education*, segregation in practice was still widespread. Now that most clubs had black players on their rosters—and the fact that a disproportionate number of elite players were black—rather than outright hostility, the racial attitudes of white players, coaches, and even managers were most often manifest in clubhouse comments and hijinks playing to racial stereotypes at the expense of black teammates. There was still a widespread perspective, however, that the likes of Brooks Lawrence were costing white players roster spots and starting roles. The second narrative derived from racial stereotypes, including the idea that while individual black players might be great athletes, their baseball IQ about the game's nuances was deficient, they lacked discipline in collaborative teamwork, and they could not be relied upon to handle the pressure of close games in tight pennant races. Neither narrative was true in how Lawrence was actually used.

If August was unkind to Lawrence, it did not seem to diminish Tebbetts's faith in him. Lawrence's complete-game four-hitter against the Cubs on September 1, while his first win as a starting pitcher since the end of July, ran his record to 17–8 and kept the Reds on pace with the Braves and Dodgers, both of whom also won that day. Two days later, in their most crucial series of the season against the Braves in Milwaukee, Cincinnati lost the first game of a doubleheader to fall 4½ back. The Reds' 5–2 lead in the third inning of the second game was quickly in grave jeopardy when the Braves loaded the bases with nobody out and Hank Aaron (with 23 home runs), Eddie Mathews (with 37), and Joe Adcock (with 34) coming up. Knowing the difference between a win and a loss was ending the day either 3½ back and still in the pennant chase or 5½ back in probably too deep a hole to dig out of, Tebbetts called on Lawrence to save the day on just one day's rest after his complete-game victory. Lawrence got Aaron on a short fly to left and Mathews to hit into a double play without a run scoring, then pitched the remaining six innings to get the win and keep Cincinnati close enough to the top that the season still mattered. The Reds won their next two games in Milwaukee to cut their deficit to 1½ games.

Lawrence was now 18–8, and Tebbetts did not take him out of the starting rotation. That was not, however, the last time Tebbetts used his best pitcher out of the bullpen in must-win games down the stretch. The Reds' next critical series was two weeks later in Brooklyn for two games. They trailed the first-place Dodgers by two with only 13 games remaining. Even though Lawrence had pitched 6⅓ innings in a start just two days before, to win his 19th, Tebbetts used him in both games as a reliever—to stanch a second-inning Dodgers rally in the first game, which they lost, and the next day to begin the ninth inning in a tie game the Reds could not afford to lose—especially not to the Dodgers. This time, Tebbetts's gamble didn't pay off. Pitching Lawrence for the fourth time in five days, Tebbetts was clearly going with his overworked pitcher because he judged him to be the best he had. Lawrence stranded two runners in the ninth, only to give up a walk-off game-winning homer to Carl Furillo leading off the 10th.

As the Reds' prospects dwindled, a desperate Tebbetts also used Lawrence in relief each of the next two days in Philadelphia in an effort to halt Cincinnati's slide. After pitching six times in eight days, including his 6⅓-inning start, Lawrence did not get another start to go for his 20th win, even as a six-game winning streak kept Reds hopes alive into the final weekend. Perhaps Tebbetts recognized that Lawrence was gassed. Either way, Birdie Tebbetts relied on Brooks Lawrence, his starting ace, to pitch in relief in critical games down the stretch. That does not sound like a manager who didn't want his best pitcher to win 20 games because he was black.

The 1956 Redlegs were probably somewhere between true contender and mere pretender. Powered by Kluszewski, catcher Ed Bailey, and an outfield trio of Robinson, Gus Bell, and Wally Post all hitting at least 28 home runs, scoring runs was not the problem. Cincinnati's failure was ultimately reducible to not having the pitching depth to compete with Brooklyn and Milwaukee. Lawrence, 13–9 in 30 starts (with 6 wins as a reliever), was the Reds' only pitcher to start at least 20 games and have a winning record; lefty Joe Nuxhall, 11–11 in 32 starts, was the only other *not* to have a losing record. Perhaps indicative of their real capacity as a team, the Reds were not in the pennant picture the next year, despite having all their core players back. Cincinnati kept backsliding, winning fewer games each year before settling into sixth place with their worst record in 10 years in 1960, the year they reverted to simply being the Reds instead of the Redlegs. Birdie Tebbetts stepped down as manager in August 1958; Brooks Lawrence was sent to the bullpen by the new manager; and Frank Robinson kept getting better on his Hall of Fame trajectory.

* * *

If Frank Robinson was baseball's most talked about black rookie entering the 1956 season—and he lived up to the hype—Elston Howard and

Roberto Clemente were in 1955. Howard was hyped principally because he integrated the New York Yankees. Hidebound by tradition, the Yankees were one of the clubs most opposed to the Dodgers' calling up Jackie Robinson. They subscribed to the conclusion of the MacPhail Report—Larry MacPhail was then team president—that integration would hurt the value of certain franchises if there was a major surge in black attendance; the report singled out the Yankees as one of the franchises whose financial value "could conceivably" be threatened. As integration became a fait accompli, and despite the outstanding performances of black players on New York's two other teams, the Yankees became adamant in their refusal to promote black prospects to the Bronx just for the sake of integrating their ballclub. General Manager George Weiss was explicit in stating that the Yankees would not be pressured to put a black player on their major-league roster by public criticism. The Yankees would not do so, said Weiss, until a black player demonstrated he had the ability to play for the Yankees, and also that he was "the right type of Negro."

Outfielder/first baseman Vic Power showed he had the ability with the Yankees' Triple-A team in Kansas City, but his 399 hits, including 79 doubles, 27 triples, and 32 homers, and .340 batting average in 1952 and 1953 were not enough to merit a promotion to Yankee Stadium, notwithstanding that first base was a position of relative weakness for the Bronx Bombers. They traded him instead to the Philadelphia Athletics, with whom he finally broke into the majors in 1954. Power's outspoken personality and the flair with which he played made him *not* "the right type of Negro." By 1955 even the Yankees, one of only four teams yet to field a black player, had to bow to public pressure, promoting Elston Howard. Not only was he the International League MVP in 1954 and able to both catch and play the outfield, Howard was also arguably the "right type of Negro" Weiss was looking for—a reserved personality unlikely to either cause any trouble or diminish in any way the incandescence of Yankee stars Mantle, Ford, Berra, or even the rascally, limited-talent (but white) Billy Martin. Howard did well in his rookie year, hitting 10 homers while batting .290 in 97 games, only 68 of which he started.

In contrast to Howard, Roberto Clemente was a much-anticipated rookie on the Opening Day roster of the 1955 Pirates, although he did not make his first start until the fourth game of the season. Ironically, given that Branch Rickey had left Brooklyn in 1951 to try to turn around the

Roberto Clemente, Willie Mays, and Hank Aaron played on 15 National League All-Star teams together, the first time in 1960. © *Photofest.*

fortunes of the ailing Pirates, Pittsburgh was one of the National League clubs on the slow track to integration. A further irony was that Pittsburgh was the epicenter of outstanding Negro League baseball in the 1930s. The Pittsburgh Crawfords and Homestead Grays were arguably the two most dominant teams in Negro League history, and legends Josh Gibson, Satchel Paige, Buck Leonard, and Cool Papa Bell all played in Pittsburgh. The Pirates did not sign any black players until after Rickey took charge of their baseball operations, and it wasn't until 1954—Rickey's fourth year in Pittsburgh—that a black player, second baseman Curt Roberts, was promoted to the major-league club. Roberts played just one full season in the majors and was not even originally signed by the Pirates.

Rickey was working for an owner, John Galbreath, who was unwilling to spend what it would have taken to sign elite black prospects the likes of those he signed for Brooklyn. That Rickey got the Pirates' hands on Clemente was only because the Dodgers, having signed him in 1954 for big bonus money, took the calculated gamble of not putting him on their big-league roster that year, leaving the native Puerto Rican outfielder vulnerable in baseball's annual supplemental draft. While Clemente quickly became a regular and played well, he did not follow in the footsteps of contemporaries Aaron, Banks, or Frank Robinson by becoming an instant superstar. Clemente batted just .282 in his first five major-league seasons, topping .300 only in his second year. The Pirates sent 12 players to All-Star Games between 1955 and 1959, none of them Clemente. His player value those five years as measured by wins above replacement was that of an average position regular on a major-league roster.

* * *

Rickey knew he had his work cut out for him when he took over in Pittsburgh in 1951, if for no other reason than that he had fleeced the Pirates for two of their best players in December 1947 when he dispatched 37-year-old Dixie Walker and a pair of expendable pitchers to Pittsburgh for third baseman Billy Cox and pitcher Preacher Roe, both of whom became core regulars on the Boys of Summer teams to come. Galbreath, whose wealth derived from real estate, was at first amenable to giving Rickey considerable authority and flexibility in spending to improve the club. That pledge, however, turned out to be dependent on immediate results that could not possibly be forthcoming, no matter the genius of Branch Rickey.

The Pirates had last competed for a pennant in 1938, losing a close race to the Cubs. Even with slugger Ralph Kiner in his prime, they had just entered their worst stretch in franchise history. And it didn't get any better under Rickey. They lost 90 in 1951, more than 100 each of the next three years, and 94 in 1955. In the middle of that string, in June 1953, Rickey traded Kiner to the Cubs. It didn't matter that Kiner had led the league in home runs each of his first seven years as a major leaguer, that twice he did so with more than 50, or that he had hit .301 for Pittsburgh since his rookie year in 1946. Rickey made the trade despite team owner Galbreath's opposition on the grounds that Kiner's prodigious blasts were the only reason anybody came to see the Pirates play. Rickey's attitude was that the Pirates could finish last just as easily without Ralph Kiner. After the 1953 season was mercifully over, Rickey traded away Pittsburgh's best pitcher—right-hander Murry Dickson, a 20-game winner in

1951—following back-to-back seasons leading the league with 21 and 19 losses.

Winning just 35 percent of their games since Branch Rickey took charge wore out Galbreath's patience. After four consecutive last-place endings, Rickey's five-year contract was not renewed after it expired in 1955. Beneath all that losing during the Rickey years, however, Pittsburgh was building the foundation for the ballclub that would ultimately win a dramatic World Series in 1960. Right-handers Vern Law and Bob Friend were called up in 1950 and 1951. Friend was one of baseball's most durable pitchers in the second half of the decade, including leading the league with 22 wins in 1958, and Law was a 20-game winner the year Pittsburgh won the pennant. Shortstop Dick Groat, a rookie in 1952, was a model of consistency. He was the league's batting champion and Most Valuable Player in 1960. Roy Face found a home in the Pirates' bullpen in 1955—the same year Clemente found a home in right field at Forbes Field—and became one of the game's top relievers in the late fifties. Although Bill Mazeroski wasn't called up to play second base in Pittsburgh until 1956—he was still a teenager—it was Rickey whom he impressed with his historically famous quickness in turning the double play.

After Rickey left, the Pirates engineered a series of trades that ultimately helped them to their first pennant since 1927. The most controversial was trading away Frank Thomas, Kiner's successor as Pittsburgh's preeminent home run threat, with 161 from 1953 to 1958. In return from Cincinnati they picked up good-hitting catcher Smoky Burgess, crafty southpaw Harvey Haddix, and tough-minded third baseman Don Hoak—all of whom played pivotal roles in the Pirates' 1960 pennant drive. Pittsburgh's other key trade acquisitions contributing to their championship season were Cardinals outfielder Bill Virdon in May 1956; Athletics catcher Hal Smith to split time with Burgess behind the plate in 1960; and Cardinals veteran southpaw Vinegar Bend Mizell to shore up the starting rotation in May 1960.

The 1960 Pirates led all the way after Memorial Day, although not by a consistently comfortable margin until mid-September. Their seven-game World Series triumph over the Yankees was epic, especially since the Yankees scored twice as many runs. The deciding game in Pittsburgh, where they were trailing 7–4 in the eighth, was one of the best seventh games ever played. Mazeroski's lead-off walk-off homer in the bottom of the ninth to break a 9–9 tie is most remembered, but it was Hal Smith's three-run shot in the eighth that brought the Pirates back from three runs behind.

* * *

Defying anyone's realistic best guess, 1960's first-place Pittsburgh and sixth-place Cincinnati traded places in 1961's final standings. While the Pirates fell to sixth despite Clemente winning his first batting title, the Reds won their first pennant in 21 years. It was just the fourth pennant in Cincinnati's 71 years as a National League franchise. Frank Robinson had his best season yet, with 37 homers, 124 RBIs, and a .323 batting average to win the MVP Award. Center fielder Vada Pinson, another outstanding young black player, was second in the league in batting, with a .343 average. Pinson was in the midst of an unusual pattern of batting over .300 only in odd-number years between 1959, his rookie season, and 1965.

With solid starting pitching—Joey Jay won 21 in both 1961 and '62; knuckleballer Bob Purkey led the league with a 23–5 record in 1962; lefty Jim O'Toole won at least 16 every year from 1961 to 1964; and Jim Maloney was a 20-game winner in 1963 and 1965 while striking out a batter an inning—the Robinson-and-Pinson-led Reds remained competitive through the middle of the decade. Their infield was fortified by sure-handed Cuban-born shortstop Leo Cardenas making the grade in 1962 and second baseman Pete Rose, a gritty overachiever born and raised in Cincinnati, doing so in 1963. Most famously in 1964, the Reds were mostly hangers-on in a race they were expected to compete in until 12 wins in 13 games beginning in mid-September thrust them from fourth place, 8½ games behind the first-place Phillies, into first place by a game with five remaining in what had become a taut four-team pennant race. Losing four of those final games condemned them to finishing second, one game shy of the top prize.

In December 1965, having just hit more than 30 homers for the seventh time and driven in more than 100 runs for the fourth time in his 10th year since breaking into Cincinnati's Opening Day lineup on April 17, 1956, Frank Robinson was traded to the Baltimore Orioles for right-hander Milt Pappas. When Jackie Robinson left the game after the 1956 season—Frank's rookie year—Jackie's and Rickey's mission was accomplished only to the extent that black players, although still in relatively few numbers, *could* make it in the major leagues as core regulars on their teams. By 1965—Frank's last year in Cincinnati—black players *had* made it. That was especially true in the National League, where 32 of the 69 position players to start at least 100 games for their teams were African American or black Hispanic from Caribbean Basin countries. In the American League, where teams were far more resistant to integration, black players still accounted for only 14 of the 63 position players to start at least 100 games. Major League Baseball had come a long way, but there was still quite a way to go.

6

BASEBALL'S MANIFEST DESTINY

The Road to Expansion

If the franchise moves of the Braves to Milwaukee, the Browns to Baltimore, and the Athletics to Kansas City were understandable, if not wholly justifiable, to America's legions of baseball fans because all were noncompetitive teams in both standings and attendance in the cities they left, the 1958 franchise moves of the Brooklyn Dodgers and New York Giants to California were perceived as mercenary, if not an outright betrayal of their fan bases. With nearly 8 million people, New York was large enough to support three major-league clubs. From 1946, America's first postwar year, through 1951, all three New York teams drew more than 1 million to their ballparks every year. After dipping below 1 million during the two years that Willie Mays was in the army, the Giants were back over that number in 1954 when the Say Hey Kid, back to baseball, excited fans like few players ever had before and helped his team win both a pennant and a World Series. Beginning in the mid-1950s, however, attendance began declining for all three teams for a variety of demographic and infrastructure reasons. New York City had become racially more diverse, with lower-income families replacing the white, middle-class families that were moving to the suburbs for nicer homes and their own lawns.

The Giants had a rich heritage—15 pennants since 1901, including two recently, in 1951 and 1954—not to mention the incomparable Willie Mays. And they had a farm system stocked with talented players like

Willie McCovey, Orlando Cepeda, and Felipe Alou who would soon make a big impact in the major leagues. The Dodgers had a recent history of excellence, winning six pennants since 1947, and established stars in their early 30s, like Duke Snider and Gil Hodges, as well as dynamic younger players like Jim Gilliam, Don Drysdale, and a hard-throwing scatter-armed kid with great potential named Sandy Koufax.

But what they also had were old ballparks in blighted neighborhoods with little or no room to expand or build new parking lots to accommodate the growing proportion of their fans now living in the suburbs. Ebbets Field, with its distinctive rotunda, was hardly considered quaint. Built for baseball in 1913, it was too small, in need of extensive and expensive renovation, and increasingly inaccessible by car or public transportation for the many fans who had moved out of Brooklyn to Queens and beyond on Long Island. The Polo Grounds, reconstructed with concrete and steel after a fire burned much of the wooden grandstand in 1911, was even older, also in disrepair, and increasingly surrounded by tenement apartments that diminished the attraction of going to Giants home games. Yankee Stadium, while certainly larger, was also beginning to show signs of age in a neighborhood that was becoming more rough-and-tumble. The Yankees, however, weren't going anywhere.

* * *

Even though his team had drawn more than a million fans every year since 1945—and would every season until they left Brooklyn—Dodgers owner Walter O'Malley was dismayed by what he considered relatively lackluster attendance when they just missed out on pennants in 1950 and '51 and won in 1952 and '53. Surmising that the Ebbets faithful would become less so—neither the ballpark nor the team's best players were getting younger—O'Malley commissioned architectural plans for a new stadium and began pressuring city officials to make land available and build parking garages at a location about two miles from Ebbets Field that is now the site of Barclays Center, a twenty-first-century-built sports arena. In New York, all urban development projects went through Robert Moses, an unelected official with a grand plan for remaking the metropolis. Arguably the most powerful city official, Moses was not inclined to see a baseball team as a sacrosanct institution that helped mold the identity of a city, or in this case a borough, and so did not consider a new, modern ballpark on prime real estate to have much civic merit. He had other plans for the area where O'Malley wanted a new home for the Dodgers but offered an alternative in the Flushing Meadows part of Queens. That was not what O'Malley wanted.

All the while O'Malley was looking to Moses for help in Brooklyn, he was being courted by Los Angeles, on its way to eclipsing Philadelphia as the country's third largest city in the 1960 census. O'Malley's preference was to keep the Dodgers in Brooklyn, but he was not above using LA's interest as leverage. He ramped up the pressure on Moses to support his plans by announcing before the 1956 season that the Brooklyn Dodgers, the reigning World Series champions, would play in Ebbets Field only two more years. The 1958 season was his deadline—either the Dodgers would have Moses's commitment to provide the real estate he wanted in Brooklyn at a cost-effective price and to build the supporting urban infrastructure, or a move to the West Coast was not out of the question.

Even though O'Malley kept insisting he wanted his team to stay in Brooklyn, by the time the 1957 season got started, with the Dodgers once again defending a pennant, rumors were rampant this would be the club's last year in New York. A preseason deal with the Cubs to swap Pacific Coast League affiliates gave the Dodgers the Cubs' former territorial claim to the environs of Los Angeles. City officials there were promising to make land available for a modern baseball stadium in Chavez Ravine. In May, National League owners granted permission for both the Dodgers and the Giants to move. In August the Giants announced they would be moving to San Francisco, and in early October the Dodgers confirmed they were indeed on their way across country to Los Angeles.

While Walter O'Malley, playing New York and Los Angeles against each other, seemed genuinely ambivalent about his choices, Giants owner Horace Stoneham was clear about his for at least as long as the Dodgers' owner was lobbying for a new stadium in Brooklyn. With attendance at the Polo Grounds having dropped below 1 million in 1953 for the first time since the war, to just fifth best in the NL—also his team's final resting place in the standings—Stoneham decided that staying in New York was a financially losing proposition. That the Giants were back over 1,155,000 in 1954 and won the World Series with Willie Mays back in *their* uniform, not that of the army, did not change Stoneham's outlook. The very next year, attendance fell to 824,112, sixth in the league, not helped by the fact that the defending-champion Giants, even with Mays, were already 9½ games back after just 21 games because the 1955 Dodgers got off to such a torrid start. And in 1956 the Giants were last in National League attendance, with just over 629,000 paying to see them drop into sixth place.

Unlike O'Malley's extensive dealings with Robert Moses and the city government for a new stadium in Brooklyn, Stoneham did not lobby, at least not publicly, for the city's help in building a new ballpark for his club, nor did he have any particular location in mind, although he did suggest in 1955 that, in all fairness, the Giants were as deserving of the city's assistance as the Dodgers. Minneapolis was Stoneham's obvious choice to relocate the Giants, since they controlled territorial rights by virtue of their Triple-A affiliate there. But California, the "Golden State"—particularly Los Angeles and San Francisco—was the place for the major leagues to be, according a report Bill Veeck presented to National League owners in 1954. His report made the practical point that two teams out west would be better than one, providing economies of scale for travel and scheduling, and either opined or warned that the American League had designs on California. As the Dodgers closed in on their Los Angeles deal in the beginning months of 1957, O'Malley suggested to Stoneham that he consider San Francisco instead of Minneapolis, which would allow the Dodgers and Giants to continue their storied New York rivalry about 400 miles apart on the West Coast. The mayor of San Francisco persistently lobbied on his city's behalf, including offering to help finance a new stadium. By August the deal was done, even though O'Malley was still not irrevocably committed to LA.

* * *

Meanwhile, in the nation's capital, the family business wasn't doing so well. The Washington Senators had been run by the Griffith family since 1920, when Clark Griffith, their manager since 1912, bought majority ownership of the franchise. The only stretch of sustained success for the old Senators had been three pennants in 10 years between 1924 and 1933. The only year since then that the Senators were in realistic contention was 1945, when they were deprived of the opportunity for a playoff to decide the American League race thanks to Hank Greenberg's dramatic ninth-inning grand slam on the final day of the season that secured the pennant for Detroit. Their next 15 years in Washington—their last 15 years in Washington, as it turned out—were dismal in performance and attendance. They ended with a winning record just once, at 78–76 in 1952. They lost at least 91 games every year from 1955 to 1959, finishing last four times. Once the Browns had left for Baltimore and the Athletics for Philadelphia, the Senators were last in the league in attendance every remaining year of the decade.

Washington's most prominent players in the 1950s were first baseman Mickey Vernon, outfielder Roy Sievers, and third baseman Eddie Yost. Vernon began his career with the Senators in 1939, beat out Ted Williams for the 1946 batting title, was traded in December 1948, brought back in June 1950, was a mainstay in the middle of the Senators' lineup the next five years, and won a second batting title in 1953. Sievers was traded to the Senators in 1954, averaged 26 homers his first three years in Washington, then exploded for a league-leading 42 in 1957 and 39 the next year after the Senators did their right-handed slugger a favor by reducing the home-run distance at Griffith Stadium by 10 to 20 feet across the breadth of left field. By the time he left Washington in 1960, Sievers's 180 homers were the most so far in franchise history. Yost, the Senators' lead-off batter between 1947 and 1958, didn't hit much for average, batting only .253, but led the league in walks four times (and twice more after being traded to Detroit).

While Bob Porterfield, a Yankees castoff, did lead the league with 22 wins and 9 shutouts in 1953, Senators pitchers in the 1950s were most renowned for giving up mammoth home runs to Mickey Mantle. The two most famous were Mantle's drive on April 17, 1953, which ticked a 60-foot-high billboard at the back of the left-field bleachers in Griffith Stadium, left the park completely, and was picked up by a kid at a distance the Yankees' publicist estimated at 565 feet from home plate, and his shot on May 30, 1956, that came within a foot and a half of becoming the first fair ball hit out of Yankee Stadium when it crashed into the famous frieze hanging over the third deck in right field. No one ever did hit one out of the original Yankee Stadium, although Mantle came close again in 1963, hitting the top of the facade in right field.

The switch-hitting Mantle's 1953 Griffith Stadium blast came on Opening Day, batting right-handed off lefty Chuck Stobbs. Half a century later, the writer Jane Leavy, working on a Mantle biography, queried a baseball enthusiast physicist about the true distance of the clout. He calculated the ball to have flown 535 feet before bouncing to where the kid picked it up. Mantle's soaring 1956 blast that almost cleared Yankee Stadium came in the first game of a doubleheader, batting left-handed against righty Pedro Ramos. Arguably the Senators' ace for their remaining years in Washington, Ramos led the league in losses four consecutive years beginning in 1958—an unprecedented feat unmatched by any pitcher since—after which he was traded away. One of the Senators awestruck by mighty Mick's blast off Ramos was Camilo Pascual, then at the beginning of his career. He had given up two long-distance homers to the Yankee slugger earlier that year at Griffith Stadium and would be victimized by Mantle again in the second game on the day the Mick almost (literally) left the yard. In all, Mantle torched Pascual for five home runs in 1956 and 11 over the course of his career.

Attendance at Griffith Stadium in the fifties was in a death-to-the-franchise spiral. Calvin Griffith, having inherited ownership of the team when his uncle Clark died in 1955, thought the reason for the Senators' decline was much more than their being noncompetitive and having a badly aging ballpark. Calvin believed that the changing demographics in the nation's capital toward an increasingly poor and lower-income African American population was bad for business, and Griffith Stadium happened to be in an overwhelmingly black neighborhood. This was in fact a central argument advanced in the "Race Question" section of the 1946 MacPhail Report, which warned that blacks would drive away white fans and threaten the value of the affected major-league franchises. By 1959 Calvin Griffith wanted out of Washington. The white suburbs of northern Virginia were a possibility. He had barely taken any initiative toward such a move before Minneapolis made an offer he could not refuse—including a major-league-ready ballpark just five years old in nearby Bloomington—despite opposition from everyone else in the Griffith family, other team owners, the United States Congress, and President Dwight D. Eisenhower.

The Griffith family's attitude toward race was at best problematic. Clark Griffith claimed later in his life that in 1943, a war year, he considered offering tryouts to Negro League stars Josh Gibson and Buck Leonard, whose Homestead Grays played at Griffith Stadium. Not only were there were no tryouts, but Griffith was among the American League owners who held out the longest against integrating their ballclubs. The apologist explanation for his stance was that Clark Griffith was well aware that Washington, DC, in the 1940s and 1950s had a very Southern sensibility, where segregation of the races was the general rule. It wasn't until 1952 that Griffith's franchise signed its first black players. Both were from Cuba. Every other major-league club had done so by then except the Cardinals and Tigers. And it wasn't until September call-ups in 1954 that the Senators became the fifth American League club to integrate their dugout, leaving the Yankees, Tigers, and Red Sox alone in defending all-white rosters. That player, too, was a black Hispanic born in Cuba. (Ramos and Pascual, also Cuban nationals, were white Hispanics.) It was not until Calvin Griffith's reign, in August 1957, that the Senators brought an African American player—right-hander Joe Black, the 1952 National League Rookie of the Year for the pennant-winning Dodgers—to Washington. His major-league career ended after seven relief appearances.

Ironically, the Senators were on the threshold of becoming quite good when they picked up and left for Minnesota in 1961. The players they brought with them from DC to the upper Midwest included slugging corner-infielder Harmon Killebrew, hard-hitting outfielder Bob Allison, catcher Earl Battey, an African American player acquired in 1960 from the White Sox, and emerging pitching ace Camilo Pascual. In 1959 Killebrew, playing third base for the Senators in his first season as a regular, led the league with 42 homers and was third with 105 runs batted in; Allison, in his rookie year, smacked 30 homers with 85 RBIs; and Pascual, whose mastery of the curve gave him a high strikeout-to-innings ratio and put him on the cusp of being an elite pitcher, was 17–10 for a club that won just 63 games. Battey in 1960 was arguably the Senators' best position player. Their exploits contributed to increased attendance at Griffith Stadium in the Senators' last two seasons in Washington, but they were still at the bottom of the league in draw. Calvin Griffith's mind was made up.

* * *

The National League's dual abandonment of New York City gave life to Branch Rickey's new visionary quest. The founding father of the farm system and the executive who dared take on the major leagues' policy of racial exclusion, Rickey believed not only that there was room for considerable growth in Major League Baseball but also that the game's future depended on it. But rather than adding expansion teams he knew would be competitively weak to the existing American and National Leagues, Rickey advocated a "third major league" where each team, because they were all new teams, would begin on a level playing field. Rickey expected that within five years the new teams and the new league would be capable of competing at the existing major-league level. In 1959 he and a handful of influential backers—most notably New York attorney William Shea, whose real priority was to replace the departed Giants and Dodgers with another major-league team in New York City—announced the formation of the Continental League, with Rickey as president. Shea said the new league would begin play in 1961.

The last "third major league"—the Federal League, organized in 1914—lasted just two years, ultimately foundering because star National and American League players did not sign on and because the upstart league was unable to win an antitrust suit in federal court. Rickey was trying now to take advantage of concurrent congressional scrutiny of baseball's antitrust exemption. After years of hearings, which most famously included testimony by Casey Stengel that left everybody wondering what it was he actually said, Rickey was gambling that rather than risk losing the exemption, major-league owners would agree to limiting to 30 the total number of player contracts each existing franchise could hold. That would leave a sufficient number of Triple-A players on the threshold of making it to the majors available for selection to start up the Continental League. For its part, the new league would respect the sanctity of reserve clause contracts. Like every other executive in baseball, Rickey believed as a matter of principle that the business model for professional baseball demanded the reserve clause.

While congressional supporters of legislation to strip Major League Baseball of its antitrust exemption used the Continental League as leverage, major-league owners lobbied hard for Congress to maintain the status quo. Their efforts paid dividends in a competing bill that declared all major professional sports, including baseball, exempt from most antitrust regulations. Moreover, Calvin Griffith's decision during the 1959 World Series to move his Senators to Minneapolis in 1961 picked off one of the eight cities the Continental League intended to place franchises in. As had happened 45 years earlier, when Federal League owners gave up the fight in the face of Major League Baseball's intractable opposition, Rickey and his investors in the Continental League were forced to back down. But it was not an unconditional surrender. Knowing they were skating on very thin ice with Congress, Commissioner Ford Frick—the baseball writer–become–National League president who replaced Happy Chandler as commissioner in 1951—and the owners agreed (some reluctantly, others less so) on Rickey's broader point about the need for the major leagues to grow beyond 16 teams.

Expansion committees were formed by both leagues. In 1961 the American League opened the season with two new clubs—one in Los Angeles and the other in Washington, to replace Griffith's departed Senators—and the National League became a 10-team league the next year by adding New York and Houston. Of the four new franchises, only Houston and New York were in would-be Continental League cities. New York had been the linchpin of Rickey's third-league ambition because he recognized the critical importance of the city's extensive financial and media outlets to the success of the Continental League. Bringing National League baseball back to New York was a necessary trade-off to placate Shea, whose financial clout and political influence helped give credibility to the Continental League proposal. Los Angeles was given a team in the American League because if the Yankees had to share their city with an expansion club, so the Dodgers would have to in theirs. The decision to place the second AL expansion team in Washington, despite the city's history of lukewarm attendance in support of its major-league team, was necessary to satisfy members of Congress, for whom not having Major League Baseball in the nation's capital was, well, un-American.

Although each league had different rules when it came time for expansion clubs to build their rosters in the fall preceding their inaugural seasons, both mandated that existing franchises could protect only 25 players on their 40-man rosters, 18 of whom had to be on the major-league club before September call-ups of the season just ended. Since the list of players made available by each team was finalized before the draft, existing National League clubs gamed the system by ensuring that their best minor-league prospects were put on their 40-man roster at the expense of marginal major leaguers or players deemed expendable. It made no difference that the general managers of the expansion Houston and New York franchises complained about the poor-quality players they had to choose from. Branch Rickey was certainly right that expansion clubs would be competitively far inferior to the 16 established big-league teams.

7

THE FIRST LATIN WAVE

Just as black players in the Negro Leagues could have—indeed, *should* have—enriched the major leagues for decades before Jackie Robinson broke the color barrier, Caribbean Basin countries, especially Cuba, could have—indeed, *should* have—been a pipeline for top-tier players. Whether introduced to the game by virtue of the close proximity of the United States, by US soldiers in various military interventions, or by American industrialists, entrepreneurs, and workers taking advantage of economic opportunity south of the border, baseball became a part of the Caribbean's cultural fabric. Even though Puerto Rico had been a US territory since the 1898 Spanish-American War, which was fought over Cuba, and its people US citizens since 1917, it was Cuba that was most mad about baseball.

The game was popular in Cuba even before the US intervention to free the island from Spanish rule. It wasn't long after independence before Cuban teams were playing major-league clubs or traveling all-stars in postseason exhibition series—and holding their own against the big leaguers. Over the years, Cuban professional leagues produced some outstanding players clearly capable of playing at the major-league level. They included the likes of Martin Dihigo, Jose Mendez, and Cristobal Torriente. The problem was that they were black Hispanics, and Major League Baseball had a closed-door policy when it came to black players. The door was not *tightly* closed, only to the extent that lighter darkskinned Cubans were able to pass as swarthy white Hispanics. Dihigo, Mendez, and Torriente could not. Consequently, of the 40 players born in

Cuba who played in the major leagues before Jackie Robinson's debut, only one—right-hander Dolf Luque, the "Pride of Havana," who won 194 big-league games between 1918 and 1935—was historically consequential.

Notwithstanding the prejudices of many white Hispanic elites, Cuba was a country where interracial coupling was not unusual and Jim Crow–like segregation was not practical. The fact that Cuba's professional baseball league was integrated and that so many of the best players were "colored" put the island nation largely off the map as far as major-league scouts were concerned. Many of the Cuban players who made it to the majors in the Deadball Era, which ended in 1919, got their big break when they were brought to play professionally in the United States by the Colombian-born owner of a Class D minor-league club with close ties to Cuba. They included Luque, journeyman catcher Mike Gonzalez, who played parts of 17 seasons in the majors in the 1910s and 1920s before becoming a highly regarded coach on the Cardinals, and Armando Marsans, mostly an outfield reserve in eight big-league seasons during the teens. Because most of the Cuban-born players making it to the majors in the teens and twenties labored under the suspicion they were at least partially black—it was quite likely many of them were, and two in fact had previously played for Negro League clubs—they were given short shrift in their opportunities to make good and had very short-lived big-league careers.

Baseball had also taken hold everywhere in the Caribbean where there was an American economic or military presence. By the 1930s Venezuela, the Dominican Republic, and Mexico had their own professional leagues, but it was Cuba that remained the regional fulcrum. The Cuban League, which played its schedule between late fall and early spring, when daytime temperatures were more comfortable, attracted the best players from elsewhere in the Caribbean. With racially mixed teams, Cuba was also a popular winter destination for ballplayers from the United States, particularly black players. Indeed, Cuba's winter league provided a cross-fertilization of black players that bolstered the quality of play in both Cuba and America's Negro Leagues. The payoff for Major League Baseball of players from the Cuban League should have been obvious—except, of course, for the major leagues' no-blacks-allowed policy.

Clear-eyed about that policy, the Washington Senators in the 1930s became the first major-league club to take an interest in scouting and signing Caribbean players, primarily because their best scout had good baseball contacts in Cuba. The Senators had collapsed competitively after winning the 1933 American League pennant, the US economy was still in the Great Depression, the club's home attendance was also depressed— near the bottom of the league—and Washington owner Clark Griffith was operating on a very tight budget. Cuba was a ready source of Latin ball-players with at least marginal big-league skills who could be had relative-ly inexpensively for franchises handicapped by minimalist and under-funded farm systems—provided, of course, they were either white His-panics or had light enough skin that they could pass for sunbaked descen-dants of Spanish conquistadors. Few, however, made it to Griffith Sta-dium before the exigency of ballplayers being drafted for World War II caused the Senators to bring up more Latin players—mostly Cuban-born—to round off their rosters, and even fewer had big-league careers with any longevity.

* * *

Notwithstanding the quality of Cuba's professional baseball league and that the Senators had staked a scouting beachhead on the island, the fact that so many of the island nation's best ballplayers were black left Cuba—and all of Latin America, for that matter—an undiscovered coun-try for the rest of Major League Baseball. Jackie Robinson changed everything because he made Minnie Minoso possible, and Minnie Mino-so put Cuba on the major-league scouting map.

Like many top-flight Cuban black Hispanic players, Minoso pursued a baseball career that included playing in the Negro Leagues, where he was discovered by a scout for the Cleveland Indians in 1948. He made the Indians' 1949 Opening Day roster, which also included Larry Doby and Satchel Paige. Cleveland was the only American League team to have black players on the roster at any time during the 1949 season, but the 26-year-old Minoso got only 16 at-bats in nine games before being sent to the Pacific Coast League for the chance to play regularly and hone his skills. Unlike Doby and Paige, both African American, the Spanish-speaking Minoso had to master a foreign language in addition to adapting to American culture. After two exceptional seasons in the PCL, Minoso was back in Cleveland on Opening Day in 1951 as a reserve until being traded to the Chicago White Sox on the last day of April in a multiteam deal.

Minoso immediately made his impact felt in Chicago. His.359 batting average in his first two months with the White Sox—a sixth-place club the year before—was instrumental in his new team's reaching and staying in first place for virtually all of June and remaining competitive until August. The White Sox finished fourth, out of the running, but with a winning record for the first time in eight years. Minoso's .326 batting average was second in the league. He was also second in runs scored, with 112—just one behind the league leader. Showing the speed and aggressiveness that made him such a dynamic player, Minoso led the league with 14 triples and 31 stolen bases. His player value of 5.5 wins above replacement was fourth best among American League position players. Minnie Minoso was better than any other rookie in baseball, including Willie Mays, in every meaningful statistical category except home runs, but it was the pennant-winning Yankees' versatile infielder Gil McDougald who spent the winter polishing the AL's Rookie of the Year Award. Minoso remained one of the American League's premier players for the rest of the decade, with eight .300 seasons in 10 years between 1951 and 1960. In 1954 he was arguably the best player in the American League, based on the WAR metric, but his team finished a distant third, and it was Yogi Berra of the second-place Yankees who got to polish a Most Valuable Player trophy over the winter.

Major league integration proved the catalyst for an unprecedented influx of players from Cuba in the 1950s and 1960s. The Washington Senators—the one major-league club that scouted Cuban players before integration—were ahead of the field in signing players from the island nation, benefiting from taking on the Havana Cubans as an affiliate in the Class C Florida International League in 1947. Of the 49 Cubans who made it to the major leagues between Robinson's rookie year in 1947 and 1961, when the Senators moved to Minnesota and became the Twins, 23 made their big-league debut in Washington.

Notwithstanding Minoso's phenomenal success in Chicago, just five of the Cubans who made it to Griffith Stadium were black, and only one—shortstop Zoilo Versalles, but not until the Senators were the Twins—eventually became a regular. Helping the Twins win the 1965 pennant, Versalles was the first Cuban-born player to win a Most Valuable Player Award, an honor that eluded Minoso. Until the franchise move, however, Washington's best Cuban-born players in the late-1950s were right-handers Camilo Pascual and Pedro Ramos, both white Hispanics. Pascual was one of the best pitchers of his generation, leading the league in strikeouts each of the club's first three years in the Twin Cities and twice winning 20 games.

Meanwhile, blessed by Organized Baseball's agreement in 1947 to allow and encourage inexperienced major leaguers and top minor-league prospects to boost their big-league chances by playing winter ball in Cuba, the Cuban League flourished in the 1950s. In 1954 the Havana Cubans, no longer a Senators affiliate, recast as the Sugar Kings and playing in the spring and summer months, were incorporated into the Triple-A International League—one level below the majors—and in 1955 became an affiliate of the Cincinnati Reds. Many of Cincinnati's best prospects on the Sugar Kings were from Cuba or other Caribbean countries. Cuban baseball fans expected, or at least hoped, there eventually would be a major-league franchise in their country. Given the political turmoil occasioned by opposition to the corrupt and repressive American-backed regime of Cuban strongman Fulgencio Batista, however, such expectations were probably unreasonable, particularly as an insurgency took shape in the mountains, political violence spread to universities and urban areas, and the regime intensified its crackdown on political opponents.

It all ended badly, of course, when Batista fled the country on New Year's Day in 1959 and Fidel Castro became the new power in Cuba. Within days of Castro's decree in July 1960 nationalizing the Cuban assets of all US companies operating in the island nation, Major League Baseball commissioner Ford Frick ordered Cincinnati's Havana franchise peremptorily moved to New Jersey. Among the Sugar Kings players making the move to the United States who would become prominent major-league players were Cuban-born Mike Cuellar, Leo Cardenas, Cookie Rojas, Vic Davalillo, and Joe Azcue. They would never play baseball in Cuba again.

Castro's crackdown on political opponents and Cuba's vibrant private sector, as well as his suppression of civil rights and liberties, resulted in US sanctions intended to cripple the Cuban economy and isolate his fledgling Communist regime. The imposition of stringent travel restrictions making it difficult to leave the island effectively ended the first wave of Cuban players coming to America. Those who had left Cuba for

American diamonds before or in the first chaotic year or two of Castro's revolution were forced to choose between staying in America year-round to pursue baseball careers (and to live in a free society) or the uncertain prospects of being able to return to the United States if they went home to their families in the off-season. Most dared not return, and many spent decades unable to visit their parents and other family members and friends they left behind to play ball in the United States. By the mid-1960s there were about 30 Cuban-born players in the major leagues in any given season, making them the dominant foreign nationals in the game. Pascual, Cuellar, Tony Oliva, Bert Campaneris, Luis Tiant, and Tony Perez took their place among baseball's best players that decade and the next. But the Cold War playing out between the United States and Castro, particularly the regime's crackdown on leaving the country, led to a lost generation of Cuban players for Major League Baseball.

The Cuban generation most affected, because they came of age in the years when the Castro regime was most repressive and political tensions with the United States at their highest, were those born between 1950 and 1970—only 17 of whom played in the major leagues, compared to 49 Cubans born between 1930 and 1950 who wore big-league uniforms. After the number of Cuban-born players in the major leagues peaked in 1968, with 32, by 1975 there were only 14, only eight in 1980, and a mere three Cubans in the big leagues in 1985. After Tiant and Perez retired in the 1980s, Jose Canseco and Rafael Palmeiro—both of whose big-league careers started in the mid-1980s—were next as the first prominent post-Castro Cuban-born players in the major leagues. Both grew up in Florida after their families fled Cuba on "freedom flights" organized by the United States and accepted by Castro as a way to defuse dissent.

It would be more than two decades after the early years of Castro's crackdown before a second wave of Cuban-born players began making their way into the major leagues. While players in the first wave found themselves cut off from their home and became exiles, the second wave had to chance the risks of defection, where a failed attempt could cost them their baseball careers in Cuba (certainly on the national team that traveled abroad), their freedom, and even their lives—and they too were separated from their families, in some cases their wives and children.

* * *

Following in the footsteps of increasing numbers of Cubans making it to the United States to play baseball as a consequence of Jackie Robinson's integration of the major leagues, players from around the Caribbean Basin began populating big-league rosters in the 1950s. Amplified by their familiarity with winter league baseball in Cuba, which also attracted outstanding players from elsewhere in the Caribbean, major-league clubs began paying attention to the talent pool in countries that loved their baseball as much as Americans. It bears mentioning that neglecting the Caribbean—so close to home—as a place to scout for high-potential players until after Branch Rickey signed Robinson speaks not only to Major League Baseball's longstanding prohibition against black players, but also of prejudice against "brown"-complexioned white Hispanics.

The first white Hispanic beneficiary of baseball's willingness to ignore complexion and look beyond America's shores was Mexico's Bobby Avila, a veteran of five Mexican League seasons when he was signed by the Cleveland Indians in 1948 and assigned to their top Triple-A affiliate that year. As one of the Mexican League's top stars, it might well have been his outstanding play in Cuba's winter league that got him noticed by big-league scouts. When he was called up by the Indians in 1949, fated to warm the bench that year, Avila was only the fourth player born in Mexico to make it to the major leagues. He was the first, however, whose professional baseball career began in the country of his birth; outfielder Mel Almada, whose seven years in the Big Time were in the 1930s; Chile Gomez, an infielder for the Phillies for two years in the mid-1930s; and Jesse Flores, a pitcher for the Athletics in the mid-1940s, all grew up in California, where their families moved when they were kids. By 1951 Avila was the Indians' second baseman. In 1954, hitting second in the order, his .341 batting average was best in the league as he played a key role in Cleveland's winning 111 games to finally snatch the American League pennant from the Yankees. By the time he left Cleveland after the 1958 season, his big-league career almost over, eight more players born in Mexico had made it to the majors.

With Avila getting more playing time in 1950 and Minoso making an open-and-shut case for himself that year in the Pacific Coast League, it was Chico Carrasquel, a white Hispanic, who became the major leagues' most consequential player from Latin America since Dolf Luque. Signed to a minor-league contract by the Brooklyn Dodgers in 1949 and dealt to the Chicago White Sox after the season, Carrasquel was only the third major leaguer to come from the ballfields of Venezuela, following in the footsteps of his uncle, former 1940s Senators pitcher Alex Carrasquel, and Chucho Ramos, whose big-league career ended after four games with the wartime Reds in 1944. Unlike his uncle, who pitched credibly without much acclaim, Chico Carrasquel was a revelation to American baseball fans, particularly in the field, where his quickness, range, leaping ability, and agility often made for spectacular plays. Carrasquel and Minoso combined to help turn around the long-stagnant White Sox fortunes with a fast-paced, aggressive dynamism that redefined the club as the "Go-Go Sox."

Carrasquel was the first of many super-athletic shortstops to come from Venezuela—a country that would become synonymous with quick and nimble shortstops, deft with glove and hands and strong of arm, as well as eventually a breeding ground for exceptional ballplayers at any position. The second was Luis Aparicio, whose rapid development in the minor leagues after being signed by the White Sox in 1954 made Carrasquel expendable. Even more dazzling at shortstop than Carrasquel, although at first more error-prone, Aparicio's rookie season in 1956 was the first of nine consecutive years he led the league in stolen bases—something no other player has ever done—and he was successful in 81 percent of his attempts. Aparicio and Carrasquel were two of only five Venezuelans to play in the major leagues between Jackie Robinson's 1947 debut in Brooklyn and Aparicio's 1963 trade to Baltimore.

The 1947 breach of the major leagues' color barrier, coupled with Cuba's being recognized as potentially fertile ground for finding ballplayers, also opened scouts' eyes to the possibilities in Puerto Rico. Although Puerto Rico was a US territory where baseball had been played for decades, only two Puerto Ricans—right-hander Hi Bithorn with the Cubs just before World War II and outfielder Luis Olmo with the Dodgers during the war years—had ever played in the major leagues before integration. The fact that so many of the island's best players were black Hispanic, as was true in Cuba, probably deterred American scouts from giving much thought to Puerto Rico as a source for major-league talent until then.

By the mid-1950s, however, black Hispanic Puerto Rican players collectively were making perhaps an even greater impact than players from Cuba as core regulars on big-league rosters. In 1953 rookie right-hander Ruben Gomez moved into the Giants' starting rotation, where he averaged more than 30 starts a year in his first six major-league seasons. In 1954 Vic Power finally made it to the majors with the Kansas City Athletics, after two outstanding seasons in the Yankees' minor-league system that failed to merit promotion to the Bronx because he was black, and went on to a creditable 12-year career. The great Roberto Clemente made his debut with the Pirates in 1955, and Orlando Cepeda—another future Hall of Famer—with the Giants in 1958, when his 25 homers, 96 RBIs, and .312 batting average made him the unanimous selection as National League Rookie of the Year.

Power, Cepeda, and Clemente, in addition to being representative of the aggressiveness and excitement Caribbean ballplayers brought to American diamonds, also came to embody negative stereotypes about Latin ballplayers that were bandied about in dugouts and clubhouses and given shelf life by baseball writers. All three were flamboyant and outspoken, especially if they felt slighted—characteristics that were not, for the most part, approved of in white America, especially coming from black men who were not even from the continental United States. Vic Power became the poster boy for Latin players as showboating individualists interested only in personal aggrandizement because of the many plays he made at first base, snatching grounders and line drives with his glove hand only rather than using his throwing hand to secure the ball. This was true of many Latin players, whose range and quickness enabled them to make an inordinate number of spectacular plays.

Orlando Cepeda's outstanding start to his big-league career—222 homers, averaging 105 RBIs, and hitting .309 in his first seven seasons— did not prevent repeated criticism that he was not a team player, that he was lackadaisical in the field, that he went into angry sulks if he was called to task by his manager, and that he made "injury excuses" for poor performance when he did in fact have chronic knee problems. He was even accused of being jealous of the accolades that went to superstar teammate Willie Mays. And Latin beats were his preferred music; indeed, like Power, Cepeda's "Cha Cha" lifestyle off the field, even in the clubhouse (which earned him that very nickname), fed the impression he cared more about having a good time than being a better ballplayer and teammate. Clemente's outspoken insistence that he be taken seriously and treated respectfully, the same as any white ballplayer, came to symbolize Latin players who were petulant and self-absorbed. He too was accused of complaining too much about aches, pains, and injuries.

The problem for Latin-born players was both language and culture. Unlike African American ballplayers who grew up in the United States and, even if demeaned and discriminated against, were part of America's cultural fabric and fluent in English, Latin players spoke Spanish and came from the more free-wheeling culture of the Caribbean islands—one that was much less race based. They had to endure the same racism of the time that African American players endured while also learning a new language and having to adapt to new foods and fundamentally different social mores. Unlike today, where interpreters are common in club-houses, teams gave little support to Latin players in their interactions with the scribes, let alone helping them to navigate their way in a new country.

Their Caribbean accents, often mocked, and their lack of proficiency in the English language contributed to perceptions that Latin players were, to be blunt, less intelligent than their white American teammates. Latin players were also accused of being unnecessarily sensitive to slights. This was a caricature that as great a player as Clemente had to live down even as he was winning four batting titles in the 1960s on his way to exactly 3,000 career hits. The culture clash between Latin players and the prevailing ethos of Major League Baseball came to a head on the San Francisco Giants in the heat of the 1964 pennant race, in the Alvin Dark affair.

* * *

If the Brooklyn Dodgers led the way in integrating the major leagues—including by fielding more black players as core regulars than any other club in the 1950s—the San Francisco Giants can lay claim to being baseball's first multicultural team. Following Jackie Robinson's instant success in Brooklyn, the Giants, still in New York, moved quickly to establish a reliable pipeline to top-tier black players by recruiting Alex Pompez, owner of the Negro League's financially struggling New York Cubans franchise, which played its home games in the Polo Grounds. In addition to his longstanding role as a powerbroker in the Negro Leagues, Pompez, a Cuban American fluent in Spanish, had strong baseball con-nections in Cuba and elsewhere in the Caribbean. Pompez's network of contacts was instrumental in the Giants' signing of Ruben Gomez in 1953 and Orlando Cepeda in 1955. Both came to the attention of Pompez playing in the Puerto Rican Winter League, where they impressed one of his top scouts.

Pompez also used his connections in the Dominican Republic to cor-ner the market on Dominican players for the Giants. As elsewhere in the Caribbean, baseball was all the rage in the Dominican Republic, which had its own professional winter league. That major-league clubs showed no interest in the country's ballplayers before the Giants "discovered" the Dominican Republic may have had much to do with the chronic political violence that resulted from General Rafael Trujillo's oppressive military rule. Pompez, however, had political connections to the highest levels of the regime, which he exploited to make it safe for the Giants to scout Dominican ballplayers.

The payoff for the Giants, now playing in San Francisco, included Juan Marichal and all three Alou brothers—Felipe, Matty, and Jesus— and that helped them build a formidable club that engaged in three epic pennant race battles with the Dodgers in the 1960s. Beginning with a one-hit shutout in his major-league debut in July 1960, in which he retired the first 19 batters he faced before an error broke up his perfect game and put him within four outs of a no-hitter, Marichal became one of baseball's all-time great pitchers. The Giants soured on outfielder Felipe Alou after outstanding seasons in both 1962—a pennant-winning year for San Francisco—and 1963 because of his outspokenness, including complaints about being underpaid for his talent level, and traded him to the Braves, with whom he would have his best years. Neither of Felipe's brothers, outfielders Jesus and Matty, contributed much to the Giants' offense.

The genesis of the Alvin Dark affair was two articles appearing in the Long Island paper *Newsday* in mid-July 1964 in which Stan Isaacs, a well-respected sports columnist, quoted Dark, the Giants' manager since 1961, as saying that "Negro and Spanish-speaking players on this team are just not able to perform up to the white players when it comes to mental alertness." The Giants, considered by many to be the National League favorite because of the strength of their lineup, were playing badly at the time. They had lost seven of their nine previous games, and Dark felt his team could have—indeed, *should* have—been maybe two or three games up in the standings instead of a game behind the not-expected-to-contend Phillies. He specifically singled out Puerto Rican–born Cepeda and Dominican-born Jesus Alou for "dumb" base-running mistakes. Giants regulars who were "Negro and Spanish-speaking players on this team" also included shortstop Jose Pagan from Puerto Rico and Marichal from the Dominican Republic, not to mention African Americans Willie Mays, Willie McCovey, and 1964 rookie-sensation third baseman Jim Ray Hart, who missed out on being NL Rookie of the Year only because Phillies third baseman Dick—then known as "Richie"—Allen was even more sensational.

Dark's remarks were disturbing on several levels. As the manager—and one who emphasized the importance of the team over the individual—he singled out a particular subset of players for criticism, which was not only inappropriate but foolish because the Giants' best players were black and Latino, and he had seriously undermined their faith in his leadership. Dark quickly tried to backtrack, claiming he was misquoted and that Isaacs presented his remarks out of context. Even if Dark had not really meant what he said, but rather was venting because his whole team was playing below their collective potential, he nonetheless betrayed prejudices that, at their most benign, were reflected in persistent casual racial and ethnic stereotypes that were not unusual in America at the time.

Coming at a time when black and Latin players were among the very best in the game, and as integration was being consolidated in the major leagues, with increasing numbers of minority players making big-league rosters as core regulars on their teams, Dark's comments were a reminder that Major League Baseball was still grappling with both the race issue and demeaning cultural stereotypes. Aside from the public relations firestorm Dark's quotes created for the Giants, the team's Latin players in particular were incensed by their manager's opinions of them, which primarily concerned their baseball work ethic. Said Dark: "You can't get Negro and Spanish players to have the pride in their team that you can get from white players. . . . You can't make them subordinate themselves to the best interests of the team. . . . They [their mistakes] are not the kind of things a manager can correct—missed signs and such—but they are inabilities to cope with game situations when they come up." And he topped it off by saying, "I only know what I've seen on this team and other baseball teams." What was particularly insidious about Dark's words was that they repeated the same arguments about "personal characteristics" attributed to black players that franchise owners had used less than 20 years earlier to justify their opposition to the integration of Organized Baseball. And these stereotypes were brought into the cultural realm when it came to Latin players from Caribbean Basin countries as they became more prevalent on big-league rosters.

While certainly insensitive and ill-informed, the racial and ethnic stereotypes held by many in America's overwhelmingly majority-white population were not necessarily mean-spirited—it was not, for example, unusual for stereotypes to be played for comic effect on television shows during the 1960s—but they were revealing of widely held perceptions in a still largely segregated society about specific minorities that many quite likely believed contained seeds of truth. In the absence of a more integrated society than there was at the time—and when it was still popular to see the United States as a great "melting pot" where all citizens of whatever background assimilated into the dominant white-majority culture that was presumed to offer the best that was possible in America—there was little understanding of cultural differences and the perspectives of minorities, and little effort was made to understand them.

Isaacs's columns hit the news in the San Francisco area in early August, when the Giants were hanging on to second place, close behind the front-running Phillies. According to James S. Hirsch in his 2010 authorized biography of Willie Mays, it was Mays who quelled a clubhouse rebellion by convincing his African American and Latin teammates not to give up on Dark because they were in the heat of a pennant race. Whether Dark's opinion of them depressed the pennant chase drive of the Giants' African American and Latin players is unknowable, particularly because of the monthlong loss of Marichal—who was 15–5 through July—with back problems, but the team lost six in a row in mid-August to fall 8½ games behind. That the Giants got back into the pennant race was only because the Phillies' monumental collapse in September breathed unexpected life into their prospects. Notwithstanding that in 1962 he had led the Giants to the pennant, Dark was unable to recover from his controversial remarks, not to mention an outside-of-baseball lifestyle that was equally controversial as far as Giants' owner Horace Stoneham was concerned. He was fired when the season was over.

* * *

Demeaning stereotypes of Latin ballplayers persisted long after the Alvin Dark affair. On the one hand, they were accused of being showboats on the diamond. On the other, they were portrayed as lazy or lackadaisical, as if soaking up the Caribbean sun. Having a "hot Latin temper" became an issue if a Caribbean-born player took physical exception to being hit by a pitch or to a hard tag or hard takeout slide; it didn't help that Juan Marichal, at the plate, took his bat to Dodgers catcher John Roseboro's skull when Roseboro's return throw to the pitcher buzzed a little too close to his ear, perhaps even nicking him.

As Roberto Clemente and Orlando Cepeda learned, when Latin players mentioned they were hurt, they were often perceived as lacking toughness or making excuses. Clemente and Cepeda also found that protesting their treatment, either in the clubhouse or to the media, earned them reproof for being cancerous to the team or childish chronic complainers. They were sometimes portrayed as innocents abroad, unable to speak the language and confused by life in America. Many young Latin players new to the majors had the same story told about them ordering the same thing they had memorized for breakfast every day because they couldn't read the menu.

Perhaps worst of all—and this happened even with the great Clemente—some newspapers quoted them in pidgin English as they struggled to answer sportswriters' questions in the clubhouse without benefit of a translator. This particular caricature of the Latin American ballplayer was captured by Garrett Morris, an African American comic actor, in his recurring role on *Saturday Night Live* in the late 1970s as Chico Escuela, a former major-league all-star from the Caribbean whose poor command of English has him limited to speaking in such trite aphorisms as, "Baseball bin berry berry good to me" and, "Keep you eye, keep you eye on da ball."

Part II

The Last of the Old-Fashioned Pennant Races

Roger Maris swings for the fences at Yankee Stadium. He batted .339 with 5 home runs and 13 runs batted in when the Yankees won 13 of 14 between September 16 and September 30, 1964, to move from 1½ games out in third place to a 3½-game lead with 5 games remaining in a tight pennant race involving three teams in the final month. © *Photofest.*

8

WEST COAST RIVALRY

The long tradition of caustic rivalry between the Dodgers and Giants was born more of community partisanship between the good citizens of Brooklyn and those in Manhattan than of frequent head-to-head battles for the National League pennant. For most of the first 40 years of the twentieth century, the Giants were a National League powerhouse and the Dodgers rarely in the race. In the 1940s and 1950s, it was the other way around. The one true exception was the Miracle of Coogan's Bluff, in 1951, that was ultimately decided by a three-game playoff, an ill-fated pitch by Ralph Branca, and the "shot heard 'round the world" by Bobby Thomson. In 1958 the two clubs took their rivalry to the West Coast, although Los Angeles and San Francisco were hardly within a subway ride of each other. It took a year in their new California surroundings for the Dodgers and Giants to become acclimated, but once they did the stakes in the rivalry they had stoked in New York became much greater because the two clubs were two of the best in baseball for the better part of the 1960s and competed directly for the right to represent their league in the World Series.

Their West Coast battles for the top spot began in 1959. 'Twas a three-team race to the finish. The two-time defending-NL-champion Braves spent most of the first half of the season on top trying for their third straight pennant. The Giants spent most of the summer in first place, powered by sluggers Willie Mays—the last remaining core position player of the Giants' 1954 World Series–winning team in New York—whose best years were still to come; 1958 Rookie of the Year first baseman Orlando Cepeda; and Willie McCovey, yet another first baseman, whose arrival in late July forced Cepeda to left field. McCovey's .354 batting average with 13 homers and 38 runs batted in was so impressive that his selection as the NL's 1959 Rookie of the Year was unanimous even though he played in just 52 games and had only 192 at-bats. The Giants' season came undone when they lost seven of their last eight games, starting with a sweep by the Dodgers in a three-game series at home that dumped them out of first place.

The Dodgers and Braves, both winning six of their last eight to get ahead of the Giants, ended the 154-game schedule with the same record, forcing the National League's third best-of-three playoff to decide the pennant winner, all since 1946 and all involving the Dodgers. This time (perhaps because they were no longer in Brooklyn?), the Dodgers won. The Dodgers' pennant was unexpected because they were in the process of rebooting for the future, while the Braves were a powerhouse, featuring Hank Aaron and Eddie Mathews, who clubbed 85 home runs between them, and a first-rate trio of starting pitchers in Warren Spahn, Lew Burdette, and Bob Buhl. Don Newcombe had been traded the previous June, leaving five-year veteran and hero of the 1955 World Series Johnny Podres and the youngsters Don Drysdale and Sandy Koufax as the core of manager Walt Alston's pitching corps in LA. Drysdale won 17, Podres 14, and Koufax—still in the process of harnessing his overpowering stuff—was 8–6 in 1959. Of the core lineup that had powered Brooklyn's Boys of Summer, Duke Snider was platooned in right field, Gil Hodges played in only 124 games, and Roy Campanella never made it to LA with the Dodgers because of a tragic car accident that left him paralyzed. To make matters more interesting, the Dodgers played in a stadium—the Los Angeles Memorial Coliseum—built for football, not baseball, with comically short dimensions in left field.

Yet they won the pennant anyway. Significant contributions from four African Americans—none of whom were elite players on the order of Jackie Robinson, Campanella, or Newcombe back in Brooklyn—were major reasons. Third baseman Jim Gilliam and second baseman Charlie Neal began their careers in Brooklyn; left-handed batter John Roseboro replaced Campanella behind the plate and would be platooned his entire career in LA, taking his days of rest whenever the Dodgers faced a righty; and Maury Wills was called up in June to play shortstop. With a far less imposing lineup than he had in Brooklyn, Alston began emphasizing run-creation strategies relying on speed and situational hitting that had been an important part of the 1950s Brooklyn Dodgers' power-driven offense but came to define the 1960s Los Angeles Dodgers. Alston's skillful management of his bullpen also made a difference. The 1959 Dodgers were the first NL pennant-winning team that did not exceed the league average for innings by starting pitchers.

* * *

Neither team was much of a factor in the 1960 and 1961 pennant races. For the next five years, however, the Los Angeles Dodgers and the San Francisco Giants were locked in mortal combat. In three tense pennant races, the National League's West Coast rivals played themselves to a virtual draw. They tied their regular-season series in 1962 and 1966 with nine wins each, and in 1965 the Dodgers held a two-game edge, winning 10 of their 18 games, which turned out to be exactly their pennant-winning margin of victory.

The two teams faced off in a fierce battle for the pennant in 1962, finishing the 162-game regular season tied with 101 victories each. Already with 100 wins, the Dodgers' four-game lead seemed secure with seven games left. They won just one. The Giants won five of seven. And for the fourth time in 16 years, the Dodgers were forced into a best-of-three playoff for the pennant. Mays hit two homers as the Giants crushed the Dodgers in the first game, played in San Francisco. The Dodgers took the second game, played in LA, in the bottom of the ninth after overcoming a five-run sixth-inning deficit. The deciding game, also in Los Angeles, surely brought back memories of Bobby Thomson's home run 11 years before when both clubs were still in New York. Nothing quite as dramatic this time, but the Dodgers blew a 4–2 lead in the ninth, giving up four runs to lose the game—and the pennant—to the Giants. Again. The World Series with the Yankees went seven games and famously ended with two outs, two runners in scoring position, and the Giants trailing, 1–0, in the last of the ninth when Willie McCovey smoked a line drive right at perfectly positioned second baseman Bobby Richardson.

With Mays, Cepeda, McCovey, and Felipe Alou the heart of their lineup, San Francisco was a potent offensive ballclub, scoring the most runs in the majors. Los Angeles was second. Even though 1962 was the inaugural year of Dodger Stadium, which became famous for being a pitchers' park, the Dodgers offense might have reminded some of the Boys of Summer back at Ebbets Field. Tommy Davis, a Brooklyn-born outfielder who didn't make it to the Dodgers until 1960 when they were already in California, led the league with a .346 batting average, 230 hits, and 153 runs batted in. Right fielder Frank Howard, the National League's 1960 Rookie of the Year, crushed 31 homers and drove in 119 runs. And Maury Wills set the new major-league stolen base record with 104 in 117 attempts, the last four of his steals coming in the three-game playoff. Unlike Roger Maris, whose record-setting 61 homers in a 162-game season the previous year came with a metaphorical asterisk because Babe Ruth's 60 in 1927 were in a 154-game schedule, Wills would have 156 games to break Ty Cobb's record 96 steals, as ruled by Commissioner Ford Frick, because that was how many games Detroit played in 1915. The Dodgers speedster did not steal his 96th base to tie the record until the 156th game of the season. Wills also stole his 97th base that day to eclipse Cobb.

LA almost certainly would have won the pennant without the need for any playoff if Sandy Koufax hadn't missed most of the second half of the season with circulatory problems in his dynamic left arm. (After years of struggling with his control, Koufax had his breakout season the previous year, going 18–13 and leading the league with 269 strikeouts in 255⅔ innings.) When he was sidelined in mid-July, Koufax had won six of his previous eight starts while surrendering only 4 earned runs in 67⅓ innings. Returning in late September, Sandy was not the same Koufax, giving up 10 runs in 8⅔ innings in three starts and a relief appearance. He started the first game of the playoff but failed to last even two innings. Although leading the league in earned-run average, Koufax finished with just 14 wins. Don Drysdale, still the putative ace of the staff, won 25 to earn the major leagues' still-singular Cy Young Award.

Aside from missing the last week of April and the first week of May, Koufax was healthy in 1963—with 40 starts, a 25–5 record, and a league-best 1.88 ERA—and Los Angeles had a relatively easy time winning the pennant. Tommy Davis won another batting title, and Howard smacked 28 homers. The Dodgers swept the Yankees in the World Series, allowing the Bronx Bombers just four runs. Koufax whiffed 15 Yankees in the series opener to set a new World Series record and won the finale, 2–1. Drysdale shutout the Yankees, 1–0, in Game Three. The Giants finished a distant third in 1963, but the next year were in a dogged fight for the pennant until, in the wake of manager Alvin Dark's complaints that his Latin and African American players left something to be desired as far their baseball mental edge was concerned, they lost seven straight in mid-August. On August 16, the day the Giants' losing streak began, Koufax pitched a complete-game shutout for his 15th win in 16 decisions. Sandy was 19–5 and had given up just 5 earned runs in 35⅓ innings in four August starts. Koufax was also suffering from debilitating arthritis in his left shoulder and did not pitch again in 1964. The Dodgers, however, were already out of the running.

The next two years, it was the Dodgers and Giants again, neck-and-neck to the finish line. Los Angeles won both times, by two games in 1965 and 1½ in 1966. The Giants began the 1965 season with a new manager. After employing only four managers over 52 years dating back to John McGraw in 1902 (succeeded by Bill Terry in 1932, Mel Ott in 1942, and Leo Durocher in 1948), they seemed to be on a four-year plan for managers since coming to San Francisco. Bill Rigney, Durocher's replacement in 1956, lasted until early in the 1960 season; Alvin Dark took command in 1961 and was fired after the 1964 season, in no small part because of his insensitive, racially tinged comments about the Giants' African American and Latin players; and now Herman Franks—the coach who'd spied on opposing catchers' signs with a powerful telescope from the Polo Grounds' center-field clubhouse in 1951. Franks also would manage the Giants for just four years, finishing second every time.

Both clubs lost a major player to injury in 1965. San Francisco's Orlando Cepeda missed almost the entire season with a bad knee he could hardly put weight on. Similarly, Tommy Davis, the Dodgers' best hitter, was out the rest of the year after breaking his ankle in an awkward slide into second base just 16 games into the schedule—against the Giants, it so happened. Cepeda's injury turned out to be a big break for Willie McCovey, who took over at first base after playing out of position in left field the three previous years, and he responded with 39 homers, second in the league, and 92 RBIs. For most of that summer, Los Angeles was on top and San Francisco not far behind. A 14-game winning streak in the beginning of September, however, allowed the Giants to blow past the Dodgers and take a 4½-game lead with just 16 left to play. In a script reversal from 1962—LA meant Hollywood, after all—this time it was the Dodgers who came roaring back to take the flag. Beginning with 13 wins in a row—including six decided by one run—the Dodgers closed out the season with a 15–1 record to grasp the pennant with 97 wins to the Giants' 95, then beat Minnesota's Twins in seven games in the World

Series. Koufax was 26–8, led the league in earned-run average for the fourth straight year, and fanned 382 batters in 335⅔ innings. His strikeout total was the highest since Rube Waddell fanned 349 back in 1904. His three-hit shutout in Game Seven against a powerful Twins lineup on two days' rest secured the Dodgers' third World Series championship since coming to LA.

The 1966 season began with Koufax and 23-game-winner Drysdale holding out together for higher salaries commensurate with their contributions in 1965. This being before free agency, both were forced to settle when Dodgers owner Walter O'Malley refused to back down from his position that players do not dictate salary demands to owners, and certainly not collectively. The Dodgers trailed the Giants and Pirates most of the summer. Winning 13 of 15 to start September, however—their two losses were to San Francisco—catapulted the Dodgers into first place, where they held off the Giants' winning eight of their last nine. LA was rescued from the possibility of having to play their third playoff for the pennant against the Giants since 1951 when Sandy Koufax won his 27th against only 9 losses on two days of rest in game 162 on the schedule. It was Koufax's sixth win in eight starts, only one of which he lost, in the final month, and the last of his major-league career.

The 1966 season ended ingloriously for the Dodgers as they were swept four straight in the World Series by Baltimore's Orioles. The Dodgers were as stymied by Orioles pitching as the Yankees had been by Dodgers pitching in the 1963 series. LA scored a total of two runs in the series, none after the third inning of the opening game. In Game Two Koufax was outdueled by a young pitcher in his last week as a 20-year-old named Jim Palmer and victimized by Dodgers center fielder Willie Davis, battling a bright sun on a cloudless Los Angeles day, making three errors—two dropped flies and an errant throw—in the fifth inning. With LA still reeling from the series loss, Koufax announced he would not be returning the next year—or any year. Forced to take frequent cortisone shots for his chronically arthritic left elbow just to take the mound, he pitched in acute pain. Only 30 years old and worried that continuing to pitch would leave his left arm crippled for life, Koufax had had enough.

Sandy Koufax retired at his peak, with back-to-back Cy Young Awards, his third in four years, and having just put together one of the greatest—if not the best ever—five-year stretches of baseball the game has ever seen by a pitcher. From 1962 to 1966 he won 77 percent of his decisions, with a 111–34 record, and had a 1.95 earned-run average. He had led the league in ERA five straight years. He completed 100 of his 176 starts, threw 33 shutouts, led the league in strikeouts three times, and struck out 9.4 batters for every 9 innings he pitched. Koufax became the first pitcher to throw four no-hitters, one each year from 1962 to 1965. The fourth was a perfect game against the Cubs in which the Dodgers didn't get a hit of their own until two outs in the seventh—the only hit Bob Hendley allowed in his eight-inning complete-game loss—and it didn't even figure in the outcome of the 1–0 game. Major League Baseball had not seen such pitching dominance since Lefty Grove went 128–33—a .795 winning percentage—from 1929 to 1933 and had his league's best ERA four years in a row.

The excellence of Sandy Koufax was unfortunate for Giants ace Juan Marichal. After winning 18 for the 1962 pennant-winning Giants, Marichal moved into the all-time greats category by putting together six 20-win seasons over the next seven years, including 25–8 in 1963, 22–13 in 1965, 25–6 in 1966, and 26–9 in 1968. In 1965 it was he, not Koufax with his league-leading 26–8 record and 2.04 ERA, who was the best pitcher in baseball, according to pitching wins above replacement. For all that, he did not receive a single vote for the Cy Young Award in any of those years because Koufax was a unanimous selection in 1963, 1965, and 1966, and the Cardinals' Bob Gibson took all the votes in 1968.

* * *

Except for 1963, when the Giants were unable to keep up with the Dodgers, either team could have won any of the pennants the other came away with at the end of their close tussles. It could easily have been the Giants with three pennants and the Dodgers with only one between 1962 and 1966, and the Giants, not the Dodgers, recognized in the baseball world as the class of the National League. The Giants, especially in retrospect but even at the time, seemed a more imposing team than the Dodgers. San Francisco's core regulars included five future Hall of Fame players—Mays, McCovey, Cepeda, Marichal, and Gaylord Perry, although Perry, whose rookie year was 1963, did not become a great pitcher until 1966 when he went 21–8. Los Angeles had three future Hall of Famers—Koufax, Drysdale, and right-hander Don Sutton, a rookie in 1966 whose best years were in the 1970s. The Dodgers' most notable position regulars were shortstop Maury Wills; Tommy Davis until his broken ankle early in the 1965 season ruined his career; center fielder

Willie Davis; outfielder/first baseman Ron Fairly; and catcher John Rose-boro.

The mid-sixties Dodgers had an anemic offense compared to the Giants—the heart of whose batting order included sluggers Mays, McCo-vey, and third baseman Jim Ray Hart, whose rookie year was 1964. Influenced by the vast dimensions of Dodger Stadium, the first in a wave of new stadium construction in the 1960s and 1970s, the Dodgers placed their bets on pitching rather than slugging. Dodger Stadium not only suppressed home runs but took away many hits. Ebbets Field it clearly was not. When they were winning three pennants in four years between 1963 and 1966, the Dodgers were in the bottom half of the league in runs and substantially below the league average slugging percentage. After scoring the third fewest runs in the league in 1964, the Dodgers, already with two of the best pitchers in baseball—Koufax and Drysdale—thought it expedient to trade slugger Frank Howard to the Washington Senators for another quality starter, lefty Claude Osteen.

Howard's power game was ill-suited for Dodger Stadium and the offense manager Walt Alston was building around speed and situational hitting. By virtue of his size—he stood at 6-foot-7 and weighed in the neighborhood of 260 pounds—and raw power, Howard hit a higher per-centage of his homers at home than his teammates, but he still had more on the road than at Dodger Stadium. The trade worked out for both the Dodgers and Frank Howard. With all due respect to the excellence of Koufax and Drysdale, the Dodgers would not have won in either 1965 or 1966 without Osteen. Howard, meanwhile, went on to power-hitting fame in Washington, although the Senators—a 1961 expansion team—were never in a pennant race.

Alston managed with the expectation that every game, especially at home, was going to be low scoring, every game was going to be close, and every run would be important. The stolen base—Wills stole 329 bases between 1962 and 1966, leading the league four times—situational hitting, and sacrifice bunts to advance baserunners were staples of the Dodgers' offense. Alston also skillfully employed his bench for any ad-vantage he could in close games. In winning the 1965 and '66 pennants, the Dodgers had the unique advantage of each of their infield regulars being a switch hitter, always enabling a favorable matchup with the pitch-er, whether right-handed or left-handed, whenever first baseman Wes

Parker, second baseman Jim Lefebvre, shortstop Wills, or third baseman Jim Gilliam came to bat.

Compensating for his mediocre offense, superior pitching was Alston's trump card and the hallmark of the mid-sixties Los Angeles Dodgers. While he had a strong cadre of starting pitchers—Koufax, Drysdale, and Osteen—that allowed him to use significantly fewer relievers than the league average, Alston was aggressive in using his relief ace in the heat of tight pennant races. From 1962 to 1965, that was lefty Ron Perranoski. In 1966 Perranoski was in a subordinate role as right-hander Phil Regan, acquired over the winter, led the league with 21 saves while winning 14 of 15 decisions. Getting the win in two games after having blown the lead and in eight others he entered with the score tied, Regan was known as "The Vulture" for picking up victories that starting pitchers thought they deserved.

As was typical of managers at the time, Alston frequently brought his relief ace into high-stress situations with runners on base earlier than the ninth inning and allowed him to pitch multiple innings. In the hectic final month of 1962, when the Dodgers were struggling to hold off the surging Giants, that may have cost his team the pennant. Perranoski pitched in 15 of LA's last 27 regular-season games, five of them for two or more innings, and then in all three playoff games against San Francisco. In only his second year, and his first in a close pennant race, Perranoski struggled with so much at stake; in 24⅔ innings down the stretch, Perranoski gave up 31 hits and 19 runs, his ERA soaring from 1.85 to 2.85. In 1965 it was a different story. Perranoski racked up 8 of his 18 saves, giving up just 2 earned runs in 36 innings, in the September stretch as the Dodgers vaulted over the Giants to win a tight pennant race.

Given how close the Dodgers-Giants pennant races were, Walt Alston was perhaps the indispensable man(ager) to LA's success. Always working with the understanding that Walter O'Malley renewed his contract for only one year at a time, perhaps no other manager was as successful with different kinds of ballclubs. Alston deftly managed the transition of O'Malley's franchise from the formidable power-based offense of the mid-1950s team he inherited and managed to their last two pennants in Brooklyn to the mid-1960s team in Los Angeles that, in almost a direct contradiction to the Boys of Summer, was distinguished by superior pitching, excellent team speed, and a reliance on small-ball strategies to score runs. And in the midst of that transition was the hybrid Dodgers team that unexpectedly won the 1959 pennant.

Casey Stengel was the only manager with a better record than Alston managing as many close pennant races. Going back to his teams in Brooklyn, Alston won four of five pennant races that were decided by two games or less, and the one he lost was 1962 in a playoff. With the exception of 1962, when they let a four-game lead with a week remaining slip away, the Dodgers under Alston's steady hand were exceptional when the pressure was on in September, particularly in games with first place on the line. He won with teams he should have won with in Brooklyn (which many managers haven't done), and—even though Koufax and Drysdale were quite an advantage to throw against other teams—he led the mid-1960s Dodgers to more success than the quality of their roster merited. Walt Alston's teams probably overachieved by winning in 1965 and 1966, particularly given the strengths of their hated rivals in San Francisco.

* * *

It perhaps *should* have been the San Francisco Giants with three pennants—1962, 1965, and 1966—and the Los Angeles Dodgers with one in 1963 (when the Giants were out of the hunt). The Giants might have won in 1964, too, had Alvin Dark not alienated his team. While Los Angeles had superb pitching to compensate for a mediocre offense, San Francisco had a powerhouse offense *and* their own dominant pitcher in Juan Marichal. The Giants had three players in the NL's top five for home runs in 1963 and 1964, and two in the top five in 1962, 1965, and 1966. With a much more potent lineup, the Giants needed substantially fewer runners on base for each run scored than did the Dodgers every year from 1962 to 1966.

In retrospect, the Giants were much like the 1956–1959 Milwaukee Braves, who perhaps *should* have won four consecutive pennants. Like those Braves, the Giants were cursed by having largely marginal major-league talent, including among position regulars, around the club's strong core of Willie Mays, Willie McCovey, Orlando Cepeda (until he was hurt), and Jim Ray Hart. Middle of the infield mediocrity, with Chuck Hiller and then Hal Lanier at second and Jose Pagan and then Tito Fuentes at shortstop, while not necessarily a fundamental weakness, was glaring when compared to the Dodgers. Manager Herman Franks lamented many years later that had he had a decent double-play combination, it would have been San Francisco and not Los Angeles that won the 1965 and 1966 pennants. The Giants, moreover, were not as potent offensively during these years as their power-hitting lineup might suggest. They were the National League's leading team in runs scored in 1962 and finished second in 1963, but otherwise fared no better than fourth in the league. And even with Marichal, San Francisco's pitching, while quite good, was not in LA's class. From 1962 to 1966, the Giants scored 9 percent more runs than the Dodgers—but also gave up 11 percent more runs.

While Marichal's 111 wins between 1962 and 1966 put him in the ranks of the game's greatest pitchers, and Hart slugged 87 homers between 1964 and 1966 to get his career off to an impressive start, and McCovey in 1965 began a string of five consecutive years with at least 30 homers (including leading the league in homers and RBIs in 1968 and 1969), Mays had the best five-year stretch of his career between 1962 and 1966, averaging 10.5 wins above replacement. He was, in fact, the major leagues' best position player each of those years, and the best player *period* in the first four, with only Koufax having a higher player value in 1966.

A fair argument can be made that Willie Mays—not his contemporary Mickey Mantle, or Honus Wagner or Ty Cobb or even Babe Ruth—is the best player to have ever played in the major leagues. (That also includes his godson, Barry Bonds, whose excellence was tainted by credible allegations of steroid use.) Not necessarily *the greatest*—that honor rightly belongs to the Babe because of his outsized impact on the game's history—but *the best*. Mays excelled in every facet of the game. He finished his career with 660 home runs, only 54 shy of Ruth's mark, and most likely would have shattered that record had he not lost two years of his youth to military service during the Korean War, and had he not been robbed of some indefinable but almost certainly significant number of home runs by the swirling, often gale-force winds at San Francisco's Candlestick Park—as close to a torture arena for right-handed power hitters as there could possibly be.

Moreover, unlike the Babe—who played in a hitters' era that he had no small role in establishing—Mays's very best years in the 1960s came in a pitchers' era, when he had to hit against the likes of Koufax, Drysdale, and Gibson. And even if Mays does not approach Ruth for league-leading black ink in the record books, consider that he was part of what can arguably be called baseball's greatest generation of players. Finally,

Mays played a much more demanding and defensively important position—center field. Ruth was no stiff in the outfield, at least when he was in his prime, but Mays was exceptional. Indeed, for all his batting prowess, the signature moment of his career was the remarkable catch he made in the 1954 World Series.

According to the WAR metric for player value, Ruth tops Mays 163 to 152 over the course of their full careers—22 years on big-league diamonds for both men, the last season for each an embarrassing imitation of when they were the real deal. (Ruth's 162 wins above replacement are as a hitter and outfielder; he earned another 20.8 as one of the best pitchers in baseball during his Red Sox years.) Bookending their best years by the baseline player value of 5 wins above replacement that denotes an all-star quality season, and allowing a season or two of relative mediocrity below 5 WAR within that stretch, Ruth's consecutive best years were from 1916 (when he starred on the mound) to his final season in a Yankees uniform in 1934, and Mays's from 1954 (after two years in the army) to his last full season in a Giants uniform in 1971. Over the course of their best years bracketed by a WAR of at least 5, Ruth had an average annual player value of 9.4, compared to 8.3 for Mays.

Mays, however, went 13 consecutive seasons in which his player value never dipped below all-star level, and only twice was slightly below the 8 wins above replacement that is defined as an MVP-quality season. After his 1951 rookie year, it was not until Mays was 36 years old in 1967 that his player value again slipped below 5 wins above replacement, but he exceeded that in three of the next four years. Ruth, on the other hand, had an uncharacteristically very poor season (at least by his standards) in the middle of his career, with a 3.5 WAR in 1925 when he played in only 98 games. Both Mays, from 1960 to 1966, and Ruth, from 1926 to 1932, had a stretch of seven straight years in which their player value exceeded the 8 WAR standard for an MVP-level performance, each averaging 10.1 for those years. Mays exceeded 10 wins above replacement four years running from 1962 to 1965; Ruth never went more than three years in a row with such a high player value, although he almost certainly would have if not for the said-to-be bellyache that sidelined him in 1925.

Of course, what Ruth had that Mays did not were 10 World Series appearances, three with the Red Sox as a top-tier pitcher and seven with the Yankees, compared with just four for Mays—the last when he was in his final year as a player in 1973, back in New York with the Mets.

Moreover, the Babe was a clutch performer in World Series play, first setting a record by throwing 29⅔ consecutive shutout innings as Boston's left-handed ace in the 1916 and 1918 series, and then setting a record with 15 World Series home runs in 36 games for the Yankees. Both records have since been broken. If the measure of any single player's greatness is the number of times his team was the only one to walk off as the proven best in the sport, then Ruth truly trumps Mays. Unlike the Babe, who was the driving force behind the Yankees' perennial success in the 1920s, Mays was unable to drive the mid-1960s Giants to dynastic mode.

Mays had one last opportunity with the Giants to do so in 1971. By now 40 years old, starting in just 116 games, and never playing more than seven in a row, Mays nonetheless hit 18 homers and was the Giants' second-best player and fifth among National League position players, based on his 6.3 wins above replacement. The Giants' best player was right fielder Bobby Bonds, in his fourth season, who smacked 33 home runs, drove in 102 runs, and had a seven-year-old son named Barry hanging around the clubhouse. Despite hitting at the top of the order, Bobby Bonds used an all-or-nothing swing that resulted in his averaging 27 homers a year in his seven San Francisco seasons and striking out a phenomenal—for the time—145 times a year. In 1970, batting exclusively in the lead-off spot, Bonds set a new major-league record with 189 strikeouts, breaking the record 187 he had set the year before.

With both Bonds and Mays getting off to fast starts—Mays had 12 home runs and a .340 batting average through June 1—the 1971 Giants soared to a 10½-game lead by the end of May. By the last week of the season, however, the Dodgers had closed to within one. On the last day of the season, Marichal pitched a complete game for his 18th win to clinch first place for the Giants in the National League's Western Division (it was the third year of divisional alignments in Major League Baseball). The Giants lost the best-of-five National League Championship Series in four games, in Game Two of which Mays hit the only postseason home run of his career. Following 646 regular-season homers for the Giants, 459 after the move from New York to San Francisco, it was his last home run as a Giant. For what it's worth, 96 of those homers—the most he hit against any team—were off Dodgers pitching.

9

THE PERILS OF GENIUS

Explaining the '64 Phillies' Epic Collapse

It was with great expectations that the good citizens of the City of Brotherly Love awoke on the morning of September 21, 1964. Their Phillies were returning from a road trip on which they won 6 of 10 games. In first place every day since mid-July, they held a commanding 6½-game lead. Only two weeks and 12 games remained. It seemed inconceivable that they would not soon be appearing in only the third World Series in franchise history. What happened next was arguably the most monumental meltdown of a frontrunner in baseball history—10 consecutive losses that not only cost the Phillies an all-but-certain pennant but had as profound an effect on a generation of their city's fan base as perhaps there ever has been.

With the exception of the St. Louis Browns, no major-league franchise had been as sorry as the Philadelphia Phillies entering the season. Not even "first in war, first in peace, last in the American League" Washington was as sad a tale of woe; the Senators won three pennants and a World Series in their first 33 years. The Phillies had won only two pennants, in 1915 and 1950, and played a grand total of nine World Series games, of which they lost eight. But the Phillies were a team on the rise. They went from 47 wins in 1961 to 81 in 1962. Even accounting for expansion adding two teams, the truly awful Cubs playing like an expansion team, and the schedule increasing from 154 to 162 games, 34 more victories in a single season was a fairly significant marker of improvement. In 1963 the Phillies not only improved further, with 87 wins to finish fourth, but from the beginning of July till the end of the season they had the third-best record in the major leagues; only the two pennant winners—the Yankees and Dodgers—played better than Philadelphia in the final three months.

The Phillies' dramatic change of direction from their decline to mediocrity and doormat of the National League since their 1950 pennant was owed to John Quinn's becoming general manager in 1959 and his hiring rookie manager Gene Mauch in 1960. Mauch spent most of his nine years playing as a seldom-used utility infielder for six different teams observing and mastering the art of the game. Carefully cultivating a reputation as a brilliant baseball strategist and tactician—a latter-day John McGraw, always outthinking whoever was managing in the opposite dugout—Mauch got the credit for the Phillies' remarkable improvement in 1962 and '63.

Quinn had been the architect of the Milwaukee teams that were a National League power in the second half of the 1950s, and just as his investment in black players paid off for the Braves—not just the superstar Hank Aaron but also role players like Wes Covington—the same would be true in 1964 when the Phillies unexpectedly competed for the pennant with five black players in key roles. In 1960 and '61 he traded for outfielders Covington and Tony Gonzalez and second baseman Tony Taylor; in 1961 he promoted Ruben Amaro to play shortstop; and in 1964 Dick Allen (then known as "Richie"), signed by the Quinn regime in 1960, became the Phillies' third baseman. Given their noxious history on the integration front, that the Phillies would not have competed for the 1964 pennant were it not for their black players was itself a terrific story.

In addition to his trades for Taylor, Gonzalez, and Covington, Quinn pulled one over on the White Sox in December 1959 by trading third baseman Gene Freese for Johnny Callison. A five-year veteran, Freese was seen by the White Sox as a perfect fit for a position they had been struggling to fill since the end of World War II. Callison was a 20-year-old outfield prospect with limited big-league experience. Freese proved not to be the answer to the White Sox' problem position, but Callison quickly became one of the best young players in baseball. In 1963 he was the third-best position player in the major leagues after Mays and Aaron, at least by wins above replacement. But Quinn's biggest-impact trade was for 32-year-old Detroit Tigers ace Jim Bunning in December 1963. One of baseball's best pitchers since winning 20 in his first full season in 1957, Bunning came to Philadelphia with a career record of 118–87 for a Detroit team that was mostly not competitive in the years he pitched for them.

Their strong ending in 1963 made the Phillies an intriguing proposition going into 1964. *Sports Illustrated*'s preseason prognostications called Philadelphia one of the "six teams with a good shot at the National League pennant this year." It was a long shot, to be sure, with the Dodgers and Giants dominating the league and the Cardinals and Reds both dangerous teams, but one that proved accurate. The *SI* preview projected Callison to be the "hitting star," and Allen to "be the top-hitting rookie in the major leagues this season." *SI* was right on both counts. Callison played in every game and, with 31 home runs and 104 runs batted in, would likely have been voted MVP were it not for Philadelphia's almost incomprehensible implosion. Allen hit 29 homers, had 91 RBIs, batted .318, and was overwhelmingly voted NL Rookie of the Year. *SI* also predicted, based on his exceptional performances in All-Star games against the National League's best hitters, that "Bunning will be tough the first time around the league and should help the Phils get off to a good start." They were right about that, too: Jim Bunning was 8–2 with six complete games, three shutouts (including a perfect game against the Mets on Father's Day), and a 2.17 ERA in his first 16 starts for the Phillies through the end of June.

The Phillies' daily lineup was much less settled than the NL's other putative contenders, and with many more weaknesses. Callison, Allen, and Taylor—a steady hand at best—were the only players Mauch wrote into his lineup every day. The Phillies started with Bobby Wine at shortstop and ended with Ruben Amaro, neither of whom caused angst in the hearts of opposing pitchers. Mauch used a lefty-righty platoon all season for catcher, first base, center field, and right field. The unexpected position platoon was in center field, where left-handed batter Tony Gonzalez—a .300 hitter against both righties and lefties, starting in all but 18 games, in 1963—had such a horrible time against southpaws at the beginning of the season (just 4-for-31 in his first 9 starts against them) that Mauch decided to platoon him with right-handed Cookie Rojas.

The most interesting aspect of Mauch's platoons, however, was his platooning the Phillies' two most dangerous hitters—Callison and Allen—in the batting order. From the beginning of the season until early

June, Mauch had right-side Allen batting second and left-side Callison third when the Phillies faced righty starters, and Callison second and Allen third when southpaws took the mound. Through the end of May with this batting order platoon alignment, Callison hit .299 with 4 homers and 20 runs batted in, and Allen, along with 24 RBIs and a .301 average, was leading the league with 10 home runs. Presumably awestruck by Allen's power, Mauch moved his slugging third baseman into the cleanup spot in June and penciled Callison third in the batting order, where both remained on a daily basis until mid-August, when Mauch went back to swapping them between second and third for the rest of the season, depending on the opposing starter.

In contrast to his skillful manipulation of position players, however, by September Mauch's starting rotation was in deep trouble. By midsummer, three of his four core starting pitchers when the season began could no longer be counted on. Art Mahaffey got off to a bad start, never to regain his manager's confidence no matter how well he pitched; 22-year-old Ray Culp was pitching with severe elbow pain every start he made after mid-May; and lefty Dennis Bennett's strong 6–3 start took a painful turn in June with left-shoulder problems that got worse as the season progressed, notwithstanding his 32 starts on his way to a 12–14 record. The underlying fragility of the Phillies' pitching woes was masked through the summer months by the excellence of Jim Bunning and lefty Chris Short, who didn't move into the starting rotation until mid-May. By the end of August, Short was 14–7 with a 1.90 earned-run average that was second only to Sandy Koufax, Bunning was 14–4 with a 2.17 ERA, and the Phillies were in first place by 5½ games. Notwithstanding that reasonably comfortable lead, the debilitating injuries to Culp and Bennett, almost certainly aggravated by their continuing to start games in pain all summer, depleted Mauch's core of *reliable* starting pitchers as the season entered its final month.

* * *

Nearly all accounts of the 1964 Phillies' collapse are all about their 10-game losing streak that started on September 21, when they had a 6½-game lead with 12 remaining, and cost them eight games in the standings in 10 days. Mauch has been blamed ever since for pitching Bunning and Short twice each on two days of rest, instead of the normal three, during those 10 days in an effort to end his team's disastrous slide.

A strong case can be made, however, that Gene Mauch's biggest blunder came five days before the start of that losing streak, on September 16 in Houston, when he chose to start Bunning, 17–4 at the time, on short rest just three days after he had thrown a 10-inning complete-game victory in San Francisco. Pitch counts were not much (if at all) on managers' minds back then, and were not recorded for posterity, but given that he faced 38 batters, gave up 7 hits, walked 2, and struck out 9, Bunning clearly threw well over 100 pitches in his 10 innings against the Giants. But Philadelphia had a comfortable 6-game lead with 145 down and just 17 to go, and Houston was not a contender. Mauch's decision meant Bunning's next regular turn would be the fourth and final game of the next series in Los Angeles, also not in contention, which meant Bunning would not start any of the three games against Cincinnati—a team that still *was* in contention, however dim their chances—at least, not on normal rest.

Why Bunning in Houston? Looking at the calendar, the most plausible explanation is that Mauch was trying to set up Bunning, his best pitcher, to start the first game of the World Series—scheduled to begin on Wednesday, October 7—on suitable rest. Ironically, Bunning would have been perfectly lined up to start the World Series by making his last five regular-season starts on normal rest, except for a quirk in the schedule that had Philadelphia concluding the season in Cincinnati with games on Friday, October 2, and Sunday, October 4, with an off-day on Saturday between the two games. Being a manager who prided himself on thinking ahead, and undoubtedly expecting his Phillies to coast to the finish line, Mauch may have reasoned that if Bunning continued to pitch on his normal schedule, his last start before the World Series would have been on September 29, giving him a full week off before Game One, which Mauch probably assumed would disrupt Bunning's pitching routine and cause him to lose his sharpness going into the World Series.

Mauch could have given Bunning four days of rest between his remaining starts, which would have had his ace making his final start of the regular season on Friday, October 2, giving him another four days off before the start of the World Series. But even if he had been willing to buck the then-conventional practice of top starting pitchers taking the mound every four days by having Bunning start every fifth—which is the norm today—Mauch most likely did not even consider such an option because—with Culp sidelined, Bennett pitching in pain, and Mahaffey deemed unreliable—the Phillies had no depth in their starting pitching beyond Bunning and Short. Mauch appears to have decided that keeping Bunning to three days of rest between starts was preferable and took the gamble of starting him on two days' rest against the woeful Colt .45s, presumably just this once, in order to align him to make his final regular-season start with the proper rest on Friday, October 2. Bunning would then have had an extra fourth day off before pitching the opening game of the World Series. It probably made little difference to Mauch that Bunning gave up 6 runs in 4⅓ innings in his Houston start because the loss had no bearing on the standings. That decision, however, began a cascade of questionable moves he made that ultimately left him little choice but to pitch Bunning and Short twice on short rest in an eight-day span in a desperate attempt to salvage a pennant that had been his team's for the taking.

* * *

If we were to characterize Mauch's managerial moves in the final 16 games with cheeky headlines, the first would be "Burning Two to Win One" for his decisions to start Rick Wise in Los Angeles on the day after Bunning's defeat in Houston and to replace him as soon as he got in trouble in the very first inning despite the Phillies already having a 3–0 lead. Mauch could have started the experienced Mahaffey, whose turn to start against the Colts was taken by Bunning, but instead chose a rookie who had just turned 19 a few days before. Mahaffey's last two starts had gone badly, but so had Wise's. His most recent, against the Dodgers in Philadelphia 10 days before, had been a disaster; Mauch yanked Wise after three batters—all of whom reached base—leaving his successors on the mound to get all of the requisite 27 outs. Here he was again facing the Dodgers, and his day was much the same—Wise faced four batters, gave up two runs, and had gotten just one out when Mauch had seen enough. With a pair of left-handed batters up next, Mauch called on veteran south-paw Bobby Shantz to get out of the inning.

It seemed like a brilliant move at the time. Shantz pitched into the eighth inning and gave up only one run of his own while the Phillies held on for the win. But it would turn into a profound mistake—one Mauch should have anticipated. Instead of showing commitment to the decision he made to start a young rookie in a late-season game during a pennant drive, Mauch replaced him in the very first inning—in effect, using two pitchers in one "starting role" that day—despite knowing that his starting rotation was in disarray and that Bunning and Short were his only two reliable starting pitchers. With a six-game lead in a season fast approaching its end, this was not a game the Phillies necessarily needed to win.

The unintended consequence of Shantz's facing 25 batters in relief of Wise was his being unavailable to pitch in dire circumstances two days (and one loss) later at Dodger Stadium, forcing Mauch to "Send a Rook to do a Vet's Job." The job was to get the final out in the last of the 16th inning of a tied game with the would-be winning run on third, two outs, and left-handed Ron Fairly now batting for LA. The rookie was lefty-throwing Morrie Steevens, pitching in his first major-league game of the season—having pitched only 12 times in the Big Time before this. Mauch's far better left-handed option was crafty veteran Bobby Shantz, but having pitched 7⅔ innings in relief two days before, he was not sufficiently rested—apparently not even to face one batter—to get out of the inning. Willie Davis, an aggressive baserunner, was edging off third. As a lefty, whether from the stretch or a full windup, Steevens was pitching with his back to the runner on third in his delivery. He was apparently so focused on the batter that he was totally inattentive to Davis—who noticed. Davis stole home to score the winning run.

But that wasn't Mauch's only failed strategy of the day. Following a leadoff single by Callison in the 14th inning of the tie game, Mauch ordered next-up Dick Allen to lay down a sacrifice bunt to move the would-be go-ahead run to second base, rather than allowing the Phillies' most feared and dangerous hitter the opportunity to drive in the run himself. Mauch did this knowing that even if the bunt attempt was successful, the pitcher's spot was up next, the result of an earlier double-switch; that he had already used seven position players off the bench; that his only option for a pinch-hitter was light-hitting Bobby Wine, batting .209; and that .238-hitting catcher Clay Dalrymple was up after that. Allen bunted successfully, leaving Mauch with only two outs and two weak hitters to try to score Callison from second. "Baseball Gods to Mauch: Sacrificing Allen? Seriously?" Surely Allen was a better bet to drive in a run than Wine or Dalrymple. The Phillies did not score. Willie Davis's game-stealing play came two innings later.

* * *

Even that loss seemed relatively inconsequential, especially after Bunning survived a ninth-inning Dodgers rally the next day for a complete-game victory. We are now where most accounts of the 1964 Phillies' historic collapse begin. When the Phillies took the field at home against the Reds on September 21 for the first of three games, their lead was 6½ ahead of both Cincinnati and St. Louis. Fourth-place San Francisco was seven back. Their lead was so strong that even if the Reds or Cardinals won all their remaining games, the Phillies needed to win only seven of their last 12 to win the pennant outright. If either competitor won 10 of their remaining 13 games—which the Cardinals in fact did—Philadelphia could have finished the season 4–8 and still gone to the World Series. It would take a perfect storm for the Phillies *not* to win the pennant.

But the atmospherics were there for a perfect storm. Despite their long-shot chances, the remaining schedule favored both Cincinnati and St. Louis, and even San Francisco. The Reds and Cardinals both had five games against the awful Mets, and the Cardinals five and the Reds three against sixth-place Pittsburgh. More importantly, however, the Reds had five games left against the Phillies and the Cardinals had three, giving both clubs the opportunity to make up significant ground against the first-place team they had to overtake. While the Giants did not have any games against the teams ahead of them, they had the advantage of playing all 12 of their remaining games against the eighth-place Cubs and the ninth-place Colts.

The Phillies, by contrast, did not have any of the National League's worst teams on *their* remaining schedule. In eight of their final 12 games they had to contend against their two closest competitors—the Reds and Cardinals—meaning they would lose ground in any game they lost. And their four other games were against Milwaukee, a fifth-place team, but one whose potent lineup was more than capable of doing serious damage to Mauch's worn-out pitching staff. Philadelphia was scheduled to close the season with three games in St. Louis and two in Cincinnati. But at the dawn of play on September 21, the pennant chances for both those teams were dim. Mauch had reason to expect that neither would be a pennant threat by then.

For the Reds, their only realistic chance of catching the Phillies depended on sweeping the series now at hand. While there was nothing at the moment the Phillies could do about the Cardinals and Giants, winning just one of the three games would leave the Reds 5½ back—a gap that would be nearly impossible for Cincinnati to close with only 10 games after that. How important would just one win against the Reds have been? Even if the Cardinals swept their upcoming two games against the Mets in New York, one Phillies win against the Reds would have left St. Louis five behind and, with 11 games remaining, also with not very much hope. The first game in that series is remembered for Cincinnati's Chico Ruiz stealing home with two outs in the sixth inning to score the only run of the game. "Phillies Victimized by Home Invasion—Again." This time the victim was Art Mahaffey, who otherwise had an excellent start. Accounts of this game mention that both managers—Gene Mauch and the Reds' Dick Sisler—were shocked (shocked!) that Ruiz dared to steal home with Frank Robinson (*the* Frank Robinson!), one of baseball's most accomplished and dangerous hitters, at the plate.

But the headline for the loss could also have been "Allen Sacrificed at the Altar of Playing for One Run—Again." After Mahaffey retired the Reds in the top of the first, Tony Gonzalez led off for Philadelphia with a single, bringing up Dick Allen, back to hitting second against right-handed starters. The Phillies had all 27 outs remaining. Rather than allowing Allen, second only to Willie Mays in offensive wins above replacement that year, to hit away with the possibility of setting up a big first inning, Mauch was playing for one run to get a lead, and for the second time in three days ordered him to bunt. Allen's sacrifice was good. Gonzalez got as far as third. That's the closest any Phillie came to scoring all evening.

The rest of the series went badly for Philadelphia. The Reds clobbered Short the next day and the Phillies once again suffered a home invasion, this time by Pete Rose swiping the plate. The next day, Bennett took a 3–2 lead into the seventh and wound up losing the game when reliever Ed Roebuck surrendered a three-run homer to Vada Pinson. The failure to take even one game from the Reds cost the Phillies three games in the standings in three days, but with a 3½-game lead and now only nine games to go, it seemed time was still on their side. Moreover, the Cardinals and Giants were both five back, presumably no longer in the picture.

Bunning, whose regular turn in the rotation would have had him starting the first game of the series with Cincinnati if not for his short-rest start in Houston, did not pitch against the Reds, but took the mound for the first of four games against the visiting Braves. He gave up three runs in six innings, taking the loss as his team was held scoreless until the eighth. For Philadelphia, losing had become contagious. The good news was that their lead was still three games over Cincinnati. No need to be desperate—yet. Gene Mauch, however, feeling his sure-thing pennant slipping away, acted in desperation by starting Chris Short in the second game of the Braves series on only two days of rest instead of Mahaffey, whose turn it was in the rotation and who had pitched so well in his previous start, even if he neglected to check on Chico Ruiz at third base; Mauch felt Mahaffey cracked under pressure when he allowed Ruiz to brazenly steal home. Short gave Mauch eight strong innings, but the game went into extra innings. The Braves scored two in the 10th. Allen hit a dramatic two-run inside-the-park homer in the bottom of the inning to keep the game going. The Phillies lost in the 12th. The Reds swept the Mets in a doubleheader. Philadelphia's lead was down to 1½ games.

Now it really was "Desperation Time," and Mauch did not handle it well as his "Reckless Endangerment of Lead" contributed to the Phillies' losing contagion. Milwaukee had whittled Philadelphia's early 4–0 lead to a single run in the eighth—an inning that ended with Bobby Shantz being brought in to get the final out with the bases loaded. Due up first in the Braves' ninth was the ever-dangerous right-handed batter Hank Aaron, capable of tying the game with one swing. In the bullpen was right-hander Ed Roebuck, the one Phillies reliever who had pitched well in September, allowing just 2 earned runs in 14 innings in seven games. But Mauch chose to stay with Shantz, never mind his being a lefty. Perhaps he was disturbed by the game-winning homer Pinson hit off Roebuck three days before. Aaron singled. Mauch stayed with Shantz against another dangerous Milwaukee slugger, Eddie Mathews, which made sense because Mathews batted from the left side. Mathews singled. Next up was right-handed Frank Bolling—hardly a dangerous hitter, his average hovering slightly above .200. Shantz stayed in. Bolling reached on an error, loading the bases. The Phillies had yet to get an out. Rico Carty, another dangerous right-handed hitter, stepped to the plate carrying a .325 batting average with 20 home runs and 80 RBIs. Roebuck the righty was warming up. Mauch stayed with Shantz the lefty. Carty tripled. The Phillies' lead was gone. Roebuck was finally brought into the game. He got three outs, stranding Carty at third. The Phillies went down quietly in their half of the ninth.

Gene Mauch had now watched his team lose six in a row, and 9 of 11 dating back to when he decided to start Bunning on short rest in Houston. With the Reds having extended their winning streak to seven, the Phillies' advantage was down to half a game. The Cardinals, having won five of their last six, had closed to within a game and a half. There were still six games to play. "Desperate Times Call for Desperate Measures," and with Culp out of action, Bennett's shoulder in debilitating pain, and Short and Mahaffey having started the two previous days, Mauch really had no choice but to send Bunning to the mound on two days of rest in a desperate effort to stop the losing. Similar to what happened in his short stint against Houston, Bunning gave up seven runs in three innings. The Braves won, 14–8. The Reds beat the Mets in a doubleheader. For the first time since mid-July, the Phillies were no longer in first place. Philadelphia was now down a game to Cincinnati, and just half a game ahead of the surging third-place Cardinals of St. Louis—the Phillies' next destination.

Had they pitched in turn in the rotation, Short and Bunning would have been available to pitch on normal rest in the season series that now mattered the most—against the Cardinals, a team the Phillies had to beat to keep from falling behind yet another sudden contender, let alone keep pace with the Reds. The unintended consequence of starting his two best pitchers out of turn against the Braves was that Mauch was now forced to use them on only two days of rest in St. Louis. Three games later, the Phillies were "Winless in St. Louis." Pitching for the fifth time in 15 days, and the third time in the last 7, in the series finale, Bunning was battered around and failed to make it out of the fourth inning. Their losing streak had reached 10 games. Philadelphia was now in third place, 2½ behind St. Louis and 1½ behind Cincinnati.

But as the 1964 season entered its final weekend, there was still hope! The Phillies could still make it to the World Series that just 10 days ago seemed such a sure thing—but *only if* they beat the Reds in their last two games in Cincinnati, *and* the Cardinals lost all three of theirs against the lowly Mets, which would have left all three clubs with identical 92–70 records, and then *only* if they went on to win the resulting round-robin playoff. And blessedly, their off-day on October 1—the Phillies' first day of rest after 31 games in 30 days—and another off-day scheduled for October 3 meant that Mauch could start Short and Bunning on their normal three days of rest. Baseball had never before had a three-way playoff series to decide a pennant winner, and it could even be a four-way tie if the Giants—now three games back—won all three of their remaining games against the Cubs in San Francisco, *and* the Cardinals were swept by the Mets at home, *and* the Phillies won both of their games against the Reds.

Except for the Phillies doing their part by beating the Reds in both teams' final two games, none of those scenarios played out. The Giants' loss on Saturday took them out of the equation. The 109-loss Mets, however, made things interesting by beating the Cardinals on Friday and Saturday. After Bunning hurled a six-hit masterpiece to shut out the Reds, 10–0, and earn his 19th win, the Phillies and Reds were tied in the standings awaiting the outcome of the Mets-Cardinals game in St. Louis. The Mets had a 3–2 lead in the fifth, but that score proved deceiving. Bob Gibson came on in relief to shut down the Mets; the Cardinals scored three times in the fifth, sixth, and eighth innings to blow out the Mets; and there was no need for any playoff—St. Louis secured the pennant outright and, for good measure, went on to win the World Series that Philadelphia had seemed sure they would play.

* * *

When it was over, Gene Mauch blamed himself for the debacle. This was telling not so much because he attempted to remove the stigma of the collapse from his players but because, in the final weeks, he may have put on himself too much of the burden to win games instead of allowing the games to play out with less urgency. Mauch was an intense manager who prided himself on his intimate knowledge of the game. He tended to be very hands-on in game management. Many of his players felt Mauch was too controlling as their manager, most notably Dick Allen, as he related in his autobiography.

Mauch's constant maneuvers to try to wrest competitive advantages—both big and small—caught up with him in the final weeks of the season. An aggressive manager who liked to force the action, particularly early in games to score the first run or in close games as the innings wound down, Gene Mauch—unlike John McGraw, the granddaddy of master strategist baseball managers, who disdained the sacrifice bunt precisely because it "sacrificed" a precious out—was willing to "sacrifice" as outs his two most dangerous run producers in the interest of playing for one run. Dick Allen and Johnny Callison, combining for 60 home runs in 1964, each laid down six sacrifice bunts that year to move a runner into scoring position. Few other managers used their most powerful hitters to sacrifice themselves so lesser lights could drive the sacrifice-advanced runner home. Of the league's other premier hitters who also hit for power, Mays had one sacrifice bunt for the Giants in 1964, and Orlando Cepeda and Willie McCovey had none; Frank Robinson did not have a sacrifice all year for the Reds; neither did Ken Boyer for the Cardinals; nor did Hank Aaron or Eddie Mathews for the Braves.

Calling on Allen to bunt in the extra-inning game Philadelphia lost when Willie Davis stole home, with two notoriously weak hitters following in the lineup, and again in the very first inning of the game they lost, 1–0, on Ruiz's steal of home, was misplaced in the context of both games, particularly since Allen was the one Phillies batter not struggling the last two weeks of the season. Beginning with Bunning's start on short rest in Houston, Allen batted .386 with 3 homers, 18 runs scored, and 13 RBIs in the Phillies' final 17 games; the Phillies as a team hit only .234, struggled with runners on base, and scored 66 runs in those games. During their 10-game losing streak, while the Phillies scored just 34 runs and batted .217, Allen hit .415, scored eight runs, and drove in five. Had Mauch let Allen swing away instead of sacrifice in those two games, the outcome of either—or both—might have been different. A victory at that point in the season, with so few games remaining, may have been all it took to permanently deflate the hopes of the Reds and Cardinals before they began their surge toward the top.

While Mauch made any number of questionable in-game decisions in the final weeks, his primary miscalculation was strategic, with ultimately unforgiving cascading effects. That was trying to win every game knowing that his starting rotation was in shambles at a time the Phillies had a comfortable lead in the standings with time rapidly running out on their pennant race rivals. They could have afforded to lose a few games, like the one in LA where Mauch wouldn't let Wise pitch his way out of even the first inning, inadvertently limiting his relief-pitching options two days later. He overreacted after the Phillies lost four in a row and 3½ games from their lead by starting Short and Bunning on two days of rest against Milwaukee. That decision might ultimately have forced him to resort to doing so a second time in St. Louis after the Phillies' lead was entirely gone. Given that his two best pitchers already had 471 innings between them and would have been more likely to pitch effectively and gain a victory on normal rest, Mauch turned possible wins into losses by panicking rather than accepting losses for the sake of maximizing the odds of winning when either started. The Phillies lost the pennant by one game. Just one additional win by both Bunning and Short, or two by either, could have changed the outcome of the pennant race.

The turning point for the season, however, was Mauch's misguided decision to start Jim Bunning on short rest in Houston on September 16, probably so his ace would be aligned to start the opening game of the World Series—still three weeks away. With a comfortable six-game lead and so little time left on the schedule, Mauch would still have had time to arrange his rotation and ensure his ace had the appropriate rest between his final regular-season starts and the start of the Fall Classic had he waited till *after* the Phillies officially clinched the pennant before starting Bunning, just once, on short rest. Mauch's planning for the World Series resulted in his best pitcher being unavailable to start against one of the remaining contending clubs—the Reds. Even then, the impact of his Houston decision could have been mitigated had he kept his ace on the schedule apparently planned. Instead, he veered off plan even before the Phillies were halfway through their 10-game losing streak. By prematurely assuming the certainty of a pennant, Mauch ended up outsmarting himself. Baseball has a way of punishing such hubris.

* * *

Gene Mauch was not fired after the Phillies' historic collapse. He may have botched the end game of a pennant race his team should have won, but the front office gave him credit for the team's unexpectedly contending for the pennant in the first place. His platooning and persistent position player substitutions to get the matchups he wanted as the game progressed masked the fact that his player talent was not at the level of the other contending teams. But to say the Phillies overachieved just to get to the point of their collapse is disingenuous. Some of the most compelling pennant races involved teams that were not expected to compete, yet did, and won—the 1914 "Miracle" Braves and the 1969 "Miracle" Mets, for example. Perhaps the 1964 Phillies peaked too early, their weaknesses catching up with them, while the 1914 Braves and 1969 Mets peaked at just the right time, coming from far behind to finish first by decisive margins and going on to win the World Series before their relative weaknesses could reassert themselves. Mauch finally wore out his welcome in Philadelphia in June 1968. He went on to manage a total of 26 years in the major leagues. He never did get to manage in a World Series.

For the 1964 Phillies, like the 1950 Whiz Kids, it proved to be that year or never. Jim Bunning won 19 each of the next two years and 17 in 1967. Chris Short won 66 the next four years. Johnny Callison had another outstanding year in 1965. Dick Allen continued his fearsome assault on National League pitching. But Philadelphia was not a factor in any pennant race. Not until the mid-1970s were the Phillies competitive again—after they traded Rick Wise, their best pitcher in 1971 with 17 wins, to the Cardinals for first-time 20-game winner Steve Carlton.

Dick Allen's career took a turn down a rabbit hole of controversy after 1964 that led to his persistent reputation as an all-around jackass and a cancer to team chemistry. Like Joe DiMaggio after his sensational rookie year in 1936, Allen held out in spring training 1965, believing the salary he was offered was less than he deserved, before finally settling with the front office. In July that year he threw a punch at highly regarded veteran first baseman Frank Thomas over a racially insensitive remark that may have been more in the nature of edgy ribbing than racist putdown—Thomas sarcastically asking whether Allen, a slugger who disdained being asked to bunt, thought he was Muhammad Ali. While the 36-year-old Thomas, now a reserve with limited playing time, was sent to Houston, Allen began being booed in Philadelphia. As he became more resentful and impolitic in his words and actions, hometown boos for the Phillies' best player only increased. Dick Allen endured five years of this in Philadelphia after his stellar rookie season. There were incidents of late arrivals, of not showing up for games, of conduct generally deemed detrimental to the ballclub. Through it all, he remained one of baseball's elite players—until he and his 177 home runs and .300 batting average in six Phillies seasons were traded to St. Louis in October 1969.

10

THE (TEMPORARY) END OF THE YANKEES' FOREVER DYNASTY

There have always been sacred numbers in baseball. For kids growing up in the 1960s they were 714 (Ruth's career homers), 60 and 61 (Ruth's and Maris's single-season home run records), 56 (DiMaggio's hitting streak), 2,130 (Gehrig's consecutive games streak), 4,191 (Cobb's total hits), 511 (Cy Young's career victories), and perhaps even 96 and 102 (Cobb's and Wills's single-season stolen base records). There were also 29 and 20. Those were the number of pennants and World Series won by the New York Yankees in the 44 years from 1921 to 1964. For Yankees fans of any age, if the back-to-back World Series defeats their pinstriped heroes suffered in 1963 and 1964 seemed unfathomable, it's because it was virtually unprecedented. The only previous time they had ever lost consecutive World Series was the first two they played, in 1921 and 1922. Even more unfathomable was the idea that fans were witnessing the end of the Yankee dynasty. Only three times since 1921 had the Yankees gone as many as three years without playing in a World Series. Little would a kid who lived and died by the Yankees who was 10 years old on the day they lost Game Seven of the 1964 Series have imagined the Yankees would not again be the best team in the American League, let alone return to the World Series, until he or she was 22. For fans loyal to their team, that was an eternity.

The end of the Yankee dynasty occurred precipitously after their second string of five pennants in five years beginning in 1960—Casey Stengel's last year as manager. They were indisputably the best team in the

American League, if not all of baseball, the first four of those years, even if it took a 15-game winning streak closing out the season to break a mid-September first-place tie with Baltimore in 1960 and finish eight games in front. They won the next three pennants by 8, 5, and 10 games before needing an end-of-the-season sprint to come from behind to win the 1964 pennant by a single game over the White Sox and two over the Orioles. As in 1960, a red-hot 22–6 month of September propelled the Yankees into the World Series. Their five straight pennants matched the five in a row won by Stengel's 1949–1953 Yankees, but while those Yankees also won five straight World Series, the 1960–1964 Yanks won only two.

The middle three years, 1961 to 1963, were when this iteration of the Yankees' forever dynasty was at its best. Rather than Ole Perfessor Stengel being given a chance to extend his extraordinary record of 10 pennants in 12 years, General Manager George Weiss went instead with Ralph Houk as manager. Almost the complete opposite of Casey in personality, Houk had been waiting in the wings since being called back to New York as a coach in 1958 after three years gaining experience managing the Yankees' top farm club in Denver. Before that he was a third-string catcher on a Yankees team so flush with talent, including Yogi Berra in his 140-starts-a-year prime, that Stengel could afford to keep him on the roster even though his role was to hardly ever play. Whatever his frustrations about lack of playing time, Houk made good use of his time, mentoring players and cultivating an astute understanding of how to manage the game.

The controlled chaos of Casey Stengel's roster management gave way to lineup stability under Houk, particularly in the infield. Whereas Stengel prized the ability of his infielders to play any position and was constantly changing who played where from one year to the next, and even within a given season, Houk identified his core regulars and stuck with them. Unless injured or otherwise unavailable, Bill Skowron at first, Bobby Richardson at second, Tony Kubek at shortstop (except for most of the 1962 season, when his National Guard unit was mobilized), and Clete Boyer at third were his everyday regulars in 1961 and 1962. Rookie Tom Tresh, who played shortstop in 1962, moved to left field when Kubek returned to baseball after serving his military commitment. Now in his 30s, Skowron was traded away and replaced at first base in 1963 by 10-years-younger Joe Pepitone. The rest of the infield remained the same.

Mickey Mantle in center and Roger Maris in right were fixtures in the outfield unless injured, which was more than occasionally for both players. Houk platooned the left-handed-batting Yogi Berra and right-handed Hector Lopez in left until Tresh took over full-time at the end of the 1962 season. Elston Howard, the regular catcher, sometimes platooned with Berra. Unlike Stengel, who made frequent substitutions based on game situations, Houk's infielders were almost always in at the end of games they started. The starting position players he substituted for most were the often-hurt Mantle and Maris in 1962 and 1963.

By establishing a regular rotation, Houk was also more conventional than Stengel in his approach to starting pitching. Unlike Stengel, he used the Yankees' best pitcher, Whitey Ford, as the ace he actually was. Stengel typically used Ford on four days of rest; Houk worked him every fourth day. After starting exactly 29 times each of the three previous years under Stengel, Ford made 39 starts in 1961 and 37 each of the next two years. While only one Yankee pitcher had started as many as 30 games in any season during the last four years of Stengel's reign, Houk had three pitchers with at least 30 starts in both 1962 and '63.

The 1961 season was a signature one in Yankees lore. Their 109 wins stood at only one fewer than the 1927 Yankees, although in the new 162-game schedule occasioned by expansion, and they had to contend against another team—the Detroit Tigers—that also won more than 100. It was a 13-game winning streak at the beginning of September that broke open the pennant race and allowed them to coast the rest of the way. The Yankees ended with an eight-game advantage over 101-win Detroit and then dismantled the Cincinnati Reds in five games in the World Series. It was also the year that Maris and Mantle dueled each other for the single-season home run record. Maris pulled away with four homers in a double-header on July 25 on his way to surpassing Babe Ruth's 60. His 61st blast came on the last day of the season. Mantle finished with 54. The Yankees as a team hit 240 homers, shattering the record of 221 held by the 1947 Giants and 1956 Reds. On the mound, pitching every fourth day, Ford had the best year of his career, with a 25–4 record, then broke Babe Ruth's pitching record by extending his World Series shutout-innings string to 32 (and counting). Lefty reliever Luis Arroyo set a new major-league record for saves in a single season, with 29, although this would be retroactive since the save was not yet an official statistic.

In 1962 the Yankees made Ralph Houk the first to lead his team to World Series triumphs in his first two years as a big-league skipper. In first place to stay by early July, the Yankees prevailed over second-place Minnesota by five games, then required seven games to beat San Francisco for their 20th World Series championship. Maris hit 33 home runs. Mantle had 30, despite missing about a month of the season, and earned his third MVP Award. Tresh was Rookie of the Year. Ford won 17 and extended his World Series shutout streak to 33⅔ innings before giving up a run in the second inning of his opening game start. Ralph Terry led the league with 23 wins. He followed up with a 1–0 complete-game gem in the seventh game of the series in San Francisco. The only run scored on a double play.

Seizing a double-digit lead in mid-August they never relinquished, the Yankees made it four pennants in a row in 1963. A strong argument can be made that the 1963 Yankees, with 104 wins, were actually a better team than the 109-win 1961 Yankees. And that's even though Mantle appeared in only 65 games, missing most of the season with a broken foot after crashing into the outfield fence in Baltimore, and Maris played in only 90 games because of back problems. The overall quality of competition in the American League was somewhat better three years into the expansion era than in the first year, but more importantly, the quality of the Yankees' pitching in 1963 was much better than in 1961. Ford, whose league-leading 25–4 record earned him the Cy Young Award as the best pitcher in the major leagues, was the Yankees' only pitcher that year to throw more than 200 innings. The other core starters on the 1961 Yankees were Ralph Terry (16–3), Bill Stafford (14–9), and Rollie Sheldon (11–5). Terry is not exactly unknown today, but the names Stafford and Sheldon do not resonate in either baseball history or Yankee lore as pitchers of a certain stature. The 1963 Yankees, on the other hand, had two 20-game winners—Ford (24–7) and Jim Bouton (21–7), and Terry won 17. Rookie southpaw Al Downing (13–5), pitching 175⅔ innings, led the league in fewest hits (5.8) and most strikeouts (8.8) per 9 innings.

Mantle and Maris, in the lineup together in only 31 of the Yankees' 161 regular-season games, combined for just 38 homers, 23 by Roger. The Yankees nonetheless lived up to their Bronx Bombers tradition. Elston Howard led the club with 28 homers and became the first black player to win the American League's Most Valuable Player Award; Joe Pepitone hit 27 in his first season as the Yankees first baseman; and Tom

Tresh, following up his outstanding rookie year, had 25. Mantle and Maris were both back for the Fall Classic. Maris was injured in the second game, trying to make a catch on a triple, and could not play the rest of the series. Mantle tied Ruth for the most home runs in World Series play when he hit his 15th off Sandy Koufax in the seventh inning of Game Four. The Yankees' ignominious sweep by the Dodgers in the World Series, as well as the extended absences of both Mantle and Maris, are heavy counts against the 1963 Yankees being better than their 1961 club.

The Yankees' fifth consecutive pennant in 1964 was won under their third manager in five years. Notwithstanding Ralph Houk's joining Hughie Jennings of the 1907–1909 Tigers as the only managers in major-league history to win pennants their first three years at the helm, his talents were judged more valuable in the front office. Promoted to general manager, Houk named Yogi Berra, now at the end of his stellar career, to succeed him in the dugout.

It was not easy for either Berra or the Yankees in 1964. With Berra having difficulty making the transition from teammate to exercising authority as the manager, the Yankees spent most of the year trying to catch the Orioles and White Sox. By mid-August, following a six-game losing streak and the famous Phil Linz harmonica incident, Yankees executives had all but decided that Berra's managerial tenure would be limited to this one season. The incident in which Linz, a utility infielder, continued to practice a child's song on his musical instrument on the bus following a tough loss to pennant rival Chicago after Berra told him to stop seemed to confirm he could not control his own ballclub. And then . . . the Yankees got hot. They won seven of their next nine to get back into serious contention by the end of August. They didn't clinch the pennant until the next-to-last day of the season and ended with just a one-game margin of victory, but an 11-game winning-streak that began midmonth, with 143 games down and 21 to go, all but assured them the pennant heading into the last week.

Mantle and Maris were both back from injury, although the Mick was rarely in at the end of games, to help preserve his legs. Mantle's 35 homers and 111 RBIs were both third in the league, and his .303 batting average placed fourth. New York's come-from-behind pennant, however, was almost certainly a consequence of calling up 22-year-old right-hander Mel Stottlemyre in mid-August to bolster the starting rotation and

trading for right-hander Pedro Ramos, a veteran starting pitcher, to solidify their bullpen in early September. While Ford went 17–6, Bouton
18–13, and Downing 13–8 that year—all of whom made at least 35
starts—it was Stottlemyre's 9–3 record in 12 starts, including winning
five consecutive starts in September that proved critical to winning the
pennant. Ramos was available on waivers because he was having the
worst year of his career. Berra did not necessarily need Ramos to fill a
void in the bullpen—rookie Pete Mikkelsen had 12 saves by the end of
August and second-year reliever Hal Reniff had 8—but chose the veteran
starter over his less experienced relievers to preserve victories in the final
weeks of the season. Pitching in 13 of the Yankees' final 27 games down
the stretch, all in relief, Ramos surrendered just 3 earned runs in 21⅔
innings with 8 saves and a victory.

The Yankees acquired Ramos after the September 1 deadline for eligibility in the World Series, but they sure could have used him. Yankees
relievers gave up 11 runs in 13⅓ innings. Mikkelsen surrendered a three-
run homer to Tim McCarver in the 10th inning of Game Five that gave
the Cardinals a three-games-to-two edge when the series returned to St.
Louis. With Ford having to retire from the series in the sixth inning of the
opening game because he lost feeling in his left hand, Berra was forced to
rely on Stottlemyre and Bouton to carry the starting load. Bouton won
both his starts; Stottlemyre went up against Cardinals ace Bob Gibson
three times, beating him in Game Two, surrendering one run in seven
innings in Game Five, but lasting just four innings in Game Seven. Mantle was the batting star for the Yankees, hitting .333 with 3 home runs and
8 runs batted in. The first of his three homers, a ninth-inning walk-off to
win Game Three, broke the record of 15 he shared with the Babe. Mantle's 18 World Series career home runs remains the record.

* * *

The St. Louis Cardinals had gone 18 years since their last pennant and
World Series championship in 1946. The foundation for their pennant
was set in the mid- to late 1950s, beginning with third baseman Ken
Boyer's debut in 1955. Now one of baseball's premier players, Boyer,
whose brother Clete was the Yankees third baseman, had hit at least 23
homers and driven in at least 90 runs every year but one since his second
year (1956) and was a .300 hitter five times. After being acquired as a
minor-league prospect from Cincinnati, Curt Flood took charge in center
field in 1958, becoming the Cardinals' first black position regular for an

entire season. In 1959 the Cardinals traded with the Giants for first base-man Bill White, a highly regarded young black player whose future in San Francisco had dimmed only because the Giants also had Orlando Cepeda and Willie McCovey to play first base, and *somebody* had to go. And an ace was born on July 30, 1959, when Bob Gibson threw an eight-hit 1–0 shutout against Cincinnati in his first start in the major leagues.

By 1963 the Cardinals were ready to contend. Julian Javier, a black player from the Dominican Republic, was at second base, teamed with shortstop Dick Groat, now three years removed from his 1960 MVP season with the Pirates. Catcher Tim McCarver was in his rookie season. Boyer and White were second and third in the league in runs batted in. Groat was third in batting average. Groat, White, and Flood each had more than 200 hits, making the 1963 Cardinals the first team with three 200-hit players since the Tigers had four in 1937. Veteran lefty Curt Simmons, once a Whiz Kid, won 15; Gibson and Ernie Broglio won 18. Finishing second with 93 wins, 1963 was the best year in St. Louis baseball since their 1949 bid for the pennant fell a game short of the Dodgers.

The last day of the 1963 season was also the final game in the career of Stan Musial. Like Ted Williams, he got a hit in his final at-bat and then left the game. Williams hit a home run; Musial also drove in a run on an RBI single, after which he was replaced by a pinch-runner. It was the 3,630th hit of his career—second only to Ty Cobb at the time—and his 1,951st RBI, fourth-most in history when he retired, after Ruth, Cap Anson, and Gehrig. In 22 seasons, all with the Cardinals, Musial had a lifetime batting average of .331 and won seven batting titles. Musial never led the league in home runs, but the 475 he hit in his career were second to Mel Ott's 511 in National League annals through 1963.

The 1964 Cardinals made for a compelling story with their dramatic surge at season's end to overtake Philadelphia's collapsing Phillies. The pivotal moment for St. Louis, however, was not in those frenetic final weeks, but at the trade deadline on June 15 when they made what turned out to be one of the most lopsided trades in history, acquiring Lou Brock (and two no-names) from the Chicago Cubs for pitchers Broglio (whose presumed best years to come never materialized) and Bobby Shantz (whose best years were behind him). The Cardinals had lost 10 of 12 and were mired in eighth place when they traded for Brock. It was looking like 1964 would be a major disappointment for the Redbirds, especially after how well they did the previous year. And except for Flood in center field, with Musial gone, the outfield was a major weakness. Immediately establishing himself as an impact player whose speed and nuisance factor on the bases would bedevil opponents the way Maury Wills did for the Dodgers, this marked the real beginning of Lou Brock's Hall of Fame career. Taking over in left field and hitting second behind Flood, Brock batted .348 and stole 33 bases in 103 games for the Cardinals, helping them to the best record of any team in the majors after he came to St. Louis.

The core Cardinals players were at their best when it counted the most, as St. Louis won 22 of their final 32 games to overtake Philadelphia. Brock had his best month—30 runs scored, 17 driven in, and a .364 batting average; Flood batted .358 and scored 26 runs; White had a team-leading 29 RBIs in September; Boyer smashed seven of his 24 homers and drove in 26 of his league-leading 119 runs batted in; and Bob Gibson sealed his reputation as an intimidating, refuse-to-lose master on the mound by winning eight of his last 10 starts, picking up his 19th win pitching the final four innings in relief in the pennant-clinching game on the last day after going eight innings in a start two days before, then winning two of his three World Series starts—including all 10 innings in Game Five and another complete game in Game Seven three days later—while striking out 31 Yankees in 27 innings for a new series record.

The World Series ended on October 15. The very next day, in a pair of stunning developments, the Yankees fired their manager, Yogi Berra, and Cardinals manager Johnny Keane announced he would not be signing a new contract with St. Louis. Days later, in yet another stunning develop-ment, Keane became the new manager of the Yankees his Cardinals had just vanquished. This turn of events was occasioned by the front offices of both clubs deciding in August that their managers were not up to the task of winning a pennant. Berra's Yankees appeared to be slipping out of contention, and Keane's Cardinals, in fourth place and 11 games out on August 23, were already written off. Cardinals owner August Busch fired his general manager and was already considering managerial candidates for next year. Keane, reading the tea leaves, was in contact with the Yankees, whose front office was also in the hunt for next year's manager. Even though both managers turned their teams around and got them to the World Series, the die was cast. Berra's fate was sealed and Keane wanted no part of the new contract Busch had no choice but to offer his World Series–winning manager.

The move did not work out well for either Keane or the Yankees. After leading the majors with 99 wins in 1964, the Keane-managed Yankees fell to 77 wins and sixth place in the American League the next year. Keane was declared a failure after the Yankees opened 1966 with only four wins in 20 games. Ralph Houk returned to the dugout after two years in the executive suite. The Yankees finished that year with the third-worst record in the major leagues.

* * *

The last team to have an extended run of even two pennants in five years and fall so completely off the table after winning their last one was the Philadelphia Athletics, who went from the best record in baseball and their fourth pennant in five years in 1914 to the major leagues' worst record the very next year. That was 50 years earlier. But there were extenuating circumstances. America in 1915 had endured two years of economic recession, the Athletics' baseball dominance did not prevent a dramatic drop in home attendance, the upstart Federal League's aggressive pursuit of established major leaguers was forcing owners to pay their best players much more to keep them from jumping ship, and the A's family-based joint ownership of Ben Shibe and Connie Mack did not have the financial resources to weather that confluence of events. The Athletics had won 99 games in 1914 and never fewer than 90 the five previous years, but rather than go for another championship, Mack began dismantling his dynasty immediately after being ignominiously swept by Boston's "Miracle" Braves in the 1914 World Series. It was about the money. They finished last seven straight years.

The 1965 Yankees' fall after winning five pennants and two World Series in five years, while not quite as calamitous as what happened to the 1910–1914 Athletics, was stunning nonetheless. The core players on their five-and-two-in-five club were still there. Injuries and age surely played a role in the Yankees' worst single-season drop since Ruth suffered his "belly-ache heard 'round the world" in 1925. Mantle, Maris for nearly the entire season, Elston Howard, and Tony Kubek all missed time because of injury. Budding ace Jim Bouton, 39–20 in 1963 and '64, began the season pitching with a sore bicep, was told by the Yankees to pitch through the pain, and ended up 4–15. Famous for throwing so hard his cap would fly off his buzz cut as he released the ball, Bouton had thrown out his arm and never did recover as a power pitcher.

But also undermining their cause was that the 1960–1964 Yankees were not as formidable as their five pennants in a row would suggest. Besides the 1961 expansion diluting the overall talent level in the league, there were no American League teams coming out of the 1950s that were positioned to challenge the Yankees the way Boston had in 1949 and 1950 and Cleveland did from 1951 to 1956. Chicago's White Sox, whose 1959 pennant occurred when the Yankees were beginning their transition into a post-Stengel era, slid backward. Baltimore's Orioles, who unexpectedly competed with the Yankees into mid-September 1960, were still in the process of building a consistently competitive ballclub. The same was true of Minnesota's Twins in the early 1960s. And Detroit's Tigers had been a middle of the pack team for a decade when they suddenly burst forth with 101 wins in the 1961 expansion season, still finished far behind the Yankees, and then returned to being a midpack team until after the Yankees sank into oblivion to finish out the sixties.

Moreover, while true to the tradition since the days of Ruth and Gehrig of being the Bronx Bombers, unlike past teams in their dynastic succession, the five-and-two-in-five Yankees offense was fueled almost entirely by the power game. Led by the M & M Boys—Maris and Mantle, usually batting third and fourth—40 percent of their runs scored on "Ballantine Blasts" (as broadcaster Mel Allen called them, in deference to the Yankees' beer sponsor, for those of us watching or listening at home). The Yankees in those years were consistently below the league average in productive outs that advanced runners on the bases. And managers Ralph Houk and Yogi Berra both persisted in batting Bobby Richardson first or second in the lineup despite the fact that his on-base percentage exceeded .300 just once between 1961 and 1964. Given Richardson's insisting on hitting his way on base, his .266 lifetime batting average be damned, Stengel astutely had him eighth in the order more often than not.

Most significantly, with the exceptions of Mantle and Ford, Maris in 1961 and '62, Bouton in 1963 and '64, and Howard as baseball's best catcher for the first half of the sixties, the other core regulars on the 1960–1964 Yankees stood out much less relative to other players in the league than is typical for dominating ballclubs. When Mantle and Maris were healthy, and after Tom Tresh took charge in left field as a rookie late in the 1962 season, the Yankees' outfield was probably as good as

Despite both losing significant time to injury in 1963, Roger Maris and Mickey Mantle combined for 356 home runs for the 1960–1964 Yankees that won five pennants and two World Series in five years. *National Baseball Hall of Fame Library, Cooperstown, NY.*

any in the American League. With the exception of Hector Lopez, who was closer to a replacement-level player in performance than to an average major-league starting position player, the Yankees had virtually nobody off the bench capable of playing every day in the outfield the many times either Mantle or Maris was hurt. They got away with that in their pennant-winning years. In 1965 they did not. The Yankees' infield, while solid defensively, was not as good as its reputation. None of their core regulars, first to third—Bill Skowron and then Joe Pepitone at first base, Richardson, Kubek, and Clete Boyer, whose defensive brilliance at third base was overshadowed by Brooks Robinson—were better than the average starting major-league infielder; Richardson was closer to marginal than average in the spectrum of player value.

The once-vaunted farm system the Yankees built in the 1930s, which provided infusions of high-quality major-league-ready players with regularity to keep the big-league club consistently competitive, had hollowed out by the 1960s. This trend should have been apparent in the last half of the 1950s. Whereas the beginning of that decade saw the Yankees bring up Ford, Mantle, and Gil McDougald—three of the best players in the American League in the 1950s—as well as Skowron and Howard, the new blood from the Yankees system in the late 1950s were the likes of Kubek and Richardson, good players, to be sure, but more typical of an average major-league regular than the bright young stars the Yankees used to promote to keep their dynasty going. Much of the refreshing of the Yankees roster since the mid-1950s had been through trades, and in the five-and-two-in-five years there was little change among the core regulars from either trades or the farm system. The most prominent players promoted from their minor-league affiliates in the early 1960s were Tresh, Pepitone, Bouton, Downing, and Stottlemyre. All had their moments and contributed to Yankees pennants, but only Mel Stottlemyre was an enduring impact player.

The atrophy of the Yankees' minor-league player pipeline was a direct consequence of the club's reluctance in the 1950s to scout, sign, and develop top-tier amateur black ballplayers. After Elston Howard was promoted to the Bronx in 1955, the Yankees did not have a single black player who was a genuine major-league prospect play for their Triple-A affiliates until Al Downing made it to Richmond in 1962. He was promoted to the Yankees the next year in June. Howard, Hector Lopez—acquired from Kansas City in 1959 and used mostly as a platoon starter in the outfield—and Downing were the only black players of consequence for the Yankees in the first half of the 1960s. Major League Baseball's decision in the mid-1960s to institute an annual amateur draft in which clubs selected based on the previous year's standings, from worst teams to best, meant that franchises with the best scouting and the most money could no longer corner the market on potential major-league prospects as the Yankees did in the 1930s and 1940s.

It was not as though the Yankees did not have any talented prospects in their minor-league system. In 1965 they promoted infielder Horace Clarke to Yankee Stadium; in 1966, outfielder Roy White and southpaw Fritz Peterson; in 1968, right-hander Stan Bahnsen; and in 1969, outfielder Bobby Murcer and catcher Thurman Munson. (Clarke and White were black.) All six became established better-than-average major-league players. Murcer, a top-tier prospect whose minor-league development was interrupted by two years serving stateside in the army during the Vietnam War in 1967 and 1968, was saddled by accolades suggesting he was the next Mickey Mantle, same as Mantle was supposed to be the next Joe DiMaggio. He turned out not to be, but Murcer, White, and Munson all flirted with being elite players at some point in their careers. Clarke replaced Richardson at second base in 1967 and was much the same kind of player, except marginally better. Peterson and Bahnsen had similar careers pitching for the Yankees and other teams; both were .500 pitchers, Peterson with a career 133–131 record and Bahnsen at 146–149. Other newcomers the likes of catcher Jake Gibbs, outfielders Steve Whitaker, Roger Repoz, and Bill Robinson, pitcher Dooley Womack, and infielders Mike Ferraro and Bobby Cox—yes, *that* Bobby Cox—were not as advertised or not yet ready.

* * *

The 1964 pennant marked the end of a remarkable stretch extending from Babe Ruth through Joe DiMaggio to Mickey Mantle. The three successive superstars defined the championship teams they played for, appearing in all but one of the Yankees' first 29 World Series; the 1943 exception was only because DiMaggio was in army fatigues instead of pinstripes. It also was the beginning of the end of the Yankees' Mantle era. The next three years were all losing seasons for the Yankees. The last time the Yankees endured consecutive years on the wrong side of .500 was 1917 and 1918, and they had not had a losing record three years in a row since 1911 to 1915.

By the advent of divisional alignment in 1969, Mel Stottlemyre and Joe Pepitone were the only players from the 1964 Yankees remaining as core regulars. Stottlemyre was by now one of the league's premier pitchers. Pepitone, having traded places in the outfield with Mantle to accommodate the Mick's battle-scarred mid-30s legs, did not live up to his once-brimming potential for a very successful career—undermined considerably by his unwelcome playboy persona. Whitey Ford was forced to give up the mound in May 1967 because of circulatory problems and unrelenting pain in his elbow. In addition to his exceptional .690 career winning percentage (236 wins vs. 106 losses), Ford appeared in 11 World Series, setting the records for most starts (22) and most wins (10), including three consecutive shutouts on his way to breaking *pitcher* Babe Ruth's mark for consecutive scoreless innings in the Fall Classic.

Mickey Mantle's last days in baseball, even after shifting to first base in 1967, were an exercise in agony. During his last five years in the outfield, 1962 to 1966, Mantle was in at the end of only 226 of the 504 games he started. He had seen his career batting average dwindle from .309 in 1964—his fourteenth year in pinstripes—to .302 after the 1967 season. He had 518 home runs—the fifth most in history. His first home run of the 1968 season tied Ted Williams for fourth on the all-time list. His 17th of the season—a pitch deliberately grooved by Detroit's Denny McLain, who won his 31st game of the year that day—on September 19, before only 9,063 fans at Yankee Stadium, put him ahead of Jimmie Foxx's 534 for third on the all-time list. The next day he homered off Red Sox ace Jim Lonborg, giving him 536. Mantle played in each of the Yankees' seven remaining games that year. He had just one hit in 18 at-bats. Mantle called it quits at the end of the year, his career batting average now at .298. It was not a Ted Williams ending, or even a more modest Stan Musial one, for one of the game's greatest players.

* * *

Willie Mays had surpassed Mantle in career home runs in 1965 and was 51 homers ahead of him when Mick retired in 1968. The baseball world had a spirited debate, dating back to the mid-fifties, when both played in New York, about who was the better ballplayer—the Giants' Mays or the Yankees' Mantle—recognizing that both were indisputably among the best there ever was. Both were exceptional hitters with uncommon power, although Mantle's was from both sides of the plate. And both came to the majors with outstanding speed in the field and on the bases.

Mays maintained that speed until age started getting the better of him. Playing for a franchise that was still justifiably called the Bronx Bombers, Mantle was never going to steal as many bases as the Say Hey Kid—he finished his career with 153 compared to Willie's 338—but his innate speed was also severely compromised by the devastating knee injury he suffered in the 1951 World Series on a fly ball hit by . . . Willie Mays. He had played in just 96 regular-season games. Mantle would play in 2,305 more, having never fully recovered from the injury, not to mention many others he would suffer.

In their youth, Mays was probably the more complete player because of the extra-bases threat he represented by his intuitive aggressiveness on the basepaths. Mays was also a much better outfielder. Mantle, however, was the more dangerous hitter. Through the 1962 season, when Mantle won his third and final MVP Award, a persuasive case could have been made for either having a very slight edge over the other on baseball's Mount Olympus. Mantle had led the league in homers four times, won the Triple Crown in 1956, made a run at Ruth's single-season home run record in 1961, and was the best player in the major leagues based on the WAR metric from 1955 to 1957 and the best in the American League in five of seven years between 1955 and 1961. Mays had led his league in batting once, homers twice, triples three times, and stolen bases four consecutive years (136 total steals between 1956 and 1959), and he was the best player in the National League six times and baseball's best four times since 1954.

Beginning in 1962, however, Mays put together the four best years of his career while Mantle, hobbled by yet another horrific leg injury in 1963, was in decline, effectively putting an end to the "who's better?" debate. From 1962 to 1965 Mays belted 186 homers, batted .308, and averaged 10.8 wins above replacement—the highest four-year average since Ruth's 11.2 WAR between 1921 and 1924. He also played in 180 more games—the equivalent of more than a full season—than Mantle those four years, during which the Mick hit 99 homers and batted .297.

More unfair to Mantle was a parallel debate about his place in the pantheon of Yankees greats. In some respects, Mickey Mantle, the all-American boy with a wild side, never eclipsed the always professionally dignified Joe DiMaggio as a Yankee icon. Although not as good defensively in center field, Mantle was in fact the better player. Strictly by the stats, with the exception of Mantle's huge 536 to 361 edge in home runs,

DiMaggio has the more impressive batter's résumé—a lifetime average of .325, and nine seasons, including his first seven, with at least 100 runs batted in. Mantle exceeded 100 RBIs four times, never in consecutive seasons, and his career high of 130 in 1956 was exceeded by the Yankee Clipper on four separate occasions. In a comparison of their first seven full seasons in the major leagues, however—DiMaggio from his rookie year in 1936 until he went off to war after the 1942 season, and Mantle from 1952 to 1958—Mantle's average annual player value was 8.6 wins above replacement, appreciably better than DiMaggio's 7.0. DiMaggio's career-high WAR was 9.1 in his iconic 56-game-hitting-streak 1941 season; Mantle had four seasons better than that, including back-to-back years in 1956 and 1957 when his player value was 11.3 wins above replacement.

Both were heroes to the Yankees fans who grew up watching them play, but like Ted Williams, Mickey Mantle was destined to pale in comparison to Joe DiMaggio, in part because DiMaggio so carefully cultivated and protected his aura. This was particularly true in the 1950s, when Mantle was at his best, because DiMaggio was still a recent memory. It was hard for Mantle to compete with *that* and the increasingly sanctified legacy of the Great DiMaggio, notwithstanding the awe-inspiring distances of his home runs and a Triple Crown in 1956. DiMaggio was always going to be better—better defensively, more clutch, a true leader. It didn't help that Mantle's own manager, Casey Stengel, was often hard on him and seemed disappointed that the best player (by far) in the American League, and perhaps even in the major leagues, was somehow not better than he was. Part of it was certainly perceptual; the golden-haired boy, who enjoyed alcohol-fueled good times with running mates like Ford and Billy Martin, seemed immature, as though he wasn't taking baseball all that seriously. Sometimes it seemed that the gimpy-kneed Mick wasn't giving it his all on the ballfield. At the beginning of the 1960 season, General Manager George Weiss was quoted by the *Saturday Evening Post* as saying that Mantle should be better than DiMaggio, "but he hasn't come close to proving it yet."

Prove it perhaps he finally did in his 1961 chase, alongside teammate Roger Maris, of Babe Ruth's record 60 homers. Ironically, the burnishing of Mantle's previously maligned halo was at the expense of much less fan enthusiasm for the idea that Maris would be the one to break Ruth's record. Mantle was enjoying the chase, playing for the love of the game.

Maris was a reluctant superstar, uncomfortable with such focused attention, for whom baseball seemed more like arduous work than fun. It also
helped that new Yankees manager Ralph Houk did not find reasons to
criticize his best player.

At the end, what can be said is that throughout his career and beyond,
while Mickey Mantle came to be idolized as a conquering hero, human
and accessible, Joe DiMaggio was worshipped as an infallible god, cold
and remote. It was a dichotomy that fit both who they were and perhaps
what their fans wanted to see in them. Both were exceptional ballplayers.
Both were the face of the Yankees. DiMaggio, extraordinarily prideful,
mounted the pedestal of fan worship, was careful not to do anything to
damage his reputation as "Baseball's Greatest Living Player," and kept a
chilly distance and reserve from the world. Mantle was a relatable hero
with human dimensions, even a tragic hero given the career he might
have had had he not suffered the injury he did in the 1951 World Series.

II

WAITING IN THE WINGS WHEN THE YANKS WENT DOWN

Three American League clubs were positioned to take advantage of the Yankees dynasty coming to an end, or at least its first prolonged interruption since 1921. Baltimore's well-balanced Orioles showed signs of becoming the team to beat for years to come. Now managed by former Yankees outfielder Hank Bauer, they held first place far more days than either New York or runner-up Chicago in the 1964 pennant race before being overtaken by the Yankees for good on September 19. Minnesota's Twins, although not in the pennant action in 1964 but with two 91-win seasons before that, were on the threshold of being either a dominant team riding a powerful lineup or a persistent disappointment because of deficiencies in pitching, defense, and perhaps even clubhouse cohesion, much as the late-1940s Red Sox had been. While both the Orioles and Twins looked to be pennant race competitors for much of the rest of the decade, for Chicago's pitching-focused White Sox, whose nine-game winning streak to end the season came up one game short in 1964, time was probably running out to win a pennant.

The White Sox had been consistently competitive since 1951 but had the misfortune of being so during the time when the Yankees dominated the American League landscape from 1949 to 1964. Their one pennant in 1959, which ended 40 years of wandering in the wilderness as allegorical penance for the 1919 Black Sox scandal, capitalized on the fact that the Yankees apparently forgot they were the Yankees and played uncharacteristically poorly. (Actually, the Yankees were in transition from the team that won nine pennants the previous 10 years to the one that won the next five in a row.) The turnaround for Chicago finally putting the Black Sox behind them began with the arrivals of Frank Lane as general manager in 1948, southpaw Billy Pierce in 1949, second baseman Nellie Fox in 1950, and a dynamic outfielder and new manager—Minnie Minoso and Paul Richards—in 1951. Pierce, Fox, and Minoso were all acquired in trades that ended up benefiting Chicago far more than the teams that gave them up, helping to build Lane's "Trader Frank" reputation as an astute dealmaker. All three players had breakout seasons in 1951, Richards's first year as a big-league manager, helping the White Sox to 81 victories, up from 60 the year before.

Lane and Richards's blueprint emphasized as core principles pitching, defense, and speed. Pierce was one of the best pitchers in baseball in the 1950s, and Fox was the best all-around second baseman in the game after Jackie Robinson shifted over to third base and the outfield in 1953. It was Cuban-born Minoso, however—one of the few black players to star in the American League during the fifties—who gave the White Sox their identity. Taking advantage of his batting prowess and assertiveness on the bases, the White Sox became the most aggressive team in baseball, so much so that their fans began urging them to "Go! Go!" whenever one of their faster players got on base. Richards left Chicago in the closing days of the 1954 season, just after the White Sox reached the 90-win threshold for the first time since the Black Sox scandal broke in 1920, for the opportunity to become both manager and general manager of the Baltimore Orioles. Lane resigned after the 1955 season amid increasingly strained relations with the latest heir to the Comiskey family–owned franchise (since granddaddy Charles in 1901). But the tenets of their philosophical approach remained. The only problem was that Casey Stengel's Yankees and the Cleveland Indians, managed by Al Lopez, were superior clubs. Chicago was the league's third banana every year from 1952 to 1956.

The Cleveland part of the problem changed in 1957 when Lopez left the Indians to become manager of the White Sox. Two years later, after finishing second twice, Chicago was in the World Series. Minoso was no longer there, however, having been traded to Cleveland after the 1957 season for right-hander Early Wynn and outfielder/third baseman Al Smith. In his seven years in Chicago, Minoso batted .307, reached base in more than 40 percent of his plate appearances, scored 100 runs four times, drove in 100 runs three times, and led the league in triples three times, in stolen bases three times, and in doubles once. He was an unalloyed star. Wynn was also an unalloyed star, although six years older, coming to Chicago with 235 major league victories—including four 20-win seasons in the six years he pitched for Lopez in Cleveland—and the versatile Smith had been a core player on Lopez's Indians in a career that began in 1953.

The 1959 White Sox snatched the pennant on the back of a 41–16 record in July and August. Instead of Minoso, it was Luis Aparicio, an acrobatic defensive shortstop and speedster on the bases, who took the lead in carrying on the "Go-Go" tradition. Having already led the league in steals each of his first three years beginning in 1956, Aparicio's 56 stolen bases in 1959 were the most in the major leagues since George Case swiped 61 in wartime 1943. By now the best all-around shortstop in the American League—though not in Chicago, where the Cubs' Ernie Banks also played—Aparicio finished second to teammate Nellie Fox in the American League's Most Valuable Player voting. Smith's 17 homers were second on the team to catcher Sherm Lollar's 22, but he might be best remembered for the beer that was poured on his head during the World Series when a fan attempting to catch a home run let go of his cup while Smith looked up helplessly as the ball sailed over the left-field wall.

Paced by Aparicio and Fox at the top of the order, the 1959 Go-Go Sox were in some ways the second coming of Chicago's 1906 "Hitless Wonders" Sox. Their .250 team batting average was only sixth in the eight-team league, and only two American League clubs scored fewer runs than Chicago. And like their 1906 forebears, arguably more "punchless" than "hitless" wonders, the 1959 White Sox—with only a quarter of their runs scoring on the strength of a home run, far below the American League average of 32 percent—necessarily relied on small-ball strategies. They were the major leagues' most proficient team in advancing baserunners. Their 113 steals were by far the most in baseball; indeed, the most since the 117 swiped by the 1949 Dodgers. It was also the ninth straight year the White Sox led the league in stolen bases. Since 1951 the Go-Go Sox accounted for nearly a quarter of the league's total stolen bases, averaging more than twice as many as any of the seven other American League teams.

And like their 1906 forebears, the 1959 White Sox were the stingiest team giving up runs in the American League. Wynn turned in his fifth and final 20-win season by leading the league with 22 as the ace of Lopez's pennant-winning pitching staff. Right-hander Bob Shaw's 18–6 record was the best in the league. Pierce, at 14–15, had a disappointing year and did not get a start in the World Series, apparently because Lopez thought the lefty would not fare well against Dodgers batters. Lopez also had a pair of relievers he used interchangeably in the late innings—Turk Lown and Gerry Staley—who tied for the league lead in saves, with 15.

Most of the core players on the 1959 team—including Fox, Smith, Lollar, Wynn, Pierce, Lown, and Staley—were over-30 veterans fast approaching their end-of-career horizons. Early Wynn, stuck on 299 career victories, was released after losing his last three starts and seven of his last eight in 1962; back with Cleveland, he finally won his 300th in July 1963. Luis Aparicio, although still in his prime with 269 stolen bases (on his way to a career total of 506), was traded to Baltimore in 1963 in a multiplayer deal that included getting in return 40-year-old Hoyt Wilhelm, whose exceptional command of the knuckleball allowed him to defy his ancient baseball age. It wasn't until 1963 that the White Sox got back to 90 wins and not till 1964 that they competed in a late-season pennant race. Exceptional pitching was the foundation for the White Sox' return to competitiveness. Southpaws Gary Peters, 20–8 in 1964, and Juan Pizzaro, 19–9, and right-hander Joel Horlen headlined the starting rotation. Wilhelm had the first of five consecutive seasons with an ERA under 2.00, averaging 61 games and 108 innings in relief. The White Sox were in the third of six straight years leading the league in fewest runs allowed. Their 98–63 record in 1964 was the franchise best since the 1919 Black—er, White—Sox.

Although the White Sox exceeded 90 wins and finished second for a third straight year in 1965, Chicago was never in a pennant race that Minnesota controlled from the end of July. Al Lopez retired after the season (although he returned for brief managerial cameo appearances in 1968 and 1969). Lopez could be forgiven if he had a complex about being a perennial number two. In his first nine years as a manager, his teams finished second to Stengel's Yankees seven times and finished first twice. In each of his last three years as a full-time manager, his teams finished second, twice more to the Yankees. Compared to the accomplishments of the heavyweight managers in baseball history, Lopez had a modest résumé of only two pennants and a 2–8 record in World Series games. In his 15 full seasons as a major-league manager, however, including his first six with the 1951–1956 Indians, Lopez never had a losing record. His .584 career winning percentage is the fifth highest since the start of the twentieth century. Al Lopez was masterful in keeping the White Sox, a much less imposing team than he had in Cleveland, competitive during his reign as their manager from 1957 to 1965.

* * *

Before stumbling badly in 1964, coming home sixth with a losing record, Minnesota's 91 wins in both 1962 and '63 had established them as a rising power in the American League—one, of course, whose way was blocked by the seemingly forever Yankees dynasty. The change of scenery from the nation's capital to Minnesota's Twin Cities was just what was needed to turn around the hapless "first in war, first in peace, last in the American League" Washington Senators franchise. In truth, however, it was in DC that the foundation players for the Twins' 1965 pennant—the power-hitting tandem of Harmon Killebrew and Bob Allison, pitching ace Camilo Pascual, and hard-hitting catcher Earl Battey (becoming a regular in 1960 after three years as a backup in Chicago)—got their start. Promoting southpaw Jim Kaat to join the starting rotation and Zoilo Versalles to play shortstop their first year in Minnesota in 1961; calling up Rich Rollins to play third base in 1962, Jimmie Hall to be their center fielder in 1963, and Tony Oliva to become their right fielder in 1964; and their June 1964 deals for Cleveland right-hander Jim "Mudcat" Grant to bolster the starting rotation and 35-year-old Cincinnati reliever Al Worthington to solidify the bullpen were seminal moves that set the Twins up to displace the five-in-a-row Yankees in 1965.

A power-driven offense was Minnesota's singular strength. In 1963 the Twins blasted 225 home runs—at the time, the second most in history after the 240 by the 1961 Yankees—including 45 by Killebrew, 35 by Allison, and 33 by Hall in his rookie year. In their disappointing 1964 season, they clobbered 221 homers. Killebrew led the league in home runs for the third straight year and had his fourth straight 40-homer season (and fifth in six years) with 49. Oliva had a sensational rookie season, with 32 homers and 94 runs batted in while leading the league with a .323 batting average.

Except for losing the World Series in seven games to the Dodgers, the 1965 Twins gave a command performance despite the extended absences of their right-handed ace and most dangerous slugger. When Pascual went on the disabled list in late July, he was 8–3 and the Twins' lead was four games, about where it was when he returned six weeks later. The Twins were six games up when Killebrew, tied for the league lead in homers, was injured in a collision at first base in early August. By the time he returned for the final 10 games of the season, Minnesota was coasting to a runaway pennant with a comfortable 9-game lead. Oliva won his second batting title in his second season; Versalles, an unheralded shortstop and lead-off batter, had a year far better than anyone would ever have expected and was voted the American League MVP; Kaat won 18; and Grant had a dominant season, with a 21–7 record and leading the league in wins, winning percentage, and shutouts. The Twins' 102 victories set a new franchise record—topping the 99 won by the 1933 Senators—that has yet to be surpassed.

Minnesota got off to a ragged start the next year in defense of their American League bragging rights and ended up second to Baltimore, a club as dominant in 1966 as the 1965 Twins had been. Killebrew was healthy, playing every game, and his 39 homers and 110 RBIs were second to Orioles' Triple Crown winner Frank Robinson. Leading the league in hits for the third straight year, Oliva's .307 batting average was second in the league. Jim Kaat's 25 wins were the most in the American League. Versalles and Grant, however, returned to the more modest performance levels that defined their careers. Allison, starting the season platooned in left field, played sparingly in the final three months because of a wrist injury. Pascual was mostly ineffective and made only two starts in the second half of the season because of shoulder and elbow problems. Traded back to Washington—to the expansion Senators—after the season, Camilo Pascual's 145 wins (against 141 losses) were the second most in franchise history after Walter Johnson's 417 victories for the original Washington Senators.

* * *

In Baltimore, the transplanted St. Louis Browns began building a winning tradition when they unexpectedly competed for the 1960 pennant. Tied with the Yankees atop the AL standings as late as September 14, they finished with an 89–65 record for their first winning season since moving to Baltimore six years earlier. The Orioles' surprising competitiveness was fueled by their newfound ability to score runs; they were third in runs after being last in the majors the two previous seasons, and last in the league in five of their first six years in Baltimore. While Gus Triandos, the O's catcher since 1955, and outfielder Gene Woodling, of

New York Yankees fame in their five-and-five-in-five years, provided veteran leadership, it was third-year third baseman Brooks Robinson and first-year players Ron Hansen at shortstop and first baseman Jim Gentile whose breakout galvanized Baltimore's resurgent offense. Led by a trio of young starters—righties Chuck Estrada and Milt Pappas and lefty Steve Barber—none older than 22, the Orioles also surrendered the fewest runs in the league. They were backed up by already ancient 37-year-old Hoyt Wilhelm in the bullpen.

The architect of the Orioles' sudden rise to competitiveness, which they sustained for more than two decades, was Paul Richards, both their manager and general manager since 1955. If in the pantheon of 1950s managers Casey Stengel was the eccentric Ole Perfessor–cum–mad scientist and Al Lopez the skilled practitioner-engineer, Richards was the philosopher king. In 1955 as he was settling in as the Orioles' new manager, he published a book, *Modern Baseball Strategy*, parts of which were serialized in four successive issues of *Sports Illustrated* that spring. Richards provided his readers thoughtful explanations of how modern 1950s managers thought about strategy and tactics. In a significant contrarian viewpoint to the time-honored contention among old-timers that the current generation of players was less schooled and practiced in the fundamentals, Richards wrote that the game had changed, not just with better equipment but with more sophisticated strategies, particularly on defense, to make offensive execution—bunting for hits, for example—much more difficult.

Understanding that it would take time to build a winner, Richards in his GM role steadily improved the Orioles through player acquisitions, developing a coherent system of minor-league affiliates, and systematizing instruction. Hansen, Robinson, Pappas, Estrada, and Barber were all signed to their first professional contracts by Richards' Orioles. Richards picked up Wilhelm on waivers in 1958, then designed the oversized catcher's mitt to handle the unpredictable breaks of Wilhelm's nightmarish-to-catch (as well as to hit) knuckleball and acquired Gentile on the cheap from the Dodgers in 1959 because his promotion to the majors was blocked by Gil Hodges.

Richards came to the Orioles with a well-earned reputation for insight and ingenuity. He left with a bolstered reputation for also building the foundation for competitive teams—just not for his own managerial tenure in either Chicago or Baltimore. Richards left Baltimore at the end of

August 1961 to take charge of another building project, this time as GM of the National League–expansion Houston Colt .45s, preparing for their first season the following year. Although the Orioles were in third place on a pace to win 94 games when Richards left, they were not keeping pace with either the Yankees or the Tigers, both of whom ended up with more than 100 wins in the American League's first expansion year. Baltimore wound up winning 95, a distant 14 games behind New York and six behind Detroit. Gentile blasted 46 homers and drove in 141 runs. Orioles pitchers gave up the fewest runs in the majors.

By the time he left Baltimore, Richards had laid the groundwork and principles for developing multiple generations of position players and pitchers to keep the Orioles consistently competitive into the 1980s. He wrote a small manual on baseball strategy, tactics, and playing techniques that was distributed to managers at all levels in Baltimore's farm system to ensure that players in development learned to play ball the "Orioles Way." His manual emphasized fundamentals, stressed the importance of situational awareness, and prescribed repetitions and drills that translated from practice to games that counted. Richards provided the template, modified along the way by longtime Orioles minor-league manager and major-league coach Cal Ripken Sr., for six Orioles pennants between 1966 and 1983.

Although the Orioles backtracked in 1962, their then-franchise-record 97 wins in 1964 were a stark reminder that they might just be the best team in baseball, even though 'twas the Yankees' red-hot September that won the pennant. Defensively superb third baseman Brooks Robinson was the near-unanimous choice for American League MVP, batting .317, hitting 28 homers, and leading the league with 118 RBIs. Boog Powell had replaced the departed Gentile as the Orioles' top power threat, with 39 homers. The Orioles, meanwhile, had traded for shortstop Luis Aparicio, giving up Wilhelm as part of the deal, and for 35-year-old Stu Miller, another knuckleball specialist, to take Wilhelm's place in the bullpen. Aparicio led the league in steals for the ninth consecutive year, with a career-high 57. Taking advantage of the Yankees' 1965 collapse, however, were not the 94-win third-place Orioles, but Minnesota's 102-win Twins.

In 1966 their positions were reversed. The Orioles won their first pennant—only the second in Browns-Orioles franchise history—by nine games over the Twins and went on to shock the Dodgers by winning the

World Series in a four-game sweep. They got the best of Drysdale twice and Koufax once. Shutting out the Dodgers on four hits in Game Two to beat the seemingly unbeatable Sandy Koufax, in what turned out to be the last game Koufax would ever pitch, was the coming-out party for Jim Palmer, 15–10 in his second year and still just 20 years old. Wally Bunker, whose own second year as a 21-year-old had been marred by blisters and a sore elbow, followed up with a six-hit shutout in Game Three, and lefty Dave McNally, who had gone 13–6 and led Orioles pitchers in starts and innings pitched in his fourth big-league season, closed out the series the next day with a four-hit shutout of his own. Both Bunker and McNally won by 1–0 scores. The only run in McNally's masterpiece was courtesy of a home run off Don Drysdale, the Dodgers' *other* ace, by Frank Robinson, playing his first year in Baltimore after 10 outstanding seasons with the Cincinnati Reds.

Even today, more than 50 years later, the Reds sending Frank Robinson to the Orioles primarily for Milt Pappas is considered one of the worst trades any team has ever made. It really shouldn't be. It was trading a superstar to acquire a decent, though hardly elite, pitcher. Robinson may have just turned 30, but he was still a great player, as shown by the 33 homers and 113 RBIs he had for Cincinnati in 1965. Pappas was four years younger and had a career record of 110–74 as an Oriole dating back to 1958. The Reds had a pair of 20-game winners in 1965, including Jim Maloney—one of the best young pitchers in baseball—so it was not intuitively obvious they needed Pappas to bolster their pitching, especially not at the expense of their most feared hitter. While Pappas struggled in his first year in Cincinnati, going 12–11 with a 4.29 ERA, all Frank Robinson did was hit 49 homers, drive in 122 runs, and hit .316. Nobody else in the American League was close in any of those Triple Crown categories.

"F. Robby," as he was often called in the Baltimore papers, embellished his Hall of Fame résumé by batting an even .300 in his six years with the Orioles, for whom he hit 179 of his 586 career home runs. Pappas was hardly the loser that lopsided trade often makes him out to be. Although he lasted less than three years with the Reds, Pappas had back-to-back 17-win seasons late in his career with the Cubs and won an additional 99 games in the eight years he pitched after his first eight in Baltimore, to finish with 209 major-league victories.

12

BASEBALL'S LAST GREAT PENNANT RACE AND THE IMPOSSIBLE DREAM TEAM

Three years after the Cardinals, Phillies, Reds, and Giants went into the final weekend of the 1964 season with a shot at the National League pennant, four American League teams—the Minnesota Twins, Boston Red Sox, Detroit Tigers, and Chicago White Sox—separated by less than two games, entered the final weekend of the 1967 schedule with a chance to go to the World Series. That gave the AL the distinction of having the last great pennant race in Major League Baseball's original structure of two leagues, two pennant races. Beginning two years later there would be two pennant races in each league, the result of a second round of expansion that led to realigning both leagues into Eastern and Western divisions, with the first-place division winners facing off in a league championship series to play for the pennant.

On the strength of excellent pitching that masked their meek offense, the White Sox held first place without interruption from mid-June to mid-August, holding a 5½ -game lead at one point. Shades of Chicago's 1906 "Hitless Wonders" White Sox that managed to win the pennant with by far the lowest batting average in the American League and the fewest extra-base hits, including just seven home runs, and then shocked the 116-win Chicago Cubs to win the World Series, the White Sox had the second lowest batting average (.225) of the major leagues' 20 teams in 1967. Only one AL and two NL teams scored fewer runs. The Tigers, second to the Red Sox in runs scored and second to the White Sox in fewest allowed, were rarely in first place after early June but also never far from the top. The Twins got off to an unexpectedly slow start, fired manager Sam Mele (who managed them to the pennant just two years before) in early June when their record stood at 25–25, and had the second-best record in the league the rest of the way under Mele's replacement, Cal Ermer. Only the Red Sox—a team that finished ninth, just half a game ahead of the last-place Yankees in 1966, and not expected to rise much higher in 1967, let alone compete for a pennant—had a better record, by one win with the same number of losses, after the Twins changed managers.

It wasn't until the final weeks of August that the pennant race shaped up to be a four-team race to the finish. From August 20 through September 11, the four teams were never more than 2½ games apart. On September 6, all four were tied for first. Going into the final weekend, the four were separated by 1½ games. The Twins at 91–69 were in the best position, one game up on both the Red Sox and Tigers with two to play at Fenway Park on Saturday and Sunday. If the Twins won both, the Tigers would be the only team that could possibly tie them for the pennant—*provided* they won all four of their remaining games against the Angels. Detroit, at 89–69, could win the pennant outright by winning its final four games *only* if Minnesota split its weekend series in Boston. If the Twins won one or the Red Sox both games, the Tigers would still need to win at least three to force a playoff with one or the other team.

In an ironic counterpoint to 1949, when the Yankees had to win both weekend games in their home stadium to beat out the Red Sox for the pennant, Boston, at 90–70, was in the same position now—having to win both games at Fenway to finish ahead of Minnesota. To avoid a playoff, they also had to count on the Tigers doing no better than splitting their final four games of the season and the White Sox losing at least one of their last three games. As the fourth-place laggard, having just lost twice to last-place Kansas City but still only 1½ games behind, the White Sox, with an 89–70 record, faced the biggest challenge going into the final weekend. They needed to win all three of their remaining games against eighth-place Washington, *and* for the Red Sox to sweep the Twins, *and* for the Tigers to win no more than three of four—and that would only give them a tie for first with Boston and maybe also Detroit, if the Tigers won three of four. None of those things happened. The White Sox didn't make it past Friday.

* * *

The White Sox had done well to finish fourth the previous year when they transitioned from highly esteemed manager Al Lopez, who retired, to Eddie Stanky, hard-nosed and canny in his playing days to make up for his lack of size. The new manager was handicapped by injuries that sidelined two of his best hitters—shortstop Ron Hansen and third base-man Pete Ward—for much of the season, and one of his left-handed pitching aces, Juan Pizarro, had to battle through shoulder problems that ultimately forced Stanky to drop him from the starting rotation. After having hit above the league average the last three years of the Lopez regime, the 1966 White Sox had the lowest batting average in the majors and hit the second-fewest homers, forcing them back toward the identity of Chicago's 1950s Go-Go Sox.

The White Sox were expected to be at least on the margins of the pennant race in 1967 because of their excellent pitching, and they had Ward and Hansen back. On June 11, when they took over first place, White Sox pitchers had given up by far the fewest runs in the majors. Even if hardly formidable, their offense was at least respectable; they were sixth in the league in scoring. On August 13, when the Twins completed a three-game sweep to knock them out of first place for the first time in 62 days, the White Sox were still the stingiest team in the majors, but now they were last in the American League in runs. ChiSox batters had hit only .218 collectively in their time at the top.

Just when it looked like the White Sox might fade, falling to three games behind on September 11 after losing a doubleheader, they turned around to win nine of their next 11. Chicago's prospects actually seemed good at the start of play on Wednesday, September 27. With 157 games down and five to go, they were tied for second with the Red Sox, only a game behind the Twins, and the Tigers were half a game behind them. Even better, their five remaining games were against two of the league's worst teams—last-place Kansas City and eighth-place Washington—while their competitors for the pennant were all playing tougher teams, including Boston and Minnesota with two games against each other on the final weekend. Chicago lost all five games, scoring a total of five runs against the two teams with the worst ERAs in the league. They were shut out in three consecutive games, including 1–0 in their 160th game of the season on Friday that officially eliminated them from contention. The

White Sox ended the season three games out of first, equaling their largest deficit of the year.

Chicago's difficulty scoring caught up with them at the worst possible time. Posting a 16–14 record in the final month, the White Sox hit just .214 as a team, had an awful .276 on-base percentage, and scored two runs or fewer in 12 of their final 30 games. Only two teams, both long since eliminated from contention, did worse than the White Sox' hitting 18 percentage points *below* the league-wide batting average for September. Their pennant race rivals all hit much better than the league average for the month—the Twins by 16 percentage points, the Tigers by 22, and the Red Sox by 24. Their ineffectual offense subverted continued great pitching; White Sox pitchers allowed fewer than one baserunner per inning in September and had a superb 2.17 earned-run average in the final month—by far the best in the league.

Just like 60 years before, when the 1904–1908 White Sox had the best record in the American League in that five-year span but with only the 1906 Hitless Wonders championship to show for it, so did Chicago have the best five-year record of any AL team from 1963 to 1967—except they did not win even one pennant. Applying their five-year winning percentage to a single 162-game season, the 1963–1967 White Sox would have finished one game ahead of the Twins and two ahead of the Baltimore Orioles, both of whom won only a single pennant and had a losing season in the mix. And just like the 1904–1908 White Sox, Chicago's 1963–1967 team did so with a historically weak offense for a contending team. But whereas their 1906 Hitless Wonders ancestors were better than league average in runs-to-hits ratio and scoring total runners on base, the 1967 "hitless wonders" were substantially below league average in both measures of offensive efficiency. It was a wonder they did as well as they did to compete at all in 1967.

* * *

Of the four contenders, the Detroit Tigers had gone the longest without a pennant. Their last was won on the final day of the 1945 season when Hank Greenberg, who returned in July from more than four years serving in World War II, hit a ninth-inning grand slam to send the Tigers to their fourth World Series in 12 years. They beat the Cubs in seven games. Any expectations the Tigers had to compete for pennants in the years ahead—particularly with a pitching staff that included southpaw Hal Newhouser, whose 29 wins in 1944 and 25 in 1945 made him the

American League's Most Valuable Player both years, and right-hander Dizzy Trout, a 27-game winner in 1944 with 18 in 1945—the Tigers' expectations to compete for pennants in the years ahead were shattered by the Red Sox and Yankees, with their rosters replenished by star players returning from wartime service. The closest the postwar Tigers came to a pennant was finishing second in 1950, three games short of the Yankees, then in year two of their five-and-five-in-five string of championships.

With the exception of 1952 and 1953, when they won just 36 percent of their games, the Tigers spent most of the fifties as a middle-of-the-pack ballclub hovering around the .500 mark. Gone by the mid-fifties were their best players in the postwar years—Newhouser, whose ailing left shoulder significantly diminished his innings and effectiveness beginning in 1950, and third baseman George Kell and his .325 batting average in seven years with Detroit. By the late-1950s, however, the Tigers had a handful of star players helping to keep the club respectable. Breaking in at shortstop in 1953 with a league-leading 209 hits and moving to center field in 1958, Harvey Kuenn led the league in hits four times and batted over .300 in all but one of his seven full seasons in Detroit. Without ever playing in the minor leagues, Al Kaline won the 1955 batting title in only his second year at the age of 20, making him the youngest player ever to have done so. Frank Lary and Jim Bunning, both right-handers whose rookie year was 1955, gave Detroit a formidable duo of top-tier starting pitchers into the early sixties.

After winning the batting title with a .353 average in 1959, Kuenn was part of a blockbuster trade that sent him to Cleveland in exchange for outfielder Rocky Colavito, whose 42 home runs had just led the league. Detroit gave up a singles-and-doubles guy for a power hitter just reaching his prime in what became one of the most lopsided trades of veteran players in baseball history. While Kuenn's career quickly fizzled, Colavito played four years in Detroit, knocking out 139 homers before being traded to Kansas City after the 1964 season. Colavito's best year in baseball was 1961, when his 45 homers and 140 RBIs helped the Tigers to 101 wins. The 1961 season was also arguably the best year of Al Kaline's career. Batting third, just ahead of Colavito, his .324 batting average was second in the league. The best batting average in baseball that year belonged to their teammate, first baseman Norm Cash, who hit .361 in his second season as a regular. Cash also whacked 41 homers and drove in 132 runs. Despite that firepower, 23 wins by Lary, and 17 by Bunning, the 101-win 1961 Tigers could not keep up with the 109-win 1961 Yankees. Three losses in a row in New York in the beginning of September started an eight-game losing streak that extinguished Detroit's hopes. It was the second time in franchise history the Tigers won 100 games and finished second—the same thing happened in 1915—and only the fifth time for any team in major-league history.

Although the Tigers had not been in a late-season pennant hunt since then, they would have been a good bet in 1967 to capitalize should the previous year's runaway pennant-winning Orioles falter. Kaline, Cash, catcher Bill Freehan, and Dick McAuliffe, making the switch from shortstop to second base, gave Detroit high-quality veteran leadership. Freehan, about to enter his fifth year in the majors at the age of 25, was a rising star. The left-handed hitting McAuliffe, famous for an unusual batting stance in which he stood facing the pitcher and holding his bat out over the plate as though he were a sentry daring anyone to sneak by him, had hit 93 homers in six seasons. Besides Kaline, the Tigers had a surplus of capable outfielders, including power-hitting right-hander Willie Horton, who totaled 56 homers in 1965 and '66; left-handed batter Jim Northrup; and the defensively excellent though weak-hitting Mickey Stanley. Detroit looked to have solid starting pitching led by mercurial right-hander Denny McLain, whose 16–6 record as a 21-year-old in 1965 and 20 wins in 1966 established him as a top-tier pitcher; southpaw Mickey Lolich, trying to recover from a poor season in 1966 after going 18–9 and 15–9 in 1964 and '65; and right-hander Earl Wilson, arguably Detroit's best pitcher in 1966, with a 13–6 record and excellent 2.59 ERA after being cast off by Boston at the trade deadline.

Marred by injuries that hit their pitching staff particularly hard, the Orioles were out of the pennant picture early. Detroit's opportunity to take advantage was undercut by injuries to Horton, who was hobbled for much of the season, and Kaline, who missed a month because of a broken hand. Although the 1967 Tigers spent very little time in first place, they were never far from the top. Lolich, 6–1 in September with shutouts in his last three starts, and Wilson, 4–1 in the final month to finish with a league-high 22 wins, were the pitchers most responsible for keeping Detroit in the picture down the stretch. The Tigers' four games with the Angels, scheduled for the last three days, ended up being back-to-back doubleheaders on Saturday and Sunday because of a Friday rainout. After splitting their Saturday doubleheader, Detroit began Sunday knowing they could tie the winner of the Minnesota-Boston game for first place and force a playoff for the pennant *only* if they won both their games against the Angels. They won the opener and took a 3–1 lead into the third inning of the second game, only to watch McLain and reliever John Hiller give up the lead—and any chance for a pennant.

* * *

Two years after dominating the league in 1965, the Minnesota Twins were trying to reassert themselves as the team to beat in the American League. Their blockbuster move to return to the top in 1967 was a trade for Angels ace right-hander Dean Chance to complement lefty ace Jim Kaat, whose 25 wins led the league the previous year. Chance won 20 and Kaat 16. Harmon Killebrew had another monster season, with 44 home runs. Veteran Bob Allison rebounded from an injury-plagued year to hit 24 homers. Rod Carew, the Rookie of the Year, finally solved the franchise's long-standing (since the late 1930s in Washington) second base problem. Cesar Tovar—playing center field, third base, and second base when Carew was fulfilling his military reserve obligations—had more plate appearances than any player in the majors.

The Twins would have been the class of the league, taking account of their core players, except for their maddening inconsistency. Even after the departure of Sam Mele, who was neither an inspired nor an inspiring manager, Minnesota played roller-coaster baseball. Energized at first by his departure, the Twins fought their way into the heat of the pennant race by mid-July, stumbled backward in a seven-game losing streak, got hot in the first half of August to move into first place for the first time after completing a three-game sweep of the White Sox, played .500 ball for three weeks after that, then spent all of September either in first—but by never more than one game—or no more than one game behind.

Two days off before their final two-game series at Fenway Park allowed new manager Cal Ermer to set up his two aces for a season finale showdown with Boston. Jim Kaat, at 16–13 and winner of all seven of his previous starts in September, took the mound on Saturday with a chance to clinch the pennant for Minnesota. Should the Twins *not* prevail in Kaat's start, Chance, at 20–13, was lined up to pitch Sunday's 162nd game on the schedule—with the pennant going to the winning team. They were on hostile ground, facing a team that had not won a pennant in 21 years.

* * *

The six years that passed after Ted Williams launched his 521st home run at Fenway in his last major-league at-bat on September 28, 1960, were long and dismal for Boston's Red Sox. On the final day of the seventh season since then, Carl Yastrzemski stood at the plate against Twins ace Dean Chance in the bottom of the sixth—the bases loaded, nobody out, his team down 2–0, with a chance for Red Sox redemption— the very pennant at stake. The previous day, Yaz had gone 3-for-4, his three-run 44th home run of the year in the seventh inning securing the victory that pulled Boston into a first-place tie with Minnesota, bringing it down to this 162nd game to decide the 1967 American League championship.

Yastrzemski was a worthy successor to Williams as the face of the Red Sox. Not only did he take Williams's position in left field the very next year, in 1961, but Yaz had become one of the most proficient hitters in baseball. He won a batting title in 1963 at the age of 23. He had already led the league once in hits and three times in doubles. And this year, he refined his power stroke. The most home runs Yastrzemski had hit in any prior season was 20. When the 1967 season was over, Yastrzemski had 44 homers—tied for the most with Killebrew—121 runs batted in, and a .326 batting average to win the Triple Crown, so now he had that in common with Ted Williams, who twice accomplished the feat. Although Baltimore's Frank Robinson had done the same thing the previous year, there would not be another Triple Crown winner in either league for 45 years, until Miguel Cabrera in 2012. And Yaz had something else in common with Williams—a controversial reputation for being less a team player than a self-absorbed one.

The best the Red Sox had done since Williams was sixth place in 1961. Their eight consecutive losing seasons, dating back to the last two years of Williams's career, constituted Boston's longest stretch of futility since the 14 years immediately after they sold Babe Ruth to the Yankees in 1920. Recognizing that his franchise was not likely to escape the gutter absent a fundamental change in approach, owner Tom Yawkey decided late in the 1965 season, as his club was well on its way to 100 losses, to promote Dick O'Connell to be general manager, replacing longtime Yawkey crony Pinky Higgins. O'Connell had held numerous midlevel positions in the Red Sox front office and was liked and respected by the owner, but was not in the mold of the pals Yawkey had relied on to run the team since buying the club in 1933. Yawkey gave O'Connell license to make his own *informed* decisions on how best to move the club forward. The Red Sox for decades had been known as a franchise that prized star status and personal relationships, contributing to their enduring reputation for being a country club of good-old-boy individuals rather than a cohesive team. The Red Sox were also known for biases that greatly influenced the makeup of their major-league roster.

Most notoriously, those biases were racist. The Red Sox were the last team to integrate, finally, in late July 1959, when infielder Pumpsie Green was brought up to Boston. Right-hander Earl Wilson joined the big-league club soon thereafter. While Higgins, the Red Sox manager at the time, was outspoken in his opposition to having black players in his major-league dugout, O'Connell, then the club's business manager, understood that failing to give Green a roster spot after his strong spring training reeked of racial prejudice. Higgins was let go as manager before Green was promoted, only to return the next year to a situation where going back to a whites-only Red Sox roster was untenable. Despite having starred at shortstop for the Red Sox' Triple-A club in Minneapolis, Green was never given a fair shot at holding a starting job in Boston; he started in just 169 of the 327 games he played for the Red Sox over four years. Notwithstanding Higgins at the helm, Wilson broke into the starting rotation in 1962 and was the team's best pitcher after fellow righty Bill Monbouquette in the first half of the 1960s. Wilson was 56–58 in his Red Sox career before being traded to the Tigers in June 1966 as a consequence of his protesting to the front office about being racially harassed by the proprietor of a Florida bar during spring training. In 1965 second baseman Felix Mantilla and outfielder Lenny Green, both established major leaguers before coming to Boston, became the first black position players to be day-to-day regulars in the Red Sox lineup.

Now general manager, O'Connell promoted George Scott to play first base for the Red Sox in 1966 and Joe Foy to play third. Both had outstanding rookie seasons, with Scott hitting 27 homers. O'Connell also acquired right-hander Jose Santiago from Kansas City to join the starting rotation and in June traded with Kansas City again for ace reliever John Wyatt and outfielder Jose Tartabull. Santiago was a white Hispanic from Puerto Rico, Tartabull was a black Hispanic from Cuba, and Scott, Foy, and Wyatt were African American. All were instrumental in Boston's dramatic turnaround from nearly scraping the bottom to the top of the

American League the next year. Besides Yastrzemski, they joined a core of young players in Boston that included right fielder Tony Conigliaro, a spectacular slugger who knocked out 24 homers as a rookie in 1964, led the league with 32 in 1965, and followed up with 28 in 1966; shortstop Rico Petrocelli; and right-hander Jim Lonborg. The Red Sox looked to have a promising future, particularly when they promoted the switch-hitting Reggie Smith, also African American, in 1967 to play center field. How soon they might be competitive in a league that included the Twins, Orioles, Tigers, and White Sox remained to be seen. Nobody expected it would be so soon—in 1967.

Boston's new look as the season opened included a new manager. His name was Dick Williams, promoted from managing Boston's top farm team in Toronto. O'Connell liked what he saw of the no-nonsense Williams in Toronto and wanted his "losing is not tolerable" attitude in Fenway to motivate the younger players and, when necessary, put cynical veterans—even the Great Yaz—in their place if their sense of entitlement outpaced their commitment to the team. The Red Sox hovered around the .500 mark for the first three months of the season. Had they finished with a record around .500, it would have been a very successful year. Instead they torched the league in July to move into the pennant fray. They did not fade, as many expected, in August and September. Along the way O'Connell picked up infielder Jerry Adair from pennant race rival Chicago and catcher Elston Howard, whose résumé included nine World Series with the Yankees, to bolster the club with off-the-bench, spot-start veteran leadership.

Tragedy struck in mid-August as the Red Sox were pushing to catch up. With two outs and nobody on in the bottom of the fourth in a scoreless game, Tony Conigliaro was hit flush in the face by a pitch from Angels starter Jack Hamilton. Just a month earlier, the 22-year-old Conigliaro had become the second-youngest player in history (by 65 days) to hit 100 home runs, after Mel Ott. His line statistics were 20 homers—giving him 104 for his career—67 RBIs, and a .287 batting average when he went down at the plate as though shot. There were serious concerns he might become the second player in major-league history to be killed by a pitch; Cleveland's Ray Chapman had suffered a fatal beaning exactly 47 years and two days before, on August 16, 1920. Given his talent and accomplishments, Conigliaro's being hit by that pitch was immediately considered among the greatest tragedies to occur on the diamond—right behind Chapman's death and alongside the horrific sight of Cleveland's brilliant young left-hander Herb Score, still just 23, being smashed in the face by a line drive in 1957. Serious injury to his left eye was thought to have ended Conigliaro's young career, seemingly on a Hall of Fame trajectory with hundreds more home runs to come, right then and there.

The Red Sox won on the fateful day Conigliaro went down, the first in a seven-game winning streak that put them into first place for the first time since Opening Day. They spent the entire month of September either tied for first or no more than a game behind. Now in game 162, the Red Sox and Twins tied atop the standings, his team behind 2–0, and down to their final 12 outs, Yastrzemski smacked a bases-loaded single up the middle to drive in the tying runs. Scoring the first of those runs was Jim Lonborg, Boston's ace, whose bunt single off Twins ace Dean Chance started the rally. Lonborg was working toward his 22nd win of the season, tying Detroit's Earl Wilson for the league lead.

Chance and Lonborg had both pitched four days before on just two days of rest so they would be available for the season finale on their normal three days between starts if the pennant race was still undecided. With Boston trailing Minnesota by two games at the time, but with two days off before their weekend showdown, both managers probably felt this a necessary gamble to ensure their aces pitched twice in the last five days of the season. In their game 162 matchup, both pitching for the pennant, Lonborg threw a complete game, Chance lasted just one batter after Yastrzemski's single, and Boston won, 5–3, making it to their first World Series since 1946.

* * *

Three days later, the well-rested St. Louis Cardinals had the first at-bat in the 1967 World Series. While the baseball world was riveted by the American League's down-to-the-wire pennant race and captivated by the "Impossible Dream" story of the Red Sox, the Cardinals were the hands-down best team in baseball. The Cardinals never led by less than 10½ games—their final margin of victory—after their 117th game of the season. Following two dispiriting years for the Gateway City after their Cardinals took advantage of the Phillies' 1964 implosion, storming from 6½ games behind with only 13 to go to snatch the pennant and then take down the Yankees in seven exciting games to win the World Series, St. Louis was proud to say, "We're back!"

Of the core 1964 players, Bob Gibson, Lou Brock, Curt Flood, and Tim McCarver remained as fast-lane players still in their prime. Except for second baseman Julian Javier, the entire 1964 Cardinals infield was gone after 1965, including 11-year veteran Ken Boyer, whose historical legacy is obscured by the fact that he was a direct contemporary of three outstanding Hall of Fame third basemen—Eddie Mathews and Ron Santo in his own league, and Brooks Robinson in the other. In May 1966 St. Louis made a trade that would have as much impact in 1967 as the Broglio-for-Brock trade in June 1964, sending right-hander Ray Sadecki, 20–11 when they won the 1964 pennant, to San Francisco for power-hitting first baseman Orlando Cepeda, whose career prospects were un-certain at best because of severe knee pain that limited him to just 33 games in 1965, almost all as a pinch-hitter. In August 1966 the Cardinals called up southpaw Steve Carlton for good. After that season ended, they traded Charley Smith, Boyer's replacement at third, to the Yankees for Roger Maris.

Thus fortified, the 1967 Cardinals survived their ace, Bob Gibson, being out for nearly two months from mid-July to early September with a broken leg. He finished the season with a 13–7 record. Cepeda carried the club in July and August, with 14 homers, 54 RBIs, and a .341 batting average on his way to being the NL's unanimous MVP; St. Louis catcher McCarver was second in the voting. Brock's 52 stolen bases led the league, giving him 222 steals in the 572 games he had played for St. Louis since June 1964, as did his 113 runs. Flood batted .335.

The last World Series the Red Sox had played was a classic seven-game affair in 1946 against the Cardinals that turned on Enos Slaughter scoring the winning run from first base on a relatively routine hit into center field when Boston shortstop Johnny Pesky, almost certainly not expecting Slaughter to try for home, hesitated on his pivot and held the ball a beat too long before throwing to the plate. The 1967 series between the same two franchises was another classic, with the same seven-game outcome. Yastrzemski continued his torrid hitting by batting .400 in the series with 3 homers and 5 runs batted in. Lonborg, unable to start the first game against Gibson because he had pitched the pennant-clinching game on the final day of the season, took a perfect game into the seventh inning of Game Two before walking Flood with one out and did not lose his no-hitter until Javier doubled with two outs in the eighth for the Cardinals' only hit of the game. With the Red Sox trailing the series three games to one, Lonborg also won Game Five to keep Boston's hopes alive. Pitching on just two days of rest in Game Seven, however, Lonborg gave up seven runs in six innings. Gibson, on three days' rest, surrendered two runs on three hits. Brock set a World Series record by stealing 7 bases, scored 8 runs, had 12 hits, and batted .414. Gibson had complete-game victories in all three of his starts, giving up just 5 runs in 27 innings while striking out 26 batters. Maris, a veteran of five Yankees World Series, had the best Fall Classic of his career, batting .385 with 7 RBIs.

* * *

The Cardinals were back in the World Series the next year. The Red Sox weren't. It didn't help that Lonborg took half a year to recover from a wintertime skiing injury. Instead, it was the Detroit Tigers winning their first pennant in 23 years, and doing so in commanding fashion, with 103 wins and a 12-game advantage over second-place Baltimore. Willie Horton hit 36 homers, Bill Freehan and Norm Cash both had 25, and Jim Northrup contributed 21. Al Kaline missed more than a month with a broken arm from a pitched ball but hit .309 in the 63 games he played after returning to action. These were no small feats in 1968—the Year of the Pitcher—when the league batting average was .230, Yastrzemski's .301 average was best in the league, and the only other American Leaguer qualifying for the batting title hit .290. On the pitching side, Denny McLain made 41 starts, completed 28, and finished 31–6 to become the first major-league pitcher since Dizzy Dean, 34 years before, to win 30 games.

While McLain was making headlines chasing 30 wins—he started the final month with 26 and reached the 30-win threshold with three starts to spare—what the Cardinals' Bob Gibson did that year was nothing short of phenomenal. After pitching just seven innings in each of his first two starts, Gibson never went fewer than eight in any of his 32 starts thereafter. From the end of May until the end of July he completed every game he started—a streak that ended only after he threw 11 innings in a game that went 13, after which he finished his next six starts. He ended the season with a 22–9 record that really didn't do justice to his 28 complete games in 34 starts, league-leading 13 shutouts—5 of them in a row in June—and 1.12 earned-run average.

Like Detroit, St. Louis got off to a fast start and coasted to the pennant. It might have mattered, however, that they went into the World Series losing seven of their last 11 games, because the Cardinals squandered a three-games-to-one lead despite another brilliant World Series for both Gibson and Brock. Gibson set World Series records by striking out 17 batters in the opening game and 35 batters in the 27 innings he worked; Brock batted .464, once again stole 7 bases—giving him a World Series–record total of 14, matching Eddie Collins, who played in 13 more series games—while tying a series record with 13 hits. Gibson beat McLain in the first and fourth games of the series but was outdueled by lefty Mickey Lolich in a game that turned on Curt Flood—an exceptional defensive center fielder—misjudging a fly ball into a triple that scored two runs. For Lolich, 17–9 that year, it was his third complete-game victory of the series.

Detroit won the World Series in part on a gamble by manager Mayo Smith to play Mickey Stanley, his regular center fielder, at shortstop in lieu of weak-hitting Ray Oyler, who hit all of .135 that year, in order to have all four of his outfielders—the three others being Horton, Northrup, and Kaline—in the lineup. (The left-handed-batting Northrup and Kaline had been mostly platooning in right field since Kaline's return from injury.) Stanley's preparation for his World Series role was starting the final six games on the schedule at shortstop. Smith's maneuver worked. Stanley made only two errors in 30 chances at shortstop; Kaline hit .379 and drove in 8 runs—the most in the series; Horton scored 6 runs and batted .304; and Northrup broke open a must-win Game Six with a grand slam that was the centerpiece of a 10-run inning. The 1968 World Series was the last that guaranteed the participants would be the teams with the best regular-season records in their respective leagues.

* * *

By the time divisional alignment came to baseball in 1969, the White Sox were as bad they had been in the late 1940s. The Tigers and Red Sox were both still good teams, but far outclassed in the new American League East by the Orioles. The Twins, however, won the first two AL Western Division titles in 1969 and 1970, only to be swept in the American League Championship Series both years by Baltimore. In 1969 Killebrew led the league with 49 homers and 140 RBIs, and Carew won his first of eight batting titles in Minnesota, with a .332 average. In 1970 Carew was batting .376 in mid-June when his season all but ended with a broken leg in a collision at second base; Killebrew hit 41 homers; and Oliva led the league in hits for the fifth time while batting .325. In 1971 the Twins began a decade of tepid performances.

Playing in persistent pain because of debilitating knee injuries, Tony Oliva won his third and last batting title in 1971, missed virtually the entire next season, and was able to return for four more years only because the new designated hitter rule meant he didn't have to play the field. Harmon Killebrew, whose career with the Twins was spent alternating primarily between first and third base, was let go in 1974. He was a defensive liability wherever he played, but you can't argue with the 559 home runs the Killer hit for the franchise, 84 for the old Senators in Washington. When he retired in 1975 after one year in Kansas City, his 573 home runs were fifth all-time behind Aaron, Ruth, Mays, and Frank Robinson. After 12 years playing for the Twins, the last three at first base, Rod Carew, with his .334 batting average, was traded to the Angels in 1979 because of his outspokenness about not being paid what he felt he was worth.

Had they won the 1967 pennant, the Twins' legacy for the years they had two of the most dangerous hitters in baseball in their lineup would be far different than it is today. They would have had two pennants in three years, to be followed by their winning the first two division titles in the American League West. Instead, the team that featured sluggers Killebrew, Oliva, and Bob Allison and pitchers Camilo Pascual and Jim Kaat when they won the 1965 pennant and, beginning in 1967, Carew and Dean Chance, is often considered one that underachieved for the talent on hand. The Twins, however, may have been fated to win no more than the one pennant they did. The Yankees dynasty was still going strong in the early 1960s when Minnesota first emerged as a would-be contender, followed by the Orioles beginning their own record of excellence, dominating the American League in 1966 and in the first years of divisional alignment and the league championship series.

13

EXPANSION DECADE

For baseball traditionalists, who believed (then as always) the game was not played as well as in the good old days when they first fell in love with the sport, the 1961–1962 expansion was discomfiting not only because the number of major-league clubs increased from 16 to 20 or because two 10-team leagues seemed too large. They also worried that expansion would necessarily dilute the quality of major-league rosters, that the carryover effect would persist for years, and that Major League Baseball might never return to being the elite league it was. In the short term, that was certainly correct. The addition of 100 players to fill the rosters of four new clubs in just two years meant that many minor-league players not yet ready to play at the major-league level were promoted nonetheless; that any number of players whose big-league talent ceiling had been established as reserves off the bench would become regulars; and that some veteran players, including those with impressive résumés, whose careers were nearing an end got the opportunity to extend their playing livelihoods rather than go forth into retirement or coaching. And it was not just the expansion clubs for whom they would play that would be affected; long-established teams also felt the impact because of the need to backfill for players they lost in the expansion draft.

The number of major leaguers whose official rookie seasons were in 1961, when the new Washington Senators and Los Angeles Angels came into existence, increased to 90 from 69 in 1960 and an annual average of 64 the five previous years. In 1962, when the New York Mets and Houston Colt .45s joined the show, 107 rookies played in the major leagues.

Bench players in the mid- to late 1950s—like Felix Mantilla, Roman Mejias, Leon Wagner, and Norm Larker—became regulars in the early 1960s, although among this group only Wagner stayed a regular for more than a year or two. And esteemed veterans like Gil Hodges, Duke Snider, and Eddie Yost got to hang on a little bit longer—although, again, not for very long.

The impact of expansion was most profound in the American League, particularly its effect on the quality of pitching. Although runs per game increased only marginally, from 4.4 to 4.5, in the AL expansion year of 1961, the collective league earned-run average jumped from 3.87 to 4.02 and home runs per club increased from 136 to 153. Outsized performances by Detroit first baseman Norm Cash, winning the batting title with a .361 average while belting 41 homers and driving in 132 runs, and Roger Maris, with his 61-homer season, were explained away in part by the dilution of pitching talent forced by expansion. In fact, 1961 was the only time in his career that Cash hit 40 homers, had 100 RBIs, or batted .300. Cash hit .272 in his 17-year big-league career, but take away 1961 and his career batting average was just .264. The Tigers slugger hit better than .300 against eight of the 10 AL teams but feasted in particular on the pitching of the expansion Senators, against whom he batted .431.

As for Maris, it was not as though he was not already an established home run hitter—his 39 homers in 1960 were just one shy of league-leader Mickey Mantle's 40—but 13 of his record-setting 61 in 1961 were hit off the first-year Senators and Angels, and 12 were off pitchers who were either in their rookie season or playing their first full year in the majors. Home run number 61—the one that eclipsed Ruth and earned Maris a decades-long figurative asterisk because he had 162 games in which to top the Babe—was hit off Red Sox rookie reliever Tracy Stallard, pitching in just his 47th major-league game.

But to whatever extent such worries were genuine, as opposed to just change resistance, the baked-in idea that expansion necessarily meant the dilution of major-league talent was misplaced for at least three reasons. The first was that the US population had more than doubled since the beginning of the twentieth century, when the major leagues became set for the next 60 years with two leagues of eight teams each. Not only should one have presumed a corresponding increase in the number of boys growing to be elite athletes, but improvements in diet and health care meant the proportion of such athletes relative to the general population was likely greater. The emergence of transcontinental jet travel, meanwhile, meant the entire country was open to Major League Baseball as never before. In the first half century, when the major leagues' geographic scope did not extend west of the Mississippi, there were any number of outstanding players in the Pacific Coast League who made their careers there rather than coming east to play ball. Finally, the major leagues were now taking advantage of a talent pool they knew about but long ignored because of a deliberate policy of racial exclusion. Certainly, from the 1920s through the 1940s, the Negro Leagues had enough players capable of playing in the all-white major leagues to support the addition of two to four expansion teams at any time.

A second expansion was in fact inevitable. The postwar baby boom dramatically increased the young adult population. The accompanying economic boom created an unprecedented consumer culture in which recreation became a higher priority. Television brought major sports to the eyes of people all over the country. With recreational options, including places like Disneyland and resort vacations, and television helping professional football become at least as popular as baseball across America, the power brokers in Major League Baseball were interested in increasing their game's exposure. That meant expanding the major leagues' geography to new cities where there was strong community interest in having a team.

* * *

The first expansion had been a qualified success. Branch Rickey proved correct in his prediction that the newborn franchises selecting from among the proportionally few unprotected players on existing 40-man rosters would be left at a major competitive disadvantage—the reason he gave for expansion to take the form of a new major league in his Continental League proposal.

The Los Angeles Angels, who changed their name to the California Angels in 1965, anticipating a move to a new stadium in Anaheim the next year, were the most successful of the original expansion clubs. The Angels benefited from their hastily arranged ownership group, led by Hollywood's "Singing Cowboy," Gene Autry, tapping former Braves manager Fred Haney to be general manager. Former Giants manager Bill Rigney, perceived as having the patience and skill to develop players and build a winning team from the ground up—the virtual definition of an expansion franchise—was who Haney wanted in the Angels dugout. Both were astute evaluators of players and well connected to baseball professionals informed about rising minor-league talent. The Angels came out of the expansion draft with a solid outfielder named Albie Pearson, a hard-drinking playboy pitcher named Bo Belinsky, and a pair of 19-year-olds—shortstop Jim Fregosi, left unprotected by the Red Sox, and right-hander Dean Chance, whom they acquired in trade immediately after he was selected by the expansion incarnation of the Washington Senators. The four quickly became stars in the City of Stars. Only Fregosi and Chance went on to become top-tier major leaguers.

After losing 91 games in their inaugural season, the Angels were the surprise of 1962. They were in first place on Independence Day. Everyone knew they would not prevail, but still they finished a surprising third with 86 wins. The 1962 season was indeed too good to be true. Even as Fregosi became baseball's best shortstop in the 1960s and Chance became one of the league's premier pitchers—including winning the Cy Young Award as the major leagues' best pitcher in 1964 with 20 wins, 11 of which were shutouts, and a major league–best 1.65 ERA—the Angels would not be as successful again under Rigney. Not until eight years later, under a different manager, did the Angels again win as many games, and not until 1978—their 18th year in existence, when they won 87—did they better that mark.

Washington's new Senators, meanwhile, continued in the losing tradition of Washington's old Senators. The expansion Senators began their history with four consecutive 100-loss seasons and did not have their first winning season until 1969, when baseball celebrity manager Ted Williams, in his first year managing at any level, led the team to 86 wins. The star of that team was their physically imposing, supersized left fielder, Frank Howard, hailed in the nation's capital as "The Capital Punisher." Coming from the Los Angeles Dodgers along with third baseman Ken McMullen in 1965, Howard played seven years in Washington, knocking out 237 home runs—more than any other player had ever hit playing for either the original or the expansion Senators. Leading the league with 44 homers in both 1968 and 1970, Howard's 48 home runs in 1969 were second to the 49 by Harmon Killebrew, a former Washington slugger now in Minnesota. Notwithstanding Howard's punishing power, McMullen was the best all-around player on the Senators the five years they played together in DC.

* * *

The 1962 NL-expansion Houston franchise, in a knowing nod to Western mythology, took as its nickname the iconic Colt .45 sidearm—a gun that helped keep the law in Texas and win the Wild West, and so why not (eventually) the National League pennant? That would be a very long time coming. Houston was nothing if not consistent its first seven years in the league, losing between 90 and 97 games every year between 1962 and 1968 and never doing better than eighth place. Like the Angels with Haney, the Colts hired an esteemed manager—Paul Richards—to be their GM. Richards resigned as Orioles manager during the 1961 season specifically to take on the challenge of building an expansion team from scratch. That was a losing proposition because of the poor-quality players the existing NL teams made available in the expansion draft. Of the prospects younger than 25 drafted by Houston, only Bob Aspromonte, their third baseman from 1962 to 1968, panned out as a position regular, and he was more a marginal than average big-leaguer. At a time before baseball instituted an orderly amateur draft in 1965, Houston did outbid other teams in signing highly regarded high school prospect Rusty Staub. After just one year in the minors, 19-year-old Staub made the Colts' 1963 Opening Day lineup, batting cleanup no less, and remained Houston's most prominent player until traded after the 1968 season.

A confluence of factors contributed to a franchise name change in 1965. The assassination in Dallas of President John F. Kennedy besmirched Texas's gun culture. The manufacturer of Colt firearms was threatening to sue about licensing and merchandizing rights. And Houston became mission control center for America's ambitious space program to send a man to the moon by the end of the decade. Houston's baseball team turned from celebrating the past with Colt .45s to anticipating the future with Astros. That year they also opened a new domed stadium representative of the space age—the first of its kind, even if Walter O'Malley had originally conceived of a fully enclosed covered stadium for his Dodgers in Brooklyn. Likely in the spirit of Texas braggadocio, some took to calling the Houston Astrodome one of the "Eight Man-Made Wonders of the World," adding it to the renowned list of seven. It was an architectural feat at the time, especially given the expanse of the baseball playing field it covered. The first year of indoor baseball proved challenging; fielders had difficulty tracking popups and fly balls against the dome, and the solution to that problem—a coat of paint over many of the dome's panels—so significantly diminished the nurturing rays of the sun that the natural grass specifically bred to thrive indoors died instead. The next year, the Astros became the first team to play on artificial turf.

Neil Armstrong took "one giant leap for mankind" on the moon in July 1969. Mission control was in Houston. Coincidentally, Houston's Astros reached .500 for the first time, with 81 wins and 81 losses—not exactly reaching the moon, still less the stars, but progress. Staub was no longer in Houston, but the Astros featured a pair of excellent position players, both small in stature—center fielder Jim Wynn and second baseman Joe Morgan—and right-handers Larry Dierker and Don Wilson seemed destined for solid careers. Moving into the starting rotation as an 18-year-old in 1965, Dierker was the ace of the Astros staff for the next 12 years, including 20 wins in 1969. Wilson was a mainstay in the rotation for eight years beginning in 1967 until his untimely death, apparently a suicide, in January 1975. Wynn was a power hitter. Unfortunately, the dimensions and atmospherics of the Astrodome did not play well for power hitters. Of the 223 home runs he hit in his 11 years in Houston, only 93 were at the Astrodome. Morgan played six years for Houston, not including the 1968 campaign when he was sidelined the entire season with a torn ligament. Not yet the superstar he would become in Cincinnati, Morgan demonstrated his menace as a baserunner by stealing 131 bases in 166 attempts between 1969 and 1971.

* * *

In terms of endearment, none of the 1960s expansion teams were as successful as New York's "Amazing" Mets, even as they struggled and were ridiculed for being a truly terrible team. Indeed, the especially comical ways they lost made them all the more lovable. They lost 100 games five times in their first seven years, including a record 120 in their inaugural season. They lost the first nine games they ever played. Less than a month later, they began a 17-game losing streak. They won as many as two in a row eight times in 1962, and their longest winning streak that year was three games. They lost 25 percent of their games in 1962. In 1966 they lost fewer than 109 games for the first time, with 95 defeats, and were rewarded with a ninth-place finish. Two years later they finished ninth again, one game out of the cellar, losing just 89.

In the midst of all that losing, the Mets moved from Manhattan, where they began by playing in the Polo Grounds, to Queens following the opening of a brand-new stadium named after Bill Shea, the New York lawyer who had financially backed Branch Rickey's Continental League initiative for the sole purpose of replacing the dearly departed Giants and Dodgers. Shea Stadium was built in Flushing, Queens, precisely where city urban-planning czar Robert Moses had insisted the Brooklyn Dodgers' proposed new and improved ballpark to replace decrepit Ebbets Field should be.

"Meet the Mets." Those were the first words of the jingle that introduced the broadcast of Mets games on WOR-TV in the New York metropolitan area. So who were the Mets in their early years? They were, first and foremost, their first manager—Casey Stengel. Fired by the Yankees—for having made the mistake of turning 70, he said—Stengel was an inspired choice by the Mets' new team president and general manager, George Weiss, the Yankees' GM from 1947 until he was asked, apparently more graciously, to leave along with Casey. Before he became the phenomenally successful manager of the 1949–1960 Yankees, Stengel survived nine years managing bad NL teams with banter and irreverence—which he carried with him through his Yankees years—that both entertained and diverted attention from how poorly his teams played. Those attributes were much appreciated when it came to building a loyal following for the Mets. His quirky running commentary, crafty insights, and wry asides about the Mets' many baseball flaws and incessant losing gave little offense, seemed to explain it all, and laid the groundwork for the hapless Mets becoming more popular in New York than the storied and increasingly stale Yankees franchise.

Just as they first played in the Giants' old stomping grounds, the early Mets also traded on bringing back to New York veterans of Brooklyn's adored Dodgers, gone but hardly forgotten. Their 1962 club included legendary Brooklyn first baseman Gil Hodges; middle-infielder Charlie Neal, the man who displaced Pee Wee Reese at shortstop in the Dodgers' last year in Ebbets Field; and right-hander Roger Craig, whose victory in Game Five of the 1955 World Series helped finally bring a championship to Brooklyn. Hodges homered on Opening Day, making his the very first home run hit by a New York Met, but played in just 54 games. Craig led the Mets with 10 victories and the majors with 24 losses, which were the most since 1935. Jack Fisher in 1965, also pitching for the Mets, is the only pitcher to have lost that many since. Left-hander Al Jackson, taken from the Pirates in the expansion draft, gave the 1962 Mets two 20-game losers. (He lost 20 again in 1965.) The next year Duke Snider, Brooklyn's answer to Mays and Mantle, returned to New York to play for the Mets. Like Hodges, Snider was clearly playing out the end of his career. Notwithstanding playing in the Polo Grounds those two years, it was former Brooklyn Dodgers and not former New York Giants who were making a name for the Mets.

Aging 1950s-era stars from other teams also came to the Mets for late-career finales. The inaugural 1962 Mets included former Phillies center fielder Richie Ashburn and former Pirates slugger Frank Thomas. Ashburn led the Mets with a .306 batting average and Thomas with 34 homers and 94 RBIs. And in 1965 former Braves ace Warren Spahn, with 356 wins to his credit, came to Shea, perhaps for the sole purpose of allowing him to quip about having pitched for Casey Stengel both "before" (with the 1942 Boston Braves) and "after" (with the Mets) he was a genius. The young Mets in the mid-sixties who made the most lasting impression were Ed Kranepool, their first baseman from 1964 as a 19-year-old to 1967, whose career—exclusively with the Mets—lasted until 1979, and scrappy second baseman Ron Hunt, distant runner-up to Pete Rose in the 1963 NL Rookie of the Year voting, who played the first four of his 12 major-league seasons in a Mets uniform.

And then the Mets caught a lucky break. His name was Seaver: George Thomas Seaver. The lucky break? The Braves so couldn't wait to sign the University of Southern California right-hander in 1966 that they did so during his college season, in violation of major-league rules. Suddenly a free agent, he was pounced on by the Mets.

* * *

Milwaukee's Braves were one of two established teams on the move in the 1960s. After watching their attendance drop every year, from a franchise high of 2.2 million in 1957 to 767,000 in 1962, Braves owner Lou Perini began looking for an out. It appeared not to matter to the good citizens of Milwaukee that Hank Aaron was still in his prime, that Eddie Mathews was still one of the best players in baseball, that Warren Spahn led the league in wins in 1960 and 1961 and won 23—matching his career high—as a 42-year-old in 1963, or that the much younger Joe Torre was on his way to becoming arguably the best catcher in baseball in the middle-sixties, his power and batting prowess more than making up for his defensive liabilities. By 1964 Perini was exploring the option of relocating his team to the South's most up-and-coming commercial metropolis—Atlanta, Georgia. Perini ended up selling the Braves instead, but the new ownership group followed through on his initiative and Atlanta's interest in attracting a major-league team. After only 13 years in Milwaukee, the Braves were now Atlanta's Braves.

Two years later, in 1968—after just 13 years in Kansas City—the Athletics left the Midwest for Oakland, California. Their roster in a perennial state of makeover, with few players staying long enough to become hometown fixtures, their woeful attendance was hardly a surprise. While the 1960s Braves in Milwaukee were a middle-of-the-pack club, the Athletics in Kansas City performed more like an expansion team during their short-lived history in western Missouri.

Notwithstanding that none of the first expansion teams had been competitively successful and that their prospects seemed dim for the foreseeable future, by the late 1960s the major leagues were ready for a second round of expansion. In an effort to head off Rickey's late-fifties Continental League initiative, Commissioner Ford Frick outlined a path to expansion that would ultimately add eight cities to baseball's major-league geography—the same number as Rickey proposed for his "third major league." Frick's gambit was to accept the inevitability of expansion by adding two clubs to each league immediately, which was duly accomplished in 1961 and 1962, and two more teams to each league later in the decade. While Frick had no answer to Rickey's protests that expansion teams grafted into the existing major leagues would necessarily be at a serious competitive disadvantage for many years to come, he did have an inspired answer to the unwieldy ultimate prospect of two 12-club leagues. Perhaps mindful of baseball's late-nineteenth-century history, when the National League ultimately faced an existential crisis after expanding from eight to 12 teams in 1892, only to downsize back to eight in 1900, Frick proposed the two leagues would be split into two divisions of six teams each.

Baseball's hand was forced by the Athletics' abandonment of Kansas City in 1968, which outraged a powerful US senator from Missouri. Needing to head off the risk of congressional legislation that might jeopardize the reserve clause, Major League Baseball moved quickly with expansion plans, including a new team in Kansas City. So it was that in 1969, franchises in Kansas City and Seattle were added to the American League and Montreal and San Diego in the National League. This new wave of expansion did not include any of the eight cities the Continental League had envisioned for its lineup, although four of those cities—New

York, Minneapolis, Houston, and Atlanta—did now have major-league teams.

The American League's divisional alignment adhered to the country's continental geography. Both Kansas City and Seattle were placed in the Western Division, which also included the first-round expansion Angels, while all six teams in the AL East were established teams, although the Senators were still suffering the competitive burden of their 1961 creation. In the interest of competitive balance, the National League's approach to East and West was an affront to geographers and cartographers. Since the NL West had a traditional historical rivalry between the Dodgers and Giants out in California, the NL's other great rivalry—between the midwestern Cubs and Cardinals—was put in the East. To accommodate them in the NL East, the National League placed Atlanta, a southeastern city, and Cincinnati, east of both Chicago and St. Louis, in the NL West. The NL's two new expansion teams in San Diego and Montreal, whose team name derived from the phenomenal success of the 1967 International and Universal Exposition in Montreal commemorating the 100th anniversary of the confederation of Canada as a self-governing country within the British Commonwealth of Nations, were assigned to the division that conformed with their location—the Padres in the West, the Expos in the East.

Adjustments in the American League's divisional alignment would soon be made because of franchise moves and yet another expansion eight years later. The newborn Seattle Pilots turned out to be a bust, finishing last in the AL West, and relocated to Milwaukee in 1970. The man who made that happen was Allan "Bud" Selig, the owner of local automobile dealerships and the largest public stockholder in the Braves before they moved to Atlanta. Waging an aggressive campaign to bring Major League Baseball back to Milwaukee, Selig organized an ownership group to rescue the bankrupt Pilots, brought them to "Brew-Town," and nicknamed them the Brewers. Two years later, the franchise was shifted from West to East in the AL's division makeup because the Senators, having failed to attract many to their new ballpark in the nation's capital, moved west to the Dallas–Fort Worth area, where they became the Texas Rangers. Dallas was one of the eight cities where Rickey had planned to place a Continental League team.

Eight years later, in 1977, the American League added another would-be Continental League city—Toronto, making it six of eight now in the

The nation's capital would be without a baseball team for a third of a century after the 1961-expansion Washington Senators moved to Texas to become the Rangers in 1972. The expansion Senators' last manager was Ted Williams (in a jacket on the left). *Courtesy of the Library of Congress.*

major leagues (including New York, home of the Mets)—when it expanded from 12 to 14 clubs, seven in each division. Faced with a lawsuit over Selig's purchase and relocation of the Pilots, and with a new domed stadium recently built with public money, the AL awarded the second expansion franchise that year to Seattle. Major League Baseball was back in the Pacific Northwest.

Many baseball purists decried the two-division concept because it necessarily meant the end of the indisputably best team in the league going to the World Series. Henceforth, the winner in each division would face off for the pennant in a league championship series. Since the LCS would be distinguished from the World Series by being a maximum of five games instead of seven, and since any outcome is possible between good teams in short series, it was likely that on many occasions the team with the lesser record would prevail, sometimes even against a club that was clearly the better ballclub over the course of the 162-game schedule. On the other hand, baseball fans across the country could now be engaged by four pennant races instead of two.

As if to prove the point, in 1968 the last of the old-fashioned pennant races with only one winner in each league was a snooze. Both races were effectively over by the Fourth of July as the Cardinals overwhelmed their opponents in the National League and the Tigers did the same in the American League. In 1969—the first year of divisional alignments—both East and West in the American League turned into runaways, but the two division races in the National League were close, compelling affairs. And one of them involved an expansion team—not either the newborn Expos or Padres, but the Amazing Mets.

14

LET'S GO, METS

Durocher on the Other Side of a Miracle

Nobody saw them coming. The Mets, that is. They had escaped the cellar in the last year of unitary leagues by a single game ahead of the Houston Astros. It was only the second time in their seven-year history they had not finished last, and the first time they lost fewer than 90 games. They finished the 1968 season with a 73–89 record. In the new divisional alignment of the National League, the Mets were thought most likely *not* to finish last in the six-team Eastern Division *only* because the newborn Montreal Expos were an expansion team. Although the Mets were not expected to contend any time soon, they had two major strengths going for them entering the season: a firm but patient manager whose understated ways were well suited to molding the future of a hapless expansion franchise, and a young, dynamic starting rotation led by third-year right-hander Tom Seaver, second-year lefty Jerry Koosman, and rookie right-hander Gary Gentry, backed up by a flame-throwing Texas-born prodigy named Nolan Ryan.

The manager was Gil Hodges, the very same stolid, reliable, and productive first baseman who helped make the Brooklyn Dodgers of the late 1940s and 1950s not only the National League's best team but also the endearing "Boys of Summer." He was also an original Met, courtesy of the expansion draft, until he was traded to the expansion Washington Senators in May 1963 for the opportunity to become manager. The Senators improved every year under his command, rising from last place to sixth in 1967 and raising his profile in the baseball universe. Still the worst team in baseball, the Mets were developing and acquiring young talent and optimistically looking toward a future where they would be regarded as a bona fide major-league club instead of lovable losers. Not only did Hodges have the old Brooklyn pedigree the Mets had used to help build their fan base, but he was perceived, correctly, as a successful manager, even if the Senators—an expansion team like the Mets—never had a winning record.

Core players of the 1969 Mets already there when Hodges arrived in 1968 included catcher Jerry Grote, shortstop Bud Harrelson, left fielder Cleon Jones, right fielder Ron Swoboda, and Seaver, whose 16–13 record the year before made him the first Mets player to win a major performance award, Rookie of the Year. Koosman, Ryan, and center fielder Tommie Agee joined the brood in Hodges's first year as manager. What Hodges knew about Agee, obtained in a trade from the White Sox, was that he'd hit .326 against his Senators in 1966 and 1967. Koosman became the first Mets pitcher to approach the 20-win threshold, with a 19–12 record in 1968—the Mets already had six 20-game losers—and came within one vote of giving the Mets back-to-back Rookies of the Year, losing out to Johnny Bench. Ryan was still a work in progress, exhibiting the same control difficulties Sandy Koufax did early in his career.

The Mets began the 1969 season as they had every other of their existence—with an Opening Day loss, this time to Montreal, an expansion team. (I was at Shea Stadium for that game. My dad thought we should be there for the historical significance of the game—the first ever played by the Expos.) When Seaver beat the Dodgers on June 3 for his 8th win of the year, it was the first time that late in any season that the Mets went over .500. They were in the midst of an 11-game winning streak—by far the longest in their young history. Although trailing by nine games, the Mets were second in the NL East at the June 15 trade deadline when they made a consequential deal for a much-needed power-bat for their lineup—right-handed-batting Expos first baseman Donn Clendenon, whom Hodges employed in a first-base platoon with left-handed Ed Kranepool.

Even with Clendenon, the 1969 Mets were not a potent offensive club. Their team on-base percentage, batting average, and slugging percentage were substantially below the league average. Eight of the other 11 National League teams scored more runs. Cleon Jones, however, had a career year, his .340 batting average third in the league. Agee, primarily a leadoff batter in the Bobby Bonds mold of hitting for power and striking out a lot, knocked out 26 home runs and whiffed 137 times. Pitching was where the Mets excelled. Seaver, already top-tier, became an elite pitcher in 1969, with a 25–7 record and 2.21 earned-run average to win the Cy Young Award and finish second in the MVP voting. Koosman was 17–9 with a 2.28 ERA, and Gentry 13–12.

* * *

As the 1969 season got underway, however, the Mets were an afterthought. The St. Louis Cardinals were the presumptive favorites to win the first-ever NL East division title, if for no other reason than their complete dominance of the single 10-team unitary league in 1967 and 1968. They had Bob Gibson, Lou Brock, Curt Flood, Tim McCarver, and Steve Carlton. And the player they traded Orlando Cepeda for—Joe Torre, who changed positions from catcher to first base—was still in his prime, while over-30 Cepeda gave evidence in 1968 that he might be entering his declining years. If any team in the NL East seemed poised to mount a challenge to the Cardinals' supremacy, it was the Chicago Cubs, now managed by Leo Durocher, personally controversial but still widely praised for his baseball acumen. Despite his 1,375–1,088 record in 16 years managing the Dodgers and Giants, Durocher, perhaps doing penance for his brash personality, had not managed anywhere since being fired by New York's Giants in 1955 until, at the age of 60 in 1966, he was called upon to revive the fortunes of the once-proud Cubs franchise.

Having won 10 National League pennants in the 39 years between 1906 and 1945—although no World Series since 1908—the Cubs had fared very badly in the 20 years since then. Under 12 different managers, several of them more than once, the Cubs finished as high as third just once (in 1946) and had endured 17 losing seasons in 20 years. So dysfunctional was the franchise that for two years—1961 and 1962—the team was managed by a system of rotating "head coaches," an innovation whose time quickly came and went. They were not yet the "lovable losers" of late-twentieth-century lore.

Notwithstanding their never-in-it teams, the Cubs had two Most Valuable Players in the 1950s. Leading the league in home runs and RBIs in 1952 for fifth-place Chicago, left fielder Hank Sauer won the award in 1952, his third straight 30-homer season. Sauer hit a career-high 41 two years later, at 37 years old, before age brought a swift conclusion to his career. Shortstop Ernie Banks won back-to-back MVPs in 1958 and 1959 despite his team's losing record both years. Signed directly from the Negro Leagues to become the Cubs' first black player in September 1953, Banks quickly emerged as a superstar in the class of Willie Mays and Hank Aaron. Banks was an anomaly among shortstops in historical context because he hit with unprecedented power for the premier defensive position on the diamond. From 1957 to 1960, Banks averaged 44 homers and 123 RBIs a year and led the league twice in each category. The only shortstop prior to him who was a persistent power threat was Vern Stephens, who averaged 33 homers between 1948 and 1950 for the Red Six and whose 214 home runs as a shortstop when he retired in 1955 stood as the record until Banks hit his first homer of the 1960 season.

By the time he moved to first base in 1962 because age (he had just turned 31) and assorted leg injuries had compromised his range in the middle infield, Banks had 298 career home runs—278 of them as a shortstop, a record that stood until Cal Ripken Jr. passed him in 1993. Taking account of his offensive productivity, Ernie Banks was the best all-around shortstop the major leagues had seen since at least Arky Vaughan in the 1930s, if not Honus Wagner before him, and would be until the early 1980s when Robin Yount, Ozzie Smith, and Ripken made the grade. Having started 1,121 games at short through 1961, Banks started 1,226 more for the Cubs at first base before calling it a career in 1971. He hit an additional 243 homers as a first baseman to give him a career total of 512.

Banks, whose sunny disposition lit up daytime-only-baseball Wrigley Field, was certainly the most popular player in Chicago near the end of his career in the 1960s, but he was far eclipsed in performance by third baseman Ron Santo and left fielder Billy Williams. Santo was a top-tier defensive third baseman with a potent bat of his own, hitting at least 30 homers four years in a row from 1964 to 1967, and one of the National League's top five position players in the 1960s, based on wins above replacement. Few third basemen in baseball history played at the elite level Santo did. Many consider the fact that it took until 2012—two years after his death—before he was finally voted into the Hall of Fame by the Veteran's Committee to have been a travesty of justice. Williams, a left-handed power hitter and an exceptional ballplayer in his own right, was perhaps best known for his durability. Between September 22, 1963, and September 2, 1970, Williams played in 1,117 consecutive games (five as a pinch-hitter), shattering Stan Musial's streak of 895 as the new National League record. Williams's streak was surpassed by Steve Garvey in 1983. With 392 home runs and a .296 batting average in his 16 years playing for the Cubs, Billy Williams was elected to the Hall of Fame in 1987, his sixth year on the writers' ballot, who apparently valued his contributions far more than they did Santo's.

Even with Santo, Williams, and Banks providing a measure of grace, dignity, and top-flight talent, and second baseman Glenn Beckert and shortstop Don Kessinger at the beginning of promising careers, the Cubs team Durocher inherited in 1966 was not good enough to play competitive major-league baseball, whether for a "manager" or a "head coach." In his first year at the helm, the Cubs were the not-so-lovable losers of 103 games and the worst team in the league. They ended up 7½ games behind the ninth-place Mets. But Leo Durocher was nothing if not persistent. Focusing on developing players' fundamentals and not allowing his team to accept losing as a tolerable condition, Durocher turned the Cubs into a winning ballclub. Perhaps most significantly, Durocher moved two right-handers at the beginning of their careers—Ferguson Jenkins and Bill Hands—from the bullpen into the starting rotation. With his first of six straight 20-win seasons in 1967, Jenkins quickly joined the ranks of elite pitchers. In the last two years before divisional alignment, Durocher's Cubs finished third in both 1967 and 1968.

* * *

The 1969 Cubs got off to a fast start, winning 11 of the first 12. On June 15, they were 41–19 with a nine-game lead over the second-place Mets. Losing four of six to the Mets in mid-July, however, proved a harbinger of things to come. One of those losses, on July 9 at Shea Stadium, was a near-perfect game pitched by Tom Seaver that was broken up after 8⅓ innings by rookie outfielder Jimmy Qualls, playing in only his 18th major league game. It was just the 12th hit of his career. (I was scoring at home.) Seaver's 14th win of the season that day cut the Cubs' lead to 3½ games. But a month later, Chicago was back up by 8½ games. As for the overachieving Mets, by August 13 they had dropped to 10 games back in third place. Chicago seemed in complete command of the NL East, only for long-suffering Cubs fans to see it all unravel in September. The Cubs went 9–18 in the final month as the Mets—24–8 in September—surged past them to 100 wins and a final 8-game margin of victory in the NL East.

Riding the momentum of winning nine of their last 10 on the schedule, the Mets swept the NL Western Division–champion Atlanta Braves in the five-game National League Championship Series and then, quite improbably, defeated the far-superior Baltimore Orioles in the World Series in five games. It was quite an eventful World Series, with more than its share of unusual circumstances and improbable heroes. When Seaver lost the opening game, an Orioles rout of the Mets seemed likely. But New York won Game Two, 2–1, on a two-out top-of-the-ninth single by the light-hitting Al Weis, a .215 hitter during the season who went 5-for-11 in the series. Center fielder Tommie Agee made two exceptional catches in Game Three at Shea Stadium to preserve a Mets win. In Game Four it was right fielder Ron Swoboda, not known for his defensive proficiency, who made an unbelievable swan dive/belly flop catch in the ninth inning to rob Brooks Robinson of a hit that might have won the game for Baltimore. Instead the game went into the 10th inning. The Mets won on a controversial final play in the bottom of the 10th on a well-executed sacrifice bunt by backup catcher J. C. Martin, pinch-hitting for Seaver, on which Orioles reliever Pete Richert's throw to first to retire the batter-runner hit him in the back, allowing the winning run to score. Martin, however, was running inside the baseline, against the rules. He should have been called out for interference and the ball declared dead. Long before the era of video challenges, the umpires didn't make that call. The Mets were up three games to one.

It all ended the next day with the Mets getting another consequential break. With the Mets trailing 3–0 in the sixth, Cleon Jones either was or wasn't hit by a pitch that skipped into the Mets dugout. The umpire called the pitch a ball until manager Gil Hodges emerged from the dugout holding a baseball scuffed with shoe polish. Jones was awarded first base. Donn Clendenon, acquired in June to bolster the Mets lineup, followed with his third homer of the series—he also batted .357 in the five games—and the Mets were back in the game. An inning later, they tied the score on a home run by Weis, who hit only two all season. In the eighth the Mets scored twice more to polish off Baltimore and seal their destiny as one of baseball's greatest miracle teams.

* * *

Leo Durocher certainly knew something about miracles. He was the manager who presided over the 1951 Giants' Miracle of Coogan's Bluff that wiped out the Dodgers' presumed-insurmountable 13½-game mid-

August lead. Now he was on the other side of a miracle, to the Brooklyn Dodgers' spiritual heirs, no less—the New York Mets.

Most likely, the Cubs lost a division title that seemed firmly in hand in mid-August because Durocher drove his starting position regulars to exhaustion. Rather than give them appropriate rest as needed during the long, hot summer to ensure they were prepared for the September stretch, Durocher started five of his core regulars—Ernie Banks, Don Kessinger, Ron Santo, Billy Williams, and catcher Randy Hundley—in at least 145 of the 163 games the Cubs played in 1969, and all five played in the field in at least 151 games. Glenn Beckert would have done so, too, had he not been sidelined nearly all of June with a broken finger. Hundley was the starting catcher in each of the Cubs' first 68 games, including seven doubleheaders, and played the entire game—including eight extra-inning games—in all but three of them. Playing the most demanding position on the diamond, Hundley caught 89 percent of the Cubs' total innings in 1969. Kessinger and Santo played an even higher percentage of innings at shortstop and third base. Their weariness was particularly damaging when the Cubs suddenly found themselves in September having to first fight off the Mets, and then catch them.

September witnessed the complete collapse of the Cubs' offense. Chicago scored the fewest runs and had the worst team batting average, on-base percentage, and slugging percentage in the National League down the stretch. Hundley batted .151, Kessinger .186, Banks .208, Beckert .211, and Santo .244. Their runs per game dropped from 5.1 the first three months, to 4.2 in July and August, to 3.3 in September, when the 11 other NL clubs averaged 3.7 per game. The Cubs scored no more than three runs in 14 of their 18 losses in their final weeks.

While Durocher was playing his core regulars virtually every day, Gil Hodges was careful to give his everyday players—Agee, Jones, and Harrelson—occasional days of rest. He platooned or mixed-and-matched at every other position. When the Mets were making their push to overtake Chicago, his players were not on the brink of exhaustion. Their average of 3.8 runs per game in September was only slightly below their season average of 3.9. The hard-charging Mets outscored their opponents 121 to 80 in the final month, compared to the nose-diving Cubs, who were outscored 88 to 128. Unlike Hodges's skillful use of his entire roster, Durocher went to his bench to spot-start position players only to replace

Beckert when he was hurt and to try various players in right field and center—both positions of significant weakness.

Even for a time when managers still relied on a four-man rotation, Durocher overburdened his starting pitchers. Ferguson Jenkins (21–15 in 1969), Bill Hands (20–14), Ken Holtzman (17–13), and Dick Selma (10–8) started 90 percent of the Cubs' games and accounted for 72 percent of team innings pitched. Jenkins and Hands each made more than 40 starts, and Holtzman started 39. Hodges, by contrast, used five starters. Seaver, Koosman, and Gentry each started between 32 and 35 games, and Don Cardwell and Jim McAndrew both started 21. When September came around, Mets pitchers were far more effective in the stretch drive for the division title, better than in any other month. Their starters' earned-run average was 2.07. Seaver had complete-game victories in all six of his starts and a 0.83 ERA, Koosman was 5–1 with a 2.40 ERA, and Gentry was 4–1 with a 2.19 ERA. Durocher's overworked starting pitchers posted a 3.84 ERA in September. After having already made 35 starts and thrown 261⅓ innings through August, Jenkins was 3–4 with a very high 4.68 ERA in seven September starts. Holtzman, at 1–5 with a 4.56 earned-run average, was not any better in his seven starts. Even though his starting pitchers were giving up more runs in September than any other month, Durocher was unwilling to trust his bullpen in the crucible of the September stretch. After appearing in 14 of the Cubs' 30 games in July with an excellent 1.27 ERA, ace reliever Phil Regan pitched poorly thereafter, compiling a 5.70 ERA in 22 games; his earned-run average was 6.23 in September.

* * *

The Chicago Cubs had now gone 61 years without a World Series championship and had not won a pennant since 1945. If not an epic collapse on the order of what happened to the Phillies in 1964, Leo Durocher had to endure the humiliation of his club having blown a commanding lead in mid-August and losing to a team that nobody expected would contend any time soon. In the 45 games left after August 13, the Cubs lost 18 games in the standings to the Mets.

Neither team finished closer than five games from the top in any of the next three years. In Chicago, Ernie Banks retired gracefully at the end of the 1971 season. Leo Durocher left somewhat less gracefully—fired in 1972 at the All-Star break with his team in third place, barely over .500 at 46–44. Ferguson Jenkins and Ron Santo were traded to American League clubs following the 1973 season, as was Billy Williams a year later. In New York, the most significant change was the sudden death of manager Gil Hodges during spring training in 1972. Yogi Berra, on the Mets coaching staff since being fired by the Yankees after managing them to the 1964 pennant, was given charge of Hodges's team.

A month after being dismissed in Chicago, Durocher resurfaced in Houston as the Astros' manager. Following their 82–80 season in 1973, he was fired one last time, his managerial career coming to an end with a lifetime record of 2,008 wins and 1,709 losses. Durocher's second stint as manager, from 1966 to 1973, was far less successful than his first, from 1939 to 1955. This was certainly because neither his Chicago team nor his Houston team was as good as his 1940s Dodgers and 1950s Giants. But it was also because Leo Durocher either did not, could not, or refused to adapt to a different time. Durocher acknowledged as much in his well-regarded 1975 autobiography *Nice Guys Finish Last*. Writing disparagingly about how "the new breed" of ballplayers was spoiled, selfish, in it for the money, not as dedicated to the game or to improving as players, and more than willing to disrespect and question their manager's authority, Durocher complained that "[y]ou can't tell them what to do." And major-league executives were complicit by reining in the authority of their managers. "If the manager is going to be respected," he wrote, "the players have to know that they cannot go to the front office without your [the manager's] permission." "*I'm a guy who had to do it my way*," he concluded (italics are his)—"Whether you like it or not." Those were the last lines in his book.

A tough taskmaster (and a rogue in his personal life), Durocher was an inspiring manager when he led the 1951 Giants to their improbable pennant, although he was not above cheating—witness coach Herman Franks stealing signs from the center-field clubhouse in the Polo Grounds with a powerful telescope. Durocher was not an inspiration to the Cubs in 1969. Indeed, his last years as a manager were characterized by some of his best players in Chicago and Houston profoundly disliking him—and wondering about his baseball savvy as well. He was seen as arbitrary and arrogant. Worse, Durocher was perceived as behind developments in the game and even disinterested in the dugout. The way Durocher criticized his players and laid blame on them for mistakes and defeats suggests he did not have the same respect for them—whether their work ethic, mastery of the skills of the game, or understanding of its nuances—as he did for his players in the 1940s and '50s, especially in his handling of rookie Willie Mays in 1951.

A common affliction of former players and managers from any era is their conviction that subsequent generations, for all their talent, do not understand and do not play the game with the same excellence as players in their times did. Firebrand managers with that attitude—especially those with insufferable egos like Durocher, who was twice as old as most of his players when he managed in Chicago and Houston—invariably alienate a much younger generation of players. This is not to say that older managers must be patrician types. Indeed not. Walt Alston, six years younger than Durocher and more or less in the same generation, was demanding and exacting as manager of the Los Angeles Dodgers, but in a way that showed respect for his players and had them believing in his skills and leadership. If Alston was like the tough, wise, and gracious uncle who was firm but understanding with the kids, Durocher was the petulant uncle always bothered by the kids, and so was disliked, disrespected, and even mocked.

* * *

Unlike with the 1964 Yankees, Berra did not lead the 1972 Mets to a pennant his first year as manager. The Mets won 83 and finished third for the third year in a row. Unlike with the Yankees, Berra was back for a second year. With Yogi insisting, "It ain't over 'til it's over," his 1973 Mets captured baseball's heart again by coming from behind to win a very mediocre division with just 82 wins, three games above .500, and then toppling, as they had the Orioles four years before, the much-better 99-win Cincinnati Reds in the NLCS to win the pennant. The Mets were in last place at 12½ games back on Independence Day. They were last on August 5, 11½ games out. They were still last on August 30 with a 61–71 record, but had whittled their deficit to just 6½ games. Inspired by relief ace Tug McGraw's rallying cry—"You Gotta Believe!"—to uplift his teammates, the Mets once again had a September to remember, winning 21 of 29 games to take the division title by 1½ games over St. Louis. It wasn't until their 155th game of the season that the Mets were back over .500; they had last had a winning record in late May. Ten of McGraw's 25 saves came in September. Pitching in 14 games the final month, he allowed just 2 runs in 31⅓ innings.

Third baseman Wayne Garrett, a rookie during the 1969 campaign, and right fielder Rusty Staub, acquired from Montreal in 1972, were the most potent batters on a team with the second-worst batting average in the majors. Only one of the major leagues' 24 teams scored fewer runs. Pitching, as usual, was the key to the Mets success, even though Seaver—whose 19–10 record and league-leading 2.08 ERA earned him a second Cy Young Award—was the only one of their three top starters with a winning record. Koosman was 14–15 and Jon Matlack, the 1971 NL Rookie of the Year, had a 14–16 record. And shortstop Bud Harrelson endeared himself to Mets fans by brawling with Pete Rose after a collision at second base in the Mets' stunning takedown of the Reds in the 1973 NLCS.

This time, however, the Mets were unable to beat a superior team in the World Series—Oakland's Athletics—despite Koosman's three-hit shutout in Game Five giving them a three-games-to-two advantage. Staub had an exceptional series, batting .423 and driving in six of the Mets' 24 runs. The sentimental moment of the series came in the 12th inning of Game Two when Willie Mays drove in the winning run (and later came around to score himself) on a single up the middle off Oakland relief ace Rollie Fingers. It turned out to be his next-to-last at bat and the last hit of his major-league career. Mays was 41 years old and worn down when he came to the Mets for his swan song in May 1972. He was brought back to New York to end his career specifically because New York was where it began, and where he was likely the city's most beloved baseball figure when the Giants skipped town for San Francisco. The Willie Mays that Mets fans saw play in 1972 and '73 was not even a pale imitation of the Say Hey Kid—power hitter, aggressive baserunner, and brilliant center fielder—who played for the New York Giants. Mays finished his career with 660 home runs. His game-winning hit in the World Series was a beautiful grace note on which to go out.

* * *

The 1969–1973 New York Mets won two division titles and two pennants in five years, almost entirely on the strength of their pitching—specifically Tom Seaver's durable right arm. In contrast to Jim Palmer's poised and elegant delivery, Juan Marichal's reach for the sky with his left leg, and Bob Gibson's flying off the mound as he released the ball, Seaver's drop-and-drive delivery was distinctive for being so deep that his right knee often scraped the dirt on the mound.

At the trade deadline in June 1977, the last-place Mets outraged their fans by trading Tom Terrific to Cincinnati. In 10 full seasons with the

Mets, Seaver averaged 35 starts a year, never with fewer than 32, completed 46 percent of his starts, threw 39 shutouts, struck out 200 batters nine years in a row, led the league in strikeouts five times and in ERA three times, had four 20-win seasons, and won three Cy Young Awards, the third in 1975. He had a fifth 20-win season in 1977, including his 7–3 record with the Mets before he was unceremoniously sent away. Seaver finished his career in 1986 with 311 wins, 198 with the Mets.

Even with Seaver, Koosman, and Matlack headlining their pitching staff, the Mets collapsed after their implausible trip to the World Series in 1973. Their 91 losses in 1974 were the most since the 101 games they dropped in Seaver's 1967 rookie year. The Mets rebounded to a winning record in 1975, finishing third with the same number of wins they had in 1973, but Yogi Berra failed to survive the season. He made it to August 5th. A big reason why was that he learned the lesson of Leo Durocher's lament about "the new breed" of ballplayer when he, as manager, suspended Cleon Jones, no longer playing regularly, for refusing in front of all his teammates to go into a game as a defensive replacement. The Mets' front office at first refused to back their manager on the suspension but backed down and released Jones after Berra refused to relent. Team executives made it quite clear, however, they were not happy with Yogi's handling of the situation. They used the excuse of the Mets' poor play to fire him soon thereafter.

Part III

Shifting Balances in the Game and the Business of Baseball

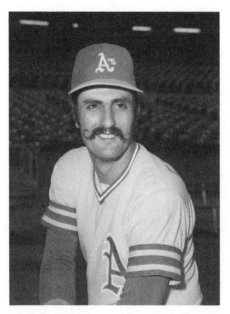

Indicative of the countercultural times in American society in the 1970s, many teams began allowing players more latitude in their appearance while in baseball uniforms, including longer hairstyles and facial hair. Rollie Fingers, the Oakland A's relief ace when they won three consecutive World Series from 1972 to 1974, was renowned for his mustache. *National Baseball Hall of Fame Library, Cooperstown, NY.*

15

RACE, WAR, CULTURAL UPHEAVAL, AND BASEBALL IN AMERICA

The United States entering the 1970s was in the midst of tectonic changes that shaped and would define the cleavages in America's culture, society, and politics for decades to come—to this very day, in fact. A series of political assassinations—beginning with President Kennedy in 1963 and including black militant Malcolm X in 1965; civil rights leader Martin Luther King Jr., shot to death in April 1968; and presidential candidate Robert F. Kennedy, brother of the slain president, killed in June 1968—roiled the country. Racial tensions were manifest in urban rioting and avowed segregationist George Wallace's victory in five Southern states as a third-party candidate in the 1968 presidential election. The country was fully engaged in the Vietnam War, which wasn't going well. Traditional cultural mores were being upended.

Major League Baseball, being a sport, was ostensibly far removed from having to grapple with these issues, excepting, of course, for the impact they had on the lives and attitudes of ballplayers, a growing pro-portion of whom were black. There was always a divide between baseball executives and players—it could not have been otherwise, since their relationship was always contractual, between employer and employee—but now it was becoming more acrimonious as players, like Americans across the country, began asserting themselves in an effort to influence outcomes affecting their lives. By pressing ahead with integration in the 1950s, despite considerable resistance from many owners and concerns about the number of black players on big-league rosters, especially in starting roles, baseball may have been at the forefront of the civil rights movement, but the major leagues reverted to embodying, through silence and in some cases complicit actions, a traditionalist conservative outlook that may have hearkened back to nostalgia for an America that once was, but was now behind the times.

President Lyndon B. Johnson signed the Civil Rights Act on July 2, 1964. The new federal law was intended to end institutional segregation in the United States of America once and for all. On that date, 18 of baseball's 20 major-league teams played ball. Of the 162 players in the starting lineups that day, 52 were black. Only 14 of them were on American League clubs; the AL was still lagging far behind the NL in black players on major-league rosters and in starting roles. Although every major-league team had been integrated since 1959, when the Red Sox finally put a black man on their roster, 1964 was the first year that every team had at least one black player in its starting lineup or starting rotation for the entire season. Unlike during the entirety of Jackie Robinson's career, when most clubs' guiding principle was that a black player had to be exceptional to win a starting job and keep his position over multiple seasons, in the beginning years of the 1960s, as movement toward the Civil Rights Act picked up steam, baseball was again at the leading edge of race relations in America by becoming more inclusive in giving black players of more modest ability than the likes of Mays, Banks, Aaron, and Frank Robinson the opportunity to succeed in a starting role.

Black players, however, even those who were core regulars, while perhaps no longer having to struggle for acceptance in the major leagues, still had to contend with stereotypical prejudices and inequality in how they were treated. In Florida, where most clubs held spring training, segregationist sentiment was hardly dented by the passage of civil rights legislation. At many spring training camps, black players—even major leaguers—confronted overt discrimination in local housing, eating, and entertainment options. During the season, many black players faced discrimination in housing in the big-league cities they called home because of white property owners' concerns that black families—even those of baseball stars—would negatively impact property values. For black players trying for their shot in the major leagues, racial prejudice and inequality was a burden their white teammates did not face if they were assigned to minor-league teams in the South. Team executives, for the most part, provided little in the way of support or pushing back on the community, either turning a blind eye or just being insensitive to the daily hassles black players had to endure.

The Civil Rights Act and the Voting Rights Act that followed in 1965 were hardly palliatives to racial prejudice and even hatred that die-hard white segregationists had for blacks, especially in the South. And it was to the South, the city of Atlanta, where the Milwaukee Braves moved in 1966. Most of their best players—Hank Aaron, Felipe Alou, Rico Carty, Mack Jones— were black, and the Braves' first year in Atlanta happened to be an election year in which staunch segregationist Lester Maddox, arguing that states' rights trumped federal law, was elected governor on a platform advocating a return to Jim Crow Georgia. Notwithstanding the attitudes of likely most of the Braves' new fan base, Atlanta had both a growing black population and ambitions to become the most dynamic center of commerce in the American South by attracting businesses and investment, a goal that required *not* being tarred as virulently antiblack.

The Braves' new fan base was also happy to have a major-league team in Atlanta, and Hank Aaron was, well, pretty darned good. Outstanding, actually. Since at least the early 1960s, when injury-prone Mickey Mantle began to fade, Aaron was the second-best player in baseball after Willie Mays, and he was three years younger. His first year in Atlanta, Aaron led the league with 44 home runs and the majors with 127 runs batted in. His second year, he led the league in homers again, with 39. In 1969 his 44 home runs were one fewer than Willie McCovey for the league lead and helped power Atlanta's Braves to the National League's Western Division title in the first year of divisional alignment. It was the Braves' first postseason appearance since they won a second straight pennant in Milwaukee in 1958. It was the first time Atlanta had a first-place team in professional sports. And six of Atlanta's core players were black: Aaron; fellow outfielders Alou, Carty, and Tony Gonzalez; first baseman Orlando Cepeda; and shortstop Sonny Jackson. That the Braves were wiped out by the Mets in the National League Championship Series was hardly Aaron's fault; he hit .357 with 3 homers and 7 RBIs. While Aaron originally had misgivings about his team's moving to the Deep South, he complemented his continuing excellence on the ballfield in Atlanta with civic engagement in the city.

* * *

At a time of considerable racial ferment in the United States, Aaron, like other black players, had to endure the ugliness of racist abuse, particularly as he closed in on baseball's most sacred record—the 714 career home runs by Babe Ruth. The idea that a black ballplayer should displace the Babe as the all-time home run king was anathema to many whites, who held views that blacks were inherently inferior. (The Babe himself, by the way, was taunted with racial slurs by bench jockeys during his playing days based not on the color of his skin but the broadness of his nose, suggesting the possibility of an interracial affair in his family history.)

Hank Aaron came to Atlanta with 398 career home runs as a Milwaukee Brave. In 1966 not even Willie Mays, who began the season with 505, was thought to be a threat to Ruth's record. Aided by Atlanta's Fulton County Stadium being a good home-run park—190 of the 335 homers he hit as an *Atlanta* Brave were at home—by the end of 1972, Aaron had eclipsed Mays and, with 673 homers, was now within 41 of the Babe. He was also now increasingly the target of virulent racist hate mail, including threats to his life. Going deep 40 times in 1973, Aaron was forced to spend an entire off-season just one home run shy of the all-time career record. That fall, Maynard Jackson, four years younger than the 39-year-old Aaron, became not only the first African American to be elected mayor of Atlanta but the first to be elected mayor of any major city in the South.

On Opening Day in Cincinnati in 1974, Aaron homered in the very first inning off Jack Billingham, giving him exactly 714. Forced by Commissioner Bowie Kuhn to play one of Atlanta's next two games in their season-opening series in Cincinnati, rather than sitting them out to assure he would hit the record-breaker in front of his home fans, Aaron went 0-for-3 in the third game of the year. On April 8, 1974, in the Braves' home opener against the Dodgers, Aaron walked in his first at-bat against southpaw Al Downing. At bat again in the fourth with a runner on base, his team trailing by two runs, Aaron went deep to left to tie the game . . . with his 715th career home run. "What a marvelous moment for the country and the world," said Vin Scully, the voice of the Dodgers. "A black man is getting a standing ovation in the Deep South for breaking the record of an all-time baseball idol."

Hank Aaron left the Braves at the end of the season with 733 home runs. He hit 22 more in his final two years, back in Milwaukee with the

American League's Brewers. Just as there were those who would claim Babe Ruth was still the all-time home run champ because he hit 714 in 3,300 fewer plate appearances, or because he played only 154 games a year whereas 15 of the 23 years Aaron played were 162-game seasons, or even because the first three years of Ruth's career were exclusively as a pitcher, there are people today who consider Aaron's 755 home runs—and not Barry Bonds's 762—to still be the record. The difference, of course, is that Aaron never shortcut his way to challenging Ruth's record, whereas Bonds allegedly did by using steroids.

Scully, as on so many occasions when he had the call, was dead-on about the moment and the man. Carrying himself with grace and dignity through a career that began when black players were few and not necessarily wanted when he debuted as a Milwaukee Brave at the age of 20 in 1954, then enduring the indignities of prejudice directed at him in spring training in Florida and in many big-league ballparks, and ultimately the venom that came his way as he stood on the threshold of history (and even after), Hank Aaron himself became "an all-time baseball idol," widely respected and admired by Americans, black and white. He was not controversial. He was celebrated. He was not an angry black man. He was an American success story, a black man born in Alabama, the heart of the Jim Crow South, whose extraordinary accomplishments reinforced the importance of the civil rights movement.

* * *

For contrast, there was Dick Allen. A black man born in Pennsylvania's coal country, eight years younger than Aaron and an outstanding ballplayer in his own right, Allen was as polarizing a figure in baseball as Aaron was unifying. Because of his outstanding rookie season with the Phillies in 1964, including playing well even as his team imploded around him in the last weeks of September, and the controversies that would dog him the rest of his career—which concluded with 351 homers, 1,119 runs batted in, a lifetime .292 batting average, and a .912 on-base plus slugging percentage—Allen's baseball reputation is an appropriate cautionary tale about what could happen to an African American ballplayer who did not conform to expectations for black ballplayers in the 1960s, when major-league integration was a fait accompli but nonetheless still a work in progress. Dick Allen was Major League Baseball's first black militant at a time when urban violence engulfed American cities across the country and black militants were scaring the overwhelming majority of Americans, black and white, in the late 1960s.

In addition to still having to overcome the likelihood of greater skepticism about their level of talent and commitment compared to white players of comparable ability, black players also were expected to conform to the norms of professional baseball culture established in the bygone era of segregated Major League Baseball—even though those norms were often transgressed by renegade personalities who happened to be superstars or fan favorites, Babe Ruth included. There was little tolerance for cultural diversity, and especially not for grievances about prejudice and discrimination that—against the backdrop of the civil rights movement at the time—black players, even major-league stars, continued to face. As in white-collar professions at the time, black players were expected to passively submit to the norms of the white ballplayers' world. The fact that all team executives, every major-league manager, and nearly all the coaches were white men reinforced the culture.

Allen's rap as a clubhouse cancer, which may be the only reason he is not in the Hall of Fame (not yet, anyway), is probably less because he was misunderstood or deliberately divisive than that he was outraged and outspoken about his sense of grievance. He chafed at the Phillies' lack of support around the racial taunts he endured playing on Southern teams in their minor-league system; at being introduced by the Phillies to their fans as "Richie"—which he thought was intended to make him seem a man-child, in keeping with the paternalistic attitude many whites still had toward black men; and at the racism in the booing he endured at home in Connie Mack Stadium. It should be noted that Philadelphia's racist reputation was a consideration for Curt Flood, along with his belief in the principle that professional ballplayers should not be treated as chattel by team owners, in his decision not to report to the Phillies after being traded for Allen, opting instead to take his case against the reserve clause that gave him no say in the trade to court. It went all the way to the Supreme Court.

Ironically, Allen's edgy assertiveness that alienated teammates and fans was not so different from Jackie Robinson's after his three-year commitment to Branch Rickey to stifle his innately aggressive personality had ended, which coincided with Rickey's departure to the Pittsburgh Pirates. But while Jackie Robinson was given some slack, even while getting his share of criticism from managers, teammates, and baseball writers, because he was the trailblazer upending the formerly all-white major leagues, Dick Allen got no such consideration. The major leagues weren't all white anymore. He was just the latest in a long line of great black ballplayers to star in the major leagues. His teammates included black players in key roles with far more modest abilities. His words and actions were perceived as playing the race card, which was considered totally inappropriate in what were now thought to be the postracial major leagues.

* * *

One month and five days after the Civil Rights Act was enacted in July 1964, both houses of Congress overwhelmingly passed the Gulf of Tonkin Resolution that authorized the president to take whatever military action he deemed necessary in the wake of North Vietnam's small-boat attacks on US destroyers. whose mission was to interdict the North's supply shipments to Vietcong guerrilla forces battling the US-backed regime in South Vietnam. Thus began a substantial escalation of American military involvement in Vietnam that saw the number of troops in-country increase from approximately 23,000 in 1964, mostly there as advisers and for logistics support, to nearly 200,000 in one year. US casualties increased exponentially, from just under 220 deaths in 1964 to nearly 2,000 in 1965. The rapidly escalating demand for boots on the ground resulted in the revitalization of the draft, which had not gone away once the Korean War was over but was very limited in scope.

More than 1.1 million Americans were drafted into the military between 1965 and 1968, more than double the number from 1960 to 1964. Notwithstanding America's new war footing and taking over strategic direction of South Vietnam's war (admittedly, a war for survival), the combined Vietcong guerrilla and North Vietnamese military forces proved a formidable and resilient adversary in the face of overwhelming US firepower, particularly from the air. By 1968 there were more than 536,000 American soldiers fighting in Vietnam. In February the North Vietnamese stunned the United States with the ferocity and lethality of the Tet Offensive, which was doomed to failure because of US military superiority but whose initial thrusts and the American casualties they caused also doomed President Johnson's aspirations to run for a second term. Nearly 17,000 American soldiers died in Vietnam that year.

Against the backdrop of racial tensions leading to urban unrest, including rioting in the streets and blocks of burning buildings in impoverished inner cities, there was little patriotic fervor for the US military effort in Vietnam, as there had been in the world wars—not even when it was couched in terms of necessity to thwart the spread of Communism in Asia, said to represent a fundamental threat to freedom and democracy worldwide and ultimately to the United States itself. As American casualties mounted, as distrust increased in the very word of the US government about how the war was going, as perceptions grew that not only was an Asian land war prohibitively costly in terms of lives and money, but that the United States was *losing* and that wartime atrocities were morally unacceptable, Americans—white and black—also took to city streets to protest the war, sometimes rioting. Many of those protests were against the draft, which not only was indispensable to the United States in fighting what many Americans increasingly saw as an indefensible war, but also widely perceived as inequitable because of the many kinds of deferments—educational and otherwise—that overwhelmingly went to well-off and middle-class, mostly white, American males. Avoiding fighting in the war, even by those who supported it, at least in principle, was a privilege for the better-off in America. It was left to those without the educational options or the resources and connections to avoid being drafted to do the fighting and, disproportionately, to die for their country.

Unlike America's previous wars in the twentieth century, the impact of the Vietnam War on Major League Baseball was close to negligible. While many established major leaguers, including elite players, voluntarily joined the bloody fray during the world wars for reasons of patriotism, none did so for Vietnam. While established major leaguers, including star players, were drafted into both those wars as well as into the Korean War—Don Newcombe, Willie Mays, Art Houtteman (a 19-game winner for Detroit in 1950), Whitey Ford, and Curt Simmons were among the most prominent drafted for Korea—none were for Vietnam.

To the extent major-league rosters were affected by the war, it was players signed up for the reserves or National Guard, to avoid being drafted, and serving their commitments during the season. In fact, according to Gary Bedingfield's extensive research on ballplayers who have served (and died) for their country, hundreds of minor- and major-league players served in the National Guard or the reserves, often through the intervention of their major-league parent clubs, seeking to keep their investment in baseball talent out of Vietnam. Unlike during both world wars and Korea, when wartime manpower requirements left no alternative, National Guard units were rarely deployed to fight in Vietnam, mostly for political reasons because of the unpopularity of the war, until after the draft was abolished in 1973. While an initial six months of basic training, two consecutive weeks of annual training, and a one-weekend-a-month individual commitment was mandatory to ensure units were combat-ready should the need arise, the reserves were likewise a safe alternative for military service to avoid the draft because President Johnson refused to mobilize them for combat tours, notwithstanding a very limited callup of the Army Reserve during the Tet Offensive.

In-season callups for players with reserve or National Guard commitments did sometimes disrupt careers and pennant races, although rarely significantly. Second-year Cubs pitcher Ken Holtzman was 5–0 in his first eight starts in 1967 before being called away in late May by the Illinois National Guard for a six-month tour of duty. He made just four more starts that season—two in mid-August and two in September—winning them all to go 9–0 for the season, leaving open the question of whether he might not have had to wait till 1973 to win 20 games. Flame-thrower Nolan Ryan believed that his in-season commitments with the Army Reserve and manager Gil Hodges's unwillingness to accommodate them prevented him from finding consistency in the four years he pitched for the Mets. (To be fair to his manager, Ryan was still in the discovery phase of his career, just as Koufax had been in Brooklyn, learning to harness and master his talent.) Hodges, on the other hand, *did* accommodate Tom Seaver's Marine Corps Reserve obligations to minimize disrupting the cycle of his starts, both with regard to his routine and the Miracle Mets' unexpected drive toward the 1969 NL East title. So too did the Red Sox with their ace Jim Lonborg, providing a private plane to allow him to make his starts and return to base during his Army Reserve commitment in the midst of their Impossible Dream pennant in 1967 that was not secured till the final day of the season.

It was easier for clubs to accommodate pitchers on reserve duty, because they ordinarily started every fourth or fifth day, than it was for everyday position players. While Lonborg was able to make all his starts during the 1967 pennant race, rival Minnesota's outstanding rookie second baseman Rod Carew, batting exactly .300 at the time, missed 16 consecutive games fulfilling his reserve obligation at the beginning of August when the Twins were battling at 4½ games behind to stay relevant in the pennant race. As it happened, with the versatile Cesar Tovar filling in for him at second base, the Twins won all but four of their games in Carew's absence and were in first place with a slim half-game lead when he returned. And while Seaver was able to make one start during his two-week tour of duty in August 1969, the Mets were without shortstop Bud Harrelson, serving with the National Guard, for nearly a month in June and July, just when they were beginning to make their move into the pennant race. Al Weis, a famously poor hitter who batted just .215 that year, stepped up to hit .250 in Harrelson's absence.

No active established major-league players saw combat in Vietnam. Future major leaguers who did fight in the war were either minor leaguers at the beginning of their careers or young men who had yet to start their professional careers. A disproportionate number were black or Hispanic. Almost all were US Army draft picks who did not have viable options to avoid being called to duty or to influence their military specialization and deployment. Some came back as war heroes, unknown to the general public because they had yet to become baseball stars. More than 58,200 American soldiers died in Vietnam. Only six were active professional baseball players; all were minor leaguers. Five were drafted, and the sixth joined the active-duty marines after a recruiter called him a coward for trying to sign up with the National Guard. Five of the six had played just one year in the minors before going to war, and the sixth had two years of experience. None were top-tier big-league prospects.

None of America's wars claimed the life of an active major-league ballplayer, even those involved in fierce fighting. Three former major leaguers died in France during the First World War, two more in the Second World War, and one in the Korean War. Although hardly a star, third baseman Eddie Grant, whose 10-year major-league career ended at 990 games in 1915, remains to this day the most prominent player to have died for his country in wartime. Killed in the Argonne Forest just a month before the November 11, 1918, armistice that put an end to the First World War, Grant would likely be lost in baseball history today were it not for his sacrifice. None of the other five former major leaguers who were American combat fatalities—Tom Burr and Bun Troy in World War I, Elmer Gedeon and Harry O'Neill in World War II, and Bob Neighbors in the Korean War—played more than seven games in the big leagues.

This did not mean, however, that active major leaguers did not face extreme combat situations in those wars, even while some of their compatriot big leaguers were criticized for working in defense industries instead, especially during World War I, or being kept from the fighting by serving in stateside or rear-area roles during World War II and Korea. In previous wars, some of Major League Baseball's best players had war stories to tell—Grover Cleveland Alexander under constant artillery bombardment in France during World War I; Bob Feller seeing combat on the high seas in the Pacific and Cecil Travis in the Battle of the Bulge in World War II; Ted Williams, his baseball career presumably flashing before his eyes, narrowly missing death or capture behind enemy lines in the Korean War by flying his shot-up fighter jet to friendly territory before crash-landing unharmed. In the Vietnam War, by contrast, those major leaguers with war stories to tell served in combat *before* they made it to the big leagues.

Giants prospect Garry Maddox had one year of minor-league ball behind him when he was drafted at the age of 19. His yearlong deployment to Vietnam in 1969–1970 exposed him to chemical defoliates being used to minimize jungle cover for the Vietcong, leaving him with skin sensitivities that made shaving a painful experience. In addition to becoming probably baseball's best defensive center fielder in the 1970s with the Phillies—"three-fourths of the world is covered by water," it was said, "the other quarter by Garry Maddox"—he was among the first permitted by his team to sport a beard because of difficulty shaving. Before Al Bumbry was the American League's 1973 Rookie of the Year, he had won a Bronze Star for valor as a platoon leader in the jungles of Vietnam. Bumbry had four years of college and one year of minor-league experience before he was called off to war; he played 13 years for the Orioles.

* * *

Related to—but on the lighter side of—the 1960s civil rights marches and antiwar protests was a counterculture movement that rebuked the very notion of conformity to traditional American values and lifestyles on the premise that they had contributed to this moment in time. The postwar Rockwellian postcard of respectful, clean-cut, church-going, patriarchal, family-oriented, small-town, middle-class strivers pursuing and living the American dream in which opportunity was open to all, although with the understanding that society's boat not be rocked (or be rocked only within limits), was to the young—the last wave of the baby boom generation, as it happened—discredited by racial inequality and a war with no clear national purpose or apparent strategy to actually win. There was significant consciousness raising about poverty and economic inequality in

America, as well as a growing awareness that women may have had the right to vote since 1920 but were still not considered equal to men in nearly anything. For many in this generation of Americans, engaging in deliberately transgressive behaviors—from listening to hard-rock bands, many of whose lyrics mocked "traditional" values and the "establishment," to smoking dope and popping psychedelic pills, to the "free love" movement, to draft-age men refusing to register with the Selective Service, to young men eschewing crewcuts for long hair and young women forgoing modest attire and skirts for jeans and more daring ensembles—were the hallmark of what the British rock group the Who called, in a 1965 song, "My Generation."

Baseball was not immune, although the major leagues' powers-that-be would have liked it to be. Franchise owners generally were conservative, both politically and socially. They saw themselves as the guardians of baseball as an American tradition, identifiable with traditional American values, as American as apple pie. They were not out to buck that tradition, even though some change seemed in order because baseball was increasingly being perceived as boring and behind the times and was rapidly being overtaken, if it had not been already, by the television-fueled popularity of football. Ballplayers making the major leagues in the 1960s were a part of America's counterculture generation. While most did not make waves because of the potential harm to their careers, some began expressing their individuality in appearance, both by growing their hair longer, rather than keeping the traditional conservative crewcut, and by finding ways to make their uniforms more form-fitting.

The Yankees' Joe Pepitone was among the first major leaguers to draw notoriety for his long hair and the tight fit of his uniform. Much (fun) was made of the blow-drier he kept in his locker. He fashioned himself along the lines of Joe Namath, the New York Jets quarterback who "guaranteed" a 1969 Super Bowl victory and was one of the first sports stars to publicly identify as a playboy. Pepitone, a Yankee since 1962, fancied himself similarly as a man-about-town—except, of course, he was no Broadway Joe. Nor was he Willie Mays, who had his uniforms tailored for a slim fit. He did not lead the Yankees to the pennant their first year after Mantle retired. His team-leading 27 home runs in 1969 were nowhere close to the league leaders, and he was not by any stretch a superstar. The next year he was no longer even a Yankee; he, his locks, and his blow-drier were traded to the Houston Astros. Some black players—Giants second baseman Tito Fuentes for one, decried by many as a "hot dog," and Reggie Jackson for another—expressed their individuality by calling attention to themselves on the playing field, including by handling routine fielding plays with showoff flair or posturing after a big hit. These were things that antagonized baseball traditionalists, including the owners who wrote out their paychecks and the baseball scribes who remembered the understated style of most of yesterday's heroes.

By the mid-1970s, longer hair—though not hippie-length—was much more prominent on players' Topps baseball cards, and major leaguers, their clubs bowing to the new reality of a major cultural shift in America, were nearly all wearing form-fitting uniforms. On the hair front, many African American players had styled Afros, although few as expansive as Cleveland outfielder Oscar Gamble's. Most owners were at first resistant to long-haired expressions of individuality before relenting to the tenor of the times. At least one, Athletics owner Charlie Finley, widely disliked by his fellow owners, not only allowed such a "subversive" look but even encouraged it, if for no other reason than to poke at the exclusive fraternity to which he belonged and which didn't want him. Thanks to Finley, facial hair, gone from the game since the end of the nineteenth century, was back with the Oakland A's, perhaps best exemplified by the cartoonish waxed handlebar mustache, complete with villainous curls at both ends, sported by ace reliever Rollie Fingers. Finley also gave certain of his pitchers a "caricature" to individualize them. At his direction, righthander Jim Hunter became Catfish. Finley thought John Odom's fifthgrade nickname was cool, so Blue Moon it was. Vida Blue's true name was so unique there was no need for Finley to think of something else.

George Steinbrenner, who bought the Yankees in December 1973, was the opposite of Finley. He insisted that rejuvenating the Yankees' winning tradition—the Yankees had not won a pennant since 1964—meant maintaining a certain decorum in appearance. So no long hair on the Yankees. Oscar Gamble had to dramatically cut back his outsized Afro after he was traded to New York in 1976.

* * *

Major-league owners were not so accommodating to their players' push for greater equality in their relationships with the front office. The civil rights battle against segregation and institutional denial to blacks of the full panoply of their constitutional rights—including unfettered access to the polls—and the widespread conviction that the government was both mismanaging and lying about its conduct in the Vietnam War fed into a fundamental narrative, particularly gripped by young adults, that nobody over 30 could be trusted, especially not those in authority. While Major League Baseball, although it had to deal with the subtext, was assiduous in avoiding having to take any position on race relations or the war other than protecting its institutional interests, it could not do so when major-league players, consistent with the calling out of inequality and authority-challenging ethos that characterized the prevailing cultural climate, began pushing back at the owners on the terms of their employment.

Institutionally, Major League Baseball hated the very idea of players' unions, and always had, mostly because of the threat they posed to the sacrosanct reserve clause that owners interpreted to keep players perpetually under club control even in the absence of a signed contract for any one season. The few players' unions there had been in the nineteenth and early twentieth centuries, and one short-lived one in 1946 after World War II, were ineffectual in negotiating with the owners, whose basic philosophy was "Just Say No." Players' unions generally died quickly from players' disillusionment and fears of antagonizing the power brokers who controlled the game.

The Major League Baseball Players Association, organized with the help of an outside attorney in 1953, primarily to keep the heat on franchise owners concerning the status and solvency of the players' pension fund, was more an adjunct to the power structure of the owner-run enterprise called Major League Baseball than an independent union acting on behalf of the players' best interests. The MLBPA did not engage in collective bargaining with the owners on behalf of the players. It had no full-time professional staff. And since 1960 it had a legal adviser who reassured the owners that his "primary concern will be what's in the best interest of baseball," not the players, and who told a congressional hearing in 1964 that major-league players "have it so good" they "[don't] know what to ask for next." The last thing the owners wanted was a real players' union led by an outsider with relevant labor relations and negotiating expertise they could not control.

The one issue the players did care about was the owners' contributions to their pension fund, which the owners agreed to in 1946 as a means of short-circuiting player support for the short-lived American Baseball Guild organized by Robert Murphy. By the mid-1960s the current pension fund was due to expire, and several influential players—Robin Roberts and Jim Bunning at the forefront—wanted their union to be led by a practiced negotiator to ensure that the fund was not only maintained but also enhanced by greater contributions from the significant increase in television broadcast revenue for the All-Star Game and World Series that went into funding their pension plan. Into that environment stepped Marvin Miller, a tough-minded longstanding labor relations negotiator most recently with the United Steelworkers of America, one of the country's most powerful unions. Like Murphy, Miller did not come from the baseball world.

Marvin Miller was *institutional* Major League Baseball's worst nightmare. He upended the longstanding paradigm promoted by owners and the commissioner of baseball, who ostensibly stood for the "best interests of the game" rather than the best interests of the owners, that conditioned players to believe that the structure and integrity of Major League Baseball would be destroyed by an activist union—especially one devoted to a "fair deal" for the players, to borrow President Truman's words from his 1949 State of the Union Address calling for a wide range of domestic policy reforms, including fair wages and antidiscrimination in employment. So conditioned, many players were at first wary and skeptical of Miller, whom the owners tarred by innuendo with the odor of a stereotypical corrupt union boss with mob ties, such as portrayed in the 1954 Academy Award–winning film *On the Waterfront*, and in 1960s real life by Jimmy Hoffa, among whose crimes was misusing funds from the Teamsters' Union pension fund. Perceptions matter, and even though Miller was anything but the bare-knuckles firebrand many Americans thought union leaders to be, baseball's owners were perfectly fine with the insinuation, even if they didn't come right out and say it. Results, of course, matter more. And Marvin Miller got results, making the owners' nightmare come true and winning the allegiance of his union's membership. Well, most of them, anyway.

Catching the owners in an illegal redistribution of money from the pension fund and sidestepping their refusal to fully disclose the value of their television contract, Miller earned the players' trust by negotiating an agreement in which players no longer had to contribute to the fund and that included a fixed pension contribution from the owners instead of a percentage of the television contract that the owners would not allow the union to study. But Miller did not stop there. In his first years as executive director of the players' union, Miller negotiated a series of collective bargaining agreements with Major League Baseball that chipped away at the owners' stranglehold on players' rights. In 1968, in the first-ever collective bargaining agreement for any sport, Miller secured a substantial boost in the minimum major-league salary, increased meal money allowances, standardized contracts, and formalized procedures for player grievances. Two years later he got the owners to agree to have player grievances heard by an independent arbitrator—a concession by the owners with consequential implications that did not, for the moment, cover the reserve clause, because neither the owners nor the union wanted to address the issue pending the outcome of Curt Flood's case, still in litigation, against baseball's antitrust exemption. Marvin Miller had the patience to wait until the time was right.

Ironically, Bowie Kuhn, whose promotion in February 1969 from National League assistant general counsel to commissioner of baseball was for want of any better alternative to replace William Eckert, proved to be the perfect foil for Marvin Miller. Eckert's seven-year contract to serve as commissioner was terminated after just three years because he was seen as ineffectual and too passive in the role. Kuhn's hardline opening stance as the owners' spokesman at the beginning of negotiations over the first CBA probably reassured them he'd have their backs as commissioner, but just weeks after assuming the office, faced with players threatening en masse not to sign contracts for the upcoming 1969 season, Kuhn backed down to union demands on a new pension agreement. Angrily embarrassed, Kuhn made it his mission thereafter to assert the prerogatives of an all-powerful czar, as had baseball's first commissioner, Judge Kenesaw Mountain Landis.

Those, however, were different times. Landis took charge right after the Black Sox scandal that impugned the integrity of the game itself. Kuhn's efforts to circumvent the union to impose disciplinary actions without due process were almost always overturned when they went to arbitration and had the unintended consequence of strengthening Miller's standing with the players—as did the hard line Kuhn took on the reserve clause whenever the issue came up. If Kuhn and the owners believed the players would not stand united if the owners held fast to what they *knew* was in the best interests of baseball, they proved very mistaken.

'Twas Marvin Miller had the leverage.

16

FROM PITCHERS RULE TO THE DH RULE

The year 1968, in no particular order: The Tet Offensive escalates the war in Vietnam to near-intolerable levels for Americans. Walter Cronkite, America's preeminent evening news anchor and arguably the most trusted man in America, declares, "[I]t seems now more certain than ever that the bloody experience in Vietnam is to end in a stalemate," effectively yanking the pillars out from under the government's rationale for being there. Embattled by the Vietnam War—"Hey, hey, hey, LBJ, how many kids did you kill today?"—President Johnson decides not to seek reelection. Martin Luther King Jr. is assassinated. Robert F. Kennedy is assassinated. The television highlights of the Democratic National Convention in Chicago are more about protests and protester-police violence in the streets than about politics. There's rioting in Paris. The Soviet Union crushes Czechoslovakia's democratizing Prague Spring by sending in the troops. George Wallace runs as a third-party candidate. Richard Nixon has a secret plan to end the war in Vietnam. Nixon beats Vice President Hubert Humphrey to become 37th president of the United States. The Rolling Stones release a song with a hard-driving samba beat, a terrific guitar solo by Keith Richards, and Mick Jagger putting seductive menace to words that seemed to summarize it all in "Sympathy for the Devil." And 1968 was the Year of the Pitcher. It came exactly 60 years after another Year of the Pitcher—1908, back in baseball's deadball days.

The years 1963, when the upper strike zone was expanded from the armpits to the top of the batter's shoulders, to 1968 were the lowest-scoring run environment in Major League Baseball since Babe Ruth's home runs ushered out the Deadball Era in 1920. Even though reliable bullpens were by now an established necessity and American League pitchers completed less than 23 percent of their starts and NL pitchers finished 27 percent of theirs, these were years of dominant starting pitchers who typically took the ball every four days, threw hard, and expected to finish what they started. There were 43 20-game winners. Eighteen pitchers threw 300 innings in a single season and another 28 threw at least 275 innings. Sandy Koufax struck out more than 300 batters three times, and Sam McDowell did so once. And 12 qualifying pitchers averaged more than one strikeout an inning—something that had been done only three times before, and not once until Herb Score fanned 9.7 batters per 9 innings in 1955, his rookie season.

In the last seven years of his major-league career before calling it quits at the age of 30, because he could not tolerate the pain in his "left arm of God" any longer, Koufax made strikeout victims of more than 26 percent of the batters he faced, 1,910 returning to the dugout in the 1,807⅔ innings he pitched. In 1962 Koufax became the first qualifying pitcher in history to strike out more than 10 batters per 9 innings—10.5, to be exact—a mark McDowell, another left-handed power pitcher, exceeded when his strikeout ratio was 10.7 per 9 in 1965. Pitching for the Cleveland Indians, McDowell never had the privilege of pitching for a competitive team but was every bit as overpowering as Koufax. Sudden Sam, as he was not-so-affectionately known by those who confronted him with a bat, struck out 1,829 batters in 1,736 innings—one-fourth of those who stepped to the plate against him—between 1964 and 1970, exceeding a strikeout an inning six times in seven years. Don Drysdale and Bob Gibson, and, by the late 1960s, Tom Seaver and Ferguson Jenkins, also had fearsome reputations as hard throwers against whom it was dangerous to dig in.

There had been a significant decline in scoring since major-league teams averaged 4.5 runs a game in 1962, beginning with a precipitous drop to 3.95 runs a game in 1963—the lowest since the wartime years of 1943. By 1967, scoring was down to 3.77 runs a game. Even then, nobody expected what happened in 1968. The number of complete games increased 15 percent, from 782 to 897. Shutouts were up by 24 percent, from 274 to 339. Major-league hitters were held to a collective .237 batting average, down from .242 the previous year and the lowest in major-league history, including the nineteenth century. Just six batters hit over .300, five of them in the National League. Carl Yastrzemski won the American League batting title with a .301 average, only one other batter in the league hit .290, and just nine batted .275 or better.

The Year of the Pitcher began with four complete-game shutouts on opening day by Mel Stottlemyre, a 1–0 winner; Chris Short and Dean Chance, both winning by 2–0; and Sonny Siebert. Don Drysdale pitched a four-hit complete-game shutout in his first start of the season three days later, which is significant because on May 14, Drysdale pitched the first of six complete-game shutouts in a row—five on three days of rest and one on four—to break the record of 55⅔ consecutive shutout innings held by all-time great Walter Johnson since 1913. Johnson's string, however, included only four complete-game shutouts, following an Opening Day start in which he pitched eight scoreless innings after surrendering a run in the first, as well as the equivalent of a complete game in three relief outings in which he did not surrender a run.

The first two of Drysdale's shutouts were tight 1–0 victories, and the third was 2–0. His streak was at its greatest jeopardy after 44 innings in the ninth inning of a game on May 31 against the Dodgers' hated-rival Giants when Drysdale loaded the bases with nobody out on two walks sandwiching a single and proceeded to hit batter Dick Dietz with a pitch, presumably forcing in a run. Since he was more than 11 innings shy of the record, it is quite likely that plate umpire Harry Wendelstedt did not have history in mind when he voided the hit-by-pitch by declaring Dietz made no effort to evade the pitch, as the rule book stipulates he must. The bases were still loaded and there were still no outs, but Drysdale got Dietz on a short fly to left, got the next batter to hit into a force play at the plate, and retired the Giants' last hope on a popup to first. Drysdale pitched a shutout in his next start to get him within two innings of Johnson's record. After four shutout innings in his next start, the Phillies finally scored against Drysdale to end his streak at 58⅔ innings.

On June 6, two days after Drysdale's sixth straight shutout and two days before his scoreless-innings streak came to an end, Bob Gibson pitched a three-hit shutout against the Astros. That evened his record at 5–5, which belied the fact that Gibson's earned-run average was a superb 1.52. Then Gibson got down to business. Throwing shutouts in each of his next four starts, Gibson ran his streak to five in a row, putting Drysdale's record for consecutive shutouts in peril less than a month after it was set when the two aces took the mound against each other in Los

Angeles on July 1. The Dodgers ended the drama early by scoring a first-inning run—the only run Gibson allowed that day as he beat Drysdale to run his record to 10–5 and drop his ERA to a microscopic 1.13. Gibson went on to win 15 games in a row—all complete games, 10 of them shutouts—with one no decision. Allowing just 7 runners on base by hit or walk every 9 innings, his ERA during that stretch was 0.68. He gave up just 6 runs in his 12 starts in June and July, throwing 108 innings. At the end of the season, Gibson's 22–9 record with 28 complete games, 13 of them shutouts, in 34 starts was impressive enough; his 1.12 earned-run average was bettered in the twentieth century only by Dutch Leonard in 1914, whose 0.96 ERA was accomplished in 80 fewer innings.

On August 24, when Gibson's 15-game winning streak came to an end in a 6–4 loss to Pittsburgh in which three runs were unearned, Detroit's Denny McLain lost back-to-back games for the first time that season. McLain's record stood at 25–5, and with five weeks to go and starting every fourth day, he figured to have as many as nine starts to win the five games he needed to become the first 30-game winner since Dizzy Dean in 1934. Unlike Gibson, already well-established as an elite pitcher, McLain stood in the ranks of the very good with potential to be great. He had been a 20-game winner in 1966, his second season as a core regular in the Tigers' starting rotation, but dropped to 17–16 in 1967. It took McLain just five more starts to win his 30th game, and the start after that he won his 31st—the most by an American League pitcher since Lefty Grove won 31 in 1931. Grove finished that year, which was in a hitters' era, with a 31–4 record and league-leading 2.06 ERA. McLain finished his season with a 31–6 record and 1.96 earned-run average, which was only fourth in the American League in this Year of the Pitcher. Cleveland's Luis Tiant, 21–9 in 1968, led the league with a 1.60 ERA and in shutouts with 9, while striking out 264 batters in 258⅓ innings.

The day before McLain won his 31st game of the season, the Cardinals' Ray Washburn pitched a no-hitter at San Francisco's Candlestick Park, walking five and striking out eight. His no-hitter came the very day after the Giants' Gaylord Perry outdueled Gibson to win, 1–0, on his own no-hitter at Candlestick in which he walked two and struck out nine. Back-to-back days. Same ballpark. Same two teams. Back-to-back no-hitters. It was Washburn's fourth shutout of the year and his seventh complete game. There were five no-hitters in 1968, including a perfect

Denny McLain, 31–6 in 1968, is the only pitcher since the Great Depression to win 30 games. No pitcher has won more than 27 in the half century since. © *Photofest*.

game by Oakland's Catfish Hunter on May 8—the first in the American League during the regular season in 46 years.

* * *

As riveting as the extraordinary pitching performances of 1968 were, Major League Baseball recognized that hitters being mired in a new dark age was not the kind of game fans wanted to see. If pitchers were king of the hill, baseball's solution was to lower the hill. The summit of the mound from where the pitcher began his windup with his back foot on the rubber had officially been 15 inches since 1903. In some ballparks, most notably Dodger Stadium in the days of Koufax and Drysdale, it was even higher, as there was little effort to enforce height. Pitching from up high allowed pitchers to generate greater momentum at the moment they released the ball, and the greater angle gave their stuff more movement. This was a particular advantage to hard-throwing pitchers.

Drawing the inevitable conclusion that pitchers had it too good, the maximum height of the pitching mound was reduced by one-third the very next year, to 10 inches. At the same time, the strike zone was shortened back to where it had been before 1963, between the batter's armpits and the top of his knees, giving pitchers less space to work with, and umpires in practice began calling it tighter than that. That combination of changes had a profound effect in 1969. It helped that a second round of expansion—four new teams—diluted the overall quality of major-league talent, perhaps especially among pitchers. Team scoring increased overnight, from 3.42 runs a game in 1968 to 4.07. Major League Baseball's collective batting average increased 11 percentage points to .248. The number of .300 hitters doubled from five to ten in the National League and increased from Yastrzemski alone in 1968 to six in the American League.

Meanwhile, in the eight-team Triple-A International League, average runs per game in 1969 jumped from 3.98 the previous year to 4.48, the league batting average from .252 to .269, and, to pitchers' chagrin, the league ERA from 3.60 to 4.24. Why? A new experimental rule was in effect that allowed managers to use a designated hitter for the pitcher. The DH experiment in one of baseball's three Triple-A leagues, just below the major-league level, was a direct consequence of the Year of the Pitcher. If lowering the mound and shortening the strike zone weren't going to reestablish a more acceptable balance pitchers and batters, baseball needed a more drastic fallback option. The very concept of a designated hitter for the pitcher was controversial because baseball had always been played with all nine men in the lineup having the dual role of playing a position in the field and taking his turn at bat. That was elemental. Everybody, including the pitcher, was a two-way player.

While hitting and fielding one's position were both disciplines that required concentration and mastery, fielding was more an athletic endeavor that did not require the exacting demands of hitting. Players could focus on improving their hitting without sacrificing much in the way of time and effort on fielding practice. Pitching, on the other hand, was a discipline even more exacting than hitting, if for no other reason than that the pitcher is the only player who has a role on every play. Position players have a say on any given play only when a ball is hit or thrown to them, or just once every nine times through the batting order. Pitchers, whose effectiveness is the key determinant in how games unfold, must necessarily focus on their craft to give their team the best chance to win. Batting practice is just that for pitchers—*practice*—rather than a rigorous effort to refine their skills. A great many pitchers love to hit, even if they aren't very good at it, but all realize that their priority for team and livelihood is mastering their pitches, control, and command of the game. Hence, historically, while there have been a number of very good hitting pitchers—Babe Ruth (who was great and went on to devote his full time to the discipline of hitting), Wes Ferrell, Red Ruffing, Bob Lemon, Don Newcombe, Warren Spahn, and Don Drysdale, to name the most prominent—pitchers in general are notoriously bad hitters. They are the closest thing to an automatic out in the batting order.

The idea of designating a pinch-hitter to bat for the pitcher had been bandied about, infrequently and quickly forgotten, since the nineteenth century. Such a rule had been considered by baseball owners three previous times. The first time was following the 1905 season when Connie Mack, fresh from his Athletics being limited to a .155 batting average in their five-game World Series loss to the New York Giants (in which his pitchers went 1-for-13), made the argument that advocates of the designated hitter would seize on 70 years later—that fans would much rather watch an actual hitter rather than a feckless pitcher bat. Mack had two more practical reasons as well. A designated hitter would allow young players who would otherwise just be sitting on the bench get in-game batting experience as part of their grooming to become position regulars, and it would avoid pitchers tiring themselves out having to run the bases in games they were pitching in the hot summer months. Getting little positive response, Mack did not raise the issue when the major-league rules committee met later that winter. The second time was in 1914 by team owners in the upstart Federal League, which unilaterally designated itself a "major" league. They decided against such a provocative move. The last time was after the 1928 season when National League president John Heydler proposed the idea. No action was taken.

Mack's suggestion in 1905 followed back-to-back seasons when team scoring dipped below four runs a game for the first time in over a decade. Although it would have clearly distinguished the Federals from the two well-established major leagues, a DH rule would not have prevented the

Federal League from its inevitable collapse after just two seasons. The third time the DH concept came up in 1928, generating offense was hardly a problem; it was the middle of the Lively Ball Era, when .300 hitters were bountiful and pitchers certainly welcomed pitching to their fellow pitchers—the one guy they'd face in most games who was an easy out.

In 1973, four years after the DH experiment did *not* ruin baseball as fans knew it in the International League's exercise of the concept, the designated hitter came to Major League Baseball—but only in the American League. Scoring and batting averages in both leagues increased in 1969 and 1970—the first two years of the new expansion, the lower mound, and the smaller strike zone—but declined in both 1971 and 1972. While the two leagues were comparable in their 1969 recovery from the Year of the Pitcher, the American League lagged behind each of the next three years. From 1970 to 1972, AL teams averaged 7 percent fewer runs, batted .245 compared to the NL's .253, and had a league-wide slugging percentage 12 percentage points lower than the .374 mark put up by National League hitters. The offensive difference between the two leagues was most pronounced in 1972, with NL teams averaging 3.9 runs a game, compared to the AL's 3.47, and hitting for a much higher batting average (.248 to .239) and slugging percentage (.365 to .343). AL pitchers' contributions at the plate amounted to a .145 batting average and .182 slugging percentage, almost exactly the same as how NL pitchers fared at the plate in 1972.

Faced with those numbers, American League club owners voted in favor of adopting the DH rule. The National League was opposed. Major-league owners collectively agreed that the AL's use of a designated hitter taking the pitcher's spot in the lineup would be a three-year experiment beginning in 1973, after which there would be another vote on the future of the DH. Traditionalists were opposed on principle, especially to the idea that the designated hitter could evolve into a highly specialized position for those who could hit but not do anything else well on the ball field. Others worried that the DH would diminish the importance of managerial decisions—and the second-guessing of them that helps feed fans' enthusiasm for the game. Most obviously, the DH rule meant managers were spared from having to decide when and whether to pinch-hit for the pitcher. Instead, AL managers' decisions about whether and when to replace the pitcher could be determined entirely by his effectiveness and the game situation. But there were also a great many enthusiasts for the new rule precisely because it meant more offense. And who wants to watch a pitcher hit, anyway?

Introducing the DH into the American League made an immediate difference. Offensive numbers were up in both leagues in 1973, but much more so in the AL. With designated hitters combining for more home runs than batters at any of the fielding positions, scoring was up in the American League by nearly 30 percent, compared with 11 percent in the NL; the league batting average increased by 20 percentage points in one year, to .259; and AL batters' slugging percentage was up nearly 40 points, to .381. (NL batters collectively hit .254 with a .376 slugging percentage.) Designated hitters hit a collective .257; NL pitchers, still taking their turn at bat, hit a pathetic .149. The DH experiment was a smashing success. After three years, the American League made it permanent. The National League continued to play baseball the old-fashioned way, with pitchers having to bat for themselves.

* * *

The DH also had a profound and immediate impact on how American League managers used their pitching staffs. While NL managers were still having to make the fraught decision of removing an effective pitcher—even their ace—for a pinch-hitter late in a close game, especially if their team was behind by a run, AL managers were able to keep their starting pitcher in the game for as long as he was pitching well, even late in the game on the losing end of a pitchers' duel, because the pitcher didn't have to take his turn at bat. The difference was stark. In the first four years of the DH rule, 1973 to 1976, just under one-third of all starts by American League pitchers ended as complete games, compared to about 23 percent in the National League. Nineteen American League pitchers threw more than 300 innings between 1973 and 1976, six more than once and Gaylord Perry three times, compared to just three in the National League. In both 1973 and 1974, seven AL pitchers had more than 300 innings pitched. The last time any league had that many pitchers throw more than 300 innings was the NL in 1908.

More telling of the impact the DH rule had on the game longevity of starting pitchers was the fact that in the American League, losing pitchers going the distance in games they started increased to 32 percent of total complete games in the first four years of the designated hitter. The last time losing pitchers accounted for such a high percentage of complete games—other than in the American League in 1945, the year of greatest impact on major-league rosters during World War II—was in the Deadball Era and the very beginning of the Lively Ball Era in 1920 and 1921. Complete-game losses by NL pitchers remained at about 13 percent of the total—only slightly less than from 1963 to 1968.

No American League manager was even close to as extreme in making his starting pitchers go the distance as Oakland's Billy Martin in 1980 and 1981, whose Athletics, in contrast to the Yankees he previously managed in the new DH era, had a weak bullpen. In 1980 his five starting pitchers—Rick Langford, Steve McCatty, Mike Norris, Brian Kingman, and Matt Keough, all right-handers—none of whom were established big-league starters, started all but three of the A's 162 games and completed 94 of them. The next year they finished 60 of their 109 starts in a strike-shortened season. That percentage of complete games had not been seen since the deadball days. Before the A's in 1980 and 1981, the last time a major-league team had half as many complete games as scheduled games was in 1954, when Phillies pitchers threw 78 complete games and Indians pitchers 77 in a 154-game season. Martin's strategy was ultimately unsustainable and probably explains why none of his five starters were as effective after 1981.

The percentage of complete-game victories by American League starting pitchers was about 7 percentage points higher than in the National League, but also at about the same level it was in 1968—the Year of the Pitcher. Rather than this being inconsistent with the much higher percentage of complete-game losses, it more accurately reflects that the DH rule did not cause AL managers to rethink their use of relief pitchers—especially relievers the quality of Oakland's Rollie Fingers, New York's Sparky Lyle, Detroit's John Hiller, or Minnesota's Bill Campbell—to save tight ballgames in the late innings. Because of the designated hitter, managers had the luxury of allowing starting pitchers to go the distance in games they had well in hand or were pitching well on the short end of the score. But when it came to holding on to a slim lead, especially if the opposing team got the tying run on base, there was every incentive to bring in their relief ace to save the day. Fingers entered the game with runners already on base in 197 of the 283 games he pitched between 1973 and 1976, when he was arguably the best reliever in baseball. For Lyle, the numbers were 165 of the 250 games he pitched in relief those same years. In 1973, when Hiller led the league with 38 saves and was 10–5 in relief, 52 of his 65 relief appearances came with runners on base. When Campbell led the league with 31 saves and went 13–9 in 69 relief appearances for Boston in 1977, he walked into a runners-on-base situation 59 times.

Although spared from having to make pitching changes based on whether to pinch-hit for offensively deficient pitchers late in the game, the percentage of complete games by American League starting pitchers began to decline after 1976. By 1990, complete games had dropped from about 24 percent in the American League at the end of the 1970s to 10 percent—exactly the same percentage as in the National League, where complete games accounted for about 15 percent of all starts a decade earlier. In both leagues the percentage decline in complete games since 1976 was explained entirely by a steady decline in complete-game wins—a metric different, to be clear, from the percentage of complete games that are victories. In close games certainly, but also to avoid having starting pitchers throw any more innings than absolutely necessary in games where their teams had a big lead, managers in both leagues were in sync in relying on their bullpens to secure wins. The percentage of victories for which a reliever got credit for a save surpassed 50 percent in the NL for the first time in 1987, and in the AL in 1988.

It would not be incorrect to suggest that a manager's reliance on his relief ace to save victories in close ballgames, even if his pitcher in the game was still keeping opposing hitters at bay, betrayed a defensive posture of not wanting to risk a loss by staying some undefinable moment too long with that pitcher. In a much more expansive media environment than the past, where managers' decisions and players' performances in game-critical situations were being dissected and analyzed to an unprecedented extent, that was certainly part of it. But it was also sound strategy because of how specialized bullpens were becoming, the quality in terms of command and their arsenal of pitches—often just a singular "out" pitch—of teams' ace relievers, and the emergence of those ace relievers as closers to put an emphatic exclamation point on a victory. It was no accident in the American League during the 1980s that clubs with a top-tier relief ace—the Yankees, for example, with Goose Gossage and then Dave Righetti; the Royals with Dan Quisenberry; the Blue Jays with Tom Henke; and, at the end of the decade, the Athletics with Dennis Eckersley—were among those with the fewest complete-game victories, notwithstanding having good starting pitchers and the flexibility that the DH gave managers to making pitching changes based entirely on game circumstances.

While the designated hitter rule might not have had the enduring effect of allowing American League managers to have their starting pitchers, especially their ace, go for the complete game in any start they were winning and pitching effectively, it continued to make a difference in the number and frequency of pitching changes between the two leagues. In addition to calling in relievers based on game circumstances when the opposing team was at bat, NL managers—unlike their AL counterparts— still had to contend with their pitchers being in the batting order. Many pitching changes in the National League continued to result from decisions to pinch-hit for the pitcher. The number of pitching changes in the two leagues was approximately equal, at 2.1 per noncomplete game between 1961 and 1972, when the rules were the same for both leagues. After the DH rule went in effect in 1973, NL managers typically averaged about 2.1 pitching changes in noncomplete games, compared to about 1.7 by AL managers through the early 1980s and 1.8 until the late 1980s. In 1990 the figures were about 2.3 in the National League and 2.2 in the American League. Perhaps somewhat surprisingly, starting pitchers averaged about the same ratio of innings-per-start most seasons in both leagues, with or without the DH.

* * *

For Major League Baseball, the designated hitter rule was an unqualified success, even if it was—and continues to be—limited to just the American League. While there remains some sentiment that all of Major League Baseball should play by the same rules—specifically, DH or no DH in both leagues—the fact that the two leagues were different turned out to be a good thing. For one thing, the DH difference has become a distinguishing characteristic of the two leagues. For another, it has promoted a spirited and endless—but endless in a good way—debate about the merits of the DH rule.

The DH rule did immediately boost scoring in the American League, as it was intended to do—by nearly 30 percent the first year alone. It also reestablished the AL's once-upon-a-time reputation for being a hitters' league. By eliminating the requirement that pitchers must bat for themselves, it may have widened the window for several American League pitchers to showcase that they could dominate a game from beginning to end in the manner that National League hurlers like Koufax, Marichal,

Gibson, Seaver, and Jenkins did in the 1960s and early 1970s. Most notably, Nolan Ryan in 1973, making 39 starts—the same as he had in 1972—pitched 26 complete games, compared to 20 the previous year, accounting for 42 more innings that helped him to 383 strikeouts—exactly one more than the record 382 Koufax fanned in 1965.

Some have argued Ryan would have had more than 400 strikeouts if he had been able to pitch to opposing pitchers, as Koufax did, instead of designated hitters. This argument ignores the fact that Ryan also did not have to hit, and so never had to leave the game for a pinch-hitter. In 16 of his 39 starts, Ryan either threw a complete game or pitched into the ninth inning in games that were decided by two runs or less—close enough margins that he might have been removed for a pinch-hitter in any of them when his turn came to bat in the late innings had there not been a DH to do his hitting for him. He was 10–6 in those starts in a season he finished with a 21–16 record. Only two of his starts were no-decision, and he had four in which he pitched extra innings.

One thing the DH rule did not do, at least at first, was cause teams to fill a roster spot with a player whose sole baseball skill was hitting. That kind of position specialization was a significant concern of at least one team owner when the DH concept was discussed in 1928. To be sure, in the 1970s oft-injured power-hitting outfielders Tony Oliva and Willie Horton were both able to extend their careers as full-time designated hitters—Oliva the last four years of his career, beginning in 1973, and Horton the last five years of his beginning in 1975. Some, like Don Baylor, Jim Rice, and Dave Kingman, were exceptional hitters but questionable outfielders at the beginning or the middle of their careers, and others entering the twilight of their careers, like Carl Yastrzemski and Reggie Jackson, split time as both position players and designated hitters. Young players being groomed to be in-the-field position players as soon as they were ready might start out in a DH role, as Orioles first base prospect Eddie Murray did in his 1977 rookie year. Baseball's first true professional DH was Hal McRae, an outstanding all-around player until at the age of 22 he suffered devastating leg and shoulder injuries that prevented him from sustaining a career as an everyday outfielder. In 1976 he became the Royals' regular DH, playing the outfield occasionally and hitting .298 with 115 home runs and 645 RBIs the next eight years.

By 1990 the DH was a specialized position for professional hitters only, to the extent they had already proven themselves as good-hitting position players. The stigma that a DH was much less than a complete ballplayer, held by many veterans, was by now evaporating with the realization it could lengthen careers. Especially after a fruitful career as a position player, there was no longer reason to be ashamed of any player's continuing ability to defy baseball age, which manifests itself most savagely in the field, because of his prowess with the bat. Harold Baines, seven years an outfielder, and Paul Molitor, 11 years an infielder, both went on to double the length of their careers as designated hitters.

Ted Williams, for whom hitting a baseball was all that mattered and playing defense an inconvenient if necessary afterthought, would have approved. Joe DiMaggio, who prided himself on his all-around skills and retired in part because he felt he was becoming a stumblebum in center field, would have been appalled. Don Drysdale and Bob Gibson, both of whom were decent hitters for pitchers—29 homers for the former, 24 for the latter—would have dumped the designated hitter on his ass, same as they would any other hitter trying for a better toehold against them.

17

O'S AND A'S AND THEIR WINNING WAYS

The first half dozen years of the divisional era in the American League were dominated by two clubs—the Baltimore Orioles, who won five of the first six Eastern Division titles and the first three pennants in the new East-West alignment, and the Oakland Athletics, who won five consecutive Western Division titles between 1971 and 1975 and followed the Orioles' three straight trips to the World Series with three straight of their own, all of which they won. Baltimore's "O's" were the epitome of a model franchise; Oakland's "A's" somehow succeeded despite being more akin to a dysfunctional family. Both won because they had a cadre of outstanding players as core regulars. And both teams got started on their winning way by young managers who were in rabble-rouser mode, hearkening back to the early twentieth-century days of John McGraw. They were Earl Weaver, 37 years old when he took charge of the Orioles at the All-Star break in 1968, and Dick Williams, a year older than Weaver, whose claim to fame was leading the 1967 Impossible Dream Red Sox team to an improbable American League pennant in his first year as a major-league manager.

Weaver, Williams, and Billy Martin—another rabble-rouser whose 1969 Twins won the AL West and a date with Weaver's Orioles in the first American League Championship Series in his managerial debut when he was 41—were part of a new generation of managers who had been scrappy ballplayers of at best modest ability only recently removed from tenuous playing careers. Weaver's 13-year playing career was all as a minor-league second baseman; Williams's 13 years in the majors were mostly as a reserve infielder/outfielder; and Martin was an overachieving second baseman on Stengel's 1950s Yankees best known for the fun-loving company he kept with Mantle and Ford. What they lacked in playing skills, they made up in baseball smarts and (as understood in today's vernacular) attitude. They were fiery, bringing new excitement to going nose-to-nose with the umpires. They were disciplinarians. They fought with their players—rhetorically, if not physically, although Martin in particular was not averse to fisticuffs with his. They were bombastic and did not suffer fools gladly. In the case of both Williams and Martin, that meant also fighting with the club owner. But most important, all three were an immediate success.

It's not as though baseball did not have more than its share of feisty, combative, profane, in-your-face, downright nasty, and altogether un-pleasant managers since the days of McGraw. Leo Durocher, to name but one, was certainly not going to win any Mr. Congeniality awards with major-league umpires. Every manager has had his moments of lunatic behavior, often calculated for effect on the umpires, the home crowd, or (perhaps most importantly) his players. But as the twentieth century marched on from its early barbarism, major-league managers in general had followed in the footsteps of Connie Mack, Joe McCarthy, and Bill McKechnie in becoming more self-contained. There was no question who was boss, but along with that responsibility they accepted accountability and an obligation to always demonstrate control. Williams, Weaver, and Martin broke with the paradigm of managers as paternalistic commanding presences, exemplified in the 1960s by the likes of Walt Alston, Ralph Houk, and Al Lopez—sort of a "father know best (so do what I say), but dad will fight the good fight if there is injustice on the playing field" model. The newcomers brought instead a "must always be fighting to survive in the Darwinian world of major-league baseball" attitude with them to the dugout. They were extraordinarily effective managers, with creative tension the buzz in their dugouts.

* * *

Frank Robinson was the heart and Brooks Robinson the soul of the Baltimore team Earl Weaver took charge of at the All-Star break in 1968. They were the only core regulars over 30 on an otherwise relatively young club destined for greatness. Weaver had managed in the Orioles farm system at every level since 1957, developing players and proving himself. Named to the coaching staff as manager-in-waiting at the beginning of the season, now Weaver's wait was over. Nobody was going to catch Detroit in 1968, but the Orioles were only a game and a half worse the rest of the way under the fiery Weaver, finishing second.

Entering the 1969 season, Weaver had the makings of a formidable club to challenge Detroit for the American League's first Eastern Division title. Boog Powell, a left-handed power hitter, and Brooks anchored the infield corners. Up the middle were second baseman Davey Johnson and Mark Belanger at shortstop. Left to right in the outfield were Don Buford, Paul Blair, and F. Robby. All except for Buford and Belanger—the latter's range, quickness, and sure-handedness on defense making up for his weaknesses as a hitter—were regulars on Baltimore's 1966 championship team; Belanger took over for 10-years-older Luis Aparicio in 1968 when the 12-year veteran shortstop was traded back to the White Sox for Buford. Left-handed batter Elrod Hendricks and right-handed Andy Etchebarren shared the catching duties.

Pitching was still a big question mark. A rash of arm problems and injuries that plagued the 1966 team's outstanding core of young starting pitchers—lefties Dave McNally and Steve Barber, and righties Wally Bunker and Jim Palmer—fatally undermined Baltimore's chances in 1967. The Orioles had given up on injury-plagued Barber and Bunker but were hopeful that budding phenom Palmer had recovered from the arm and shoulder problems that cost him two years and seemed possibly the end of his career. Fresh off a 22–10 record, including winning his first 12 decisions under new manager Weaver in 1968, McNally was the indisputable ace of the staff. Hedging their bets, the Orioles over the winter traded for Mike Cuellar, also a southpaw, whose signature pitch was the screwball. Cuellar had gone 36–32 for the Astros the three previous years. And Weaver was happy with his bullpen.

Baltimore got off to a fast start in baseball's new world of divisional alignments, winning the first three AL East titles by decisive margins of 19, 15, and 12 games. In 1969 and 1970 the Orioles were in first place to stay by the end of April; in 1971 it took them until early June. They won 109, 108, and 101 to become the third team in history—after the 1929–1931 Athletics and 1942–1944 Cardinals—with 100 wins three years in a row. In each of those years, another team in the AL East had at least 90 victories, so Baltimore was not in a division of patsies. Baltimore went on to sweep each of the first three American League Championship Series, beating Western Division winners Minnesota in 1969 and '70 and

Oakland in 1971. Winning the World Series proved more problematic. The 1969 Orioles were upended by the not-supposed-to-be-there Mets in five games. In 1970 they needed just five games to defeat the Cincinnati Reds in a series that featured one spectacular defensive play after another by Brooks Robinson. And in 1971 the Orioles went down in seven games to the Pittsburgh Pirates.

With the arguable exception of the Minnesota Twins, whose lineup featured Rod Carew, Tony Oliva, and Harmon Killebrew, the Orioles had the AL's most potent offense. Batting first, Buford was the Orioles' catalyst, with an on-base percentage of .405. Missing at least 18 games each year, mostly at the manager's discretion to account for his being in his early 30s, Buford had the distinction of scoring exactly 99 runs in each of the three straight years Baltimore went to the World Series. Batting third and fourth, F. Robby and Powell were at the center of things in all three of their pennants. Robinson batted .299 and belted 85 home runs from 1969 to 1971 while missing 69 games because of assorted injuries. Homering in both games of a doubleheader on September 13, 1971, Frank Robinson became the 11th player in major-league history to hit 500 home runs, a little more than a month after Killebrew hit his 500th. Powell slugged 37 homers and drove in 121 runs in 1969 to finish second to Killebrew in the MVP voting, and was elected Most Valuable Player in 1970 on the back of 35 homers and 114 RBIs. Brooks Robinson, like F. Robby and Buford already in his 30s, added to his collection of Gold Gloves—12 and counting in 1971—and hit 61 home runs those years. Blair and Belanger were also recognized as the best defensively at their positions, and Blair added 54 home runs.

Even if the pitchers were second-tier stars compared to the two Mr. Robinsons, an exceptional starting rotation, backed by terrific defense, was what most distinguished this Orioles team. Palmer, McNally, and Cuellar were the best threesome of starting pitchers in the American League, and quite possibly in the majors, since Cleveland's Lemon, Wynn, and Garcia in the 1950s. Cuellar (23–11) and McNally (20–7) topped the 1969 O's in wins, and Palmer's 16–4 record led the league. All three were 20-game winners in 1970, and in 1971 they were joined by Pat Dobson, acquired over the winter from San Diego, to become only the second team in history, after the 1920 White Sox, to have four 20-game winners on staff. No club has had four 20-game winners since; neither has any team since had as many as three 20-game winners in back-to-back seasons. Both these facts are likely to stand the test of time, at least until there is a fundamental change in the prevailing paradigm of relying on relievers to finish up for starting pitchers.

Baltimore's winning ways came to a temporary end in 1972. The Orioles began that season with a major handicap of their own doing, having made the same mistake the Cincinnati Reds had in 1966 by trading the now-37-year-old Frank Robinson to LA and getting four unproven prospects in return. From 1966 to 1971 the only player in the American League *possibly* better than Frank Robinson was Boston's Carl Yastrzemski. The Orioles quickly learned that, regardless of his age-related diminishing performance, F. Robby's productivity and leadership were impossible to replace. They could have used his fiery on-the-field leadership going for a fourth-straight division title and pennant in 1972, when they held a 1½-game lead on September 1, then lost 17 of their final 29 games to finish third, 5½ games behind Billy Martin's Tigers. Pitching was not the problem: Palmer again won 20, all four of their primary starters had ERAs under 3.00, and for the fourth year in a row the Orioles gave up the fewest runs in the majors. Without Frank, the Orioles' offense struggled mightily. Their .229 team batting average was second lowest in the league, and only the four teams with the fewest wins in the American League scored fewer runs.

With Brooks and Boog Powell showing their age and 35-year-old Don Buford retiring after a very subpar year, the Orioles were now in rebuilding mode. Thanks to a strong farm system where prospects were taught to play baseball the "Orioles Way," Baltimore recovered quickly in 1973, finishing on top of the AL East by eight games, their 97 wins the most in the league. For much of the summer, the division race was a tight affair, with Baltimore, New York, Detroit, and Boston all in contention through mid-August. But winning 17 of 19 in the middle of August, including 14 in a row, allowed the Orioles to open up a six-game lead by the end of the month, which they widened by winning 21 of their final 32 games. Baltimore's rising stars in their first or second years were outfielders Al Bumbry (a left-handed batter) and Don Baylor (right-handed), who platooned in left field, and second baseman Bobby Grich. The 1973 Orioles dramatically ramped up their offensive game, batting .266 as a team and scoring just four runs fewer than Oakland's league-leading 758, and their stellar pitching and defense gave up the fewest runs in the majors for the fifth straight year. Palmer was a 20-game winner for the fourth year in a row to win his first of three Cy Young Awards. Cuellar won 18 and McNally 17.

The Orioles' 1974 defense of their division title seemed doomed on August 29 when they started the day eight back of the division-leading Red Sox with a losing 63–65 record and only 34 games to go. They went on to win 28 of those games, including 16 of their last 18 and a season-ending 9-game winning streak to finish two games ahead of the rapidly improving Yankees. Baltimore accomplished this despite Palmer, in the midst of eight 20-win seasons in nine years, spending nearly two full months on the disabled list with arm problems and going only 7–12. Cuellar won eight of his last nine decisions, all complete games, including all six in September, to finish with 22 wins. In his 17th year as Orioles third baseman, 37-year-old Brooks Robinson had the last good season of his career, batting .288 and winning his 15th consecutive Gold Glove Award. He would win another the next year, which proved to be his last as a regular. By the time he retired in 1977, Brooks Robinson could lay claim to being Baltimore's most beloved player. Cal Ripken Jr. has a more recent claim to the title of most popular Oriole ever, but his popularity is really based more on respect and admiration for his unfathomable work ethic.

* * *

Earl Weaver's Orioles failed to advance to the World Series in either 1973 or 1974 despite having the best record in the league, falling victim in the ALCS both times to the new most dominant team in the American League, if not all Major League Baseball—the Oakland Athletics. No sooner had Baltimore won three straight American League pennants at the beginning of the divisional era than the Athletics in 1972 began their own string of three pennants in a row. They also won three World Series in a row. It was a tour de force by a franchise that had gone from being an early twentieth-century dynasty in Philadelphia, winning nine of the American League's first 31 pennants, to 40 years in the baseball wilderness, 13 of them in Kansas City from 1955 to 1967, before finally finishing atop the AL West in 1971.

Unlike the former St. Louis Browns, who systematically, if patiently, built a winning tradition in Baltimore, the Athletics became a punchline for ineptitude and dysfunction after Chicago businessman Arnold Johnson bought out Connie Mack and moved the storied Philadelphia franchise to Kansas City. That didn't change when Johnson's death in 1960 necessitated finding a new owner. He was Charles O. Finley, another Chicago-based businessman. K.C.'s Athletics had losing season after losing season. There were 10 managers in 13 years, only two of whom were around for two full seasons. Their best player in the 1950s was flashy first baseman Vic Power, who debuted with the A's their final year in Philadelphia and was traded to Cleveland in June 1958 for an outfielder named Roger Maris, whose 28 home runs that year and 16 the next aroused the Yankees' interest. Two years later, Maris was a New York Yankee. Before the Athletics arrived, Kansas City had been home to one of the Yankees' top farm clubs. Even though the A's were an American League rival, under Johnson they still seemed to be a Yankee farm club, with promising prospects going from what had once been a frontier town to the big city. Maris joined Hector Lopez, Clete Boyer, Ralph Terry, Art Ditmar, Bobby Shantz, and Ryne Duren as former Kansas City A's in pinstripes. All were instrumental to the Yankees' kickstarting their second string of five consecutive pennants.

Even though Finley put an end to Kansas City being a player pipeline to the Yankees, the Athletics had little continuity in core regulars from one year to the next. Their longest-tenured core regulars in the 1960s, each for five years before being traded elsewhere, were second baseman Jerry Lumpe, shortstop Wayne Causey, and third baseman Ed Charles. In 1964, Kansas City fans were entertained by the power tandem of Jim Gentile and Rocky Colavito, whose combined 62 homers were not enough to prevent the Athletics from finishing dead last with 105 losses. The next year, Colavito and his 34 home runs were in Cleveland, Gentile was gone in early June, and the Athletics had a new teammate—well, a mascot, anyway—"Charlie O," a real live mule. Charlie Finley was determined that his team would be, if not a competitive success, an attraction. The mule was a part of that. Finley also built a zoo and a sheep pasture, minded by a shepherd, beyond the outfield fence; installed a popup mechanical rabbit behind the plate to hand the umpire new baseballs; introduced a yellow cab to taxi relievers in from the bullpen; and outfitted his ballclub in sleeveless yellow uniforms with green trim that were hardly in the traditionalist mold.

These sorts of shenanigans did not endear him to his peers in Major League Baseball's conservative, traditionalist owners' clubhouse. And it didn't help his standing in the local community, or among his fellow owners, that Finley repeatedly purged his baseball executives, went through seven managers in his first seven years as owner, and alienated players with his stinginess, the pettiness of suddenly imposed club rules, and arbitrary disciplinary actions. Local officials and the media were antagonized by Finley's lobbying for capital improvements and better terms on the ballpark, threatening to move the franchise elsewhere if there was no commitment to publicly finance a new stadium, and calling Kansas City "a horse-shit town." As the 1967 season drew to a close, it should not have come as a surprise to the good citizens of Kansas City when Finley announced his intention to move the Athletics to Oakland, where the modern multipurpose stadium opened in 1966 for the Oakland Raiders football team was more than suitable for a major-league baseball team.

As bad as they were, by the time the Athletics left KC for Oakland, they had the makings of a pretty good team, one that would quickly morph into a short-lived dynasty. Called up in July 1964 to play short-stop, Bert Campaneris led the league the next three years in stolen bases. Catfish Hunter made the starting rotation as a 19-year-old in 1965, and Chuck Dobson as a 22-year-old in 1966. Rick Monday took over in center field in 1967. Reggie Jackson and Sal Bando both had a taste of Kansas City in 1967, although neither did much that year with their opportunity. All were signed as amateurs by the Kansas City Athletics, as was future Hall of Fame reliever Rollie Fingers. And they all helped the Oakland Athletics rise to greatness. But the man who took Oakland's Athletics to the top was Dick Williams.

* * *

Notwithstanding his being the guiding hand behind Boston's 1967 Impossible Dream team, Williams had an unpleasant parting of ways with the Red Sox. His hard-driving ways and contentious relationships with star player Yastrzemski and team owner Tom Yawkey wore out his welcome. He was fired with nine games remaining in 1969. When Williams returned to managing after serving as a coach in Montreal, it was in 1971 to take charge of Finley's Athletics—a team on the cusp of greatness. The team Finley entrusted to him featured Jackson in right field and third baseman Bando entering their prime, and shortstop Campaneris already in his. Hunter was by now one of the best pitchers in baseball, and he would be joined by lefties Vida Blue in 1971 and Ken Holtzman in 1972 to give the A's one of baseball's best starting rotations. Williams also benefited from his predecessor's having moved Fingers from the starting rotation in August 1970 to the bullpen, where Fingers found his true calling.

Dick Williams had a dynasty on his hands, but a very dysfunctional one due in no small part to the constant interference of Oakland's mercurial owner, not to mention Finley's miserliness when it came to player compensation. As well as the A's played as a team, they were "all for one and one for all" only on the ball field, not in their factionalized, roughhouse clubhouse, where there was open feuding among players and near-universal hatred of cheapskate Finley. Yet by winning the AL West every year from 1971 to 1975, the Athletics became only the third team in history after the 1949–1953 and 1960–1964 Yankees to finish first in five consecutive years. The 1972–1974 A's were the first team to win three straight World Series since the 1949–1953 Yankees, and Oakland did so with having to first survive the league championship series, whose best-three-of-five format left very little room for a poor start in the series. The A's had a killer instinct that would have made the five-and-five-in-five Yankees proud. In five Septembers, the A's were never not in first place. And this they did dressed in green and gold uniforms and white cleats, to which the players added their own individual facial hair styles.

Williams, however, managed only the first three of the five division titles and two of the pennants and World Series championships before he tired of Finley and quit as a result of the owner's various controversial interventions during the 1973 season, including the World Series against the Mets. Most blatantly, Finley attempted to deceitfully manipulate Oakland's roster in the middle of the World Series by claiming Mike Andrews was injured to have him replaced on the roster after the second baseman committed two critical errors in the 12th inning of Game Two that cost them the game. For Williams, that was the final straw in putting up with Finley. It was Alvin Dark who managed the A's to their third straight World Series in 1974 and a fifth straight division title in 1975. Dark had his own problems with Finley telling him how to manage his club. Among other things, Finley insisted the A's 25-man roster must include sprinter Herb Washington, the world record holder for the 50- and 60-yard dash, for the sole purpose of being a designated runner at the expense of an actual baseball player.

Dark was fired after the 1975 season. Although he was likely gone anyway, it didn't help Dark's case for staying a third year that he was quoted as telling a local congregation in testifying about his Christian devotion that (paraphrasing), while the Oakland owner should be praised for bringing the A's to World Series heaven, Finley was not going to the real heaven because he was not right with God. As for Herb Washington, he appeared in 105 games in 1974 and early 1975, and five more in the 1974 postseason, without a single plate appearance. All were as a pinch-runner. Successful in only 65 percent of his 48 stolen base attempts during the regular season, Washington was hardly an elite basestealer. He was unsuccessful in two stolen base attempts in the 1974 ALCS and was ignominiously picked off first base as the would-be tying run in Game Two of the World Series for the next-to-last out of the only game the A's lost.

The 1971–1975 A's had an explosive offense that combined power and speed. Reggie Jackson blasted 154 home runs, twice leading the league. Bando hit 105, and Gene Tenace added 154 after becoming a regular in 1973, starting at either catcher or first base. Campaneris stole 178 bases in their five-year run, including a league-leading 52 in 1972; Billy North stole 137 in three years after he became Oakland's regular center fielder in 1973; and Jackson complemented his power game with 89 steals of his own. Left fielder Joe Rudi, a .284 hitter those five years with 84 home runs, earned such a reputation for consistency and coming through in clutch situations that he might have been baseball's most overappreciated underrated player. Oakland's pitching, while perhaps not the equal of Baltimore's, was tough to beat. Hunter won 20 four years in a row from 1971 to 1975. Blue won both the Cy Young and MVP awards in 1971, his first full year in the majors, when he went 24–8, completing 24 of his 39 starts, led the league with a 1.82 earned-run average and 8 shutouts, and struck out 301 batters in 312 innings. Excelling in odd-numbered years, Blue won 20 in 1973 and 22 in 1975. Ken Holtzman was the Joe Rudi of the pitching staff—a model of consistency. Then there was Rollie Fingers to wrap things up when necessary, saving 102 of the A's 476 victories from 1971 to 1975.

* * *

By this time it was clear the Oakland A's dynasty was coming to an end, and not just because despite their AL-best 98–54 record in 1975 they fell prey to the Red Sox in the ALCS, swept in three games. Of course, they no longer had Catfish Hunter and his 88 victories from 1971 to 1974. His departure was the beginning of the A's unraveling, and it was all Finley's fault. The owner's refusal to make payments on an annuity clause in Hunter's contract, because he was unhappy he wouldn't get a tax benefit, led to arbitration and a ruling that Finley had violated the terms of his ace pitcher's contract. Catfish became a free agent quickly and was snapped up by a rival owner, the Yankees' George Steinbrenner. The Hunter case proved to Oakland's players that Finley was not only mercurial and a tightwad, but disreputably untrustworthy. And Steinbrenner's showing that he was definitely not cheap when it came to paying star players was certainly not lost on the rest of the A's top-tier players— or on Charlie Finley.

Then came the independent arbitrator's decision that because pitchers Andy Messersmith and Dave McNally played the 1975 season without a contract, they were now free agents. No matter that major-league owners were determined at first to head off free agency, Finley knew that outcome was unrealistic in negotiations with an increasingly potent players' union that had successfully called the owners' bluff in the short-lived strike at the beginning of the 1972 season. As the owner of a small-market team whose annual attendance was in the bottom half of the league every year they dominated the AL West—except one, 1972, when the A's were fifth in attending fans—Finley also knew he could not afford the lucrative multiyear contracts that big-market owners like Steinbrenner could offer top-tier players.

Knowing full well that all of the A's core players were intending to take advantage of the Messersmith decision and play the 1976 season without contracts to make themselves free agents, Finley decided on a scorched-earth policy. He renewed all of their contracts with the maximum-allowed 20-percent salary cut. Predictably, his players refused to sign. Seeking value for his best players, Finley traded Jackson and Holtzman to the Orioles just days before the 1976 season for veteran right-hander Mike Torrez and Don Baylor. As the June trade deadline approached, with the Athletics already effectively out of the running for a sixth straight division title, Finley tried to cash in by selling Blue to the Yankees for $1.5 million and Rudi and Fingers to the Yankees' rival Red Sox for $2 million, only to be foiled when Commissioner Bowie Kuhn voided both deals. With the owners still at loggerheads with the players' union on free agency, Kuhn did not want to set a precedent for small-market franchises to conduct annual fire sales of pending free agents, believing it would ruin the competitive integrity of the game. Kuhn later established a cap of $400,000 on cash transactions for players. Blue, Rudi, and Fingers stayed in Oakland.

Finley's A's suffered a massive exodus of free agents that sank the club to last place in the AL West in 1977 with the third-worst record of the major leagues' 26 teams. Vida Blue still belonged to the A's only because he had agreed to sign a new three-year deal to facilitate his sale to the Yankees, which Finley now had to pay. Oakland's Athletics were in freefall; the A's attendance was by far the worst in the majors; and Finley, in addition to going to court against Kuhn's decision to void his cash deals with Boston and New York, wanted out. He lost his case in court: The most attractive buyer for the A's intended to move them to Denver, and the city of Oakland refused to allow the franchise to break its long-term lease on the municipal stadium.

It was not until 1980 that the stars aligned for Charlie Finley to get out of baseball, for Major League Baseball to be rid of him—the commissioner and most owners despised the man—and for Oakland to keep its team. Ironically, it was Finley's hiring of the ever-controversial Billy Martin to manage the A's in 1980 that allowed all that to happen. Martin's hard-charging managerial style and the emergence of the dynamic Rickey Henderson, stealing 100 bases in his first full season, led the A's from 108 losses in 1979 to second place and 83 wins in 1980. Attendance more than doubled, a local buyer stepped forward, and Finley profited from the deal.

* * *

Although taking a back seat to the Red Sox in 1975 and the Billy Martin–led Yankees revival the three years thereafter, the Orioles remained a very good team. Recovering from the arm problems that ruined his 1974 season, Jim Palmer had another stretch of four 20-win seasons from 1975 to 1978 and won the Cy Young Award in 1975 and '76. In the meantime, the Orioles retooled. By 1979 Palmer had been joined in the starting rotation by right-hander Dennis Martinez and lefties Mike Flanagan and Scott McGregor, giving Baltimore a top-tier foursome. Brooks Robinson had been replaced at third by Doug DeCinces, good for 15 to 20 home runs a year and solid defensively even if he was no Brooks at the hot corner. Baltimore's new power batters were right fielder Ken Singleton, Lee May the DH, and 1977 Rookie of the Year Eddie Murray at first base. They won the AL East handily in 1979; their 102 wins were the most in baseball, and they went to the World Series, which they lost—as they had in 1971—in seven games to the Pirates. In 1980 the Orioles had the dubious distinction of becoming just the seventh major-league team in history to win 100 games and not finish first; they were the first in the division era to win 100 and finish second in their division because the Yankees won 103.

These were also the years that Orioles manager Earl Weaver became . . . Earl Weaver. The Earl of Baltimore's formula for success was pitching, defense, a strong bench, and, most famously, "Praised be the Three-Run Homer!"—the subtitle of his chapter on offense in *Weaver on Strategy*. Although none of his teams ever led the American League in home runs, he was explicit in believing "the home run is paramount because it means instant runs." The only years his Orioles lacked consistent power were 1972 to 1974. Otherwise, Weaver always had a pair of dangerous power hitters who delivered in the middle of his lineup— Frank Robinson and Boog Powell, when the 1969–1971 Orioles won three straight pennants; Lee May and Don Baylor in 1975; May and Reggie Jackson in 1976; and May, Singleton, and Murray after that.

The flipside of his emphasis on the almighty homer was his disdain for run-creation strategies, especially sacrificing precious outs to advance baserunners. In this, Weaver's philosophy was the same as that of John McGraw, who believed the same thing even in the Deadball Era when scoring opportunities were routinely set up that way. An analysis of his team's sacrifice attempts shows, however, that it wasn't until after 1975 that Weaver actually adopted that approach in practice. Like McGraw, Weaver also managed in a base-stealing era and was not averse to stolen bases, provided he had players like Al Bumbry with both good speed and a talent for the art. Failed attempts, however, "can be destructive," Weaver wrote, "particularly at the top of the order, because it takes the runner off the base paths ahead of your home run hitters."

By the mid- and late seventies, enabled by the DH rule that allowed him to think more expansively about his bench, Weaver had resurrected Casey Stengel's philosophy for platooning and made it his own. Since pinch-hitting for the pitcher was no longer necessary, Weaver constructed his bench for enhancing his flexibility to pinch-hit for position players for batter-pitcher platoon advantages in key situations in the game and to make defensive substitutions. Weaver had a plan for every Baltimore Oriole. Everybody played, and he expected them all to contribute. While every core regular other than catcher met the major-league qualifying minimum of 502 plate appearances on Weaver's 1969–1971 Orioles, by the late 1970s the only Orioles position players assured of finishing games they started were Murray, DeCinces, Bumbry, and rookie short-stop Cal Ripken in 1982. Ken Singleton, the most feared hitter in Baltimore after Eddie Murray, was often replaced in the late innings for defense. Weaver always had a combination of four or five lefty and righty outfielders on the bench to call on whenever he thought necessary. While Singleton and Bumbry started most often in right field and center, Weaver usually had a left-field platoon—most famously the left-handed batter John Lowenstein and right-handed Gary Roenicke, who in 1982 combined for 45 home runs.

* * *

Earl Weaver, of whom it might be said no manager this side of John McGraw was as astute a baseball strategist, announced he would retire after the 1982 season. It had been a combative thirteen and a half years at the helm of the Baltimore Orioles, both in his in-your-face confrontations with umpires and with his players—most famously his pitching ace, Jim Palmer, 240 of whose 268 major-league wins came in the Weaver regime. The 36-year-old Palmer had his last Palmeresque season in Weaver's presumed farewell year of 1982, going 15–5, his best winning percentage since he was 16–4 in 1969, Weaver's first full year as manager.

It looked at first that Weaver was going to go out on a sour note. The Orioles got off to a terrible start and didn't climb out of last place till mid-May. Although they had fought to within 3½ games of first by the All-Star break, on Friday the 13th in August they were back to eight games behind division-leading Milwaukee—a team that seemed on the cusp of taking command of the AL East. From then till the end of the season, the Orioles were nearly unbeatable, winning 35 of their last 50 games. They were 27–5 from August 20 to September 20. As the gods on baseball's Mount Olympus would have it, their final series of the season was Milwaukee coming to Baltimore for four games at the beginning of October. The Brewers did so with a three-game lead. Three games later—all Orioles victories—the teams were tied, setting up a 162nd game showdown for the division title.

It was Jim Palmer, 13–1 since the beginning of June, against fellow veteran Don Sutton. It would have been the perfect ending—Palmer, the great pitcher near the end of his own career whose opinions always seemed to clash with his manager's, winning the last regular-season game for Earl Weaver, putting both into the ALCS. Perhaps they could go out together as World Series champions. Instead, the Brewers crushed the O's, 10–2, putting an end to Weaver's attempt to engineer a dramatic come-from-far-behind division title, perhaps a pennant, and maybe even a World Series title in his last year as manager. The postgame outpouring of sentiment in Memorial Stadium for Earl Weaver at the presumed end of his career—Weaver came out of retirement in June 1985 to right a struggling Orioles team that was playing below expectations—was something to behold. As the love rained down that first Sunday in October 1982, Weaver's managerial record stood at 1,354 wins against 919 losses—a career winning percentage of .596 not the equal of twentieth-century managers Joe McCarthy's .615 or Billy Southworth's .597, but ahead of John McGraw's .591 with the Giants.

The Orioles may have fallen one game short in Weaver's farewell, but he left them well positioned to win the AL East the very next year under his successor. Perhaps Weaver's defining legacy for Baltimore moving forward was his decision to move Cal Ripken Jr., son of highly esteemed Orioles coach Cal Ripken, from third base to shortstop. At 6-foot-4, Ripken was considered by many too big to play shortstop. Weaver thought otherwise. Having played 44 of the Orioles' first 47 games at third, including starting every game there (27 total) since May 30, Ripken was Weaver's starting shortstop beginning July 1 for each of Baltimore's remaining games. He ended up the American League Rookie of the Year. May 30, 1982, turned out to be the first of 2,632 consecutive Orioles games Cal Ripken played before voluntarily agreeing to sit one out on September 20, 1998.

18

THE RISE OF THE BIG RED MACHINE AND THE RETURN OF DODGER BLUE

"**B**ad trades are part of baseball. Who can forget Frank Robinson for Milt Pappas, for God's sake?" This was Susan Sarandon's classic line as Annie Savoy in the 1988 movie *Bull Durham*. Yeah, it was a bad trade, given that Frank Robinson wasted no time in winning the Triple Crown and leading the Baltimore Orioles to a World Series championship in 1966. And while the Cincinnati Reds dropped from fourth place and a very respectable 89 wins with Robinson in 1965 to seventh place and 76 wins without him in 1966, the deal was not as devastating to the Reds as Annie's critique might imply. By the end of the decade, Cincinnati had a strong cadre of players including Pete Rose, now playing in the outfield, slugging third baseman Tony Perez, first baseman Lee May, and 1968 Rookie of the Year catcher Johnny Bench. In 1969 the Reds finished third in the new NL West; Rose had his fourth 200-hit season, batted .300 for the fifth consecutive year, and won his second batting title; Perez broke out with 37 home runs and 122 runs batted in; May hit 38 homers and drove in 111; and Bench had 26 homers with 90 RBIs.

The Los Angeles Dodgers were having a more difficult time recovering from Sandy Koufax's unexpected decision to retire after the 1966 World Series and their decision to trade the centerpiece of their infield, shortstop Maury Wills, to Pittsburgh for light-hitting shortstop Gene Michael and third baseman Bob Bailey. Wills was nowhere near the ballplayer Frank Robinson was, but Wills for Michael and Bailey was not exactly a great deal for the Dodgers; Wills batted .302 for Pittsburgh in

1967, while Michael batted 100 points below that for LA and Bailey hit but .227. After two eighth-place endings, however, Wills was brought back to play shortstop; center fielder Willie Davis had the first of three straight .300 seasons—the only three in his career, it turned out; veteran southpaw Claude Osteen won 20 for the first time; and the 1969 Dodgers were back to a winning record.

Both teams were potential contenders in the NL West going into 1970, but neither was a sure bet to be consistently competitive in the years ahead. The Reds had the advantage of relative youth—none of their core regulars were over 29—and a robust offense that led both major leagues in scoring the two previous years and outpaced the runner-up team in home runs by 29 in 1969. There were questions about their pitching, however, made even more urgent when their ace Jim Maloney blew out an Achilles tendon running out a ground ball in just his second start of the new season. The Dodgers, on the other hand, were an older club in transition whose starting rotation no longer had Don Drysdale, forced by shoulder problems to retire at the age of 33. No one could have predicted the Reds and Dodgers would dominate the National League for most of the 1970s, between them winning eight pennants in nine years between 1970 and 1978.

* * *

Cincinnati had a new manager in 1970. His major-league career was limited to one year playing second base for the last-place 1959 Phillies and one coaching for the 1969-expansion Padres. He was 36 years old, prematurely gray, and unknown to most of the baseball world. But the Reds knew his managerial potential from when he managed their Double-A affiliate to the best record in the Southern League two years earlier. By the end of the 1970 season, all of baseball knew who he was. He was Sparky Anderson.

After only the sixth game of the season, Anderson's Reds were never anywhere but in first place on their way to winning the NL West by 14½ games over the Dodgers. They were 13 games better than NL Eastern Division champion Pittsburgh, whom they swept three straight in the NLCS to win the pennant, after which they were trashed in five games by Baltimore in the World Series. Bench led the majors in home runs (45) and runs batted in (148), batting .293 to win the MVP Award. Perez was third in the league in homers (40) and was tied for second in RBIs (129). Center fielder Bobby Tolan led the majors with 57 stolen bases while batting .316. Rose also hit .316 and tied for the major-league lead in hits with 205. Anderson proved a master manipulator of his starting rotation and bullpen as Cincinnati's team earned-run average improved from 4.11, fourth worst in the league in 1969, to 3.69, second best in 1970. Gary Nolan, recovered from two years of arm problems after a promising 1967 rookie season, won 18. Jim Merritt, acquired the previous year from Minnesota, won 20. Wayne Granger led the majors with 35 saves, and Clay Carroll had 16 saves of his own.

Reality struck hard the very next year. Losing 11 of their first 15 games, the Reds were a distant memory in the pennant race by the end of April, leaving many to wonder whether Cincinnati had returned to being a middle-of-the-pack baseball team. Twenty-year-old lefty Don Gullett's 16–6 record in only his second big-league season was the best thing about the Reds' season. Smarting from being one of only five NL teams with a losing record in 1971, Cincinnati made one of the most consequential trades in major-league history with Houston, sending first baseman Lee May (and his 39 homers) and second baseman Tommy Helms to the Astros for second baseman Joe Morgan, veteran infielder Dennis Menke, unproven 24-year-old outfielder Cesar Geronimo, and right-hander Jack Billingham. The departure of May and the arrival of Menke allowed Anderson to move Tony Perez from third to first, which was more suitable for Perez's defensive skill set. Thus reinforced, Cincinnati went on to win four division titles, three pennants, and two World Series the next five years, averaging more than 100 wins a year.

The Reds won 95 and their division by 10½ games over Houston in 1972, defeated the 96-win Pirates in the NLCS, and rallied from a three-games-to-one deficit to force a seventh game in the World Series before falling to Oakland. Although the Reds were even better in 1973, they had to rally from fourth place and an 11-game deficit behind LA at the end of June. Winning 24 of 31 games in July thrust them into the pennant race, and winning 14 of 16 from late August to mid-September vaulted them from second and 4½ games behind into a commanding position in the NL West. The concern of baseball traditionalists that the new divisional format could result in a pennant going to an undeserving team in a five-game league championship series seemed validated when the 99-win Reds lost the 1973 NLCS to the 82-win Mets. It was a stunning defeat for a clearly superior ballclub with the best record in baseball to a team that finished just three games over .500 with only the fourth-best record in the National

League. The vaunted Reds' offense was shut down by the Mets' top-flight pitching, which held them to a .186 batting average and only 8 runs in the five-game series.

* * *

As in 1973, the 1974 Reds found themselves having to make up a large early season deficit to the Dodgers. Trailing by nine games in late May, they had by far the best record in the majors the rest of the way, but this time the Dodgers did not relinquish the lead. Cincinnati's 98 wins were second most in the major leagues; LA's 102 were the most. After having little trouble beating Pittsburgh in the NLCS, the Dodgers were upended in five games in the World Series. Four of the five games were decided by the same 3–2 score.

Still managed by Walt Alston, in his 21st year in Dodger blue, the 1974 Dodgers made two trades prior to the season that were pivotal to their winning the division title. They traded longtime center fielder Willie Davis to Montreal for reliever Mike Marshall, whose 92 outings in 1973 set a new record for games pitched, and then sent Claude Osteen, third-banana behind Koufax and Drysdale in 1965 and 1966, to Houston for power-hitting Jim Wynn to replace Davis in center field. Even without Osteen, Los Angeles had a formidable starting rotation, featuring veteran right-hander Don Sutton, veteran southpaw Tommy John—acquired from the White Sox in 1972—and righty Andy Messersmith, picked up in 1973 from the Angels down the freeway in Anaheim. Messersmith won 20 and Sutton 19 for the 1974 Dodgers. Wynn's 32 home runs were third in the league. And the Dodgers had in place their infield for the long term, first to third, Steve Garvey, Davey Lopes, shortstop Bill Russell, and Ron Cey.

The most notable developments in LA's season, however, were John's blowing out the ulnar ligament in his left elbow on July 17 and Marshall's pitching in a not-to-be-believed 106 of the Dodgers' 162 games. His team's lead down to 5½ games from 10½ a week earlier, Tommy John took the mound on July 17 with a 13–3 record. Delivering a pitch, he heard a pop in his throwing arm that immediately left him with "nothing" on his pitches. The injury would have been career-ending had orthopedic surgeon Frank Jobe not proposed revolutionary surgery to replace the injured ligament with a tendon from Tommy's right wrist. The surgery took place on September 25, a week before the season ended. Nobody knew whether Jobe's "Tommy John surgery" would allow the pitcher to resume his career. John was already 31 years old and had 124 major-league wins. Missing the entire 1975 season, John returned in 1976 to pitch effectively for another 14 years, adding 164 victories to finish his career 12 wins shy of the coveted 300 mark in 1989 at the age of 46.

Los Angeles got off to a good start in 1975 and held first place for the entire month of May. It took that long for Sparky Anderson's Cincinnati Reds to get into gear and become "The Big Red Machine" that would be the most dominant team in baseball that year and the next. The Reds began the year with Bench set behind the plate, Rose in left field, Perez at first, Morgan at second, and Davey Concepcion at short. Concepcion was one in a long line of quick and agile Venezuelans to star at the position,

The first seven batters in the starting lineup for Cincinnati's "Big Red Machine" in all four games of the Reds' sweep of the Yankees in the 1976 World Series were Pete Rose (third base), Ken Griffey (right field), Joe Morgan (second base), Tony Perez (first base), Dan Driessen (the designated hitter), and Johnny Bench (catcher). *National Baseball Hall of Fame Library, Cooperstown, NY.*

dating back to Chico Carrasquel and Luis Aparicio. Anderson platooned the left-handed-batting Geronimo in center field with George Foster. Ken Griffey, another left-sided batter, was platooned in right field. "Who's at third?" was the operative question in the first weeks of the season. At the end of April, with his team barely above .500 at 12–11, Anderson was particularly dissatisfied by the lack of production at third base. His solution was genius. The amenable Rose became Cincinnati's new third baseman and the power-hitting Foster the everyday left fielder. Griffey continued to sit against lefty starters.

From the day Rose moved to third base, the Reds won 95 of their 138 remaining games. Although the 1975 Reds did not breach the .500 mark for good until their 41st game in late May, they had a 12½-game lead by mid-July, went into the final month leading by 18½ games, and then built on their lead to finish with a 108–54 record and a 20-game advantage over second-place LA. Cincinnati's .667 winning percentage was the best by a National League club since Brooklyn's 1953 Dodgers were .682 in a 154-game schedule, and their 108 wins was the most by any NL team since the 1909 Pirates won 110. After sweeping the Pirates in the NLCS, the Reds outlasted the Red Sox in an epic World Series still considered by many to be the best ever played. The series was not decided till the final inning of Game Seven, when Joe Morgan drove in the winning run with two outs in the top of the ninth to break a 3–3 tie. Fresh off that signature season of the Big Red Machine, Cincinnati started the 1976 season strong, went into first place for good on May 29, and finished with 102 wins, 10 games ahead of second-place LA. Sweeping the Phillies in the NLCS and the Yankees in the World Series, the 1976 variant of the Big Red Machine is the only team in the divisional era to go undefeated in the postseason.

The 1975–1976 Reds were an offensive juggernaut. That was their identity, so much their calling card that the quality of their pitching— particularly starters Gary Nolan and Don Gullett, not to mention a first-rate corps of relievers—was often overlooked. Cincinnati led the league in scoring by wide margins both years. Pete Rose topped the 200-hit threshold both years, the seventh and eighth times he had done that in his 14 years in the big leagues. He was now within 238 hits of 3,000. Joe Morgan had two of the best back-to-back years of any second baseman in history and was the major leagues' best position player and the National League's MVP both years. He batted .324 those years and got on base 46 percent of the time. He could also hit with power and was a premier basestealer, swiping 127 bags in 146 attempts. In the middle of the lineup were Johnny Bench, Tony Perez, and George Foster. Concepcion and Geronimo, both best known for their defensive excellence, had matured as hitters and were no longer easy outs. Geronimo batted .307 in 1976, joining Griffey, Rose, Morgan, and Foster—all of whom hit .300 the previous year—to give the Reds five .300 hitters among their core regulars.

* * *

The dominance warranty on Cincinnati's Big Red Machine expired in 1977 with the return of Dodger blue to the top of the NL West. Having interrupted the Reds' dominance of the league by taking the division in 1974, Los Angeles was poised to become the National League's best team whenever Cincinnati lost its edge. Walt Alston, the Dodgers' manager since 1954 when they were still in Brooklyn and the only manager LA fans had known, retired in 1976, at the age of 64, after 23 years at the helm. He had presided over 2,040 Dodgers victories and 1,613 losses, seven National League pennants—five in Los Angeles—and four World Series championships, his first and most noteworthy being in 1955 when Brooklyn finally won it all. Replacing Alston was Tommy Lasorda, whose 14 years pitching in professional baseball included small parts of three seasons in the majors. Managing in the Dodgers' minor-league system since 1965, Lasorda finally earned a promotion to Alston's coaching staff in 1973. His elevation to manager was a momentous change for the Dodgers. While Alston was taciturn and all-business, Lasorda was an infectiously enthusiastic motivator who bled Dodger blue.

Taking advantage of a much better pitching staff and Cincinnati's slow start to the 1977 season, Lasorda's first year as manager was a resounding success. The Dodgers won on Opening Day and trailed in the standings only three days in April. They won 98 games and their division by 10 games. They won the NLCS handily, beating Philadelphia, only to run into Reggie Jackson and the rejuvenated New York Yankees in the World Series. Reggie's three home runs on three pitches in the sixth and final game of the series not only sent Los Angeles down in defeat but earned him the sobriquet "Mr. October." It was pretty much the same story in 1978, except the Dodgers spent most of the summer trailing their California rivals in San Francisco. In the end, they held a commanding 9-game lead with 12 games remaining, let down their guard to see they final margin of victory over second-place Cincinnati dwindle to 2½ games, again beat the Phillies handily in the NLCS, and again lost the World Series in six games to the Yankees.

Typical of Dodgers teams since Brooklyn's 1949–1956 Boys of Summer were assembled, the 1977 and 1978 club had a central core that would play together for many years, dating back to their 1974 pennant and extending to 1981 when they won both the pennant—their fourth in eight years—and, finally, the World Series. Their starting infield of Steve Garvey, Davey Lopes, Bill Russell, and Ron Cey was the same for nine years, from 1973 to 1981. Garvey was perhaps overrated because of his extraordinary consistency. He batted .309 in the nine years the Dodgers infield was intact, typically in the .304 to .319 range, and could be counted on for around 200 hits, 24 homers, and 105 RBIs every year. Cey averaged 26 homers a year between 1975 and 1980 but, even with the good fortune to play in the mass media market of Los Angeles, had the misfortune of being a National League third-base contemporary of both Mike Schmidt—arguably the best at his position in history—and Pete Rose. Lopes, likewise overshadowed at second base by Joe Morgan, stole 291 bases between 1974 and 1978.

As expected of the Dodgers since the days of Koufax and Drysdale, their pitching was a strong point. Tommy John, back from the surgery that bears his name and a 20-game winner in 1977, and Don Sutton, who won 21 the next year, were their top starters. Unlike the 1960s Dodgers, whose success was primarily because of their superior pitching, the midseventies Dodgers were a much better offensive ballclub. Lopes was a constant threat to steal at the top of the lineup, and right fielder Reggie Smith, Garvey, Cey, and left fielder Dusty Baker in the middle of Lasorda's batting order posed a formidable threat for opposing pitchers to navigate. All four crushed more than 30 homers in 1977, contributing to LA's league-leading total of 191—the most by a Dodger team since the Boys of Summer clubbed 201 in 1955.

Had the Dodgers not been so good in 1977 and '78, the Big Red Machine would have rumbled on even as it began shedding some of its parts. Finishing second both years, Cincinnati was never in contention in 1977, and in 1978 was doomed by a poor month of August resulting in a deficit too great to overcome when LA sputtered in September. With the loss of Don Gullett to free agency and the "final" return of Gary Nolan's arm and shoulder problems in 1977 (which had already cost him two years of his career, 1973 and 1974), the Reds could no longer paper over their pitching weaknesses—not even after their June 1977 trade for Tom Seaver, whose New York excellence continued in Cincinnati with a 14–3 record the rest of that season and a 16–14 mark in 1978. Sparky Anderson's vaunted bullpen went from having the second- and third-best relievers' ERA in the National League in 1975 and '76 to the second- and third-worst in 1977 and '78.

The Reds' offense, however, remained potent. George Foster led the league in home runs and RBIs both years, and in 1977 was the fifth Cincinnati Red to win the MVP Award in six years. His 149 RBIs in 1977 were the most in the majors in 28 years. On May 5, 1978, Pete Rose became the 13th player to reach 3,000 hits, and on June 14 he began a much-watched assault on Joe DiMaggio's 56-game hitting streak that ended on the first day of August after 44 games, which tied Willie Keeler's National League record set 81 years earlier in 1897. Rose batted .385 during his streak but just .302 for the season. He was 37 years old.

* * *

It has been fashionable to pinpoint the end of Cincinnati's baseball dominance to the trading away of Tony Perez less than two months after winning the 1976 World Series. While his leadership and performance were indisputably important to the Reds' success, 10-years-younger Dan Driessen was waiting in the wings for an opportunity to play regularly. It should be remembered, however, that the life expectancy of most baseball dynasties, defined here by the core players of a championship-caliber team, is about five years. After four NL Western Division titles, three National League pennants, and two World Series victories in five years from 1972 to 1976, the Big Red Machine was aging out and in need of tuning up. Perez, Rose, Morgan, and two of their top four starting pitchers in 1976 were already in, or approaching, their mid-30s.

Notwithstanding the accomplishments of the players, and even their manager, Reds executives were not big on sentiment. The trade of Perez to Montreal so that Driessen could play first base was not the beginning of dismantling the Big Red Machine so much as the beginning of a slow attrition. Once Cincinnati had a chance to celebrate its native son Rose's collecting his 3,000th hit, with the added bonus of chasing the great DiMaggio, they did not offer him the free-agent contract he felt he deserved, causing Pete to leave for Philadelphia. Also not returning for the 1979 season was manager Sparky Anderson, whose contract was not renewed. Under their new manager, the Reds came from behind to narrowly beat out the Houston Astros for the Western Division title in 1979, making it eight consecutive years that either Cincinnati or LA won the division. After being swept in the NLCS, the Reds also said goodbye to Joe Morgan.

The 1972–1976 Cincinnati Reds probably cannot stand the scrutiny of comparison to various teams of the Yankees' forever dynasty, but were arguably as dominant a team as the National League had yet seen. With four pennants in five years and winning at least 100 games four times, the 1906–1910 Chicago Cubs established an unsurpassed record of dominance with a dynamic, multifaceted offense that was obscured by superb frontline pitching and a terrific defense memorialized in unforgettable prose ("These are the saddest of possible words, Tinker-to-Evers-to-Chance"). But they were a Deadball Era team at a time when baseball's bottom dwellers were worse, perhaps even far worse, relative to the norm of the bottom-tier clubs the Reds played against. The 1942–1946 St. Louis Cardinals also won four pennants in five years, but two of those pennants were during World War II. Brooklyn's 1949–1956 Dodgers, with Jackie Robinson, Snider, Campanella, and Pee Wee Reese—like the Big Red Machine led by Morgan, Bench, Rose, and Perez—were an offensive juggernaut with less-than-imposing pitching. The 1972–1976 Reds, however, were far more dominant in league context.

The Reds dominated the league primarily by virtue of their variegated attack, blending batting prowess (exemplified by most of the lineup), aggressiveness (epitomized by Rose), speed (Morgan and his many steals), and power and clutch hitting (Rose, Morgan, Bench, Perez, and Foster). Rose batted .316 those five years. Bench had 142 homers and four 100-RBI seasons. Perez hit 115 home runs. Morgan batted .303, had an on-base percentage of .431, added 108 home runs and 310 stolen bases, and averaged 9.3 wins above replacement—far ahead of anybody else. Three of the Reds' core four are in the Hall of Fame based in large part on those five years, and Rose would have been a first-ballot selection had his gambling addiction and lapse in judgment for betting on baseball more than 10 years later not put him on Major League Baseball's permanently ineligible list.

To their detriment was that, while the Big Red Machine had a deadly efficient offense, their pitching was relatively pedestrian. Cincinnati's adjusted earned-run average—which normalizes ERA to the context of the time and the team's home park—was always around the league average; only in 1975 was it much better. Anderson was unable to sustain a great starting rotation because of persistent injuries. Gary Nolan and Don Gullett, the Reds' two best starting pitchers from 1972 to 1976 and two of baseball's best when healthy, missed substantial time on the disabled list, Nolan for two full years in 1973 and '74 and Gullett in 1975 and '76. Neither pitcher had career longevity after Gullett beat the Yankees in the opening game of the 1976 World Series and Nolan finished them off in Game Four. Anderson was able to compensate for injuries to his frontline starters and otherwise generally average starting pitching by having an excellent corps of relief pitchers to back them up. Rather than relying on an ace reliever and journeyman pitchers in the bullpen, Anderson made sure to have two, and usually three, dependable relievers who could close out games. Sparky Anderson was the first manager of a great team to make his bullpen the strength of his pitching staff and the centerpiece of his pitching philosophy.

19

SPARKY'S HOOK

Anticipating the Quality Start

While jump-starting his Hall of Fame managerial career as ship's captain of the mighty Big Red Machine, Sparky Anderson became the notorious "Captain Hook" for his propensity to remove starting pitchers early in games if they were struggling, even if his team was ahead, rather than allowing them to overcome adversity and pitch into the late innings. Anderson established this pattern in his very first year as manager in 1970 when, leading the Reds to the World Series, he allowed his starting pitchers to complete only 32 games—the fewest ever by a first-place National League team. The three teams that year with fewer complete games were the three worst teams in the league. With 25 wins and a major-league-record 60 saves, 12 of which were on behalf of a game-winning reliever, Anderson's calls to the bullpen figured directly in 72 percent of Cincinnati's 102 victories, far outpacing the league average of 58 percent. Two years later the Reds became the first team to win a pennant with the fewest complete games (25) in their league. With 28 wins, including 15 saved by another reliever and matching their record of 60 saves set two years before, the 1972 Reds' bullpen accounted directly for 77 percent of the team's 95 wins, again far outpacing the league average of 55 percent.

But it wasn't until 1975, when the Reds became the Big Red Machine, that Captain Hook really became *Captain Hook*. Although Cincinnati starters combined for 75 wins, the most of any team in the league, only 18 were complete-game victories. Anderson's starting pitchers went the distance only 22 times that year, including four losses, which was not only the fewest complete games by a first-place club in major-league history—one fewer than the 23 thrown by the 1966 Baltimore Orioles—but last in the major leagues. Of the 23 other major-league teams, the team with the next-fewest complete games was last-place Chicago in the NL East with 27. Anderson called on his bullpen 277 times, which responded with league-leading totals of 33 wins in relief and 50 saves, according to the new—and still current—definition of "saves" that went into effect that year. In all but 26 of the times he made a pitching change, Captain Hook relied on just four relievers—Rawly Eastwick (5–3 with 22 saves in 58 games), Will McEnaney (5–2 and 15 saves in 70), Clay Carroll (7–5 and 7 saves in 56), and Pedro Borbon (9–5 with 5 saves in 67 games).

Up to now, Anderson typically allowed his starting pitcher to stay in the game for as long as he was effective. That paradigm changed—for that year only, it turned out—at the end of June, by which time the Reds' lead was up to seven games. Through the first three months and 77 games of the 1975 season, Cincinnati starters threw 18 complete games, which was on par for that time frame in his first five years as manager. But while in previous years Anderson's starters completed a comparable (though slightly less) number of starts in the second half of the season, from July till the end of the 1975 season—a total of 85 games—Anderson allowed his starting pitchers to go the distance only four times.

Notwithstanding his extraordinary success with the 1975 Reds, Anderson once acknowledged being sensitive about the Captain Hook appellation, noting he was booed even by his daughter for pulling a starting pitcher relatively early in a game, and while he certainly would not admit it had a bearing, Captain Hook was somewhat reformed in 1976. Even though his starting pitchers were not as effective relative to the rest of the league's starters as in 1975, Anderson let them pitch 33 complete games, one-third more than the year before. Moreover, while he typically removed his starting pitchers about 65 to 70 times a year in the middle of innings, almost always with runners on base, in 1976 he did so only 49 times, meaning Anderson was more willing than before to let them pitch out of trouble. The Reds' bullpen nonetheless again led the league with 31 relief wins and 45 saves. Allowing his starters more opportunity to finish games lasted but one year and might have had a premature end because, despite the addition of Tom Seaver in 1977, Cincinnati's starting rotation in Anderson's last two years as manager was not as good as it was when he was winning five division titles in seven years. The Reds fell short of the division title both years, and in 1978—after which Anderson was unceremoniously fired—his pitchers notched only 16 complete games, half of them by Seaver.

Except for 1973, one of the four years his Reds had the National League's best record, Anderson gave his starting pitchers fewer innings than the league average every year he was their manager. Cincinnati pitchers averaged the fewest innings per start in the league three times, and in 1975—the best showing of the Big Red Machine—only Philadelphia's starters averaged fewer innings. But this was not because he was diminishing the importance of starting pitching, nor because the Reds did not have good starting pitchers. Each of Anderson's division-winning teams had at least two starting pitchers who had very good if not outstanding years: Gary Nolan (18–7), Wayne Simpson (14–3), and Jim Merritt (20–12) in 1970; Nolan (15–5) and Ross Grimsley (14–8) in 1972; Jack Billingham (19–10) and Don Gullett (18–8) in 1973; Gullett (15–4) and Nolan (15–9) in 1975; and Nolan (15–9), Gullett (11–3), and Pat Zachry (14–7) in 1976.

Anderson was able to be aggressive in giving the hook to his starters at early signs of trouble because he had a very strong bullpen, particularly from 1970 to 1976. Every year of that stretch, Anderson always had two exceptional relievers—Carroll and Wayne Granger in 1970 and '71; Carroll and Borbon from 1972 to '74; and Eastwick and McEnaney, along with Borbon, in 1975 and '76. But Sparky was judicious in his use of the bullpen, not some Captain Hook run amok. From 1970 to 1975, Anderson used *fewer* relief pitchers in games his starters failed to complete than the league average every year but one, even while he was consistently below the league average, usually far below, in allowing his starting pitchers to complete games.

* * *

Having a good bullpen with depth, almost unheard of before the 1950s, was recognized as an essential component to successful teams by the time Sparky Anderson became a major-league manager in 1970. Deeper bullpens and dedicated ace relievers gave managers the flexibility to remove their starting pitcher earlier in games to avoid being blown out and the confidence to be able to pinch-hit for a starter still pitching well in the late innings of close games or to relieve him in the middle of an inning should trouble arise. Perhaps no team proved this more than the

1966 Baltimore Orioles, whose starting pitchers were in at the finish of only 23 of their starts for a team that won 97 games. Manager Hank Bauer relied on five principal relievers who combined for 49 of the Orioles' 51 saves to navigate Baltimore to a decisive American League pennant. He needed only one, however—Moe Drabowsky—just one time, to pitch in the Orioles' World Series sweep of the Dodgers. Drabowsky pitched 6⅔ innings in relief with 11 strikeouts, including a record six in a row, to get the win in Game One, after which Baltimore starters pitched three complete-game shutouts to complete the sweep.

As important as having a quality bullpen had become, however, starting pitching was still what mattered most. Managers in both leagues expected their starting pitchers to have the stamina to pitch into the late innings—and to want to finish what they started—and to have the fortitude and guile to pitch their way out of trouble. The best starting pitchers were given more latitude to pitch out of late-inning trouble than others in the rotation, in part due to the respect they earned by virtue of being the best, but even they were sometimes relieved in tight spots. If the game was a blowout in their favor, managers almost always allowed the starting pitcher to go for the complete game. That counted for pitchers in salary negotiations at a time before free agency. There was no consideration of limiting a pitcher's time on the mound, either to pitch counts in any one game or innings-pitched over the course of a season, not even for top-tier pitchers who often approached or exceeded 300 innings. Lesser-caliber starting pitchers were on a shorter leash by their managers and less likely to finish what they started unless they were on the upside of a big lead or having a great day on the mound. Still, their managers expected them to last at least through the middle innings and typically let them try to work their way out of trouble unless they weren't getting outs, were obviously struggling with their command, or were pitching in a critical game where the manager felt there was no margin for error.

Even as the percentage of complete games was relatively stable—at about 25 percent in the 1960s, down from about a third of games started for most of the 1950s—and the percentage of saves increased from about a third of team victories to close to 40 percent, 14 pitchers combined for 28 seasons with 20 complete games in the 10 years from 1960 to 1969. In 1970, when Anderson debuted as manager, four pitchers threw at least 20 complete games. The most by a Reds starter that year was 12, by 20-game winner Jim Merritt. Sparky was well on his way to upending the still-prevailing wisdom that strong starting pitching led by an ace (or two) capable of going the distance in any given start was the foundation for precisely the kind of sustained success his Cincinnati Reds were soon to achieve.

* * *

"For five innings it's the pitcher's game," Anderson was quoted as saying in Tom Adelman's book on the 1975 season, *The Long Ball: The Summer of '75*. "After that it's mine." Sparky Anderson was years ahead of his contemporaries in implicitly recognizing the value of the quality start, a metric developed in the 1980s by Philadelphia sportswriter John Lowe to gauge how well a starting pitcher did his job, defined as pitching at least six innings and allowing no more than three earned runs. Rather than allowing them to try to overcome adversity and pitch into the later innings, Anderson's quick hook for starting pitchers who ran into trouble, even if the Reds were ahead, was not so different from what other managers, going back to Casey Stengel and Walt Alston, had been doing for years. What was different was Anderson's inclination to take out his starting pitcher relatively early in the middle innings, especially with runners on base, if that pitcher was *not* giving him a quality start along the lines that would later be devised by Lowe. In his division-winning years, more than 75 percent of the times he allowed his starter to go at least six innings, it met the future definition of a quality start. Anderson was consistent as Reds manager in wanting a quality start and giving an early hook to pitchers not giving him one.

The lack of patience Sparky Anderson had for starting pitchers not giving him a quality start was apparent in all four of the World Series his Cincinnati Reds played. In the 23 series games he managed, Anderson did not once allow his starting pitcher to go the distance. In only 10 of those 23 games did a Reds starter throw six or more innings, and eight of those 10 were, by later definition, a quality start. In five other games, three in 1972 against Oakland and two in 1975 against the Red Sox, Anderson removed his starting pitcher before the sixth inning even though the pitcher was on pace to give him a quality start. Two of those were Games Six and Seven of the 1972 World Series, both must-win for Cincinnati because Oakland had a three-games-to-two lead. Anderson removed Nolan in the fifth inning of Game Six after the A's tied the score at 1–1 in a game the Reds eventually won to even the series, and he pinch-hit for Jack Billingham in the fifth inning of Game Seven with the

Reds trailing, 1–0. That move paid off when Billingham's pinch-hitter drove in the tying run, but reliever Borbon gave up two runs in the sixth that proved decisive in Cincinnati losing the game and the series.

Of the 59 pitching changes Anderson made in the 23 series games he managed, 18 were to remove his starting pitcher in the middle of an inning to stanch a rally. He did so in all four games of the Reds' 1976 World Series sweep of the Yankees, despite each of his four starters walking off the mound with a quality start. Twenty-one other times Sparky used his hook to replace a relief pitcher in trouble in the middle of an inning. The frequency with which he replaced pitchers in the middle of an inning in World Series games was out of sync with Anderson's approach in the regular season, when he never once in his nine years as Cincinnati manager exceeded—and was often substantially below—the league average in bringing in relief pitchers with runners already on base. But the World Series is, of course, for much higher stakes.

Tom Seaver, however—still very much in his prime—*was* routinely allowed to go the distance when he took the mound after being acquired from the Mets in June 1977. Seaver made 20 starts for the Reds after the trade, 14 of which were quality starts, and pitched 14 complete games while recording a 14–3 record. Anderson let him pitch into the eighth inning in all but three starts he made that year for the Reds. The next year, despite 28 of his 36 starts being quality starts, Seaver finished the season with just 8 complete games—the first time in his career, dating to 1967, that he had fewer than 13 completions. Seaver, however, was now 33 and had gone into the season having thrown nearly 3,000 innings, perhaps influencing Anderson to give him the hook in the late innings even when he was pitching effectively. He pitched at least seven innings in 30 of his 36 starts and into the eighth in 16.

* * *

Anderson left his hook in Cincinnati, however, when he moved to Detroit to manage the Tigers in 1979, which was clearly evident from the number of complete games and average innings pitched by his new corps of starting pitchers. He was also now in the American League, where having a designated hitter for the pitcher allowed him to continue with a pitcher having a quality start without needing to consider whether to pinch-hit for him in the late innings of a tight game for the purpose of scoring a necessary run. Anchored by Jack Morris, a workhorse who virtually ensured a strong performance and many innings every time he took the mound, and including Dan Petry and Milt Wilcox when he arrived, and Walt Terrell beginning in 1985, Detroit's staff gave Anderson a deeper and more consistent starting rotation in the 1980s than he had with the Reds. Morris got the Tom Seaver treatment; Anderson allowed him to pitch for as long as he could, and even go the distance, so long as he was pitching effectively. In the 388 times he took the mound for Anderson before leaving Detroit as a free agent in 1991, Morris averaged 7⅓ innings a start and had 231 quality starts, winning 190 while losing 142. Thirty-eight percent (151) of his starts were complete games. The rest of the staff was given less leeway, but as long as they were giving Anderson a quality outing, he let them go deep into games.

From 1983 to 1988, when Anderson managed his most competitive Detroit teams, winning two division titles and finishing second twice, the Tigers were consistently *above* the league average in complete games and innings per start and *below* the league average in number of relievers used. Except for Detroit's 1984 World Series–championship season, Detroit's starters those six years were always either second or third in most innings per start, on the opposite end from where Cincinnati's starting pitchers were under Captain Hook.

After they got off to a terrific 35–5 start to take early command of the AL East, Anderson seems to have adopted the same approach with the 1984 Tigers that he used with the 1975 Reds once they had broken away from the pack in their division race. As if to limit starting-pitcher innings in anticipation of postseason baseball still months away, Captain Hook was less willing to allow his pitchers to carry even a quality start too deep into games. Tigers pitchers had 9 complete games in 46 starts through the end of May, after which Anderson allowed them to go the distance just 10 more times in the four months and 116 games that remained. Morris pitched complete games in seven of his first 12 starts through May, but was in at the end of only two of the 23 games he pitched the rest of the way. Come the World Series, though, Jack Morris pitched complete-game victories in the first and fourth games of the Tigers' five-game wipeout of the San Diego Padres, making him the only pitcher to ever pitch complete games for Captain Hook in a World Series. Morris would likely have gone the distance in the opening game of the ALCS as well, but was taken out with the Tigers comfortably ahead, 6–1, after seven polished innings.

Likely coincidentally, 1984 was also the only season in his 17 years as Detroit's manager that Anderson had a relief corps as effective as he'd had in Cincinnati from 1970 to 1976, with lefty Willie Hernandez (9–3 with 32 saves) and righty Aurelio Lopez (10–1, 14 saves) appearing in a total of 151 games between them. In a year where the Tigers accomplished the rare feat of spending every day in first place, were 15 games better than the second-best team in the American League, and won the World Series handily, their starting pitchers completed only 19 games— the league average was 28—and their six innings per start was third worst. Logging the second-most relief innings in the American League and allowing the fewest walks and hits per inning, Detroit's bullpen had by far the best relievers' earned-run average in the American League. Hernandez, pitching in 80 games—just one game fewer than half a season—won both the Cy Young and the Most Valuable Player awards.

In contrast to 1984, the deficiency of his bullpen caused Sparky to sheath his hook down the stretch the next time Detroit won the AL East in 1987. Nine of the Tigers' 33 complete games came after September 1 as Detroit battled Toronto into the final weekend for the division title. Rather than being capricious with his hook, as many frustrated Reds starting pitchers believed a decade earlier, Anderson was quite considered about when to call in relief. But unlike the Big Red Machine and the 1984 Tigers, whose superior bullpens allowed him to use his relievers with Captain Hook regularity, his 1987 Detroit team had a formidable starting rotation that led the league with 88 quality starts, when the league average was 73, and a mediocre corps of relievers. He managed his pitching accordingly.

* * *

Even though the so-called quality start was not yet in vogue as an explicit statistic, Anderson intuitively understood its meaning and acted on that principle. In both Cincinnati and Detroit, he wanted the quality start, and he was quicker than most managers to use his hook when he did not get it. Sparky Anderson's insight ultimately redefined for managers and front offices alike their expectations for starting pitchers. In the quarter century that Anderson managed in the major leagues, complete games declined from 22 percent in 1970, his first season in Cincinnati, to just under 7 percent in 1995, his final year in Detroit. There were 852 complete games in the major leagues in 1970, with 11 pitchers throwing at least 15. In 1995 there were only 275 complete games, with the season high being 10 by Greg Maddux, and only nine others throwing more than six. Anderson's starting pitchers went the distance just five times—last in the American League.

National League complete games dropped below 20 percent for good in 1979. In the American League, where the designated-hitter advantage made managers' decisions about whether and when to take out the starting pitcher independent of the pitcher's hitting ability, it was not until 1984 that complete games dropped below 20 percent for good. The next year, Bert Blyleven's 24 complete games was the last time an American League pitcher topped 20. The last National League pitcher to complete 20 games was Fernando Valenzuela in 1986, when he alone accounted for nearly 10 percent of the league total.

As the concept of the quality start gained currency in the 1980s, in principle if not actually by name, the expectation that starting pitchers should be capable of finishing what they started greatly diminished in importance. Even elite starters were expected to go only as deep into the game as they could without sacrificing much in terms of the quality of their pitching performance from first pitch to last, no matter that it came an inning or two or even three before the game-requisite nine. Bullpens, and particularly ace relievers, were no longer there for damage control or to come into a *winnable* game when the starting pitcher had clearly become too weary to continue pitching effectively. They were now used preemptively to take over a *winning* game before the starting pitcher, having done his job with six or seven quality-start innings, might begin to lose his command.

The emphasis on a six- or seven-inning quality start being acceptable in a nine-inning game placed a premium on shutdown relief to preserve the accomplishment. It was inevitable, therefore—as did in fact take shape in the late eighties and early nineties—that the concept of quality starts would lead to defining specific roles for relief pitchers, including who got which late inning. Sparky Anderson, who used his top relievers interchangeably depending on the game situation rather than any specific inning when he managed the Big Red Machine, was *not* at the leading edge of *that* bullpen innovation.

20

MARVIN MILLER TIME

Not the (Presumed) End of Baseball History

From almost the beginning of major-league time, dating back to the formation of the National League in 1876, franchise owners—the barons whose money made possible the business enterprise of Organized Baseball—considered player contracts sacrosanct to their operation. Early on, in 1880, they developed the stipulation of a contractual reserve clause that bound players to their club for another year even after their contract expired unless they were released or dealt to another club, which would then inherit the contract. The reserve clause was seen as an absolute necessity to ensure continuity, and hence stability, in the professional sport. Otherwise, in the absence of long-term deals, which clubs initially were unwilling to give even star players, each off-season would be a mad scramble, as every player would be a free agent negotiating with multiple clubs for the best deal. Franchises would not be able to count on roster continuity, including the marketing of star players identifiable with their team, from one year to the next. The obvious downside of the reserve clause from the perspective of the players—especially the best players— was that they lacked leverage with the owners when it came to negotiating a fair-market-value salary based on their performance. Their only leverage was to threaten to sit out the season or quit the game—a high-risk bluff if the owner called it, because they were still technically bound to their club by the reserve clause.

The reserve clause seemed immune from legal challenge. There was virtually no precedent for players to rely on. There was one, however, for the owners. In its battle for survival after self-declaring as a "major league" in 1914 and aggressively pursuing established major leaguers, the upstart Federal League took to federal court the proposition that the reserve clause, by binding players to their club even when their contracts were up, was restraint of trade that monopolized the baseball business, putting the American and National Leagues in violation of federal antitrust law. Although the Federal League folded after two years, in large part because major-league owners enticed their star players to stay put by offering lucrative multiyear contracts, the Federal League case regarding the reserve clause lived on, ultimately finding its way to the US Supreme Court in 1922.

In a decision that Major League Baseball surely regarded as game saving, the court unanimously upheld a lower court ruling in favor of the established major leagues. The foundation for the court's conclusion was that there was no violation of federal antitrust law because, since the transportation required between states to play games was "a mere incident, not the essential thing," baseball could not be said to be interstate commerce. Alluding to the reserve clause, the very last sentence of the decision stated that "the restrictions by contract that prevented the plaintiff [the Federal League's Baltimore club] from getting players to break their bargains" were "not an interference with commerce among the states." In an article for the *Baseball Research Journal* in 2009, current Supreme Court justice Samuel Alito explained that the decision, which has since been widely derided, relied on the more limited definition of interstate commerce then prevailing and was consistent with the jurisprudence of the time.

The 1922 decision would stand the test of time. It was upheld in *Toolson v. New York Yankees*, when the Supreme Court ruled in 1953 that the reserve clause in pitcher George Toolson's contract allowed the Yankees to reassign him in their farm system when he failed to make the major-league club in 1949 rather than let him negotiate a new contract with another franchise. And it was upheld by the Supreme Court again in the 1972 Curt Flood case. Neither of those decisions was unanimous; both featured strongly worded dissents.

The 1946 MacPhail Report on the fundamental challenges facing Major League Baseball as the country emerged from the Great Depression and World War II was less sanguine that the reserve clause, at least as then worded, would hold up to player challenges in federal court. Labor law expert Robert Murphy's ill-fated effort earlier that year to organize a players' union in the ferment of labor activism in postwar America greatly alarmed the owners. Although his rollout of the American Baseball Guild included securing the right of arbitration in player salary disputes as a primary goal, Murphy deliberately shied away from explicitly targeting the reserve clause. That did not prevent him from making the provocative statement that "the days of baseball serfdom would soon be over."

Washington Senators owner Clark Griffith understood where this was headed. He would know. As one of baseball's premier pitchers nearly 50 years earlier when Ban Johnson was targeting established stars to jump to his American League startup, Griffith was the most influential activist in using his position as vice president of the Players Protective Association to convince a great many National League players to hold off signing new contracts until after the NL owners negotiated with the union about their grievances. The owners didn't, and many players jumped leagues, giving the AL instant "major league" credibility. Now a franchise owner himself, Griffith not surprisingly was adamantly opposed to player activism. In April 1946 Murphy, accusing Griffith of illegally counseling his team's players not to join the American Baseball Guild, filed charges with the US National Labor Relations Board. Griffith's response was to say he was indeed opposed to Murphy's union because it would inevitably challenge the reserve clause, and "baseball can't exist without the reserve clause." The MacPhail Report hammered home the point, calling the reserve clause "the fundamental upon which the entire structure of Professional Baseball is based."

While the failure of the *Toolson* case may have settled the matter in the courts, by the late 1950s the reserve clause was being debated in congressional hearings on big-league sports. Legislation could change everything. Still, there was no budge as far as Major League Baseball was concerned, and the owners were able to secure enough allies in Congress to head off laws that would have limited baseball's antitrust exemption. But now it was Marvin Miller's time, and baseball would never be the same.

* * *

Since becoming executive director of the Major League Baseball Players Association in 1966, Miller had proven himself an unintimidated ally of the players, relentless especially in improving their leverage on issues that mattered—first the pension plan, followed by collective bargaining, then independent arbitration of player grievances. Some players, most famously Carl Yastrzemski, were slow to come around, buying into the owners' contention that the business of Major League Baseball was necessarily different from that of other industries and that to mess with it would undermine both an all-American tradition—baseball was the national pastime, after all—and the structural integrity of the game itself. Miller was careful not to assault the reserve clause prematurely, knowing he had to have the trust and full backing of the players when he did so. He also had the advantage of the current generation of players whose careers began in the 1960s being, like countless young Americans, skeptical of authority and more willing to challenge what they believed to be unfair. Miller had their back, and they had his.

The first challenge to the reserve clause in Miller's time as leader of the players' union was initiated not by him, but by veteran outfielder Curt Flood after the Cardinals traded his contract to the Phillies in October 1969. Flood had played 12 years in St. Louis, batting .293 in 1,738 games. He was a cornerstone player on the Cardinals' 1964, '67, and '68 pennant-winning ballclubs, teaming with Lou Brock at the top of the order to jump-start the offense. Soon to turn 32 and having just hit .285 in 1969 (following .335 and .301 the two previous years), Flood figured to have several productive seasons ahead of him, with 2,000 hits a benchmark to achieve in 1970; he was 146 hits shy and had averaged 178 hits the five previous years. But he had no interest in going to Philadelphia, in part because of that city's reputation as both racist and nasty, including the press, when it came to the shortcomings of their professional sports teams. Even after the Phillies offered him a $100,000 contract, up from the $90,000 he made his last year in St. Louis, Flood refused to go, deciding instead to challenge the reserve clause that gave the Cardinals carte blanche to trade him.

After consulting with Miller and being assured of the union's support, Flood notified Commissioner Bowie Kuhn in a letter drafted by Miller that he would not be reporting to the Phillies. "After twelve years in the Major Leagues," Flood explained, "I do not believe I am a piece of property to be bought and sold irrespective of my wishes." He asked that all major-league clubs be informed of his availability for the 1970 season, essentially saying he wished to be a free agent able to consider offers from different teams. The commissioner wrote back that "your present contract has been assigned in accordance with its provisions by the St. Louis club to the Philadelphia club." Flood announced that he would see Major League Baseball in court, drew criticism for asserting that the reserve clause was "indentured servitude" and made him feel like a "slave," and, when told by Howard Cosell in an interview on ABC-TV's *Wide World of Sports* on January 3, 1970, that "$90,000 . . . isn't exactly slave wages," answered, "[A] well-paid slave is, nonetheless, a slave." The fact he was a black man saying this, earning as much money as he did, at a time when black militancy was scaring whites across the country, made him an unsympathetic figure in much of the public eye. It did not go unnoticed that while black players were among the strongest backers of their union, prominent stars like Willie Mays and Hank Aaron kept quiet about Flood's gambit.

Curt Flood lost his case in the court of public opinion before he lost in court—first in the federal court in the Southern District of New York in 1970, then in a federal appeals court, and finally in the Supreme Court, which affirmed the lower court's ruling by a 5-to-3 majority in 1972. Flood's rhetoric about "indentured servitude" and "slavery" while America was dealing with racial strife and fighting a war in Vietnam made him an unsympathetic character. As the ever-provocative Cosell pointed out, Flood had just earned $90,000 playing baseball at a time when the median family income in the United States was less than $9,000, according to Department of Commerce data. Even in the major leagues, where the average salary in 1970 was about $29,000, Flood was being paid close to the top tier of players; only 10 players in 1970 earned more than $100,000—the salary the Phillies offered Flood to play in Philadelphia. It also didn't help that there was widespread sentiment among Americans that the country's moral grounding was being undermined by a lack of respect for tradition and institutions of authority. Flood's suit directly undermined a longstanding cornerstone, however unjust it might have been, of a revered American institution—Major League Baseball. Most of the sports coverage about Flood's case was negative, making precisely the point that, should he win in court, baseball as legions of fans over a century had come to know it would be irrevocably damaged.

It is likely not coincidental that in denying Flood relief from the reserve clause in the case he brought before the Southern District of New York, the judge's opinion made note of the "unique place" baseball held in "our American heritage"; nor that Supreme Court justice Harry A. Blackmun, in affirming that decision two years later, began his opinion with a nostalgic exposition on the history of baseball in which he listed 88 baseball personages dating back to the nineteenth century whose exploits "provided tinder for recaptured thrills, for reminiscence and comparisons, and for conversation and anticipation in-season and off-season"—some of whom, like Germany Schaefer, Jimmy Austin, and Moe Berg (better known as the catcher who was a spy), would not have been familiar to most people reading the decision. Many thought Blackmun laid it on a bit too thick. Because Flood's case was brought before the courts as an antitrust suit, the lower court, the federal appeals court that upheld that decision, and the Supreme Court ruled that the 1922 Supreme Court verdict that exempted baseball from antitrust statutes still held.

While upholding baseball's antitrust exemption, however, both the Southern District and Supreme Court opinions suggested it was out of step with the times. The Southern District judge who first ruled on the Flood case offered the view that Major League Baseball and the players' union should negotiate "an accommodation on the reserve system that would be eminently fair and equitable to all concerned." Justice Blackmun, in his majority opinion, called the 1922 exemption an "aberration" because subsequent Supreme Court rulings held that other interstate professional sports were not similarly exempt, but said it still applied to baseball for the reason that Congress had failed to do anything about it despite numerous opportunities, including specific legislation, to do so. If baseball was to be stripped of its antitrust exemption, Blackmun wrote, the burden was on Congress, not the courts, to take action.

Two justices dissented from the decision, claiming that players were "victims" of the reserve clause, which was in fact "an unreasonable restraint of trade," and that the majority erred in leaving it up to Congress to pass legislation ending baseball's exemption. The third justice in dissent, Thurgood Marshall, the only black man on the court, would have remanded the case back to the district court on the grounds that the collective bargaining agreement between Major League Baseball and the players' union, having made the reserve clause "a mandatory subject of bargaining," might override the antitrust exemption. In that case, federal labor statutes, not antitrust laws, would apply. Marshall's dissent surely piqued the interest of Miller, not necessarily because he hadn't thought of that himself, but because Marshall, from the highest bench in the land, put a light on that avenue.

* * *

On March 20, 1972, the day oral arguments in the Curt Flood case were heard by the Supreme Court, Major League Baseball stood on the precipice of its first leaguewide players' strike. Ever. Spring training was nearing its end; April 5th was Opening Day. With baseball's collective bargaining agreement about to expire, the owners were unexpectedly taking a hard line on modestly increasing their contributions to the pension fund to make up for inflation since the last CBA was negotiated in 1970. Outraged, the players threatened to strike. The owners wanted to call their bluff. Miller was worried the union's leverage would be irreparably damaged if the players went on strike only to cave when the realization hit that this could go on, without pay, for some time. Rallied by Oakland A's star Reggie Jackson, all but one of the 48 player reps demanded Miller lead the union on a strike. The players were in effect calling the owners' bluff. They went on strike on April 1—April Fool's Day. Opening Day came and went with no games. The players stood firm. Realizing their revenue losses from canceled games—particularly from national TV broadcast rights—could very soon become prohibitive, it was the owners who caved. The strike ended on April 11. Four days later the season picked up from it would have been on that date according to the major-league schedule. None of the 86 games lost to the strike were made up.

There was widespread booing of the players when they took the field their first games back after staring down the owners, but for Marvin Miller this was a seminal moment for the players' union. The players proved they would stand united in defense of their interests. The owners were shocked into realizing that they could not intimidate the players to back down. They had overplayed their hand on a small issue. Miller's union had clout and demonstrated its willingness to use it—especially on matters of importance, like the reserve clause. It didn't matter that two months later Curt Flood lost his case before the Supreme Court. The courts had made clear that while baseball's antitrust exemption still stood, it was an anachronism even in modern jurisprudence. All that Marvin Miller needed was an opening—and the appropriate player.

While Miller was biding his time for that propitious moment, the MLBPA scored another victory by getting the owners to agree in the 1973 collective bargaining agreement to binding salary arbitration for unsigned players with at least two years in the major leagues, with an independent arbitrator deciding between either the player's salary demand or his club's salary offer if the two sides could not negotiate their differences. The new CBA also mandated that any player with 10 years in the majors and five with his club could not be traded or sold to another club without his consent. In December 1973, Cubs' third baseman Ron Santo, who had 14 mostly stellar big-league seasons behind him, all with the Cubs, vetoed a trade that would have sent him to the California Angels. Having just traded for 22-year-old third baseman Bill Madlock, who batted .351 in his September call-up with the Texas Rangers, the Cubs no longer wanted or needed the 33-year-old Santo. The veteran third baseman *did* approve being traded across town to Chicago's White Sox.

But the most significant development leading toward a direct assault on the reserve clause came in December 1974 when Peter Seitz, the independent arbitrator to hear player grievances as agreed to in baseball's 1970 collective bargaining agreement, ruled Oakland A's ace Catfish Hunter to be a free agent because franchise owner Charlie Finley did not live up to his side of the two-year $200,000 contract the pitcher had signed before the previous season. For tax purposes, half of each season's salary was to be deferred into insurance annuities. Hunter had the best year of his career in 1974, with a 25–12 record, leading the league in wins and earned-run average. Oakland went to the World Series for the third consecutive year and won for the third straight time. Despite the excellence of his pitcher and the success of his club, Finley did not make any of the obligated deferred-salary payments even after Hunter's attorney began pressing the matter in August. As soon as the World Series ended, Hunter, with the full backing of the union, declared his contract voided by Finley's failure to abide by its terms. Hunter's grievance went before the three-person arbitration panel—which included Miller representing the union, an attorney representing the owners, and Seitz—in November. That month, Hunter was also named the American League's Cy Young Award winner for 1974. Seitz was persuaded by the evidence; by the end of the year Catfish was a free agent.

Hunter was not the first-ever player bound to his club by the reserve clause to be declared a free agent. In the late 1930s, for example, future stars Tommy Henrich and Pete Reiser, both standout minor leaguers at the time, were granted free agency by Commissioner Landis, a former federal judge, on the grounds that their parent club violated major-league rules in their handling of the players' status in their farm systems. Hunter, however, was the first player to be declared a free agent by an arbitrator acting independently of institutional Major League Baseball.

Every major-league team was now free to bid for the services of one of baseball's finest pitchers. Into the fray stepped the New York Yankees, whose new owner, George Steinbrenner, was anxious to return the Yankees to their once-upon-a-time status as the best team in baseball year in and year out and whose club had just finished fourth in his first year as "The Boss." Steinbrenner wanted Hunter, and the Yankees got their man. All it took was the first multimillion-dollar contract in baseball history, the principals of which were $3.2 million over five years and a $1 million signing bonus. All of baseball surely took notice—the owners with trepidation over skyrocketing salaries if free agency replaced the reserve clause, the players with anticipation of big paydays if free agency replaced the reserve clause, and Marvin Miller with the knowledge that having player grievances heard by an independent arbitrator diluted the owners' power to dictate outcomes when it came to player contracts.

* * *

Although he gave the former St. Louis center fielder the union's full backing, Curt Flood's case was probably not the one Miller would have chosen to challenge the reserve clause had Flood not come to him for assistance. For one thing, the legal weak point of the reserve clause was the club's right to a one-year extension on the same terms if there was no agreement on a new contract that the owners interpreted could be annually renewed in perpetuity. Miller thought the best approach to force the issue on whether that interpretation was correct was for a player to play his reserve year without a contract and then petition for free agency on the grounds that the club's right to reserve his contract was for one year and one year only. Miller also believed the first means for tackling the issue should be through independent arbitration as a player grievance, per the 1970 collective bargaining agreement, rather than through the courts. As long as the Flood case was being litigated, however, Miller was committed not to muddy the legal waters or confront the owners with either a demand to modify the reserve clause or a player testing the club option for a one-year renewal in arbitration.

The time for that came soon after Hunter was granted free agency—a decision that had to do with a contract violation rather than the reserve clause. Like Hunter, Dodgers right-handed ace Andy Messersmith had an outstanding season in 1974, his 20 wins the most in the National League. Having just had the best season of his career, Messersmith wanted a multiyear contract with a provision that he could veto being traded or sold to another club. The Dodgers refused his demands; Messersmith refused to sign a new contract, and so he pitched the 1975 season without one. As it happened, Messersmith had another outstanding season, going 19–14 with a 2.29 ERA. His 40 starts, 19 complete games, 7 shutouts, and 321⅔ innings pitched led the league.

Messersmith's was an excellent test case for challenging the reserve clause—specifically, should the player and his team not agree to the terms of a new contract, what exactly did the words "the Club shall have the right by written notice to the Player to extend this contract for the period of one year on the same terms" mean? This was specific language recommended in the 1946 MacPhail Report to "remove the grounds on which the option could be attacked successfully." The players' union interpretation was that Messersmith's pitching the entire 1975 season without a new contract was the "one year" the Dodgers were entitled to in unilaterally "extending" his contract, that LA therefore no longer had an option on him, and that Andy Messersmith should be declared a free agent.

Realizing what was at stake, especially given the outcome of the Hunter arbitration hearing, the Dodgers tried to retroactively sign Messersmith to a lucrative contract for the season just ended. The pitcher said, "No thanks," but, hedging his bets against the possibility that the Dodgers and Messersmith might reach an accommodation, Miller reached out to Dave McNally, the former Baltimore ace who had also pitched the 1975 season without a contract after being traded to Montreal and failing to come to terms with his new team. McNally, who had retired in June and had no interest in ever pitching again, agreed to join Messersmith's arbitration case. With Messersmith staying the course, Seitz ruled in December that the one-year renewal provision of the reserve clause meant for one year only and that the 1975 season, when both Messersmith and McNally pitched without a contract, was that one year. Seitz was fired on the spot, as was the owners' prerogative, since both sides had to agree on the arbitrator.

Both pitchers were now free agents pending the outcome of Major League Baseball's case in the federal district court in Kansas City, where the league hoped the arbitrator's decision would be overruled. The judge, however, was not given to sentiment about baseball's hallowed place in American culture and was not persuaded by either the merits of the owners' case or their assertions that the national pastime would be irreparably damaged if Seitz's decision stood. The owners lost. They also lost on appeal to the Eighth Circuit, which they should have known had a history of upholding arbitrators' decisions. Baseball's owners did not appeal to the Supreme Court, properly understanding that—as Justice Marshall had pointed out in his dissent in the Curt Flood case—this was now a case in the realm of federal labor statutes, not antitrust laws. Messersmith was now indeed a free agent, with suitors that included the Yankees. He signed a three-year deal with the Atlanta Braves for $1 million and a $400,000 signing bonus and was booed at ballparks around the National League, including at home, because fans bought into the premise that free agency would ruin the game. McNally went back to retirement.

What next?

The judge in the federal district court that first heard the Flood case wrote in his opinion that the best solution would be for the players' union and the owners to negotiate their differences on the reserve clause "so as to find acceptance by player and club." Miller also thought this the best approach, and not just for the tactical reason of presenting the union as responsible and reasonable in negotiating a new collective bargaining agreement that included changes to the reserve system. As an economist, Miller had little doubt that unrestricted free agency—free agency for every player at the end of every contract—would both be unworkable and have the effect of suppressing, rather than raising, player salaries. He was more than willing to compromise. The commissioner and baseball's owners, however, were not. Reeling from the Seitz decision, believing that free agency would destabilize the game, thinking (probably correctly) that they had most of the country's baseball fans on their side, and calculating (probably incorrectly) that the players would ultimately back down, many owners at first wanted to take a hard line on the reserve clause, as though the Messersmith case was an anomaly they could put behind them. They imposed a lockout of all but nonroster players when spring training began in 1976, implying they might play the season with them until a new CBA was signed—one in which the union backed down from demands that the terms of free agency be negotiated.

The lockout caused Miller to recommend that players not sign their contracts for the coming season, which would effectively make them all free agents going into 1977. The owners themselves were divided. Probably a majority wanted to keep the old reserve system the way it had always been. Some understood, however, that the lockout put Major League Baseball in legal jeopardy. Many more were fearful of the chaos that would ensue if most players followed Miller's guidance to not sign contracts, thus becoming free agents. A few owners, most notably George Steinbrenner and Atlanta's Ted Turner, were inclined to support a compromise on the reserve clause and free agency, in large part because they—especially the well-capitalized Steinbrenner Yankees—would benefit competitively, at the gate, and in broadcast revenue from their ability to sign the best free agents. And then there was Charlie Finley, Oakland's maverick owner who had made a sideline of offending virtually all of his fellow owners since he first bought the Athletics. Finley wanted to call Miller's bluff. "Make 'em all free agents!" he declared, making the point that a glut of players on the market would drive down their price— precisely Miller's reason for wanting a compromise that reasonably *restricted* free agency.

Commissioner Bowie Kuhn, buoyed by the sage counsel of Dodgers owner Walter O'Malley and pressured by the likes of Steinbrenner, decided the lockout was counterproductive and would likely do more harm to the game than compromising on free agency. He ordered spring training camps reopened; Miller reciprocated by saying players were free to sign new contracts for the upcoming season; and the two sides convened to negotiate a new CBA that would, as the first federal judge hearing the Flood case suggested, "produce an accommodation on the reserve system which would be eminently fair and equitable to all concerned."

In the midst of the negotiations, Finley, all of whose best players would be free agents at the end of the season because none had signed a new contract, and having already traded Reggie Jackson and Ken Holtzman, conducted a fire sale of three of Oakland's remaining star players— Vida Blue to the Yankees and Joe Rudi and Rollie Fingers to the Red Sox—which Kuhn summarily voided for *not* being "in the best interest of baseball." If Kuhn's intention was to establish an "in the best interest of baseball" precedent for the commissioner to intervene in free agency, Miller quickly slapped that down as unacceptable. The new collective bargaining agreement finally approved in July granted all players who played the year without a contract free agency for 1977. Going forward, no player could become a free agent until he had played six years in the major leagues.

* * *

All eyes were now on the first free agent class of 1976—those who had played out their team's option year on their services without having signed a new contract. How would they fare? The class of '76 was particularly interesting because it included some players with much less than the six years of big-league service time that would be required for free agency in future years. Thirteen free agents signed multiyear million-dollar contracts, most for five years. What major leaguers looking to their future, and certainly Marvin Miller, paid attention to were the players scoring million-dollar deals who did not have the résumés of Reggie Jackson, Joe Rudi, Rollie Fingers, Sal Bando, Gene Tenace, and Bert Campaneris—just to name those on Finley's Oakland team that won five straight division titles, three pennants, and three World Series. A particular head-scratcher that drew notice was Cleveland's signing right-hander Wayne Garland to a 10-year deal worth $2 million on the basis of one 20-win year for Baltimore in 1976, prior to which he had appeared in 53 games with a 7–11 record, made just 8 starts, and thrown only 194⅓ innings in parts of three seasons—hardly a track record, many said, to justify that kind of a contract.

The first free agent class was also a feeling-out for major-league teams of both the market and the impact of player signings on competitiveness. Seven National League clubs and six in the American League, two of which were the 1977 AL expansion teams, did not make any serious bid for established veterans who had played their option year without a contract. The Cubs' general manager explained his club's passivity by saying, "Mercenaries don't win wars," to which *Sports Illustrated* in a December 1976 article summarizing how it was going so far replied, "Neither do conscientious objectors."

The clubs that were most aggressive in pursuing the best players available in the free agent class of '76 were the New York Yankees, California Angels, and San Diego Padres. For Steinbrenner, the outstanding season Catfish Hunter had in the first year of his five-year $3.2 million deal after the Seitz decision—a 23–14 record and 2.58 earned-run average in 1975—and his 17 wins helping them to the 1976 pennant validated the benefits of plunging into the free agent market for top talent, so he made

Jackson and Cincinnati ace Don Gullett offers they could not refuse. Hunter's deal was the threshold to pass, in terms of both overall value and annual compensation, but not even Reggie could get the Yankees to give him as sweet a deal as they gave Catfish. The Angels, a fifth-place club in 1976 but possessing a formidable starting rotation led by Nolan Ryan and Frank Tanana, hoped their free agent signings of Baltimore second baseman Bobby Grich and Oakland outfielders Joe Rudi and Don Baylor would pave the way to winning the AL West. Enticing Fingers and Tenace to San Diego, the fourth-place Padres probably had the less ambitious hope of simply being able to compete in the NL West. While the Yankees with their free agent acquisitions won 100 games, the pennant— their second with Catfish—and the World Series in 1977, the Angels and Padres with theirs came in a distant fifth in their respective divisions, both with losing records.

Whatever misgivings his fellow owners had about free agency, most continuing to believe it was bad for the game as they had forever known it, Steinbrenner was liking it very much for what it could do for his Yankees. First there was Hunter. Then there was Jackson and Gullett and the Yankees' first World Series victory in 15 years. Since Pittsburgh reliever Rich "Goose" Gossage was by far the best player in the free agent class of 1977, Steinbrenner wanted him too, even though Yankees relief ace Sparky Lyle had just become the first reliever to win the American League Cy Young Award and had pitched brilliantly out of the bullpen in both the ALCS and the World Series. Notwithstanding Lyle's predictable resentment and its potential impact in the clubhouse, Gossage was signed to a six-year deal exceeding $3.5 million including his signing bonus and deferred salary. The next year the Yankees went after Red Sox pitcher Luis Tiant, not only best in the class of 1978, but an ace on the Yankees' rival for supremacy in the AL East. Two years later Steinbrenner stunned the baseball world by signing the best player in the 1980 free agent class, San Diego outfielder Dave Winfield, to the richest contract in baseball history—$13.3 million for 10 years, with cost of living increases that a *New York Times* baseball columnist calculated could make the deal worth close to $25 million. In fact, Winfield earned nearly $20 million in salary alone under the terms of that contract.

* * *

The Yankees' largess and Steinbrenner's annual romp in the marketplace fed the perception that well-capitalized big-market teams would henceforth dominate the game year in and year out because they would be able to buy their way to the top. In considering the implications of Seitz's Messersmith decision, some owners and many influential baseball writers worried that free agency would lead to a competitive imbalance between flush dynasties and everybody else.

That, however, was precisely the history of Major League Baseball for virtually the entirety of the sanctity-of-the-reserve-clause era. Until 1965, when an amateur draft was instituted with teams' drafting order determined by the order they finished the previous year starting with the worst record, amateur players were free to sign with any team that offered them the best contract, which allowed the wealthiest clubs to snap up the best young talent. The less well-off clubs, who also had less money to spend on scouting, had to hope they got lucky. The wealthiest clubs were also able to ensure their best players were the best-paid in baseball, could use cash sweeteners in transactions for other teams' best players, and had a significant advantage in being able to fund productive minor-league farm systems. It was not happenstance that the Yankees, the seemingly forever dynasty, won 29 pennants and 20 World Series in 44 years between 1921 and 1964.

Lessons were learned by all sides about perceptions and risks, although there was no consensus on what they were. Indeed, there was a spectrum of opinion among both players and executive management, not to mention baseball's scribes and legions of fans. Players who signed lucrative contracts were widely perceived as greedy. Those who left the teams with which they had long been identified for a better payday were seen as disloyal. But if the owners were only too happy to play the "players are greedy and disloyal" card in the court of public opinion, they faced their own scrutiny about why they weren't spending more on quality free agent players to boost the home team's competitive fortunes. Or they were being nastily second-guessed, as they had forever been on bad trades, on why they gave a small fortune to a guy who failed to live up to the hype *after* he signed for big bucks. Teams began trying to preempt free agency by offering players higher pay and multiyear contracts.

Baseball heroes from the past, perhaps resentful of the new earning potential of the profession they had to abandon because old age comes early to a ballplayer, had new ammunition—that free agency showed the current generation of players were just in it for themselves—to make the age-old point, as old-time players always have, that baseball just wasn't the same game it used to be, that players today (whenever "today" happened to be) were not as well-versed in the nuances of the game as in their generation. Some players who played below expectations in the first year of their new contracts were overwhelmed and snakebit by the pressure of trying to justify their large paychecks. And the enormity of those paychecks cast a greater divide between them and the rest of working Americans—not that there wasn't with Babe Ruth or Joe DiMaggio or Mickey Mantle. But those guys were the rare exception to the supposed reality that most players were like most Americans striving to make ends meet, except in a professional sport.

And Major League Baseball, including the fans, learned that free agent signings, even the most coveted, could not guarantee a player's health, especially pitchers. Messersmith, winner of 39 games the two years before Seitz made him a free agent, won only 18 more games in his major-league career as injuries to his knee and elbow forced his retirement in 1979. The Yankees only got two full seasons out of Hunter before he spent extended time on the disabled list the remaining three years of his contract. Gullett, whose recent history of injuries as Cincinnati's ace did not deter Steinbrenner from giving him a six-year deal worth $2 million, was all the Yankees expected him to be in his first year with them in 1977, going 14–4, but the searing inoperable shoulder pain that sidelined him for half of May and all of August drove him from the game the next year after just eight starts. He collected two-thirds of his $2 million the next four years—in retirement. Wayne Garland legitimately earned the first year of his ten-year $2 million deal with Cleveland, then went under the knife for rotator cuff surgery in 1978. The Indians let him go in 1981 after he had gone 28–48 for them in five years, then paid him a million dollars not to pitch over the remaining five years of his contract.

* * *

The beginning years of free agency did not prove to be the disaster that many baseball traditionalists said it would be. In 1978, player salaries, now about $68.5 million, accounted for less than a quarter of the total revenue brought in by Major League Baseball, according to Miller, because television broadcast revenues were up substantially. The game in many respects was perceived as more exciting than it had been in decades, in no small part due to greater exposure on television. TV coverage was more sophisticated and better than ever in terms of both camera angles and expert analysis. In 1979 Major League Baseball signed a new national television deal worth $47.5 million annually for games of the week, the All-Star Game, and the World Series, more than twice the previous agreement. And while free agent acquisitions were almost certainly decisive in the Yankees' winning close pennant races in the AL East in 1977, 1978, and perhaps even 1980, it could not be said that the competitive balance had changed in any meaningful way. Kansas City, for example, won three division titles without delving into the free agent market, except for a number of bit players and to sign one of their own pitchers, Larry Gura, when he became a free agent after the 1978 season. Rather than the mass movement that had been warned about, the percentage of players changing teams each year was about the same as before, when transactions between ballclubs ruled who went where, perhaps even a little less.

But as a matter of principle, Commissioner Kuhn and most of baseball's owners were not at all happy about free agency. Thanks to Marvin Miller and the changes he wrought, the average major-league salary had increased from just over $44,500 in 1975, the year before independent arbitrator Seitz precisely defined the one-year-renewal provision of the reserve clause, to about $74,000 in 1977, the first season played under free agency. Steinbrenner's ambitions contributed to all players entering free agency making what many owners considered extravagant salary demands, which had a cascading effect on what three-year players were demanding, and often winning, in salary arbitration and an upward push on player earnings in general. It was inevitable that Major League Baseball would soon have its first $1 million-a-year man. On November 19, 1979, it did. Houston's Astros, having just missed out on the NL West division title by 1½ games after blowing a 10½-game July Fourth lead, signed Nolan Ryan, the best in the free agent class of '79, whose 16–14 record had just helped the California Angels to their first-ever division title, to a four-year contract for $1,125,000 a year. By 1980 the average major-league player salary was up to $143,756.

Notwithstanding their industry being more profitable than ever, baseball's owners were determined to swing the pendulum back toward themselves when it came to the free agent marketplace in the new collective bargaining agreement to be negotiated in 1980. Their main objective was to diminish free agents' leverage by insisting that any team signing a "premier" free agent had to compensate that player's former team with a player off its major-league roster. The players' union was adamantly opposed precisely because the owners' plan would neutralize free agency. Already in 1980 spring training camps, major-league players were all but unanimous in voting to authorize a strike. Neither side was quite ready for a shutdown at this time, however. The new CBA did not address free agent compensation. The owners and the players' union agreed to a joint committee to study the issue for next time.

The owners were buying time. They established a strike fund to bail out the financially weakest franchises. They took out an insurance policy to cover losses for approximately six weeks. In February 1981 they announced that because the joint study committee was at loggerheads, they would unilaterally implement their compensation proposal. Spring training began amid talk of a players' strike. A federal mediator got involved, to no avail. The union filed an unfair labor practices suit. In early June a federal judge ruled against an injunction on the owners' intended action. The players' hand was forced. On June 12, Major League Baseball was shut down for the first time by a midseason players' strike. It lasted until July 31.

Despite losing some $34 million in pay, the players' solidarity proved far stronger than that of the owners, whose own losses, according to Miller in *A Whole New Ball Game*, were "said to exceed $72 million after insurance payments" and "were probably considerably higher." The owners' strike fund was about to run out. Moreover, the longer the strike went on, the less likely there would be a sufficient number of games played to justify a legitimate postseason, and it was the league championship series and the World Series where the money was made when it came to baseball's television contract. Desperate for an end to the strike, the owners agreed to far more limited compensation—any compensation at all was a concession by the players' union, since it eroded the concept of unencumbered free agency—for teams losing a premier free agent.

After about a week of players retuning for a return to action, the All-Star Game was played on August 9, and the 1981 baseball season resumed the following day. The 712 games not played could not possibly be rescheduled. Rather than pick up the pennant races where they left off, or think creatively about a "wild card" in each division, it was decided the 1981 season would be split in two, with the teams that were on top of their divisions when the strike began, declared automatic winners of the "first half," having to face off in a preliminary "division series" round of playoffs against the team with the best record in the poststrike "second half." That, of course, meant that the first-half winners could afford to *not* be at their best down the stretch drive. They were in the postseason without ever actually having to fight for a spot, since real pennant races could hardly be said to have been considered begun before the season was even a third over, as it was on June 12.

Marvin Miller stayed on as head of the players' union for another year before retiring in December 1982. Because of him, the *business* of baseball had fundamentally changed. Through arbitration and free agency, players were no longer at the mercy of franchise owners, as they had been for a full century after the National League opened for business in 1876. But it did not change the *game* of baseball, as the ownership clique insisted and baseball traditionalists feared free agency would. It was the same game, except in the American League with its 1973-adopted designated hitter rule.

21

A NEW BOSS REBOOTS
THE YANKEE DYNASTY

On January 3, 1973, the New York Yankees were sold for $10 million by CBS, the New York media conglomerate that had bought the club eight years earlier from longtime owners Dan Topping and Del Webb for $14 million, to an investor group led by the owner of a Cleveland ship-building company, name of Steinbrenner. George Steinbrenner. To secure the requisite funding, Steinbrenner had a host of limited partners, of whom it would soon be joked they had no idea how "limited" their limited partnership with "The Boss" would be. At his introductory press conference, Steinbrenner stated he would be an "absentee owner" and leave running the Yankees to baseball professionals who knew what they were doing. "We're not going to pretend we're something we aren't," he said. "I'll stick to building ships." Famous first words.

The CBS years, which began just after the Yankees won their 29th pennant in 1964, saw the end of the "forever dynasty" that got its start in 1921 under the aegis of New York beer baron Jacob Ruppert, whose foresight included hiring Miller Huggins as manager, buying Babe Ruth from the Red Sox, enticing Ed Barrow to leave Boston for New York to be general manager, hiring Joe McCarthy as manager a year after Huggins died, and developing the best possible farm system his money could buy in the Depression-era 1930s. Since the age- and injury-related retirements of Whitey Ford and Mickey Mantle in 1967 and 1968, the closest the CBS-owned Yankees came to a pennant was 1972, the year CBS put the franchise on the market. The Yankees were within half a game of first in the AL East for four days in early September before ending up fourth, 6½ games behind, with a record just three games over .500.

The Yankees' headliners in 1972 were outfielders Bobby Murcer, whose terrific season—33 homers, 96 runs batted in, and second-in-the-league .331 batting average—finally lived up to expectations he would be at least Mickey Mantle–lite, and Roy White, quietly consistent and much better throughout his career than his stats would indicate; catcher Thurman Munson, the AL's 1970 Rookie of the Year whose orneriness made him both a natural leader and somehow endearing; and relief ace Sparky Lyle, in his first year with the Yankees after five in Boston, whose 35 saves were a new American League record. After the 1972 season ended, and in the midst of Steinbrenner's negotiations to purchase the team, the Yankees traded with his hometown team in Cleveland for third baseman Graig Nettles, whose defensive excellence at the hot corner was backed up by his 71 homers for the Indians between 1970 and 1972.

American League owners approving the sale of their league's flagship franchise to Steinbrenner had no idea what they were in for. Those in the Yankees' universe soon found out. During spring training, Steinbrenner issued an edict hearkening back to McCarthy's dress code that was a Yankees tradition—that the appropriate appearance for Yankees one and all precluded long hair and beards. The season was barely two weeks old before Steinbrenner succeeded in forcing out team president Michael Burke, a holdover from the CBS years. The new boss was not at all happy about how the 1973 season played out. After holding first place in the AL East for all of July, they won only 20 of their 54 games the rest of the way to end his first year as owner with a losing 80–82 record. Thus began Steinbrenner's obsession with criticizing his manager's moves. His manager happened to be Ralph Houk, one of the most respected dugout leaders in the game and the Yankees' last remaining link to their glory years in the 1950s and early 1960s. Houk didn't wait to be fired, as he surely would have been. He resigned on the last day of the season.

In the midst of the Yankees' August tailspin, Steinbrenner began secretive talks with Oakland manager Dick Williams about coming to New York, and Houk, now in his eighth year as Yankees manager since stepping down from the GM role early in the 1966 season, did the same with the Detroit Tigers. In both cases, they violated baseball's regulations against clubs tampering with other teams' personnel. Both cases became an issue for adjudication ultimately involving Commissioner Bowie Kuhn once the season ended. Houk was permitted to accept the Tigers' offer. Williams, despite winning two World Series, quit as A's manager because he couldn't stand team owner Charlie Finley's incessant meddling, was not allowed to manage the Yankees because he was still officially under contract to Oakland. With Williams taken off the table, the Yankees signed Bill Virdon as their new manager.

Steinbrenner's Dick Williams gambit was the first of many high-profile instances of the new boss going aggressively after specific people he was convinced would return the Yankees to their former glory. Almost exactly a year later, Steinbrenner went after another top-tier talent on Finley's club—right-handed ace Catfish Hunter, fresh off his fourth straight 20-win season, and just made a free agent by baseball's independent arbitrator because Finley had failed to live up to a key provision of his contract. In the wake of the Yankees' failing to hold the slim lead they had for most of September in the 1974 division race and losing out to the Orioles by two games, Steinbrenner and his baseball brain trust were certain Catfish would make all the difference in the year ahead. Steinbrenner, however, was serving a two-year suspension from the privileges of ownership by the commissioner for pleading guilty in August 1974 to making illegal contributions—a federal felony—to President Richard Nixon's 1972 reelection campaign. The Boss may have been officially benched, but given that Hunter was almost certainly going to get the most lucrative contract in major-league history from whichever team offered it, Yankees executives felt justified in seeking his approval—at least implicitly. Steinbrenner, aware of the terms of his suspension, said both that it was their decision and "[W]e have to get this guy."

Hunter's five-year $3.2 million deal paid significant dividends for the Yankees as Catfish went 23–14 in 1975 to lead the league in wins for the second straight year. So did the trade of Bobby Murcer to San Francisco for their comparable star, Bobby Bonds. Unfortunately, Hunter's wins and Bonds's team-leading 32 homers weren't enough to overcome the Yankees' poor start. That cost Virdon his job, never mind his track record leading the Pirates to the best record in baseball in his first year as a manager in 1972. With the Yankees out of the division race by late July and struggling to stay above .500, Steinbrenner, despite still serving time in Kuhn's doghouse, was hardly silent in his associations with team executives on "a purely social basis," which was allowed under the terms of his suspension, about what he considered to be the Yankees' underperformance. Steinbrenner not only wanted Virdon out, he wanted Billy Martin in. The Boss may have been officially sidelined, but he got his man.

* * *

Billy Martin was available because he had just been fired as manager of the Texas Rangers. They were the third team to rid themselves of Martin in six years. Martin's record of significant accomplishment was accompanied by a growing rap sheet of antagonistic relationships with players and owners. In 1969 he guided Minnesota to a runaway division title in the AL West in his first year as a major-league manager, but also punched out 20-game winner Dave Boswell in a bar fight. Twins owner Calvin Griffith did not consider him either a good citizen or an appropriate role model. He was fired. Getting a second chance in 1971 with the Tigers, Martin boosted the club's winning total from 79 to 91 his first year, then led Detroit to the AL Eastern Division title in 1972 by half a game—an anomaly occasioned by the players' strike that cost the first two weeks of the season with no effort to either make up the missed games or ensure all teams played the same number of games by the end of the season. The next year he was once again at odds with both players and upper management, and told baseball writers he had ordered his pitchers to throw at opposing hitters. Martin was fired in August.

Out of work less than a week, Martin resurfaced as manager of the Texas Rangers, who already had 91 losses on their ledger, to finish out a lost-cause season. With a fresh start the next year, he quickly turned his new team around, taking a last-place 57-win club the year before into second place with 84 wins in 1974. It was a remarkable performance for a historically hapless franchise that began as the 1961-expansion Washington Senators. The Rangers could not sustain that level of play the next year, the intensity and appropriateness of his managerial style was again an issue, and Martin was fired in mid-July 1975 with Texas buried deep in fourth place. That made him immediately available for his dream job— manager of the New York Yankees.

Billy Martin had an affinity for New York. He identified with the Yankees—his first major-league team—and was an apt pupil of Casey Stengel, his one and only manager in his time with the Yankees. He seemed to play above his abilities in the World Series, saving the seventh game of the 1952 series with a running, lunging catch of a Jackie Robinson popup around the mound with the bases loaded that seemed not to interest the rest of the Yankees' infield, and batted .500 with 12 hits as the

Yankees beat the Dodgers in six games in 1953. He also palled around with Mantle and Ford, which is what ultimately got him traded to Kansas City as a bad influence—not that Mantle and Ford needed Martin's motivating influence. He wanted nothing more than to manage the Yankees, considering it almost his birthright. Boss Steinbrenner made Martin's dream a reality, and for dramatic effect the managerial change was announced during the Yankees' annual Old-Timers' Day festivities on August 2, for which Billy Martin was present as a Yankee from the 1950s. This was the start of quite the soap opera, with Steinbrenner and Martin playing the parts of star-crossed lovers.

* * *

Back in New York, where he believed he belonged, Billy Martin was ready to return the Yankees to greatness. And return them he did, with a vengeance. In his first full year as manager in 1976, Martin had the Yankees on top of the AL East in all but the first two days of the season on their way to a 10½-game romp of their division. Hunter won 17. Nettles led the league with 32 homers. Munson batted over .300 for the fourth time in his eight-year career and won the MVP Award. The Yankees were bolstered by trades with the Angels, giving up Bonds for speedy center fielder Mickey Rivers and right-hander Ed Figueroa, and with the Pirates for second baseman Willie Randolph. After winning the fifth and final game of the 1976 ALCS in dramatic fashion on first baseman Chris Chambliss's walk-off home run in Yankee Stadium, the Yanks had their first pennant since 1964. As dominant as they were with 97 wins, however, the Yankees were no match for the Big Red Machine in the World Series. They were swept in four games despite Munson's batting .529, in part because Johnny Bench batted .533 with 6 RBIs in a compelling tour de force by the two teams' catchers.

Notwithstanding that unhappy ending, the 1976 season was one to celebrate in more ways than one. Steinbrenner's suspension, the impact of which was mostly just keeping him out of the ballpark, was lifted in spring training. He was now free to opine loudly and very visibly whenever things displeased him. And after two years playing in Shea Stadium, home of the New York Mets, while Yankee Stadium was being renovated, the Yankees were back in the House That Ruth Built. Except it was no longer the stadium that Ruth and Gehrig, DiMaggio and Mantle had played in: Field dimensions were altered, outfield fences raised, and the center field monuments were no longer on the playing field; the bullpens between the triple-deck grandstands and bleachers in left and right fields were eliminated and placed elsewhere; and Yankee Stadium's distinctive, aging facade was removed so it wouldn't fall on patrons.

Perhaps most relevant to Steinbrenner going forward was the Andy Messersmith decision on the reserve clause—a development he would exploit year after year in his effort to keep the Yankees' dynasty "forever"—or for at least as long as he shall live. The subsequent collective bargaining agreement approved by players and owners established free agency for six-year veterans as the new law of the land. Much to the chagrin of his fellow owners, very few of whom had comparable financial resources to draw upon, Steinbrenner was prepared to bid whatever it took to sign any free agent superstar he wanted.

To shore up his club for the 1977 season, Steinbrenner was attracted to Oakland's discontented-with-Finley superstar slugger Reggie Jackson, who had been traded to Baltimore for the 1976 season, like a moth to a flame. The feeling was mutual. In addition to the promise of signing a lucrative multimillion-dollar contract, Reggie craved the bigger spotlight, wanting "to be part of it—New York, New York." Sinatra couldn't have said it better, although it took Steinbrenner until 1980 before that Sinatra classic was played at Yankee Stadium at the end of every game. The Yankees also signed Cincinnati World Series nemesis Don Gullett as a free agent and solved their longstanding problem at shortstop since Tony Kubek's retirement in 1965 by trading for the White Sox' Bucky Dent, whose middle initial was "E" for Earl, not "F" as Red Sox fans would soon have it. The 1977 Yankees also began the season with a deceptively hard-throwing—especially for being a lightweight (just 160 pounds on a 5-foot-11 frame)—lefty named Ron Guidry. Although he had been exclusively a reliever in Triple-A, Guidry quickly became the ace of the staff, with a 16–7 record and 2.82 earned-run average, as Hunter, worn out from averaging 277 innings the previous 10 years, had arm problems and drifted into relative ineffectiveness.

It was a much closer call for the Yankees in 1977. They won exactly 100, finishing just 2½ games ahead of both Baltimore and Boston. They once again required five games to take down the Royals in the ALCS in dramatic fashion, coming from one run behind in the ninth to win Game Five, this time in Kansas City. As he had all season, Sparky Lyle was brilliant in relief in the ALCS, pitching in four of the five games, winning twice, and giving up a single run in 9⅓ innings. Then the Yankees

Reggie Jackson was baseball's most coveted player in the first free agency class of 1976. Reggie made good in his 1977 debut season in pinstripes, morphing into "Mr. October," with his World Series record–setting five home runs leading the Yankees to their first October triumph since 1962. © *Photofest*.

crushed the Dodgers in six games to win their first World Series in 15 years. Jackson, whose 32 homers and 110 runs batted in during the regular season showed the Boss he was worth his big contract, put an exclamation point on it by becoming Mr. October in the World Series, torching the Dodgers' pitching with 9 hits—5 of them home runs—in 20 at-bats. Reggie's three magnificent home runs deep into the night on three consecutive pitches, each of them a mammoth blast deep into the seats, in his last three at-bats in Game Six at the least rivaled, but actually surpassed, Babe Ruth's "called-shot" in the 1932 World Series for dramatic effect, if for no other reason than tens of millions were watching on TV.

Drama became melodrama in the Yankees' universe in 1978, complete with family dysfunction and an improbable ending that brought them a third straight division title, which led to the third straight time they beat the Royals in the ALCS, which led to yet another six-game triumph over the Dodgers in the World Series. This time Steinbrenner's off-season body count in the free agent market netted him hard-throwing right-handed relief ace Goose Gossage, who had just gone 11–9 with 26 saves, a 1.62 ERA, and 151 strikeouts in 133 innings in 72 games for Pittsburgh. The problem was, the Yankees already had an ace reliever—southpaw Sparky Lyle, whose 13–5 record with 26 saves in 72 games earned him the 1977 AL Cy Young Award. While one being lefty and the other righty presented the option of alternating their game-savior roles according to the circumstance of who was coming to bat when for the opposing team, in practice one was destined to be the go-to closer for the Yankees. That turned out to be Gossage, whose 27 saves in 63 games led the league. Lyle, appearing in 59 games, had just 9 saves—all but two by mid-June. Ron Guidry, meanwhile, was king of the mound, leading the majors with a 25–3 record and 1.74 earned-run average. His .893 single-season winning percentage remains the best-ever by a major-league pitcher with at least 20 wins.

The more melodramatic chapter in the 1978 Yankees' story of family dysfunction was Steinbrenner and Martin beginning a cycle, for which they became famous and that can only be described as both humiliating and entertaining, of Martin behaving in some outlandish way that allowed his boss to fire him and then hire him back. The Yankees' flagging fortunes in June and July brought out Steinbrenner's worst impulses. On July 17, with more than half the season gone, his team was scuffling in fourth place, 14 games behind division-leading Boston. The Boss was not only demeaning players, particularly pitchers he thought were playing scared, but telling Martin that left fielder Roy White should be benched or released, Munson moved from catcher to right field, and instead of playing right field Jackson should be the everyday designated hitter. Martin was besieged by Steinbrenner's incessant interference, Reggie became increasingly belligerent about the implication he was no longer a complete ballplayer, and the clubhouse was in disarray.

It all came to a head on July 17 when the Yankees were hosting the Royals. Miffed at being asked to lay down a sacrifice bunt in the ninth inning of a tie game, Jackson deliberately showed up his manager by continuing to bunt after the sacrifice sign was taken off. The Yankees lost in extra innings. Martin was livid. He benched his superstar. Jackson vented to the press. Pressed to his limits and in an inebriated state, Martin told the *New York Times* on the record that Reggie was "a born liar" and in the next breath made an unfortunate reference to Steinbrenner's conviction for illegal presidential campaign contributions. The next day, he was fired—and soon thereafter, rehired. The announcement once again was made during the Yankees' annual Old-Timers' Day festivities. With a twist: Former 1950s Cleveland pitching ace Bob Lemon, Martin's replacement after having been fired as manager of the White Sox a few weeks earlier, would continue managing the Yankees for the remainder of the 1978 season. And the next year. But Billy would be back in charge in 1980.

Steinbrenner's plan worked great in 1978. Rallying under Lemon, the Yankees were virtually unbeatable in August and September to overcome their 14-game deficit of mid-July. After 162 games, the Yankees and Red Sox had the exact same 99–63 record. It was the first time a division race would be decided in a playoff. The game was at Fenway Park. With the Yankees trailing 2–0 in the seventh inning and two runners on base, light-hitting Bucky Dent, owner of only 22 home runs in five big-league seasons, lofted one over the Green Monster in left field to give the Yankees a lead they would not relinquish, thereby earning a new middle moniker to his name that began with the letter "F" bequeathed to him by the Red Sox faithful. Reggie, as the DH, iced the victory in the eighth with his 27th homer of the season, and in the bottom of the eighth Lou Piniella, playing right field instead of Jackson, made a miraculous stop, battling the sun with the tying run on second base to save the game—and the division title—for the Yankees.

* * *

Ask the Royals about three consecutive ALCS losses to the Yankees, the Dodgers about two consecutive World Series losses, the Red Sox about being overtaken by the Yankees and losing a single playoff game for the 1978 AL Eastern Division title. All would attest that the 1976–1978 Yankees restored not only the forever dynasty's tradition of winning, but playing their best and being nearly impossible to beat when the stakes were the highest. Munson and Jackson; Randolph, Nettles, and Chambliss; Guidry, Lyle, and Gossage also revived the tradition of we-Yankees-can't-be-beat swagger. But this team's swagger had more of an edge than the cool, almost dispassionate killer-instinct professionalism of earlier teams in the Yankees' forever dynasty, especially those associated with DiMaggio, Mantle, and Berra. Those Yankee teams gave rise to witticisms such as "rooting for the New York Yankees is like rooting for U.S. Steel."

These Yankees were different because, like the 1971–1975 Oakland Athletics under mercurial owner Charlies Finley, the 1976–1978 Yankees held together as a team despite all the controversies surrounding them—their own despotic owner's constant meddling; managerial changes dependent upon whether Billy Martin was in Boss Steinbrenner's good graces or not; and personality clashes in the clubhouse often provoked by the outsized ego of Reggie, which had also been a problem for the A's. Jackson had driven in 207 runs and hit 59 home runs in his two years in New York. From virtually his first day, however, Reggie had been a distraction—from his first press conference as a Yankee when he irritated his new teammates by emphasizing "the magnitude of me"; to his put down of Thurman Munson, whose gritty, tough-minded leadership set an example of relentless competitiveness, in a print interview during his first spring training in pinstripes when he said, "I'm the straw that stirs the drink," in contrast to Munson who "can only stir it bad"; to his having a candy bar named after him in 1978; to his various run-ins with Billy Martin.

Munson, a .302 hitter from 1976 to 1978; Graig Nettles, whose defensive brilliance at third base—displayed most prominently in the 1978 World Series—may have overshadowed the 96 home runs he hit those three years; and second baseman Willie Randolph were the Yankees' most consistent players. Guidry was one of baseball's best pitchers, and Ed Figueroa's 55 wins, including 20 in 1978, were the most on the Yankees pitching staff in their three-straight pennant-winning seasons. Cat-fish Hunter's accumulating health woes, however, including a diabetes diagnosis in 1978, that limited him to just 42 starts and 21 wins in 1977 and '78, contributed to Steinbrenner's free agent focus being on bolster-ing the pitching staff for 1979. Looking for four in a row, the Boss signed Dodgers southpaw Tommy John, who had beaten the Yankees in the opening game of the World Series just past, and Red Sox right-hander Luis Tiant, three times a 20-game winner in Boston, despite both being in their mid-to-late 30s.

Steinbrenner's farsighted Lemon in 1979 and Martin in '80 plan turned out to be shortsighted. The plan unraveled when the Boss, dis-pleased by his team's slow start in 1979, fired Lemon in mid-June and replaced him with . . . Billy Martin. It didn't help that Gossage was injured in a clubhouse tussle that would sideline him for nearly three months. The Yankees no longer had Sparky Lyle to reprise his role as their closer, having concluded they didn't need two closers and traded him to Texas. The Yankees were in fourth place, eight games behind, when Steinbrenner put Martin back in the dugout. If Steinbrenner thought returning Martin to the helm would lead the Yankees to storm from far behind for a fourth-straight division title, as they had the previous year after Martin was fired, he was mistaken. The Yankees had fallen to 14 games behind on August 2 when Munson took the off-day to engage in his favorite recreational activity—flying his own plane, in this case a new executive jet he had just bought. He crashed. The Yankees had lost their competitive leader, and perhaps their most indispensable player. Thurman Munson was 32. He had a .292 lifetime batting average. The Yankees had the second-best record in the American League from that day forward, but it wasn't enough to get them out of fourth place. They gained just half a game in the standings.

Steinbrenner's Martin-in-1980 plan was aborted in late October 1979 when Billy, claiming to be defending the honor of the Yankees, got into a fight with a marshmallow salesman who said "bad things" about the Yanks. Dick Howser, a shortstop for the Athletics and Indians in the 1960s, was named manager. The most significant moves the Yankees made in the off-season were trading first baseman Chris Chambliss for catcher Rick Cerone to replace Munson and signing former Astros star Bob Watson as a free agent to take over first base. Both moves paid off. Randolph, batting .294 with a .427 on-base percentage as the Yankees' lead-off batter, had the best year of his career. Tommy John, 21–9 the previous year, was 22–9 in his second year in New York. Guidry, after going 18–8 with a league-leading 2.78 ERA in 1979, won 17. Gossage was back, leading the league with 33 saves and striking out 103 batters in 99 innings. Reggie enlivened the proceedings with 41 homers, drove in 111 runs, and batted an even .300. It was his best year since coming to the Yankees. Baltimore won exactly 100, but New York's 103 victories secured the Yankees their fourth division title in five years. And for the fourth time in five years, they faced off against the Royals in the ALCS for the right to go to the World Series. This time they lost.

* * *

Like the 1962-expansion Mets, the Kansas City Royals went from a hapless 1969 expansion club to a division title in eight years. Unlike the Mets, the Royals went from bad to respectable very quickly. They had finished second, although 16 games behind Oakland, in 1971—their third year of existence—were second to Oakland again in 1973, and in 1975 won 90 games, second once again to the Athletics. Left fielder Lou Piniella was the 1969 AL Rookie of the Year and had two .300 seasons in five years with KC before being traded to the Yankees. Second baseman Cookie Rojas and center fielder Amos Otis were four-time All-Stars. First baseman John Mayberry belted 107 homers and had three 100-RBI seasons in his first four years in Kansas City beginning in 1972. Lefty Paul Splittorff in 1973 and righty Steve Busby the next year were the Royals' first 20-game winners.

Unlike the contemporary 1976–1980 Yankees, most of whose core players—Roy White, Munson, and Guidry being notable exceptions—were acquired in trades or signed as free agents, the cornerstone players on the 1976–1980 Royals were mostly homegrown. Third baseman George Brett, second baseman Frank White, right fielder Al Cowens, and pitchers Splittorff and Dennis Leonard were developed in their minor-league system, as was outfielder Willie Wilson, most of whose 127 games in his 1978 rookie season were off the bench but who moved into the starting lineup the next year. Three of the Royals' four core regulars who came from other teams—Otis in 1970, shortstop Freddie Patek the next year, and designated hitter Hal McRae in 1973—were still unproven at the major-league level. The fourth, catcher Darrell Porter, arriving in 1977 after four years in Milwaukee, had a more established track record.

With Otis, Patek, and Splittorff in their prime and Brett, White, and Leonard reaching for the stars, Kansas City was well positioned to take advantage of the nearly wholesale implosion of Oakland's 1971–1975 dynasty because of trades and free agency. Although their final margin of victory was only 2½ games better than the A's, who had traded Reggie Jackson to Baltimore before the season began, the Royals were in command of the AL West most of the 1976 season. Brett led the league in batting with a .333 average and McRae was right behind him at .332. It took until late August in 1977 before the Royals seized first place and coasted to an eight-game margin of victory. Brett batted .312 and topped 20 homers for the first time in his career. Cowens led the club with 23 homers and 112 RBIs. Patek led the league with 53 stolen bases. Leonard was a 20-game winner and Splittorff went 16–6. And in 1978 Kansas City won the West by five games. Leonard won 21 and Splittorff 19. The 1979 Royals were never on top of the standings after their fifth game of the season. They ultimately fell three games short of the California Angels after a desultory 14–14 record in September. George Brett, however, continued on the road to Cooperstown, his .329 batting average second in the league, and Willie Wilson, in his first year as a regular, batted .315 and swiped 83 bases in 95 attempts to lead the majors.

Whitey Herzog, their manager for three straight division titles, paid the penalty for Kansas City's missing out on four in a row. Also gone were Cowens and the five-foot-five Patek, whose slumped-in-the-dugout dejection captured on television following the Royals' defeat in the 1977 ALCS said more than words ever could about the agony of defeat. With Jim Frey as their new manager, the 1980 season became the capstone year for this edition of the Kansas City Royals. They took early command of the AL West, had a 20-game lead going into September, finished 14 games in front, and finally beat the Yankees in the ALCS before losing in six games to the Philadelphia Phillies in the franchise's first World Series. Wilson batted .326 and stole 79 bases in 89 tries. Leonard was a 20-game winner for the third time in four years. Dan Quisenberry, in his second big-league season, tied Gossage for the league lead in saves, with 33; won 12 additional games in relief; and proved he didn't need to blow away batters to be very effective in a closer's role, striking out just 37 batters in 128⅓ innings of work.

But the most compelling storyline of KC's 1980 season was whether George Brett would become the first hitter to bat .400 since Ted Williams in 1941. On June 10, when he was injured stealing second base, Brett's batting average stood at just .337. Returning exactly a month later, Brett batted .494 (42-for-85) to finish July at .390. On August 17, he went 4-for-4 to bring his average up to .401. Except for three days, he stayed over .400 until a 1-for-4 day on September 5 dropped his average to .399. After getting back to exactly .400 on September 19, Brett went 0-for-4 the next day, never to return to .400 again. He finished the year with a .390 batting average, 24 homers, and 118 RBIs.

* * *

Smarting from his 103-win 1980 Yankees being swept by the 97-win Royals in the ALCS, Steinbrenner did the two things for which he had become notorious. He fired his division-winning manager, Dick Howser, and followed up by signing the best free agent on the market, San Diego outfielder Dave Winfield. In snatching the 29-year-old Winfield in the free agent bidding, Steinbrenner went all in on him being the Yankees' star of the decade—the entire decade—giving him a record-shattering 10-year deal. Winfield came to the Yankees with 154 home runs in eight years with the Padres. Replacing Howser, said by the Boss (incredibly) to be more interested in Florida real estate, with general manager Gene Michael for the 1981 season was the sixth time in the nine years he owned the Yankees that Steinbrenner changed managers—a remarkable rate of turnover by any consistently competitive team, and a dramatic break with Yankees tradition. Miller Huggins had managed the Yankees for 12 years; Joe McCarthy for 15, plus six weeks; Casey Stengel for 12 years; Ralph Houk for 11.

New York's 1981 season ended with yet another managerial change—and a pennant nonetheless. Michael had the Boss's team in first place when the season was abruptly halted in June by the players' strike. That resulted in the Yankees being guaranteed a postseason berth against whomever won the AL East in the "second half" after the season resumed two months later. That fact did not prevent Steinbrenner from harassing his manager because his team, with nothing specific to play for except to ensure they were primed for October baseball, was not playing up to his expectations. Michael took exception to sniping from the Boss. In early September he became the seventh Yankees manager to bite the dust in the Steinbrenner era. Bob Lemon was brought back to finish the season, and for however far they went in the postseason.

Things were looking good for the Yankees when they beat second-half winner Milwaukee in baseball's ad hoc division series, swept Oakland—now managed by Billy Martin—in the ALCS, and won the first two games of the World Series against the Dodgers. But it ended badly, with Steinbrenner left fuming, as the Yankees lost three consecutive one-run games where they were ahead, and then were blown out in Game Six despite having another (short-lived) lead. After losing Game Five in Los Angeles, Steinbrenner returned to New York with a bandaged hand, claiming (shades of Billy Martin in the marshmallow man incident) it was hurt when he punched out two men in a hotel elevator who insulted the honor of the Yankees. Moments after the final out was made at Yankee Stadium, Steinbrenner issued a press release apologizing to New York City and Yankees fans everywhere "for the performance of the Yankee team in the World Series."

The Boss also would never forget that Winfield, his latest superstar free agent, had just one hit in 22 at-bats in the series. There was nothing subtle about Steinbrenner's future casting of Dave Winfield as "Mr. May" in contrast to "Mr. October"—Reggie Jackson—when he needed someone to blame for the Yankees losing three-straight to first-place Toronto in a tight September pennant race five years later. As for Mr. October, notwithstanding Reggie's .333 batting average in the 1981 World Series, Steinbrenner had no interest in re-signing him when he became a free agent after the season. Reggie hit 144 home runs as a Yankee and left "New York, New York"—no longer "part of it"—with 425 for his career on his way to 563 by the time he retired after a final year back with Oakland in 1987.

22

PENNSYLVANIA HAS ITS SAY IN THE NL EAST

While Cincinnati and Los Angeles were the dominant National League teams in the 1970s, winning nine Western Division titles and seven National League pennants from 1970 to 1979, back in the East, Pittsburgh and Philadelphia finished first every year except for 1973, when the Mets snuck through. The Pittsburgh Pirates entered the divisional era as a storied franchise with roots dating back to 1882 whose record of achievement in pennants won was somewhat disappointing given their generally winning ways. From 1901 to 1968, before each league was aligned into divisions, Pittsburgh's 45 winning or break-even seasons were second most in the NL after the New York–to–San Francisco Giants' 54. The only National League club with more 90-win seasons than the Pirates' 18 was the Giants, with 29, although the Cardinals and Dodgers also had 18. But while the Giants won 15 pennants in the first 68 years of the century—and the Dodgers 13, the Cardinals 12, and the Cubs 10—the Pirates had won only seven for Pittsburgh—and three of those were in the first three years of the century, four in the first ten. The Pirates won pennants again in 1925 and 1927, then endured a long drought until 1960, although they were competitive for much of the 1930s, finishing second three times.

After Bill Mazeroski's World Series walk-off home run stunned the Yankees in 1960, the Pirates were more pretenders than contenders, operating in the wake of Los Angeles and San Francisco, until the advent of divisional play. The arguable exception was 1966, when they had a realistic shot at the pennant into the final week of the season. Hard-throwing lefty Bob Veale was the ace of a decent pitching staff that still included Roy Face as the Pirates' relief ace. Mazeroski at second and shortstop Gene Alley, always excellent defensively, had better than their typical year at the plate. Pittsburgh's singular strength that year, and throughout the decade, was their outfield. Slap-hitting center fielder Matty Alou came to Pittsburgh from San Francisco in 1966 with a career .260 batting average and immediately hit .342 to win the batting title. To prove that was no fluke, Alou hit over .330 each of the next three years. Willie Stargell in left crushed 33 homers, drove in 102 runs, and batted .315 for the Pirates in 1966, his third in a string of 13 straight years with 20 or more home runs that came to an end in 1977 only because he missed nearly 100 games because of injury. And in right field was Roberto Clemente, whose 29 homers, 129 RBIs, and .317 batting average earned him the only MVP Award of his career.

Clemente did not rise to the level of an elite player in the 1950s, hitting .300 just once with only 26 home runs in his first five years, but he surely did in the 1960s. Averaging more than 7 wins above replacement for every 650 plate appearances—an MVP-level performance year in and year out—Clemente hit .329 with 214 home runs between 1960 and the end of his career in 1972. He won four batting crowns between 1961 and 1967. And yet the typically aloof Puerto Rican–born Clemente, who spoke heavily accented English and preferred conversing in Spanish, was often criticized for any number of reasons. He was outspoken. He complained too much. He was too proud—or too much of a showoff, particularly with his throwing arm. He didn't want to play hurt. He was a hypochondriac about his health. He could have been better than he was. In the National League during the 1960s, the only two position players who *actually were better* were named Willie Mays and Hank Aaron.

Pittsburgh finally broke through in 1970, year two of baseball's new divisional era. Having built around Clemente and Stargell, still in their prime, with a trio of new black stars—catcher Manny Sanguillen, outfielder Al Oliver, and right-handed pitcher Dock Ellis—the Pirates won five of the next six NL Eastern Division titles. interrupted only by the 1973 "Ya Gotta Believe!" Mets. Only once, however, did they make it to the World Series. In the NLCS, they could not get past superior Reds teams in 1970 and 1972, a far-better Dodgers ballclub in 1974, and the prime-time edition of Cincinnati's Big Red Machine in 1975. Their one

World Series, in 1971, was a classic. If baseball fans nationally weren't familiar with the all-around excellence of Roberto Clemente despite his 17 years in the majors, they certainly were after Pittsburgh's seven-game takedown of the Baltimore Orioles. The 1971 Fall Classic was in every respect the Roberto Clemente Show; he was 12-for-29, slashing line drives all over the place, and was as exciting in the field, especially his laserlike throws, as he was running the bases.

Seeming to defy the wear-and-tear of baseball aging, Clemente batted .352 in 1970 when he turned 36 in August, .341 in 1971, and .312 in 1972. On the night of December 31, 1972—New Year's Eve—Clemente chartered a plane with a sketchy maintenance record to personally deliver relief supplies from Puerto Rico to victims of a devastating earthquake in Nicaragua. Overloaded, the plane plunged into the sea. His body was never recovered. As if fated, Clemente ended the 1972 regular season—a year in which a viral infection and foot injuries limited him to just 102 games—with exactly 3,000 hits, becoming the 11th player in major-league history to reach that threshold when he doubled off the Mets' Jon Matlack on September 30. His final hit in baseball was a first-inning single off Cincinnati ace Don Gullett in the fifth game of the 1972 NLCS. His legacy as a ballplayer already secure, Roberto Clemente's stature as a person who cared deeply about his community was only enhanced by his ill-fated humanitarian mission. He was someone truly striving to make the world a better place. He was 38 years old.

* * *

The Pirates didn't return to the top of the NL East until 1979. But averaging 92 wins while finishing second each of the next three years, it wasn't as though they crashed and burned after their 1975 division title. Pittsburgh's Pirates were just not quite as good as Philadelphia's Phillies, 260 miles due east on the Pennsylvania Turnpike. Following four years of mediocrity and five years of very bad baseball in the aftermath of their 1964 implosion, the Phillies were ready to challenge for the division title. They had a solid core of position regulars, including catcher Bob Boone, shortstop Larry Bowa, third baseman Mike Schmidt, and left fielder Greg Luzinski—all developed in their farm system—and Garry Maddox, an outstanding defensive center fielder acquired from the Giants in May 1975. They also had Steve Carlton as their ace to anchor an otherwise unimpressive pitching staff. The lefty came to them in a trade with St. Louis in 1972, thanks to Cardinals executives holding a grudge about his preseason holdout the previous year on the heels of leading the league with 19 losses, never mind that he finished the 1971 season with a 20–9 record.

Carlton's first year in Philadelphia was one of the most remarkable by any pitcher ever. He went 27–10 in 1972 for a team that had the worst record in the National League, at 59–97. No other Phillies starting pitcher won more than four games; reliever Bucky Brandon was second on the club, with seven. Carlton's dominating year included a 15-game winning streak and leading the league in wins, earned-run average (1.97), complete games (30 in 41 starts), innings pitched, and strikeouts (310). That he fell to 13–20 the next year was not out of line for an ace pitching on a very bad ballclub; the last-place 1973 Phillies finished the season with a 71–91 record.

It didn't matter that in 1976 the Pirates won 92 games, exactly the same number as when they won the NL East the previous year, because the Phillies won 30 of their first 41 games on their way to a franchise-record 101 victories. In 1977 Philadelphia again won 101, five more than Pittsburgh, this time riding a 19–1 stretch in August to open an insurmountable lead to a second division title. Their third in a row in 1978 was harder fought and not decided until they defeated the Pirates in their 161st game to eliminate them from contention. Powered by Schmidt and Luzinski, both right-handed sluggers, the Phillies' strength was on the offensive side. Mike Schmidt led the league in homers for the third straight year in 1976 and had 97 in the three division-winning years. Greg Luzinski had 95 of his own. Carlton won 20 in 1976 and a league-best 23 in 1977. Manager Danny Ozark also made good use of a flexible bullpen, in which left-hander Tug McGraw and righties Ron Reed and Gene Garber were all reliable closers.

While the 1976–1978 Phillies were good enough to rule the NL East, like the Pirates before them, they were not a league-dominating team. The Reds in 1976 and Dodgers in 1977 and '78 were the league's powerhouse clubs. All three years, Philadelphia went down in defeat in the NLCS—swept in three games by Cincinnati in 1976 and losing in four to LA the next two years. First baseman Dick Allen, having returned to Philadelphia in 1975 after leaving the City of Brotherly Love angry and embittered in 1970, stirred new passions against him with a costly error that many believed cost his team the 1976 NLCS. It happened in Game Two. The Phillies had a one-run lead in the sixth. The Reds had the bases loaded with one out. Allen muffed a line drive hit right to him, apparently trying to snare the ball while moving toward first base to double-up the runner there. The tying and winning runs scored. The Phillies were in an unrecoverable two-games-to-none hole. An impending free agent, Allen was not brought back the next year.

Philadelphia's quest to become the first National League team to win four straight division titles came to naught in 1979. Instead it was Pittsburgh resuming pride of first place in the NL East. Six and a half games behind on the Fourth of July, the Phillies failure to do better than two games above .500 the rest of the way sealed their fate long before the September stretch. Schmidt, however, blasted 45 home runs; Carlton won 18; and Pete Rose was now playing first base, having signed as a free agent in the off-season with 3,146 hits on his ledger. Playing every game, Rose batted .331 by adding 208 hits to his career total. It was the tenth time Rose had a 200-hit season, passing Ty Cobb's record of nine.

The Pirates by now had a nearly complete makeover from their team in the first half of the 1970s. Dave Parker, playing Clemente's old position in right field, was their best player and most dangerous hitter, winning back-to-back batting titles in 1977 and '78. He hit .321 with 114 homers and 490 RBIs overall in the five years from 1975 to 1979, and stole 84 bases besides. Omar Moreno, who replaced Al Oliver in center field in 1977, stole 53 bases that year and led the league with 71 and 77 steals in 1978 and '79. Southpaw John Candelaria, whose 20–5 record and 2.34 ERA led the league in 1977, was the putative ace of Pittsburgh's staff, which was buttressed by the 1978 trade acquisition of Bert Blyleven after eight stellar seasons pitching in the American League. Kent Tekulve, whose funky submarine delivery allowed him to pitch 91 games in 1978 and another 94 in 1979 seemingly with ease, excelled as a game saver. And in June 1979 the Pirates strengthened their offense by trading for third baseman Bill Madlock, a former two-time batting champion with the Cubs in the mid-1970s. Madlock batted .328 after joining the Pirates, including .342 in the final month as Pittsburgh fought off the Montreal Expos, an unexpected competitor, for the division title.

The compelling narrative of Pittsburgh's 1979 season, however, was the Pirates as "family," with veteran slugger and now-first baseman Willie Stargell in the starring role of "Pops" on a team that took their inspiration from one of the year's top disco hits, "We Are Family," by Sister Sledge & Jade. Stargell had cemented his stature as one of baseball's most feared power hitters in the early 1970s, leading the league with 48 homers in 1971 and 44 in 1973. He finished second in MVP voting both years, and was third in 1972. He belted 203 homers and drove in 627 runs while batting a robust .291 to help lead the Pirates to five division titles in six years from 1970 to 1975. Not only was Stargell still an offensive force at the age of 39 in 1979, finally winning the Most Valuable Player Award with 32 homers, he was the Pirates' spiritual leader. It was Stargell who awarded the gold merit stars for great plays and winning contributions that Pirates players affixed to their old-style pillbox baseball caps. The Pops-orchestrated fabulous '70s Show ended with a World Series triumph over Earl Weaver's 102-win Baltimore Orioles, in which Stargell himself went 12-for-30 with 3 home runs and 7 runs batted in. Just as in 1971 against the O's, the Pirates had to come from behind to win the series. In 1971 they trailed Baltimore two games to none; in 1979 it was a more daunting three games to one.

The next year it was the Phillies rebounding to fight a pitched battle with the Expos for the 1980 division crown, which was not decided until the two teams, tied at the top, met in Montreal for their final three games. After winning the first, the Phillies brought the division title back to Philadelphia for the fourth time in five years with one game to spare when Rose singled in the 11th and Schmidt knocked out his 48th home run—by far the most in the majors—to drive in his 120th and 121st runs, the most in the National League. This time they won the NLCS. It was Philadelphia's first pennant since the 1950 Whiz Kids, finally putting to rest the sting of 1964. And they did so in dramatic fashion, overcoming a two-games-to-one deficit with two victories on the road in Houston and winning the deciding fifth game in the 10th inning on a pair of doubles. Their opening game victory in the World Series against Kansas City was the Phillies' first in the Fall Classic since the first game of the 1915 series. Carlton, 24–9 during the season, and ace reliever Tug McGraw combined for the win in Game Six that made the Philadelphia Phillies a World Series champion for the first time in their history. It was also the first World Series won for the City of Brotherly Love since the Athletics way back in 1930.

* * *

Between them, the two Pennsylvania teams froze out Canada's 1969-expansion Montreal Expos when they were at their best after a decade of losing seasons. Gene Mauch, their first manager, hired to help give the club credibility, was let go after seven years at the end of the 1975 season, one victory short of the franchise winning its 500th game. The Expos' best player in their early years—and one of the best in the National League—was right fielder Rusty Staub, acquired from Houston just before the start of their first spring training in 1969. Staub played three years for the Expos, endearing himself to French-Canadian Montreal fans by learning French as best he could and being a very public presence in the community, including living in the city during the winter. "Le Grand Orange" was much beloved by the community, but that didn't stop the Expos from trading him in 1972 to the Mets, whom he helped win the NL East the next year.

Going into 1979, the Expos had yet to have a winning season. What they did have was the nucleus of a potentially great team. Third baseman Larry Parrish, in his fifth year as a regular, and outfielders Ellis Valentine and Warren Cromartie, in their third, appeared to be on the fast track to stardom. Six-year veteran right-hander Steve Rogers was one of the premier pitchers in the league. Montreal also had two budding superstars— catcher Gary Carter, a rookie in 1975, already edging out 11-year-veteran Johnny Bench as the best all-around catcher in baseball, and outfielder Andre Dawson, the NL's 1977 Rookie of the Year. All five were signed by Montreal and, except for 28-year-old Rogers, they were all under 25. Moreover, the Expos' manager since 1977 was Dick Williams, whose résumé included taking two previous clubs with young stars to the World Series—Boston in 1967 and Oakland in 1972 and '73.

As with the 1967 Red Sox, Williams guided the 1979 Expos from a losing record the year before into a down-to-the-wire battle with Pittsburgh for the NL East before being officially eliminated on the final day. While not good enough to win the division, Montreal's 95 wins were well-ahead of Cincinnati's 90 for the National League's second-best record. A similar scenario unfolded the next year when the 1980 Expos fought tooth-and-nail with the Phillies before being sent home for the winter by Mike Schmidt's 11th-inning homer in their 161st game.

What happened in 1981 was even more painful. Winning the "second half" season necessitated by the players' strike, Montreal prevailed over "first-half" winner Philadelphia in the ad hoc division series to represent the NL East in the league championship series, only to lose the pennant to the Dodgers after taking a two-games-to-one lead in the best-of-five NLCS on Rick Monday's ninth-inning home run that broke a 1–1 tie in the series finale. In early September the Expos had parted ways with Dick Williams. Team executives felt that, for the quality players he had, the Expos probably should have won at least one of the two previous division titles, and that their middling 14–12 record since the season resumed on August 10 did not portend well for a strong finishing kick. Taking his place was Jim Fanning, whose last experience as a manager was at the Single-A level in 1963. Fanning, however, was intimately familiar with the Expos' players from his extensive front office experience since 1969, first as general manager and now in charge of player development. The Expos didn't go on a tear but played just well enough to beat out the Cardinals by half a game to win the second-half title.

It turned out Montreal's window of opportunity had closed, even with Carter, Dawson, and the 1981 additions of left fielder Tim Raines and third baseman Tim Wallach giving the Expos a formidable offense and the 1982 trade for Jeff Reardon giving them a top-tier reliever. Leading the league in steals each of his first four years and stealing at least 70 six years in a row while hitting over .300 four times, Raines became one of the most dangerous lead-off batters in baseball history. But the Expos were no longer a top-tier team. After they fell to fifth in 1984, Gary Carter, the face of their franchise, was traded to the Mets. Given that he was every bit as popular with Montreal fans as Rusty Staub had been, and for many of the same give-back-to-the-community reasons, Carter's trade—especially to a division rival—in December 1984 was every bit as shocking to Expos fans as when Le Grand Orange was sent away.

For Montreal it was about the money, especially after being dealt a severe financial blow from the loss of a potentially lucrative revenue stream when Major League Baseball granted near-exclusive broadcasting rights to the Toronto Blue Jays in the most populous region of Canada, where Toronto happened to be. Still in his prime, Carter had become unaffordable to the suddenly cash-strapped Expos. Two years later they let Andre Dawson go as a free agent for the same reason, despite his being still in his prime and having hit 225 home runs in 10 years as their right fielder. He added 213 to his career total after leaving Montreal. In February 1987 the Expos traded Reardon, the league leader in saves in 1985, with 41, and second in 1986, with 35 more, to Minnesota. His 152 saves for the Expos are still the most in franchise history, including since the Expos became the Washington Nationals in 2005.

That Tim Raines was not lost to free agency in 1987 was only because major-league owners had tacitly agreed not to aggressively pursue each other's top free agents. Finding no takers, Raines was forced to return to the Expos, with whom he negotiated a new three-year $5 million deal. Having fruitlessly waited past the deadline for teams to sign their own free agents in hopes for a fair-market contract based on what star players had received in previous years, Raines could not negotiate with the Expos until May 1. Montreal was 8–13, in fifth place, on that date. Without benefit of spring training, Raines was in action the next day and went on to have an outstanding year, leading the league in runs despite missing the first 21 games, batting .330, reaching base a career-high 43 percent of the time, and hitting a career-high 18 home runs. From the day of his return, no National League team had a better record than the Montreal Expos. They finished third, four games behind the Cardinals. Had they had Raines and Dawson, the NL's 1987 MVP for the Cubs as it turned out, the Expos quite likely would have won the division title and a chance to bring the World Series to Canada for the first time.

* * *

Neither Pennsylvania team had much to say in the NL East for most of the 1980s, although three years after their 1980 championship the 1983 Phillies rode an 11-game winning streak in September to gain separation from Pittsburgh and Montreal to return to the top of the NL East. Mike Schmidt had another terrific year—his 10th of 11 consecutive seasons when his player value was at least 6 wins above replacement—leading the league in home runs for the sixth time. Carlton, closing in on 40, was still ace of the staff, but it was 30-year-old nine-year veteran John Denny, mostly a journeyman pitcher, who led the Phillies and the league with a 19–6 record. By now Philadelphia had parted ways with Greg Luzinski, whose playing the outfield like a bull in a china shop—his nickname was in fact "The Bull," although not to mock his defense—made him best suited to being a DH in the American League; Larry Bowa, their short-stop of 12 years, traded to the Cubs in 1982 for younger shortstop Ivan de Jesus; and catcher Bob Boone, whose new address in 1982 was in Cali-fornia with the Angels. As part of the Bowa-for–de Jesus deal, the Phil-lies also sent the Cubs a promising much-younger shortstop named Ryne Sandberg, whom they apparently did not see as an immediate replace-ment for Bowa.

The Phillies won the NLCS and took the opening game of the 1983 World Series against Baltimore. But this time Philadelphia, conjuring up ghosts from 1915, lost the next four. The rest of the decade was downhill from there. New ownership in October 1981 led to a change in philosophy where attention to the bottom line, with its emphasis on cost-effectiveness and profit margins, took precedence over trying to keep pace with the resurgent Mets and Cardinals. Steve Carlton pitched his last game for the Phillies in August 1986. He left Philadelphia with 318 career victories—241 for the Phillies, including four 20-win seasons—on his way to an eventual 329. Spending his entire career in the City of Brotherly Love, Mike Schmidt retired in 1989 as indisputably the greatest third baseman in baseball history. In addition to his 548 home runs—seventh on the all-time list at the time—Schmidt is one of the very few with a seat at the head table with Brooks Robinson for defensive excellence at the hot corner. The Phillies bottomed out with back-to-back last-place endings to the 1988 and 1989 seasons.

That the Pirates descended into a series of mediocre seasons in the 1980s that led ultimately to some very bad years wasn't just because their World Series–winning 1979 team had aging players at the end of a dynastic run. It didn't help that Dave Parker lost his power stroke and Kent Tekulve his effectiveness in the bullpen the next few years, that Bert Blyleven was traded back to the American League, or that Bill Madlock was not respected in the clubhouse either as a teammate or for his work ethic, despite winning batting titles in 1981 and 1983. (Madlock's perceived selfishness in terms of his personal batting statistics, as opposed to his team's success, was sometimes held up as an example of one of the things wrong with free agency.) Instead, the Pirates lost their cohesiveness once Willie Stargell, their inspirational leader, was no longer an everyday player, which happened swiftly at the age of 40 in 1980. He was the Pops of the 1979 Pirates' close-knit family. The "We Are Family" ethos and the merit stars affixed to players' caps built a unity of purpose that helped them to be more successful than they perhaps should have been. When Stargell retired in 1982 with 475 career home runs, he was probably the most beloved Pirate since Honus Wagner—more so even than the sainted Clemente, who was more admired, as both a ballplayer and a person, than beloved.

Coinciding with their dramatic drop in competitive fortunes, the mid-1980s Pirates were probably the team most publicly tarnished by the decade's baseball cocaine scandals, for which the exponential rise in player salaries brought about by free agency was sometimes blamed. With lots of time on players' hands after games, major-league clubhouses always had a frat house vibe. Former Yankees pitching star Jim Bouton wrote about this in his at the time scandalous (but actually quite tame) book *Ball Four*, published to a much-outraged reception in 1970. But before lucrative guaranteed multiyear contracts, when vices—alcohol and extramarital affairs— were more pedestrian, baseball was the overriding priority. There were always some who focused on extracurricular activities to the detriment of burnishing their baseball skills—1960s Angels pitcher Bo Belinsky was among the most high-profile squanderers of his talent—but generally, major leaguers had their priorities in order. In the first flush years of free agency, however, players got carried away, enabled by higher-than-ever salaries, in the pursuit of celebrity lifestyle enjoyments—including high-end drugs, specifically cocaine.

Players everywhere in Major League Baseball got caught up in the country's burgeoning cocaine epidemic. Cardinals star first baseman Keith Hernandez became a detriment to clubhouse cohesion when he began bingeing on cocaine and was ultimately traded to the Mets in June 1983. Although he later admitted to often playing while high on coke, Hernandez also said he was not using when he batted .344 in 1979 to win the batting title. The late-1970s/early-1980s Expos were arguably done in by the cocaine habits of so many of their best players. The city of Montreal had a particularly vibrant nightclub scene that attracted players to share in all that the festivities had to offer. By the age of 25, Ellis Valentine's presumptive outstanding career was likely ruined by coke. Hardcore drug use became a higher priority than his baseball career for the talented Valentine. Traded to the Mets in 1981, he was never again a major-league regular. Tim Raines fell into a cocaine habit after his terrific 1981 rookie season; however, under the stern tutelage of Andre Dawson, he returned his priority to baseball and away from drugs.

Baseball's drug abuse problem became a pressing matter for Major League Baseball institutionally in the early 1980s, when major leaguers were in the crosshairs of federal authorities cracking down on the drug trade. At least 30 players were using illegal drugs in 1984, according to Steven Goldman, writing for *Baseball Prospectus*. Among them were Dodgers relief ace Steve Howe and former A's and Giants ace Vida Blue, then pitching for the Royals, both of whom were suspended by Commissioner Kuhn after they were implicated by federal authorities in cocaine purchases. Kansas City star center fielder Willie Wilson and first baseman Willie Mays Aikens, who lived up to the legend for which he was named by torching Phillies pitchers for four home runs in the 1980 World Series, were wrapped up by the feds, along with Blue and another teammate, and agreed to cooperate in the case against their suppliers. Although he did not do so for Blue, Kuhn lifted the yearlong 1984 suspensions he handed down to the three others of the Kansas City Four in May.

In September 1985, seven active and former major leaguers and Pirates manager Chuck Tanner were given immunity for testimony in a federal drug trial in Pittsburgh concerning a cocaine-distribution ring that targeted baseball players. Keith Hernandez and Lonnie Smith, teammates in St. Louis in the late-1970s and early-1980s timeframe under investigation; Enos Cabell and Jeffrey Leonard, who played for Houston at the time; and three former Pirates—Dale Berra (Yogi's son), John Milner (now retired), and star outfielder Dave Parker (now with Cincinnati)—were the players called to the stand. Parker said in his testimony that he began using coke in 1977, was often high on cocaine during the 1979 Pirates' championship season, and didn't quit until 1982, when he concluded drug use was undermining his performance on the ballfield.

Faced with the public-relations problem of seemingly rampant recreational drug use by major leaguers—but oblivious to another kind of drug use, specifically, steroids for performance enhancement, that was beginning to rear its ugly head in the mid-eighties—new commissioner Peter Ueberroth wanted to institute random drug testing of players. While he was able to do so in the minor leagues, Ueberroth could not at the major-league level without the approval of the players' union, as stipulated in baseball's collective bargaining agreement. The union objected to drug testing on the grounds of players' privacy and the possibility that erroneous tests would ruin careers. Disciplinary action, however, could be taken against players who were arrested or the subject of federal drug investigations. Accordingly, in February 1986 Ueberroth sanctioned 23 players involved in the Pittsburgh drug case, including one-year suspensions for six who had facilitated the drug dealers' entreé to major leaguers. Ueberroth waived the suspensions in exchange for the sanctioned players contributing a portion of their salaries to drug rehab programs and testing for illegal drugs for as long as they remained in the game.

Dave Parker was among those players. A two-time batting champion with a .290 average and 339 home runs in his 19-year career, seven times an All-Star, and the National League's MVP in 1978, but about 300 hits shy of 3,000 when he retired, Parker was *not* a lock for Cooperstown. As one of baseball's most impactful players in the second half of the 1970s, however, he might have gotten a little more consideration in the Hall of Fame voting by the baseball writers if not for his intimate involvement in the Pittsburgh cocaine case that went to trial in 1985. In his 15 years on the ballot, he never came close to election.

Part IV

Baseball's (Almost) "All in It to Win It" Decade

The 1986 New York Mets celebrate their expected but improbable World Series championship: expected because they were baseball's most dominant team with 108 wins—the most since the 1975 Reds; improbable because they were down to their last out in the series with nobody on base, trailing the Boston Red Sox by two runs in Game Six, and came back to win the game and even the series. The Mets also trailed, 3–0, in the sixth inning of Game Seven before taking the series finale, 8–5. *National Baseball Hall of Fame Library, Cooperstown, NY.*

23

1980S AL EAST

Taking Advantage of Yankees Dysfunction

Notwithstanding his public apology to New York City and Yankee fans everywhere following the Yankees' blowing a two-games-to-none lead in the 1981 World Series, George Steinbrenner certainly did not expect that his club would not quickly return to the top of the baseball world. Neither did Major League Baseball or baseball fans nationwide. They were the New York Yankees, after all, with a tradition to uphold, and Steinbrenner had already proven he was adept at doing whatever he must—including offering lucrative contracts on the free agent market for the biggest stars available—to make that happen. The Yankees owner in fact did continue to binge on free agents and go after other teams' star players who were a year away from free agency. But Steinbrenner also predictably continued to make life miserable for his managers, replacing them with wild abandon. And the Boss continued his tortured can't live with him, can't live without him affair with Billy Martin. All to no avail.

Despite being considered a top contender for the AL Eastern Division title virtually every year in the 1980s—and contending in most of them—those years were the beginning of the franchise's longest postseason drought since they officially became known as the Yankees in 1913. It would be 15 years before the Yankees finished atop the standings again—longer than the 12 years between their pennants in 1964 and 1976. Fifteen years was three fewer than the franchise-record drought from 1903 until Babe Ruth led the way to their first pennant in 1921; the first 10 of those years, they were known as the Highlanders. Even with the Yankees not winning even once, there were no repeat winners in the AL East in any year between 1982 and 1991. Until the 1988–1990 Oakland Athletics, there were also no repeat pennant winners in the American League.

At baseball's winter meetings in December 1981, Steinbrenner announced yet another of the managerial-succession plans for which he was becoming famous. This time the plan was for Bob Lemon to remain as manager in 1982, be replaced in 1983 by the same Gene Michael he had fired in September, who in turn would manage the American League's flagship franchise through 1985. Steinbrenner had already signed Cincinnati outfielder Dave Collins, hardly among baseball's best players, to an expensive contract. The Boss's Lemon-to-Michael plan was history just 14 games into the 1982 season, when Lemon quit because he could no longer stand the aggravation of working for Steinbrenner. Michael, his replacement, lasted 86 games before he was fired and replaced by Steinbrenner aide Clyde King, the long-ago Dodgers reliever. The Yankees finished fifth in the AL East, with a 79–83 record. It was their first losing season since 1973, the year Steinbrenner became owner of baseball's greatest franchise.

Instead, 'twas the Milwaukee Brewers and Baltimore Orioles taking advantage of the Yankees' complete collapse to engage in an epic pennant race for the 1982 division title. The 1969-expansion Brewers—originally the Seattle Pilots, but rescued from insolvency and brought to Milwaukee in just their second year of existence in 1970 by new owner Bud Selig—did not have a winning season until 1978. Their best players in the first half of the 1970s were George Scott, their first baseman from 1972 to 1976, and catcher Darrell Porter from 1973 to 1976. The Brewers, however, were building the foundation for a competitive ballclub, the stars of which would be shortstop Robin Yount, promoted to play shortstop in 1974 after just 64 games in the low minors, and infielder Paul Molitor, brought up in 1978. Although New York and Boston in 1978 and Baltimore in 1979 were too good for Milwaukee to compete with, the Brewers won 93 and then 95 games to establish themselves as a realistic contender.

In 1981 the Brewers added a pair of top-tier veterans to provide ballast and leadership—catcher Ted Simmons and former A's relief ace Rollie Fingers. They won their division in the second half of the split strike season and ended up with the best record in the AL East, only to lose the ad hoc division series to the first-half-winning Yankees. High expectations heading into 1982 were dashed, however, by 14 losses in 20 games to end the month of May, prompting a change of managers to Harvey Kuenn. The Brewers had the best record in baseball the rest of the way, took first place for good on the last day of July, built up a 6½ game lead by late August, and survived a late surge by the Baltimore Orioles—Earl Weaver's last stand as manager—to win the division title on the last day of the season. It was a particularly sweet triumph for Kuenn following years of health challenges that included the amputation of his left leg below the knee.

They were the True-Blue Brew Crew but also called Harvey's Wallbangers for good reason. Their 216 home runs led the majors. Center fielder Gorman Thomas's 39 homers were the most in the majors; left fielder Ben Oglivie hit 34; and first baseman Cecil Cooper, 32. Yount, Cooper, and Molitor were the only American League players with 200 hits. Robin Yount, already one of the best players in baseball, became a superstar in 1982, leading the league in hits (210) and doubles (46) while reaching career highs in runs (129), triples (12), homers (29), RBIs (114), and batting average (.331), falling just one hit short of beating out Willie Wilson's .332 for the batting title. Yount dominated the MVP voting in 1982.

A pivotal moment in the season came on August 30 when the Brewers traded with Houston for veteran right-hander Don Sutton to bolster their rotation. Milwaukee led by 4½ games at the time but were clearly feeling pressure from the hard-charging Orioles, then in the middle of a 17–1 stretch that kept the Brewers from coasting to the finish line. Already with 254 major-league victories on the way to 324 for his career, Sutton went 4–1 in seven starts down the stretch for Milwaukee, including shutting down the Orioles—beating their aging ace, Jim Palmer—for the division title on the final day of the season, which began with the two clubs tied for first. Milwaukee needed all five games to win the ALCS and took a three-games-to-two lead in the World Series before St. Louis rallied to win Games Six and Seven. Yount capped a brilliant year with 12 hits in 29 at-bats in the World Series, and Molitor was 11-for-31.

That turned out to be the last time the Brewers won a division title as an American League club. (They were transferred to the National League in 1998.) After 11 years playing shortstop, where he was pushing all-time greats Luke Appling and Lou Boudreau as the best at the position to that point in American League history, Robin Yount successfully made the transition to center field in 1985, at the age of 29. Four of the six years he batted better than .300 were as an outfielder, and in 1989 he won his second MVP Award. Yount reached 3,000 career hits in 1992. Paul Molitor, seeming to get better with age and benefitting from the DH rule, hit .319 between 1987 and 1992, including .353 in 1987, when he began transitioning from third base to designated hitter. Unlike Yount, who retired after the 1993 season having spent the entirety of his 20-year career with the Brewers, Molitor left Milwaukee as a free agent in 1993, after 15 years, with 2,281 hits. He joined Yount in the 3,000-hit club playing for Minnesota in 1996—a year he led the league with 225 hits and batted .341 at the age of 39.

* * *

Despite the 1982 Yankees having ended the season with 15 losses in their final 21 games, Clyde King expected to be back as manager in 1983. If Steinbrenner was ever amenable to that, it came undone as soon as Billy Martin was once again available for his dream job—manager of the New York Yankees—this time because, a year after he led Oakland to the 1981 Western Division title, the Athletics lost 94 games and the fiery Martin went on a tirade against Oakland general manager Sandy Alderson. For the fourth time since 1975, Martin was the Yankees' manager. It was the 10th managerial change Steinbrenner had made in his 10 years as the Yankees' owner. The 1983 Yankees also began the year without Collins, whose disappointing 1982 season led to his being traded out of town, and a new pair of free agents—White Sox outfielder Steve Kemp and Angels outfielder/DH Don Baylor.

Kemp bombed, Baylor hit 21 homers, Dave Winfield hit 32, Ron Guidry won 21, and in June the Yankees called up Don Mattingly to play first base. The highlights of the Yankees' season, however, were lefty Dave Righetti pitching a July Fourth no-hitter at Yankee Stadium and the "George Brett Affair" later in July, where Martin got the umpires to invalidate Brett's would-have-been lead-taking ninth-inning home run into the game's last out on a technicality: The pine tar used by the Royals' star for grip on his bat extended too far up the handle. KC's protest was upheld, the ninth inning was resumed a month later from the batter after Brett's homer, and Martin's gambit of trying to argue that Brett had not touched all the bases on his home run trot was shot down by an affidavit prepared by the umpires there that day attesting that he had in fact touched 'em all. Even though they won 91 games, the 1983 Yankees were never in a pennant race won handily by Baltimore's Orioles in their first post-Weaver season.

Replacing Weaver was the relatively unknown and certainly not as charismatic or entertaining Joe Altobelli, a Yankees coach the previous year whose major-league managerial experience was three years with the Giants in the late-1970s. A 27–7 record between August 24 and September 27 put the Orioles in first place for good. Cal Ripken, with 27 home runs, 102 runs batted in, and a .318 batting average, and Eddie Murray, batting .306 with 33 homers and 111 RBIs, finished first and second in the MVP voting. Ripken had now played in 280 consecutive games. Lefty Scott McGregor led the Orioles with an 18–7 record, but a pair of newcomers to the rotation—rookie Mike Boddicker, 16–8, and second-year pitcher Storm Davis, 13–7—raised expectations that the Orioles' tradition of an outstanding corps of starting pitchers in the model of Jim Palmer, Mike Cuellar, and Dave McNally a decade earlier would continue for much of the rest of the decade, and with it a continuance of Orioles excellence.

That was not to be. Baltimore dropped 10 of its first 12 games in 1984 and never got back into the pennant race. Although Boddicker won 20 and had the league's best ERA, and Davis had drawn comparisons to Palmer in his prime and was sometimes spoken of as "Cy Future," neither provided the foundation for the kind of excellent pitching the Orioles always had during the Weaver years. They finished fifth in the AL East, although with a winning record. In June 1985 the Orioles brought Weaver back to turn their struggling club around. They finished fourth. In August the next year, with his team destined to finish last, Weaver announced he was retiring for good once the season was over.

The vaunted Orioles Way was no longer sustaining a competitive franchise. Ripken and Murray, however, were two of the best players in baseball even as their team sank into the abyss. After 13 years in Baltimore playing nearly every game every season, except for 1986 when he was injured, Eddie Murray and the 333 home runs he had hit so far were traded to the Dodgers in December 1988. The one guy who did play every game every season—and every inning in every game—was shortstop Cal Ripken. By the end of the decade, Ripken had established himself as probably the best all-around shortstop in American League history, eclipsing Milwaukee contemporary Robin Yount, who by then was in center field. In addition to being a dangerous hitter with power, Ripken proved to be an outstanding defensive shortstop, with great positioning and a rifle-accurate arm giving him terrific range. Notwithstanding the many takeout plays at second base he had to endure, Ripken's size and agility helped him to be indestructible. By the time he concluded his 10th full season in the major leagues in 1991, Cal Ripken had played in 1,573 consecutive games. His streak was already the second-longest in baseball history, behind Lou Gehrig's 2,130, and Ripken had no intention of sitting one out any time soon.

* * *

The pine tar incident had nothing to do with Steinbrenner's decision not to return Martin as manager in 1984. The 1983 Yankees not spending a day in first place probably did. Yankees legend Yogi Berra, infamously fired after leading the 1964 Yankees to a pennant in his first year as a manager, was given the helm instead. One of Berra's most controversial decisions was to convert Dave Righetti in spring training from starting pitcher to game-saving closer to replace Goose Gossage, who left as a free agent after six years and 150 saves for the Yankees. Righetti was not happy, but he excelled in the role until he too left as a free agent after the 1990 season.

Like every other club in the AL East, including the defending World Series–champion Orioles, the Yankees fell out of contention early in the 1984 season as the Detroit Tigers broke out to a 35–5 start on their way to 104 wins and a 15-game margin of victory. They are one of the few clubs in history to spend every day of the season in first place. As Steinbrenner stewed, Billy Martin was still around as his backup plan, now working as an assistant to the Boss with undefined responsibilities. Berra knew this, yet was emboldened to push back when the Boss tried to interfere with his job in the dugout. "You want me to quit?" he yelled at the Boss at one point during the season. "You'll have to fire me!" Steinbrenner did not, even after the Yankees ended the season in third place with 87 wins, 17 games out of the running. Free agent-acquisition Phil Niekro won 16 at the age of 45. Mattingly became the latest Yankees icon; his .343 batting average was the best in the league, as were his 207 hits and 44 doubles. "Donny Baseball," as he soon became known, also hit 23 homers and drove in 110 runs.

The Tigers led the majors in runs scored and the league in fewest allowed. Their front three starters—Jack Morris, Dan Petry, and Milt

Wilcox—won 19, 18, and 17 games respectively. Their relief ace, Willie Hernandez, won both the AL's Cy Young and MVP awards with a 9–3 record, 32 saves, and a 1.92 earned-run average in 80 games. Catcher Lance Parrish smacked 33 homers, and right fielder Kirk Gibson had his breakout year with 27. Second baseman Lou Whitaker and shortstop Alan Trammell, both in their seventh full season in the majors, were shaping up into both the longest-lasting double-play combination in baseball history—they played side-by-side for 18 years from 1978 to 1995—and arguably the best. Detroit waltzed through the postseason in eight games, losing only Game Two of the World Series against San Diego's Padres.

It was Detroit's first return to the postseason since they won the AL East in 1972. That season was the last stand for the veteran players that were the foundation of Detroit's 1968 champions. Al Kaline, Norm Cash, Bill Freehan, Dick McAuliffe, and Mickey Lolich were over 30 and in their declining years. Willie Horton and Jim Northrup were on the cusp of 30 and slowing down. Manager Billy Martin, whose fiery leadership style almost certainly was the difference in their winning a tight division race, not only knew this but also was well aware that Detroit's minor-league cupboard was bare. All of this made for a fraught 1973. Martin's season-long simmering about the challenges he faced, including blunt criticism about the direction of the team going forward, put him in bad graces with franchise executives. In the second of his many managerial firings, Martin was dismissed at the end of August.

Over the next five years the Tigers were in the steady, capable hands of former Yankees manager Ralph Houk, the first four of which they were a very bad team. As the Tigers' 1968 stars left the scene or assumed secondary roles, Detroit's best players in the mid-1970s all confronted life challenges. Although under the radar because the Tigers were not competitive, John Hiller was one of baseball's best relievers from 1973 to 1978, despite having survived three heart attacks in 1971. Ron LeFlore was serving time for street crime when his baseball prowess as a ward of the state drew the attention of Billy Martin, himself a youthful rabble-rouser; in six years with the Tigers that began in 1974, LeFlore hit .297 and swiped 294 bases. In 1976 the Tigers were blessed to have rookie sensation Mark Fidrych, a happy-go-lucky lanky right-hander nicknamed "The Bird" because his physical similarity to Big Bird of *Sesame Street*, and his propensity to tell the baseball exactly what he wanted it to do before throwing it endeared him to baseball fans across the country. Fidrych's life challenge came the year after he kicked off his career with a 19–9 record, league-leading 2.34 ERA, and 24 complete games in 29 starts. The next year began with a knee injury and ended in July with a dead arm after six consecutive complete-game victories in which he surrendered just eight runs. That effectively was the end of his storybook career.

The foundation for their 1984 championship was set in 1978—the rookie year of Whitaker, Trammell, Parrish, and Morris—and 1979, when the Tigers pounced on the availability of Sparky Anderson, fired by Cincinnati after the 1978 season, never mind his having been managerial mastermind of the Big Red Machine. For Anderson it was a new beginning that did not end until 1995, when he stepped down after 17 years as the Tigers' manager. Trading for Chet Lemon in 1981, signing free-agent slugger Darrell Evans in November 1983, and trading in March 1984 for Hernandez bolstered a team that already had a solid starting rotation more stable and reliable than what Anderson had in Cincinnati. The 1984 Tigers made Sparky the first manager to win World Series in both leagues. As dominant as his Tigers were in 1984, however, they were no Big Red Machine. By the end of July 1985 they were effectively out of the AL East pennant race, which the 1977-expansion Toronto Blue Jays pretty much had in hand.

* * *

It had been three years since his team played in the World Series when, in December 1984, Steinbrenner traded with Oakland for Rickey Henderson, then gave him a huge new free-agent-size contract befitting the best player in baseball—a .291 batting average, .400 on-base percentage, and 493 stolen bases in his first six years with the Athletics. Steinbrenner also gave Berra a vote of confidence that "a bad start" in 1985 "will not affect Yogi's status" and guaranteeing him the full year. The Boss's guarantee lasted for 16 games; with his team off to a 6–10 start, it was back to Billy as manager. Henderson led the league with 80 steals and 146 runs—the most scored in the majors since Ted Williams touched home 150 times in 1949. Mattingly batted .324, hit 35 homers, and drove in 145 runs—the most in the American League since Al Rosen also had 145 RBIs in 1953. Ron Guidry led the league with a 22–6 record. The Yankees finished second, two games behind Toronto. The Blue Jays put the division title away by beating the Yankees in three of four games in New York in a tight pennant race in mid-September, embarrassing the

Boss and provoking him to disparage Dave Winfield as "Mr. May." Winfield finished the season with a .275 batting average, 26 homers, and 114 RBIs, but went 3-for-13 with 2 RBIs in the three September losses to Toronto.

The Yankees having the best record in the American League after he took charge, however, did not save Billy Martin from the Boss's wrath. Billy's fate was probably sealed by an eight-game losing streak in the middle of September, during which a frustrated Martin got in a barroom brawl with Ed Whitson—a free agent signup whose 10–8 record and 4.88 earned-run average in his first year as a Yankee was not what either Steinbrenner or Martin expected. Out for the fourth time as Yankees manager, Martin was again given an undefined role in the Boss's constellation of "baseball people"—there should he be needed again.

The Yankees finished second again in 1986 under rookie manager Lou Piniella. After July, however, the Yankees were never any closer than 4½ games to catching the Boston Red Sox for the division title. Neither was any other club. Henderson was the league's top stolen-base threat for the sixth-straight year, with 87, and, with a career-high 28 homers, had added a power dimension to his offensive contributions. In two years with the Yankees, Henderson's 52 home runs eclipsed by one the total he hit his first six years in Oakland. Mattingly's 238 hits and 53 doubles led the league. His .352 batting average was second best. If the Yankees–Red Sox rivalry was not quite what it had been or would be in the future, there certainly was one between Don Mattingly and Boston third baseman Wade Boggs when it came to the art of hitting. In the three years since Mattingly became a regular in 1984, he had banged out 656 hits, including 145 doubles and 89 home runs, while collecting 368 RBIs in 474 games with a .340 batting average. Boggs, a leadoff hitter, had a .350 batting average and .437 on-base percentage, twice leading the league in both categories, on 650 hits and 290 walks in 468 games. The legend of Donny Baseball was growing, but he had still not led the Yankees to the promised land of a pennant and World Series.

For more than half the 1987 season, the Yankees, still managed by Piniella, fought the resurgent Tigers and Blue Jays for primacy in the AL East. The Red Sox dropped off the map. 'Twas a poor month of August did in the Yankees. Even with Martin on Steinbrenner's payroll (doing something), Piniella managed to keep his job all year. Mattingly had another outstanding year, with his third consecutive 30-homer season, fourth straight 100-RBI year, and a .327 batting average. The Tigers trailed the Jays by one game when Toronto came to Detroit for the final weekend of the season. Coming from behind to win the first two games by one run, the Tigers took a one-game lead heading into the season finale. A Detroit loss would force a playoff between them for the division title. Only one run scored in game 162—a home run by Tigers right fielder Larry Herndon off Jays' left-handed ace Jimmy Key, one of only three hits Key surrendered in his eight-inning complete-game loss. Frank Tanana, now relying on guile more than power, pitched a complete-game shutout to secure the division title for Detroit.

Much has since been made of Detroit's decision to trade pitching prospect John Smoltz in mid-August to the Atlanta Braves for veteran right-hander Doyle Alexander. It was a deal without which the Tigers would not have won their division. In 11 starts for the Tigers, Alexander went 9–0 with a superb 1.53 earned-run average. His 9th win in the first game of the final series pulled Detroit even with Toronto. Alexander was 36 years old and rapidly approaching the end of his career. The prospect for whom he was traded was 20 years old and just getting started on his way to a Hall of Fame career as one of a trio of great Atlanta pitchers in the 1990s—Greg Maddux, Tom Glavine, and could-have-been-a-Tiger John Smoltz.

Trades such as that, where the potential future is sacrificed for the immediate goal of winning a pennant, often provoke controversy as to whether they were worth it—especially when the prospect given up is someone like Smoltz. For the Tigers, however, the Alexander deal was correctly seen as the last best chance for them to win with their existing core group of players, nearly all of whom were over 30. The trade for Alexander did accomplish its purpose in that the Tigers won the AL East, even if their bid for another World Series was thwarted in the ALCS. Detroit fell one game short of Boston in 1988, then spent the next 17 years as a mostly very bad and otherwise mediocre club. John Smoltz surely would have helped, but his pitching excellence would not have been nearly enough to return Detroit to the postseason.

* * *

"Again" for Billy Martin came in 1988 when he became Yankees manager for the fifth time after Piniella disappointed Steinbrenner because his team did no better than fourth in 1987. There was virtually no honeymoon this time. Steinbrenner's incessant interference aggravated

Martin; Billy didn't help matters by getting into yet another fight, this time at a strip club when the Yankees were in Texas, and he was dismissed in June after losing three consecutive games in the bottom of the last inning in Detroit, dropping them from first place to 2½ games behind the Tigers. It was back to Piniella as manager. On the margins of contention most of the season, the Yankees ended up fifth, 3½ games out, in tightly bunched standings. Mattingly's power stroke was by now beginning to suffer from chronic back problems. After averaging 30 homers the previous four years, Mattingly hit only 18 in 1988. Henderson's league-leading 93 steals were his most since the 108 he swiped in 1983.

Steinbrenner's frustrations finally boiled over in 1989. The season began with yet another managerial change—veteran manager Dallas Green replacing Piniella—a pair of high-priced free agents, and without Dave Winfield, the Yankees' best player in 1988 with 25 homers, 107 RBIs, and a .322 batting average. The Yankees' signing of Dodgers second baseman Steve Sax and Padres right-hander Andy Hawkins was their first significant activity on the free agent market since 1985, not because of fiscal restraint, but rather ownership agreement not to bid on each other's high-priced free agents, which ended only because baseball's independent arbitrator exposed their collusion and punished Major League Baseball with a hefty fine. The Boss was happy to be opening his checkbook again, even though none of his free agent signings since Winfield in December 1980 met expectations, either because they really were not as good as Steinbrenner thought, their power was ill-suited to the dimensions of Yankee Stadium, or they couldn't handle the pressure of playing in New York—and especially not the pressure of their Boss's constant criticism of their efforts. For all that spending, the Yankees had yet to win another division title.

They wouldn't in 1989, either. A herniated disk forced Winfield to have back surgery during spring training that resulted in him missing the entire season. The Yankees lost seven of their first eight games, recovered to stay within striking distance for most of the summer even after trading Rickey Henderson back to Oakland in June, but lost 21 of 31 in August to set the stage for a catastrophic year. Mattingly's power stroke returned. Sax played well, his 205 hits second most in the majors, but Hawkins (15–15) had an earned-run average that was a full run higher than the 3.84 ERA in seven years he brought to the Yankees. The 4.87 ERA compiled by Yankees starting pitchers was by far the worst in the majors. Green failed to last the season. Their fifth-place finish and 74–87 record was the Yankees' worst year since 1967.

Winfield's yearlong absence did not make hearts grow fonder between him and his Boss. While the 1989 season played out, so too did acrimonious legal battles between Winfield and Steinbrenner over the Yankee owner's failing since 1982 to make annual $100,000 tax-exempt payments to the Dave Winfield Foundation for assisting disadvantaged children, as stipulated in his contract. Winfield had already sued Steinbrenner twice to make amends on the missed payments; Steinbrenner, claiming the foundation was squandering financial resources, did not do so despite court orders to make the payments; and in January 1989—before Winfield's back gave out on him—the Boss and his star player filed suits against each other over the matter. The Winfield Foundation affair was made uglier by the fact that Steinbrenner had a supposedly well-placed source providing him inside dirt on his star outfielder, including allegations that Winfield reneged on personal contributions to his own foundation and that he was engaged in unseemly, if not illegal, activity involving loans to gamblers.

The source was Howard Spira, a con man with a sordid past and questionable motives. Steinbrenner didn't so much ask him to investigate Winfield as welcome the derogatory information he had to offer and pay him for providing it. Not quite satisfied with that, especially given his debts, Spira used his shoveling dirt on Winfield's integrity to Steinbrenner's benefit as leverage to extort hush money from the Boss even after the Winfield vs. Steinbrenner affair was settled in arbitration. A *New York Daily News* exclusive in March 1990 on a $40,000 payment Steinbrenner made to Spira two months earlier, and a grand jury indictment of Spira days later for trying to extort the Boss, left Commissioner Fay Vincent little choice but to investigate the matter. The evidence led Vincent to announce at the end of July that he was suspending Steinbrenner from any involvement with his team for two years. The Boss, wanting to protect his leadership position on the US Olympic Committee, preferred to resign as managing general partner and agreed to be placed on Major League Baseball's permanently ineligible list rather than have the taint of being suspended effect his Olympic standing. Steinbrenner remained the Yankees' owner, however, even though he would have no authority over baseball decisions—despite being "The Boss"—and he could later apply to be taken off the ineligible list.

Before he was forced to step aside from running the Yankees in the summer of 1990, Steinbrenner made news on the 11th of May when Mr. May—I mean, Dave Winfield—was traded to the California Angels. Twenty-five days later, with the Yankees in last place, holding the worst record in the majors, he changed managers for the 18th time in his 18th year as franchise owner. This did not change that the 1990 Yankees were destined for their worst record since 1913, when they first officially became the Yankees. Beset by back problems, Don Mattingly, after six consecutive .300 seasons from 1984 to 1989 during which he batted .327 with 160 home runs, played in only 102 games, hit just 5 homers, and batted just .256. As for the departed Winfield, whose signing as a free agent for the 1981 season Steinbrenner expected would add to the Yankees' 23 World Series championships, that was the only year that he played in the Fall Classic in pinstripes, and the Boss never let go of his struggles against Dodgers pitching. Winfield finally won a World Series with Toronto in 1992. Steinbrenner's voluntary banishment lasted until 1993. Fay Vincent was gone by then.

* * *

Prior to the events of the 1990 season, persistent rumors that Steinbrenner would turn yet a sixth time to Billy Martin to right the Yankees' ship after their losing season in 1989 were put to a definitive end when Martin died after driving his car into a tree on wintry roads in upstate New York on Christmas Day. Perhaps the worst thing for Billy Martin was getting his dream job of managing the New York Yankees—if not the first time in 1976, simply because it was the first time and a great opportunity, at least every time after that. Martin's neediness about wanting to be in the Yankees' dugout was an unhealthy dependency exploited by George Steinbrenner. "Billy the Kid" was desperate in his need to wear Yankee pinstripes, and his Boss was an abusive bully. This not only resulted in his on-again/off-again managerial reign—sometimes even being told in advance when he would be on the dugout bench and when he would not—but also drove Martin to distraction when he was managing the Yankees, not to mention to death by a thousand cuts of anxiety and many humiliations.

Billy Martin didn't have the inner strength to appreciate that managing a major-league baseball team was the job he wanted. It shouldn't have had to be the Yankees. Martin was very good at what he did (even if he was very hard to take); there were other jobs that would have been available; and he could have done what Dick Williams finally did with Oakland owner Charlie Finley—say, "I'm not going to take it anymore," quit, and go elsewhere. Or even more to the point, Martin could have followed the example of Yogi Berra, who, after managing the Yankees to a third-place finish in 1984, was fired after only 16 games the next season and refused to have anything to do with the team Steinbrenner owned for nearly two decades after that humiliation. And Yogi, because of his great career, was even more identifiable with the Yankees than Billy Martin.

By allowing himself to be party to the seemingly eternal recurrence of the Steinbrenner-Martin soap opera, Billy Martin surely took himself out of consideration for other managerial jobs on which he might have built a greater historical legacy and earned a plaque in Cooperstown. He was one of baseball's greatest generation of managers, which included Earl Weaver, Sparky Anderson, Dick Williams, Whitey Herzog, and Tommy Lasorda. All except for Martin are in the Hall of Fame. His achievements are comparable. He led the Twins to a division title in his first year as a manager; the Tigers to a division title in his second year there; brought the 1974 Rangers and 1980 Athletics from last place and more than 100 losses to second-place finishes in his first year on the job with both teams; and managed the Yankees to consecutive pennants and a World Series championship his first time working for the Boss. Yet the longest he lasted in any one of his managerial stints was just three years, with Oakland from 1980 to 1982.

What was his problem? Billy Martin was the impetuous, behaviorally unpredictable Billy the Kid who never grew up. Williams and Weaver were also managers whose behavior was often controversial with players and owners, not to mention umpires. But however much they may have behaved like jackasses, Williams and Weaver also possessed maturity that Martin lacked. They had self-restraint and could operate in a grown-up world. Major League Baseball, after all, is a business, not a sandlot sport. Martin, by contrast, was too often reactively impulsive and reckless in his behavior. He would have had a much longer managerial career and been recognized as one of the greatest managers in history had he not been his own worst enemy.

24

SQUANDERED GREATNESS

The Rise and Demise of a Mets Dynasty

The National League's best teams in the 1970s were Cincinnati and Los Angeles, in the Western Division. In the 1980s they centered in the Eastern Division, where the St. Louis Cardinals and New York Mets won five division titles and four pennants between them in the seven years from 1982 to 1988. The three NL East titles won by the Cardinals in 1982, '85, and '87 were each by three-game margins, with the Mets finishing close behind them the latter two years. St. Louis went on to win the National League pennant all three times, and all three World Series they played were exciting seven-game affairs, of which they won just one in 1982. The two Eastern Division championships won by the Mets in 1986 and 1988 were blowouts. Featuring a high-profile slugger and a devastating power pitcher, both seeming destined to be Hall of Fame great, the Mets so dominated the league in performance and, perhaps even more so, in attitude that it was thought they would surely be a dynasty. It was not to be. The 1980s Cardinals were probably overachievers. The 1980s Mets underachieved. Their would-be dynasty played out as a Greek tragedy, with heroic figures felled by their own hubris.

The Mets went from mediocre in the first half of the 1970s, notwithstanding going to the World Series in 1973 with a record barely over .500, to quite bad in the last three years of the '70s and the first four in the '80s. Trading Tom Seaver, the ace and the face of their franchise, in June 1977 seemed a definitive statement that the Mets no longer cared about winning. The Cardinals just missed winning the NL East in both 1973 and 1974 by 1½ games. The rest of the decade was mostly treading water, alternating winning and losing seasons.

St. Louis began the 1970s relying on aging stars from the sixties, two of whom—Bob Gibson and Lou Brock—were veterans of the Cardinals teams that won pennants in 1964, '67, and '68. The third was former Braves catcher Joe Torre, for whom the Cardinals traded Orlando Cepeda in 1969. Having Ted Simmons in hand as their catcher of the future, Torre played first base and third base in the six years he was a St. Louis Cardinal. Always a dangerous hitter, Torre tore up the league his first three years in St. Louis, including leading the majors in batting average and RBIs in 1971. Traded to the Mets in 1975, he became their manager two years later, beginning his Stengelesque journey from mostly unsuccessful National League manager to one of the greatest managers of all time after he took charge of the Yankees in 1996.

Gibson followed up on his epic 1968 season—a 22–9 record and microscopic 1.12 earned-run average in 304⅔ innings pitched in the Year of the Pitcher—with 20 wins in 1969 and a 23–7 record in 1971. He retired three years later, his legacy intact as one of the game's greatest pitchers and fiercest competitors on the mound. You didn't mess with Bob Gibson. At the age of 35 in 1974, Lou Brock shattered Maury Wills's record 102 stolen bases in a single season with 118. It was the eighth time in nine years he led the league. His 938 career stolen bases were the most in history when he retired after stealing 21 in 1979. The same year Brock bowed out, a rookie named Rickey Henderson swiped the first 33 of his career.

* * *

Any doubts the Cardinals needed a reboot despite a creditable 86–76 record in 1979 were dispelled by their dismal stretch of just 5 wins in 27 games in May and June the next year. Hired to fix the mess was Whitey Herzog, who managed the 1976–1978 Kansas City Royals to three straight division titles. In late August he stepped out of the dugout to become general manager so he could focus on player moves to improve the club. The best players on his roster were Simmons, a potent run producer and six times a .300 hitter since becoming the Cardinals' catcher in 1970; shortstop Garry Templeton; and first baseman Keith Hernandez, whose .344 batting average in 1979 led the league and earned him a share of the National League's MVP Award with Willie Stargell—the first time

MVP balloting had ended in a tie. That winter, Herzog traded with the Cubs for established relief ace Bruce Sutter and, to the anger of Cardinals fans and the scorn of baseball writers, traded Simmons and Pete Vucko- vich, the Cards' best pitcher in 1980, to the Brewers. Getting two estab- lished big leaguers and prospects, it was not a bad trade on its merits. Also, Herzog had already lined up signing free-agent Darrell Porter, his catcher in Kansas City. More importantly, Herzog believed that 30-year- old Simmons's days as a catcher should be ending; Simmons's refusal to play another position made his trade inevitable.

Returning to the dugout in 1981 while remaining general manager, Herzog guided the Cardinals to the best record in the NL East—and the second best in the league after the Reds—with no postseason to show for it. In the artificially split season resulting from the players' strike that wiped out two months, neither team was in first place when the strike began and neither finished the second half in first place, so neither played in the postseason. Just before the players went on strike, St. Louis traded with Houston for Dominican-born right-hander Joaquin Andujar. After the season ended, Herzog acquired Philadelphia outfield-reserve Lonnie Smith and, in one of the most consequential trades in Cardinals history, sent Templeton to the Padres for Ozzie Smith, their defensive wizard of a shortstop. The two were just about the same age, and at this point in their careers Templeton was the better player. Both were outstanding defen- sively, but whereas Ozzie in his four years in San Diego had just one career home run, 19 triples, and a career batting average of .231, Temple- ton led the league with 19 triples in 1979, had 69 so far, along with 25 homers and a career batting average of .305 in six years with St. Louis.

The payoff was immediate. The Cardinals won the NL East in 1982, swept the NLCS to win their first pennant since 1968, and prevailed in seven games over the Brewers—for whom both Simmons and Vukovich were key players—in the World Series. Sutter led the majors in saves, with 36. Lonnie Smith was the Cardinals' best player, based on wins above replacement, batting .307 and stealing 68 bases in his first year as a regular. Ozzie Smith was right behind him in terms of player value. Neither of the next two years belonged to St. Louis. In June 1983, leading the division by a game, the Cardinals made one of the most consequential trades in *Mets* history, sending them Hernandez, the league's best all- around first baseman with a .299 batting average in over 4.000 at-bats so far in his career, for little in return. It was a deal that stoked controversy, particularly when nine losses in 10 games in September that began with the Cardinals trailing by 1½ games finished off their chances. Batting just .206 with only 15 extra-base hits and scoring a mere 21 runs in those games, St. Louis could have used Keith's bat.

* * *

On the date they acquired Keith Hernandez the Mets were in last place, doomed to finish the 1983 season there. But with Hernandez they added a second foundation piece for becoming a dynasty. The first was rookie left-handed power-hitting right fielder Darryl Strawberry, taken by the Mets as the first overall pick in the 1980 amateur draft and now, at 21, in his rookie season. He hit 26 homers and was named Rookie of the Year. In 1984 the Mets added a third and fourth piece—former Baltimore Orioles second baseman Davey Johnson to take over as manager and 19-year-old right-hander Dwight Gooden, a first-round pick in the 1982 amateur draft. Having observed Earl Weaver and his penchant for statistical notecards of possible batter-pitcher and pitcher-batter matchups, Johnson was at the leading edge of new managers embracing having baseball data analysis at their fingertips by using modern computer technology to log and array that data. Strawberry again belted 26 homers and drove in 97 runs; Hernandez batted .311 with 94 RBIs; Gooden introduced himself to the majors with a 17–9 record and a phenomenal 276 strikeouts in 218 innings (a then-record 11.4 per 9 innings) to merit being called "Dr. K"—or just Doc Gooden—and become the second Met in as many years to earn Rookie of the Year honors; and Johnson guided the Mets to an astonishing 90 wins, third most in the National League, a year after they were the league's worst team.

The Mets' final building block was the trade they made with Montreal in December 1984 to acquire Gary Carter, a 10-year veteran and already one of the best catchers in baseball history, to provide another power bat in the lineup and, more importantly, the stabilizing leadership on the field that outstanding teams require. The Cardinals also improved their club going into the 1985 season, dealing with the Giants for veteran Jack Clark to play first base and add a dangerous hitter to the middle of their lineup, and with the Red Sox for right-hander John Tudor to bolster the starting rotation behind Joaquin Andujar. Vince Coleman was promoted from the minor leagues to provide speed and a persistent stolen-base threat at the top of the order. The Cardinals were last in the majors in home runs the three previous years, including just 67 when they won the 1982 pennant, and Herzog was building his team around speed and pitching. It did not help his cause that Bruce Sutter, the league-leader in saves in three of his four St. Louis seasons, left as a free agent.

The 1985 Cardinals ended up with 101 wins, the Mets with 98. After losing two of three to fall behind the Mets when they visited Shea Stadium in the second week of September, the Cardinals won 14 of their next 15 to take a four-game lead that held up through their last nine games. Herzog found his new closer in Todd Worrell, whose first major-league pitch was on August 28; Clark's 22 home runs, accounting for a quarter of the team's total 87, were the most by a St. Louis player since 1980; the Cardinals stole 314 bases, 110 of them by Rookie of the Year Coleman; center fielder Willie McGee hit .353 to win the batting title and the MVP Award; and Tudor and Andujar both won 21. The Cy Young Award, however, went to Doc Gooden, 24–4 with a 1.53 ERA and just one loss in 19 decisions in 25 starts after Memorial Day; Carter's 32 homers and 100 RBIs made him a big hit with Mets fans; and Strawberry bashed 29 home runs. Strawberry's missing more than a quarter of the season with a torn ligament suffered in May quite possibly was decisive in the Mets losing out to the Cardinals by only three games.

Clark's two-out three-run home run in the top of the ninth overcame the Dodgers' one-run lead in Game Six in the NLCS to secure the 14th pennant in Cardinals history. They then had their own Game Six reversal of fortunes against Kansas City in the World Series. Leading by 1–0 in the ninth inning and needing just three outs to win their 10th World Series, the Cardinals were victimized by the first base umpire's erroneous "safe!" call where everyone watching on TV, if not those at Royals Stadium, could clearly see that first baseman Clark's toss to the pitcher covering was in time and that Todd Worrell's foot hit the first base bag a beat ahead of the runner. It wasn't even that close. Worrell lost his composure or his concentration, loaded the bases, then surrendered a game-winning hit to pinch-hitter Dane Iorg, only 29-for-130 during the season, forcing a seventh game. Perhaps unable to put the umpire's bad call behind them, the Cardinals played dysfunctional baseball the next day and lost Game Seven in a rout. Their 10th World Series championship would have to wait.

* * *

But it sure wasn't going to be in 1986, because the New York Mets had baseball's most dominant single season since the 1975 Big Red Machine. Posting the same 108–54 record as those Reds, the Mets won their division by 20½ games, then proved their mettle by stirring victories against the Houston Astros in the National League Championship Series and the Boston Red Sox in the World Series that seemed to confirm that their collective whatever-it-takes-to-win swagger, while obnoxious, was deserved. They had no doubt they were always the best team on the field. They were great in their own mind, which played especially well in New York since the 1980s Yankees had lost their swagger, which happened when—despite high-profile free agency signings—the team failed to live up to the expectations of a demanding owner and a demanding city fan base, perhaps made more demanding by the expectations of Boss Steinbrenner.

In addition to historically renowned players Carter (24 homers and 105 runs batted in), Hernandez (.310 batting average and 83 RBIs), and Strawberry (27 homers and 93 driven in) batting in the middle of the lineup, the Mets had Lenny Dykstra and Mookie Wilson sharing center field and platooning as the leadoff batter. In just his second year, Dykstra gave his team a gritty tough-as-"Nails" persona, which was his nickname. Gooden's 17–6 record was backed up by lefty Bob Ojeda's 18–5, lefty Sid Fernandez's 16–6, and righty Ron Darling's 15–6. Fernandez and Darling were in their third year and, coincidentally, both from Hawaii. Davey Johnson could also count on either right-hander Roger McDowell (22 saves) or lefty Jesse Orosco (21 saves) to be effective in closing out victories. McDowell would become better known for his cameo star turn as the "second spitter" in the 1992 *Seinfeld* episode featuring Keith Hernandez and playing off Oliver Stone's movie the previous year on the assassination of President Kennedy, which became an instant classic. It is not known that McDowell employed a spitter on the mound when pitching for the Mets, although the mid-1980s Mets were not above playing below the belt to win.

The 1986 NLCS also became an instant classic. The Mets faced off against the Houston Astros, their fellow 1962 National League expansion franchise. Houston's 96–66 record, outstanding on its own and good enough to win the NL West by 10 games, was 12 games worse than the Mets. While there was precedent for the league's most dominant team to be knocked off in the league championship series, as the 99-win 1973 Reds were by the 82-win Mets, it was not thought likely that anybody could beat the 1986 Mets juggernaut. But the Astros had outstanding pitching of their own, most notably 39-year-old Nolan Ryan and Mike Scott. Ryan was 12–8 and whiffed 194 batters in 170 innings in 30 starts, his best strikeouts-to-innings ratio since pitching for the Angels in 1978. That was nothing compared to Scott, whose vicious split-finger fastball propelled him to an 18–10 record, major-league-best 2.22 earned-run average, and 306 strikeouts in 275⅓ innings. The Mets' Dr. K averaged just 7.2 Ks per 9 innings.

Scott outdueled Gooden in the opening game of the NLCS, throwing a five-hit shutout and striking out 14. A homer by Astros first baseman Glenn Davis accounted for the game's only run. The day after Dykstra's two-run walk-off homer off Astros relief ace Dave Smith turned a 5–4 deficit into a 6–5 win to give the Mets a two-games-to-one advantage, Scott pitched a three-hit complete game to win Game Four, 3–1. It was Ryan against Gooden in Game Five. Both pitchers surrendered a run in the fifth. Ryan left after nine innings, giving up just two hits—one of them a home run by Strawberry—while striking out 12; Gooden left after 10 with the score still tied at 1–1. Carter won the game with a walk-off single in the 12th. With the series back in Houston, the Mets knew if they didn't win Game Six they'd have to face Mike Scott a third time in a deciding seventh game. Trailing 3–0 in the ninth, the Mets scored three to send the game into extra innings. Both teams scored in the 14th. The Mets seemed to decide things with three runs in the top of the 16th, only to have the Astros come back with two in the bottom of the inning. With the tying run on second and the winning run on first, Jesse Orosco fanned Kevin Bass to end the game and set up a date with Boston's Red Sox— and with destiny—in the World Series.

As if their dramatic 16-inning victory in Game Six of the NLCS wasn't enough, the Mets made arguably the most stunning comeback in World Series history when they were one out away from losing in six games with nobody on base, trailing 5–3. Because every team gets exact-ly the same number of outs, including in extra innings where there is no sudden death, it is theoretically possible in baseball for a team losing by any number of runs and down to their last out to come back and win. It is the number of outs that count, not time. The Mets were certainly re-minded of that in the sixth game of the NLCS, when they couldn't get three outs in the 14th after they took the lead before Houston tied the game, and in the 16th when the Astros rallied for two runs, after they had scored three, before Orosco finally got the third out. Now it was the Mets in the Astros' position. The first two batters flied out. The Red Sox never got the third out. Gary Carter, definitely a never-give-up-hope guy, singled. Pinch-hitter Kevin Mitchell singled. Ray Knight singled to score Carter, making the score 5-4. Mitchell scored on a wild pitch. The Mets had tied it! Mookie Wilson hit a ground ball to first baseman Bill Buckner that went through his legs. Mets win! Then they won Game Seven.

* * *

Just as Strawberry's baseball-related injury might have cost his team the 1985 division title, the same argument can be made for Doc Gooden's missing the first two months of the 1987 season for the non-baseball reason that he was in a drug rehab program to deal with his cocaine problem. Without him, the Mets split their first 50 games and trailed the Cardinals by six games on the day he returned to the mound. Dr. K picked up where he left off in 1984, winning five of his first six starts. The Mets were the best team in the National League the rest of the way, three games better than St. Louis, even though by the end of August they had picked up just half a game on the Cardinals. Gooden by then was 12–4 but finished with a 3–3 record in the final month.

The Cardinals' advantage was enough for them to survive a pedestrian 16–16 stretch drive to win the East with 95 wins to the Mets' 92. They were the two best teams in the National League. Coleman swiped 109 bases to become the first and, so far, only player to steal 100 bases three years in a row. Jack Clark's career-high 35 home runs set him up for a lucrative free agent contract with the Yankees after the season. The indispensable man on the Cardinals, however, was dazzling shortstop Ozzie Smith. "The Wizard Oz," defensively probably the best ever at his position, continued his emergence as a better offensive player, especially given his speed on the bases, than he is generally given credit for. Ozzie had career highs in runs, hits, doubles, RBIs, batting average, and on-base percentage. The Cardinals went back to the World Series, this time against the Twins, and again lost in seven games. Their 10th World Series championship, it turned out, would have to wait until the twenty-first century.

Whitey Herzog's Cardinals had a knack for winning close pennant races. Their 1987 division title was their third in six years, each won by a three-game margin. In both 1985 and '87, however, the Mets were the superior baseball team. Having only one historically great player—and he a defensive wizard rather than an elite pitcher or batter—that the Cardinals beat out the Mets to win the NL East in down-to-the-wire pennant races those two years reinforces the almost mythic idea in baseball that a savvy, gritty, fundamentally sound team of overachievers can outlast, over a long 162-game season, a better and more dominant team. This underdog ideal is much less realized over the course of a full season in other team sports, like football or basketball, where the teams with the best players almost always win the regular season because the best players to a much greater extent can take control of the action. Even a team that could be as dominating (and cocky) as Davey Johnson's Mets cannot afford to spot a tough and resilient rival a relatively large lead in the standings early in the season with the expectation that their overall superiority will win out.

Although St. Louis plummeted to fifth the next year and would have been of no more consequence in 1988 than any other competitive team, the Mets made sure that would not happen by building up a seven-game lead by July Fourth, fending off a July surge by upstart Pittsburgh, and finishing with 22 wins in their final 28 games to end with 100 wins and a 15-game margin of victory. Strawberry's 39 homers led the league. Left fielder Kevin McReynolds, picked up from San Diego the previous year, hit 27, and third baseman Howard Johnson, whose 36 home runs the previous year was second on the club to Strawberry, had 24. Gooden went 18–9 and Ron Darling 17–9, but the revelation among Mets pitchers was second-year right-hander David Cone's 20–3 record. Expecting to prevail against the Dodgers in the NLCS, the 1988 Mets lost in seven games.

* * *

Their 1988 NLCS loss was a disappointing coda to what probably should have been a great team and a dynasty. It took the Mets more than a decade to recover, although they remained competitive and even favored to win the NL East with essentially the same team the next two years, finishing second each time, before self-destructing in 1991. The 1986–1990 Mets were an offensive powerhouse, leading the league in scoring four times in five years. Gooden grabbed the headlines, but having Darling, Fernandez, and later Cone behind him gave the Mets arguably the best starting rotation in baseball. The Mets probably would have won five division titles in a row—instead of just two—beginning in 1985 were it not for Strawberry's injury in 1985, Gooden's rehab in '87, and shoulder problems that limited Gooden to only 17 starts and a 9–4 record in '89. The Mets, half a game behind in the 1989 race when Gooden went on the disabled list in late June, ended up six games back of the division-winning Cubs, leaving Shea Stadium's faithful to ponder whether they might have overtaken Chicago had Dr. K been healthy all season, especially since he followed that with 19–7 and 13–7 marks the next two years.

It may say more about league parity than anything else, but the Mets were the only National League team that was legitimately competitive every year from 1984, when Davey Johnson took over as manager and Dwight Gooden first teamed up with Darryl Strawberry, to 1990, by which time Dr. K was the last of the core star players from the 1986 and '88 Mets. For a team with attitude that presumed to dominate and intimidate the rest of the National League with Strawberry and Gooden, Hernandez and Carter, Dykstra and other obnoxious characters, New York's Mets turned out to be mere pretenders to greatness. Their run was one of fast and furious underachievement for what could—and maybe *should*—have been. They burned out too soon, perhaps because of undisciplined immaturity and a sort of teenage-like belief in their own indestructibility, all of which manifested itself in the wild lifestyles of the Mets' best players—most notably Strawberry and Gooden, both of whom fell prey to addictive demons—that epitomized in part an American culture in the 1980s that many condemned for emphasizing individual fulfillment rather than collective good. Gary Carter was a straight arrow not in keeping with his younger party-hearty Mets teammates, but being a bit of a scold, he had little influence on their lifestyle choices.

Strawberry played eight years for the Mets before leaving New York in 1991 as a free agent for Los Angeles, where he was born and grew up. Only 29 when he left the Mets with 252 career home runs, Strawberry hardly expected that his best years were already behind him. He did not ultimately live up to the promise of his potential. The seeds of that were his years in New York, where Strawberry's behavior in uniform and out became an unwanted distraction for the Mets, however outstanding he was as a player. On top of his own out-of-control lifestyle issues—which included alcohol and drug abuse, not to mention domestic abuse allegations in 1987—Strawberry was often accused of being less than diligent in his approach to the game; Davey Johnson, his manager, made a point of saying Strawberry was as good as anyone in baseball—when he wanted to be. Strawberry had a typical Darryl Strawberry year with the

Dodgers in 1991, hurt his back in 1992, and was never again a regular in the major leagues. Substance abuse and abusive behavior began to define Strawberry's career more than his rapidly compromised baseball prowess, especially with the bat. His last major-league season was also in New York, with the Yankees, in 1999. Strawberry finished his career with 335 homers and exactly 1,000 runs batted in.

The trajectory of Doc Gooden's career was much the same as Strawberry's. From his rookie year in 1984 to 1991, Gooden was one of the best pitchers in baseball, winning 132 while losing just 53. Although his rookie season was the only year he struck out more than a batter an inning, Dr. K remained an electrifying pitcher when he took the mound. Like Strawberry, he was unable to control his impulse toward substance abuse, even after spending the first two months of the 1987 season in rehab. Lesson not learned, living on the wild side, with all its attendant curses, remained a problem for Gooden throughout the rest of his career. In 1994 Gooden, who also had endured arm and shoulder problems, was back in rehab for cocaine. That was his last year with the Mets. Like Strawberry, he ended his career in New York with the Yankees in 2000, falling six wins short of 200. The many who remembered the phenomenal Dr. K in his first five years with the Mets lamented that he had squandered greatness.

Given the addictive sensibilities and lifestyle choices of the Mets' young stars, the trade for Keith Hernandez might have been an unfortunate reinforcement toward their undoing. The back story to why Hernandez, one of baseball's premier players and not yet 30, was made available to the Mets for okay reliever Neil Allen and an unproven minor-league pitcher was that his off-the-field activities and clubhouse influence were unwelcome by St. Louis manager Whitey Herzog. Any mystery as to why Herzog had problems with the Cardinals' best player became clear when Hernandez was implicated in a federal cocaine-trafficking investigation in the mid-1980s that revealed the extent of drug abuse among major league players. That said, whatever influence toward socially bad behavior Hernandez may have had in the Mets' clubhouse, he was a great baseball influence in the dugout and on the field of play until age and injuries diminished his abilities, beginning in the Mets' stellar 1988 season.

As for Davey Johnson, the start of his managerial career, when Strawberry and Gooden were both at the beginning of their playing days, suggested that he too might be on a Hall of Fame path that was never his trajectory as a player. In his first five years as manager, his teams never won fewer than 90 games. Johnson lasted until Memorial Day in 1990. The Mets were fourth, 5½ games out of first. Under new manager Bud Harrelson, their long-ago shortstop, the Mets had the National League's best record from Memorial Day until time ran out on the season. They ended up second, four games behind Pittsburgh. As much as he had done to make the Mets a would-be dynasty, Johnson had also presided over a team whose central core of talented players ruined their could-have-been-great careers by intemperance and lack of discipline in their off-the-field lives. Indisputably an outstanding baseball manager, which he would demonstrate in the future by turning around the competitive fortunes of four other teams and winning four division titles with three of them, Davey Johnson with the Mets was their enabler.

25

RED SOX, CUBS, AND
THE WEIGHT OF HISTORY

The specifics are remarkably similar, except for the moment the first baseman's misplay occurred. On October 7, 1984, Chicago's Cubs held a 3–2 lead over San Diego's Padres going into the last of the seventh inning of the fifth and final game of the National League Championship Series. Chicago had won the first two games in the best-of-five series as it moved to San Diego, putting them just one win away from winning the National League pennant for the first time since 1945. The Padres won the first two at home to even the series. With their ace Rick Sutcliffe on the mound in the fifth game, the Cubs were in command until the sixth inning, when the Padres pulled within one. After a leadoff walk and a sacrifice bunt that put the tying run on second with one out in the seventh, Sutcliffe induced pinch-hitter Tim Flannery to hit a grounder to first baseman Leon Durham. That should have been the second out of the inning. Except the ball went through Durham's legs, after which a single, Tony Gwynn's double, and Steve Garvey's single gave San Diego a 6–3 lead they did not relinquish. It was now 39 years since the Chicago Cubs had last been to a World Series—and 76 since they last won one.

Exactly two years and 18 days later, leading the World Series three games to two with Game Six tied after nine innings at Shea Stadium, Boston's Red Sox scored twice in the top of the 10th to take a 5–3 lead over New York's Mets. They were just three outs away from winning their first World Series since 1918, when America was otherwise engaged in World War I. Right-hander Calvin Schiraldi was pitching his second inning in relief. Called up from Triple-A in July, Schiraldi had won four and saved nine in 25 relief appearances for the Red Sox. His earned-run average was an excellent 1.41 and he had given up just 15 walks and 36 hits while striking out 55 batters in 51 innings. The first two Mets flied out. The Red Sox were one out from a World Series championship. The home-team scoreboard flashed congratulations to the visiting Boston Red Sox. But Gary Carter singled. Pinch-hitter Kevin Mitchell singled. Ray Knight singled to drive in Carter. Mitchell went to third. Now it was 5–4. With switch-hitting Mookie Wilson at the plate, veteran right-hander Bob Stanley, Boston's relief ace until his pitching struggles opened the closer's door for Schiraldi in August, came in to get that final out. He didn't. A wild pitch and Mitchell scored the tying run. Wilson then cued a grounder to first baseman Bill Buckner. It went through Buckner's legs. The winning run scored, snatching the World Series trophy from Boston's hands. The series was tied. The Mets won Game Seven. It was now 68 years since the Red Sox were World Champions.

What else could explain what happened to the Cubs in 1984 and the Red Sox in '86 but that they were cursed? That hadn't always been how to explain the two clubs' extended lack of championships. The Cubs had become known for being baseball's "lovable losers," what with the perennial smiling faces of Ernie Banks and Billy Williams, although the black cat walking in front of Ron Santo in the on-deck circle and by the Cubs' dugout at Shea Stadium in the midst of their summer of '69 collapse did give one pause about whether some sort of black magic might be working against them. And the Red Sox' competitive failures were frequently attributed to a dysfunctional clubhouse—25 cabs for 25 players, it was said. But the curse narrative was now taking shape, even if it was not (presumably) really taken seriously.

To the extent one buys into the curse narrative, in the case of the Red Sox, they brought the "Curse of the Bambino" upon themselves when owner Harry Frazee made a financially motivated baseball decision to sell Babe Ruth to the Yankees—a deal that forever changed the trajectory of two franchises and which was the foundation of the Yankees' forever dynasty. The Cubs, on the other hand, had a curse cast on them by the aggrieved owner of the Billy Goat Tavern in Chicago, who was miffed that his real-live billy goat wasn't allowed into Wrigley Field for Game Four of the 1945 World Series—a reasonable decision if for no other reason than that a cantankerous old goat might endanger the safety of the people around it.

* * *

Between their being on the wrong side of the Mets' miracle season in 1969 and finally winning the NL Eastern Division title in 1984, the Cubs were mostly the definition of mediocrity. Following Banks's retirement in 1971, along with the departures of Santo and ace Ferguson Jenkins in 1973 and Williams in 1975, the Cubs had few identifiable stars. Third baseman Bill Madlock won back-to-back batting titles in 1975 and '76, as did first baseman-outfielder Bill Buckner in 1980. Itinerant slugger Dave Kingman, whose 442 career home runs are largely lost to history because of his many deficiencies as a ballplayer, probably had the best years of his career the three seasons he played in Chicago. His 48 homers in the middle year led the majors in 1979. Despite the Cubs being consistently in the bottom half of the league in giving up runs, starting pitcher Rick Reuschel and reliever Bruce Sutter were their most prominent players in the 1970s. Reuschel's 20–10 mark in 1977 helped the Cubs to the only year between 1973 and 1983 that they did not have a losing record. Five years a Cub, Sutter led the league in saves in 1979 and 1980, resulting in his being traded to St. Louis before he entered his qualifying year for free agency.

Only the Mets had a worse record in the National League than the 71–91 Cubs in 1983. They finished fifth and sixth in the NL East. Ironically, they finished in the same order in 1984, except at the top of the Eastern Division standings. Second in the league in runs, the 1983 Cubs were probably not as bad as their actual record; their being 18–27 in one-run games suggests they played into a lot of bad luck. Pitching was the Cubs' biggest weakness in 1983. They were the only NL club with an ERA over 4.00, and their starting pitchers' earned-run average of 4.50 was by far the worst of any staff.

The turnaround of the 1984 Cubs was sparked by the breakout season of third-year second baseman Ryne Sandberg—the National League's best player that year, according to wins above replacement—and the pitching of right-handers Rick Sutcliffe and Dennis Eckersley, both picked up in trades after opening day. Those trades were probably the difference in Chicago's beating out much-improved New York to win the NL East. Eckersley, pitching for Cleveland and Boston, was one of the top starting pitchers in the American League in the late 1970s but had been less effective since then. Sutcliffe was the NL Rookie of the Year in 1979, pitching for Los Angeles, and had the best ERA in the AL in 1982 pitching for Cleveland. Both had ERAs over 5.00 when they were traded to the Cubs. At first, it wasn't any better in Chicago for Eckersley, who lost five of his first six decisions after the trade. After correcting his inefficiencies, however, Eckersley settled down to finish the season with a 9–3 record and an excellent 2.13 earned-run average after July 1. Sutcliffe's 16–1 record after becoming a Cub and 155 strikeouts in 150⅓ innings earned him the league's Cy Young Award to complement Sandberg's MVP Award. Sutcliffe and Eckersley's combined 23–3 record from the beginning of July till the end of the season spearheaded Chicago to victory. In addition to their traded-for aces, the Cubs also had the advantage of Lee Smith as their ace reliever to close out victories.

As an aside, had they closed out the Padres in the NLCS the Cubs would have faced the Detroit Tigers in the World Series, which would have been a franchise rematch of the last time they were in the Fall Classic in 1945. The winning pitcher in Game Four of that series—the game at Wrigley Field where the pub owner's billy goat was turned away at the gate—was Detroit's Dizzy Trout. He was the father of Steve Trout, a lefty whose 13-7 record was second to Sutcliffe as the best on the 1984 Cubs.

* * *

Unlike the Cubs, the Red Sox were a competitive team in the American League's Eastern Division in the 1970s before reverting to relative mediocrity in the first half of the 1980s. Boston's 1967 Impossible Dream team proved to be a one-night stand. Notwithstanding Carl Yastrzemski being the best player in the American League for the second straight year, and even had two of their other stars not been hurt—one on the job (Tony Conigliaro from his horrific beaning), the other recreationally (Jim Lonborg from a skiing accident)—the 1967 Red Sox really were more akin to their other nickname that unbelievable year. Theirs really was a Cinderella story, whose time was up once the clock struck Game Seven in the World Series and Bob Gibson took the mound for St. Louis. Shattering their glass slipper, Gibson was not about to play the part of any prince charming for the Cinderella Red Sox.

It wasn't that the Red Sox weren't a good team in the seven long years after their 1967 heroics. They were. But they were not a top-tier 90-win team, either. Powered by Yastrzemski, center fielder Reggie Smith, and

Rico Petrocelli, who moved to third base in 1971 when Boston acquired veteran Luis Aparicio to play shortstop, the Red Sox continued to be among the top-scoring teams in the American League. Yaz hit 40 homers in both 1969 and 1970 and missed out on a fourth batting title by the barest of margins in 1970, his .3286 average falling less than one hit shy of Alex Johnson's .3289. Every year except for 1972, the Red Sox were far outclassed by their competitors—most notably the Baltimore Orioles—in the first six years of divisional alignments in the AL East. The 1972 season was odd in every respect, beginning with a players' strike that cost the first 10 days of the season. The Orioles had their worst record of the decade in 1972, and because the games that were missed were not made up, the season ended with Detroit beating out Boston in their division by half a game while having played only 14 of their scheduled 18 games against each other.

As if Baltimore's dominance of the AL East wasn't enough, by the mid-1970s the Red Sox also were confronting the reality of the Yankees storming back from a decade of lost-cause seasons. The Red Sox, however, were much better positioned to compete in the near-term than they had been in 1966—the year before their Impossible Dream team. Yastrzemski, while no longer a superstar, was still a dangerous hitter. Catcher Carlton Fisk, the AL Rookie of the Year in 1972, was implicitly dueling with the Yankees' Thurman Munson for best catcher in the American League. In 1974 the Red Sox were invigorated by young players Dwight Evans taking over in right field and Rick Burleson at shortstop, and in 1975 by another pair of young outfielders—Fred Lynn in center and Jim Rice in left—that caused Yastrzemski to move full-time to first base. Most importantly, Boston's pitching—a longstanding fundamental weakness not helped by the dimensions of Fenway Park—was much improved with Luis Tiant, signed in 1971 after both Cleveland and Minnesota had given up on him because of persistent shoulder problems, and southpaw Bill Lee, who pitched well even in a ballpark unkind to left-handers. Tiant had back-to-back 20 wins season in 1973 and '74, and Lee won exactly 17 both years.

Spearheaded by Lynn, Rice, and Fisk, returning in late June from a devastating injury from a collision at the plate the year before, Boston stormed to the division title in 1975, put an end to Oakland's string of three straight championships by sweeping them in the ALCS, and engaged Cincinnati's Big Red Machine in what many still consider the greatest World Series ever played. Lynn batted .331, with 21 homers and 105 RBIs, to become the first rookie voted his league's Most Valuable Player. Rice was leading the Sox with 22 homers and 102 runs batted in and batting .309 when a broken hand on an errant inside pitch just days before the season ended finished him for the year. Fisk hit .331, with 10 homers and 52 RBIs, in the 79 regular-season games he played and then provided one of the most indelible moments in World Series history.

Although not quite the same as Bobby Thomson's game-ending pennant-winning home run in 1951 or Bill Mazeroski's Game Seven–ending 1960 World Series–winning home run, Carlton Fisk's game-ending home run in the sixth game of the 1975 World Series might be the most dramatic. It came at the end of an exciting, hard-fought game. It came in an elimination game for the Red Sox, forcing a Game Seven. And the televised imagery of Fisk slide-stepping down the first base line waving for his high fly ball deep down the left field line to stay fair and clear the 37-foot Green Monster wall has become as iconic as Willie Mays's catch in the 1954 series. In the end, Fisk's home run only bought the Red Sox another day. Bill Lee was unable to hold an early 3–0 lead in Game Seven. Cincinnati won in the ninth on an RBI single into center field by Joe Morgan. It was now 57 years since the Red Sox last won a World Series.

* * *

Three years later Boston had the dubious distinction of playing the role of the Brooklyn Dodgers in the 1978 remake of 1951's surprise blockbuster, "The Miracle of Coogan's Bluff." The Yankees were back in business, having won the division, the pennant, and the World Series in 1977, but were stumbling in a try for a second straight championship. The Red Sox, however, fortified by trading for Cleveland's budding ace Dennis Eckersley and signing free agent Mike Torrez, late of the Yankees, whose complete-game victory in Game Six of the 1977 World Series returned the forever dynasty back to its once accustomed place as world champions, had a seemingly secure nine-game lead over the second-place Yankees on August 13 with 116 down and 46 remaining. Then the Yankees did their 1951 Giants imitation. Their four-game series sweep of the Red Sox at Fenway in early September erased the entirety of Boston's lead in less than a month. Less than a week later, after losing twice at Yankee Stadium, the Red Sox trailed New York by 3½ games with 148 games done and 14 to go.

All hope abandon ye, Fenway faithful? Eckersley's 17th win, salvaging the final game of the three-game series in New York, kicked off a Red Sox surge to catch the Yankees. His 20th victory in Boston's 161st game kept the Sox within one of the Yankees going into the final day. Tiant shut out Toronto in game 162 to keep hope alive as the Yankees went down in defeat at the hands of the 90-loss Cleveland Indians, the team with which both Tiant and Eckersley had started their careers. For the second time in American League history, a playoff was needed to decide first place. One game. At Fenway Park. Having just pitched, neither Eckersley nor Tiant was available. After losing seven consecutive starts, Bill Lee had been sidelined by manager Don Zimmer since mid-August, his quirky countercultural "weirdness" not helping matters. The start in game 163 went to Mike Torrez, now with 16 wins, against his former team.

Things went well until the seventh inning, when with two outs, two runners on, and Torrez protecting a 2–0 lead, light-hitting Yankees shortstop Bucky Dent stepped into the role of Bobby Thomson and put the Yankees ahead with a three-run homer. Like Thomson's at the Polo Grounds, which would most likely have been a routine out in most other ballparks, Dent's just cleared the short-distance Green Monster. The Yankees had the lead, but that wasn't the end of the story. This reproduction of the Miracle of Coogan's Bluff was a mashup that incorporated the nineteenth-century poem "Casey at the Bat." Trailing 5–4 in the bottom of the ninth, down to their last out but with the would-be tying and winning runs on second and third, Boston icon Carl Yastrzemski, 38 years old, came to bat against the Yankees' dominating closer Goose Gossage. Of his 17 home runs, six were in September. All he needed was a single. Instead—there was no joy in Fenway, for Mighty Yaz popped out.

The 1951 Dodgers quickly recovered from their Thomson trauma, winning four of the next five National League pennants. The 1978 Red Sox did not, descending into the middle of the pack in the AL East in the first half of the 1980s. Not until 1986 did they awaken from their stupor to compete for the division title. By then Fisk had left as a free agent, and Lynn had been traded to the Angels in 1981. Yastrzemski retired after the 1983 season. Jim Rice, Dwight Evans, and reliever Bob Stanley were the only core players remaining from the 1978 team. The new Red Sox, however, featured two of the best players ever at their positions—third baseman Wade Boggs and right-handed power pitcher Roger Clemens, also known as "The Rocket."

Boggs broke in with a .349 batting average in 104 games as a rookie in 1982. The next year he led the league with a .361 batting average and reached base a league-leading 44 percent of the time—the first of five batting titles in six years and leading the league in on-base percentage six times in seven years. Boggs scored 100 runs and had more than 200 hits every year from 1983 to 1989; his seven straight 200-hit seasons were the most since Willie Keeler's eight in a row from 1894 to 1901. In 1985 Boggs's 240 hits were the most in the majors since Bill Terry's 254 in 1930—the infamous Year of the Hitter. Clemens was 9–4 in 1984, his rookie year, but only 7–5 in 1985 because of shoulder problems that limited him to just three games after early July. Boston finished fifth that year.

Since the Orioles' and Yankees' command of the AL East in the 1970s, no one club had dominated the division so far in the 1980s. The previous four division titles were won by four different teams—Milwaukee in 1982, Baltimore in '83, Detroit in '84, and Toronto in '85 so it was perhaps only fitting that 1986 should be Boston's turn. Clemens was 14–0 in his first 15 starts, with 125 strikeouts in 123⅔ innings. In April he became the first pitcher in history to strike out 20 batters in a nine-inning game, a feat he repeated in 1996—only the second time that had been done. (Kerry Wood in 1998, Randy Johnson in 2001, and Max Scherzer in 2016 are the only other pitchers to whiff 20 in a nine-inning game. No pitcher has yet gotten 21 of 27 outs by strikeout.) Boggs was hitting .400 one-third of the way through the schedule. The Red Sox won the Eastern Division handily. Boggs hit .357 to win his third batting title. Clemens finished with a 24–4 record.

If ever it seemed like luck and good fortune would be with the Red Sox in the postseason, 1986 was the year. Boston was facing elimination, down to their final out and trailing the California Angels 5–4 in the ninth inning of Game Five in the ALCS, when late-season trade acquisition Dave Henderson, a midgame substitution, homered to stave off defeat. In the 11th his sacrifice fly gave Boston the victory. The Red Sox crushed the Angels in Games Six and Seven to complete their improbable comeback from a three-games-to-one deficit and make it to their ninth World Series in franchise history, whereupon they became the team famous for being one out away from a championship that couldn't secure that all-important last out. There was much after-the-fact criticism of manager John McNamara for not replacing the virtually immobile 36-year-old Bill Buckner and his aching knees with the more agile, defensively more proficient backup first baseman Dave Stapleton. In four of the seven ALCS games and three of the first five games of the World Series, McNamara had in fact substituted Stapleton for Buckner in the late innings. That he did not do so in the 10th inning may have been for sentimental reasons, so that the veteran Buckner could be on the field when the Red Sox celebrated their first World Series triumph since 1918. If so, sentiment paid a high price.

While the coincidence of not having won a World Series since selling Ruth to the Yankees was not lost on Bostonians and New Englanders, the way they lost in 1978 and 1986 probably had many wondering whether the Babe really did curse their team—although it should be noted that the Bambino was unhappy in Boston and wanted to spread his wings in New York, where he was also likely to be paid more, much more, for his troubles (playing baseball). Four years and two division titles later, the Curse of the Bambino may have infected Roger Clemens personally. It was Game Four of the 1990 ALCS. Boston at Oakland, trailing three games to none. Clemens (21–6) vs. A's ace Dave Stewart (22–11). Bottom of the second. Oakland had just taken a 1–0 lead. Light-hitting Willie Randolph walked. Apparently unable to contain himself, Clemens had words with the plate umpire. Clemens was ejected. Both runners on base subsequently scored. Game lost. ALCS lost. It was now 72 years since they last won a World Series. And Red Sox Nation was left to wonder what *that* was about. Somewhere the Babe, back then a great pitcher himself, was likely having a good chuckle at Rocket Roger's expense.

* * *

Longtime owner Tom Yawkey died in 1976. Sentimentalized for his love for the team he bought in 1933 and regret that he did not live to see the Red Sox win a World Series, Yawkey also left behind a legacy of promoting a country club atmosphere for star players—Ted Williams and Yastrzemski among them—that undermined a sense of being teammates in the clubhouse and competitive cohesion on the playing field.

Yawkey's more pernicious legacy, however, was his franchise's indifference to its black players even *after* the Red Sox became Major League Baseball's last team to integrate in 1959. Reggie Smith, Boston's best player after Yaz when the two played together from 1967 to 1973, might have been a superstar but for the fact he was a black man playing baseball for a team with a long history of resisting integration in a city where racist sentiments were openly expressed by widespread white opposition to busing to integrate public schools. He was not happy about either situation and did not feel the Red Sox were supportive of their black players in the face of the social isolation they endured and the racial taunts they heard.

Little changed after Jean Yawkey became owner upon her husband's death. Jim Rice retired after the 1989 season having played his entire career in Boston despite harboring bitter resentment that the Red Sox provided virtually no support in dealing with the racist taunts he endured at Fenway and, especially in the 1980s, seemed disinterested in adding black players to the roster. One they did add was Ellis Burks, who Rice mentored after he became the Red Sox' center fielder in 1987 and helped navigate through the subtle (and sometimes overt) racial hostility of the city they played in and management's lack of interest or, at best, total ineffectualness in dealing with it. A more proactive public approach to supporting their black players and, especially after free agency, making the Red Sox an attractive club for black players to come play for might have gone a long way to help ameliorate the racial tensions that gripped Boston. Helping to bring a community together—baseball can have that kind of effect.

* * *

After finishing with the National League's best record in 1984, the Cubs endured four consecutive fourth-place losing seasons, then were the National League's best team again in 1989. The Cubs were able to sneak their way to the top because the decade's most dominant NL East teams—the Mets and the Cardinals—began their downhill slides that year and the Pirates, with Barry Bonds on the cusp of being a superstar, were a year away from being the division's new powerhouse team. Second baseman Ryne Sandberg, right fielder Andre Dawson, and second-year first baseman Mark Grace carried the club offensively, scoring or driving in 64 percent of the Cubs' runs. While veteran Rick Sutcliffe, with 16 wins, may have been the titular ace of the Chicago staff, it was 23-year-old Greg Maddux who was their best pitcher. Maddux had gone from 6–14 with a 5.61 earned-run average in his 1987 rookie season to 18–8 in '88, and 19–12 in '89. Beaten in the NLCS by the Giants, it was now 44 years since the Cubs last played in a World Series.

The first two games of the league championship series were played in Chicago at Wrigley Field. At night. The "lovable losers" shtick had worn thin since the departures of Ernie Banks and Billy Williams and their sunny dispositions, especially after they won their division in 1984—which wasn't the pennant, but still it was first place. That made exclusively daytime baseball and the aesthetics of Wrigley's ivy-covered outfield brick walls and absence of light stanchions, rather than their championship drought, the greater part of the Cubs' continuing mystique. It played to nostalgia for simpler times—a notion, which Major League Baseball was only too happy to play into, that the game hearkened back to America before (and at) the turn of the century, when work and social life were guided by natural rhythms from sunrise to sunset rather than the hubbub of industrial and commercial activity. The mythology of baseball—played for the love of the game and contested outdoors in daylight with the setting sun the only limit on how long they could play on if a team did not win in nine innings—had an undying appeal for being that ideal, especially in an America still reeling from the social dislocations of the 1960s and the increasing transformative power of technological innovation, never mind that the major leagues were born, nurtured, and grew in urban America in times of labor and political ferment.

It had been only a matter of time from the moment in 1981 that the Chicago Cubs went from being a family-owned franchise run by the direct descendants of Bill Wrigley, the chewing-gum magnate who bought the club in 1921, to a corporate-run franchise owned by the Chicago Tribune Company. The baseball team just part of its many business interests, the Tribune Company was determined to bring the club into the modern era. And for both attendance at the ballpark and fans tuning in to watch their games on the Tribune's nationwide cable television network, the nighttime was the right time for baseball to be played to accommodate everyone who worked or went to school during the day looking for entertainment options in the evening, which indeed was *everyone*. When the lights went up and the first night games were played at Wrigley Field in August 1988, there was a sense, especially among baseball romantics, that something ineffable had been forever lost. Wrigley day games had seemed the last mooring of the national pastime to its supposedly idyllic, if not quite pastoral, roots. Surely the gods on baseball's Mount Olympus had their say when the first night game at Wrigley had to be called in the fourth inning because of a rainstorm that refused to go away.

Whatever baseball's gods thought, the institution of Major League Baseball itself had a vested interest in night games being played at Wrigley Field, especially should the Cubs make it to the World Series. That, however, did not seem likely to happen anytime soon—not after the Cubs reverted to losing form during the three years after 1989. Given that the fates seemed to be conspiring against either the Cubs or the Red Sox winning another championship, baseball fans looking for signs that the end might be nigh as the next millennium beckoned at the end of the 1990s would have been excused for believing that should the Boston Red Sox and Chicago Cubs ever meet in a World Series that one of them must win . . . well, that just might be too much for the universe to bear.

26

HOW THE '80S AL WEST WAS WON

While the American League's Eastern Division crown went to a different club every season between 1981 and 1986, with no division winner returning to the top until the Tigers, having won in 1984, did so again in 1987, the California Angels and the Kansas City Royals were the principal players for primacy in the AL West during the 1980s even though both teams had years they were not competitive. After nearly a decade of dashed hopes, including unrealistic expectations in 1971 and hiring the best manager available in 1974, the Angels finally broke through to finish first for the first time in 1979, interrupting the 1976–1980 Royals' string of four division titles in five years. In the meantime, Angels fans enjoyed riding the Nolan Ryan Express, with a sidecar for fellow blazer Frank Tanana.

The unrealistic expectations for 1971 were raised by *Sports Illustrated* and other, exclusively baseball magazines picking the Angels as the team to finish atop the AL West. In retrospect, especially given how good the young Oakland A's turned out to be, that judgment bordered on the ridiculous. The foundation analysis for their assessment was premised on the Angels finishing third with 86 wins in 1970; shortstop Jim Fregosi being still in his prime; outfielder Alex Johnson having just won the batting title; a preseason trade for Red Sox slugger Tony Conigliaro, whose 36 homers in 1970 suggested he had fully recovered from his near-fatal beaning in 1967 (on a pitch thrown by an Angels pitcher no less); and a pitching staff that included Clyde Wright, 22–12 in 1970, and the talented young Andy Messersmith. Overlooked was the fact that the Angels had finished 1970 with 18 losses in their last 30 games, including a devastating nine-game losing streak that plunged them from three games back to 11 behind in a little more than a week—hardly an ending to forecast a division-contending club in 1971; that Johnson had a rap sheet as a toxic teammate; and that Conigliaro's right-handed power-stroke was better suited for Fenway Park than Anaheim Stadium.

Aside from Messersmith winning 20 and Wright pitching well, 1971 went badly for the Angels. They ended up going from 86 wins the previous year to 86 losses, finishing fourth. Only the San Diego Padres scored fewer runs in the majors. Fregosi had foot problems that ultimately required surgery. Conigliaro struggled to hit for power in his new environment, complained that he wasn't seeing the ball well, became a clubhouse distraction, and finally announced he was leaving the game in July. It turned out that the blind spot he had in the center of his left eye from the 1967 beaning had gotten worse. And Alex Johnson was worse than a distraction. He sulked. He showed no small measure of disdain for his teammates. He made Dick Allen look like a model citizen in the clubhouse. He was lackadaisical at best in games, as though he just didn't care. He was fined, benched for lack of hustle, and finally suspended. At first the Angels' GM refused to back his manager on the suspension, causing Angels players to lose respect for him and even their manager for yielding on the point. Alex Johnson was suspended again, this time indefinitely.

The best manager available in the summer of 1974 was Dick Williams, still under contract to Oakland despite quitting in a pique over his disdain for Charlie Finley after winning the two previous World Series. Finley magnanimously freed Williams only because he knew the Angels were no threat to upend his Athletics. Williams's time as Angels manager was not a happy experience for anyone concerned. Aside from a pitching staff that featured Ryan and Tanana at their best, the Angels were not a talented team, and Williams was not the manager to motivate them to play above their abilities. Contrary to expectations, Williams's work in turning the 1967 Red Sox into baseball's Cinderella story and his two World Series rings did not earn him the respect and attention of Angels players. They did not appreciate either his attempts to impose discipline or his outspokenness in telling them how inadequate they really were. California came in last after he took charge in the middle of the

1974 season, finished last when he managed them for a full season in 1975, and were last in the AL West when he was fired in July 1976.

The Angels' division title in 1979 came thanks in large part to their being one of baseball's most aggressive clubs in the first years of free agency. Coming to California from the first free agent class of 1976, second baseman Bobby Grich and outfielder/DH Don Baylor both had outstanding seasons in 1979; Baylor was the AL's MVP. In the off-season prior, the Angels took advantage of free agency being on the near horizon for first baseman Rod Carew and outfielder Dan Ford, acquiring both from Minnesota in separate trades. Ford had the best statistical year of his career, and Carew topped .300 for the 11th straight year. It was only fitting that back-to-back complete-game victories by Ryan and Tanana over second-place Kansas City clinched the AL West for California with four games to spare. The Angels' celebration was short-lived, however. Not only did they lose to Baltimore in the ALCS, but Nolan Ryan became a free agent and, wanting to return to his home state, signed with Houston.

Nolan Ryan came to California in 1972 in a deal that sent Jim Fregosi to the Mets. At the time, the trade was cast as a major mistake by the Angels. Fregosi was the best shortstop in baseball in the 1960s and, notwithstanding his foot problems in 1971, was just entering his 30s. Ryan was still trying to harness his awesome talent, and it was not clear he ever would. The trade turned out quite the opposite for the Angels. The Fregosi-for-Ryan deal is indeed invoked as one of the worst trades ever— on the Mets' side of the ledger. Fregosi turned out to be finished.

Ryan pitched eight years in Anaheim; was twice a 20-game winner and twice a 19-game winner for losing teams; completed 156 of his 288 starts; threw 40 shutouts, including four no-hitters, to match Sandy Koufax's total; struck out more than 300 batters five times; led the league in strikeouts every year except for 1975, when he missed as many as 10 starts because of injury; and averaged 10 strikeouts every 9 innings. The one year the Ryan Express did not, 'twas Frank Tanana, in just his second year, leading the league in Ks with 269 in 257⅓ innings. By 1978, however, Tanana's high-strikeout early years had taken a toll on his arm, and his strikeout total dropped to 137 in 239 innings. To his credit, Tanana mastered the art of pitching after he lost his blazer and remained a quality starter through the 1980s with Texas and Detroit. He won 102 for the Angels before he was traded in 1981 and would win another 138 after.

Ryan's departure was surely not the sole cause—injuries, poor pitching, and underperformance by key position players all contributed—but the 1980 Angels nose-dived from 88 wins to 95 losses. They responded by returning to the free agent market for established veterans, signing Boston outfielder Fred Lynn and Minnesota southpaw Geoff Zahn for 1981 and Baltimore third baseman Doug DeCinces and Yankees slugger Reggie Jackson for 1982. Veteran catcher Bob Boone was acquired from the Phillies prior to the 1982 season in a cash transaction. The payoff was a return to the top of the AL West in 1982 and the first 90-win season in franchise history. Reggie had something to prove, having left New York disaffected by how he was being treated, including starting far more often than he liked as the DH. Playing right field every day for the 1982 Angels, the 36-year-old Jackson led the league with 39 homers; DeCinces had the best year of his career; and Carew's .319 batting average was second in the league—not bad for a veteran the same age as Reggie. Age was in fact to be a significant problem going forward for the Angels. All nine of their position regulars in 1982 were at least 30, and three of their top four starting pitchers were over 35, including 18–8 Zahn.

The 1982 Royals, meanwhile, were at a crossroads, needing to refresh their roster but lacking the Angels' financial wherewithal to compete on the free agent market. The only free agent of any consequence they signed was their one of own, Larry Gura, after he had gone 16–4 in 1978. George Brett was still an elite player. Outfielder Willie Wilson, as much a stolen-base threat as Rickey Henderson, and sublime relief ace Dan Quisenberry were among baseball's best at what they did. KC's other core players, however, including all three of their top starting pitchers—Dennis Leonard, Gura, and Paul Splittorff—were in their 30s and moving past their prime. The Royals nonetheless competed with the Angels for the Western Division title until 10 losses in 11 games in September, including three-straight in Anaheim, finished them off.

* * *

The Angels-Royals battle for supremacy was temporarily sidelined in 1983 when the Chicago White Sox won the AL West by 20 games with the best record in the major leagues. Their division title was the culmination of a dramatic turnaround for a franchise that struggled to gain traction since losing a close pennant race in 1967 until Chicago real estate mogul Jerry Reinsdorf bought the club in 1981. The best of the White Sox' '70s show came in 1972 when, led by Wilbur Wood's 24 wins and

Dick Allen's league-leading 37 homers and 113 RBIs in his first year in Chicago for an MVP season, they finished with the second-best record in the American League, which unfortunately was also second best in their division.

Wood's 49 starts were the most since Big Ed Walsh started 49 for the 1908 White Sox. His 376⅔ innings were the most since Walsh threw 393 in 1912. Relying on the knuckleball, he had just led the league in relief appearances three straight years when new manager Chuck Tanner intuited that Wood had the stamina to start 40 times a year and go the distance more often than not at a time when complete games still mattered, all with little impact on his arm from throwing the fluttery pitch. He was right about that. Wood averaged 45 starts, 20 complete games, and 336 innings the next five years. He won 20 four years in a row from 1971 to 1974. Sixty of his 139 starts the first three of those years were on two days of rest or less.

Allen's prodigious offensive powers were too often overpowered by personal conflicts with teammates and management. The White Sox allowed their temperamental star more leeway with team rules, which alienated his teammates. He was often injured, missing much of the 1973 season with a hairline fracture of his leg. It all came to a head in 1974 when, playing through pain and feeling disrespected by his manager and fellow White Sox, Allen quit the team with three weeks to go. The 32 homers he had when he walked out on his team held up as the most in the American League. Dick Allen did not return to Chicago the next year.

Amid sagging attendance and reports that entertainer Danny Kaye was leading a consortium to buy the club and move it to Seattle, Bill Veeck organized his own group of investors to make a bid—the same Bill Veeck, "as in Wreck," whose ownership of the White Sox from 1959 to 1961 was characterized by a stirring pennant and a flair for keeping Comiskey Park fans entertained with things like fireworks displays and exploding scoreboards. The general disdain other owners had for his antics notwithstanding, Veeck's bid carried the day. Aside from winning 90 in 1977, for their best record in 12 years, the White Sox under the new Veeck ownership were on a downward trajectory. In the new era of free agency, Veeck was in no position financially to compete for players on an open market or to pay his best players a considerably higher fair-market value for their performance. As his team faltered, and attendance with it, Veeck devised new entertainments to attract fans to Comiskey Park. The most notorious was Disco Demolition Night, between games of a double-header in July 1979, which turned into a riot. With fans surging onto the field in a cloud of smoke from blowing up vinyl records and from smoking dope, the White Sox were forced to forfeit the nightcap.

Before Veeck was forced by circumstance—increasingly poor health, general isolation among his fellow owners, and vastly inadequate capitalization—to sell the franchise to Reinsdorf, he and general manager Roland Hemond set the White Sox in a better direction with their decision late in the 1979 season to turn the club over to rookie manager Tony LaRussa. Signing veteran free agent catcher Carlton Fisk before the start of the 1981 season was the new owner's signal to White Sox fans that he was serious about turning around a team that had lost 90 the previous year. In that vein, Reinsdorf also did not replace either LaRussa or Hemond with a manager and GM of his own choosing. Budget constraints, however, forced the trade of center fielder Chet Lemon, their best player, after the 1981 season before he became a free agent the following year, when they would lose him for nothing. Three times a .300 hitter since his rookie year in 1976, Lemon was beyond what Reinsdorf felt he could afford, especially now that they had Fisk.

Carlton Fisk was the heart and soul of the 1983 division-winning White Sox. His leadership, offensive productivity, and guidance of a young pitching staff was well worth the $2.9 million five-year contract the White Sox were paying him. He helped mold right-handers LaMarr Hoyt and Richard Dotson into a pair of 20-game winners. Left fielder Ron Kittle, the AL's 1983 Rookie of the Year; designated hitter Greg Luzinski; right fielder Harold Baines; and Fisk combined to drive in 380 of the White Sox' major-league-best 800 runs. In consolidated American League standings, the White Sox were only one game better than the Baltimore Orioles, winners of the AL East. After winning the opening game of the ALCS, the White Sox were outscored 18–1 as Baltimore won the next three games and the pennant. Chicago's major-league-best 99 wins for the season were deceptive because they were the only one of the AL West's seven teams with a winning record. While crushing weak division opponents by going 55–23 against them, the White Sox were only 44–40 opposing teams in the much-better AL East.

The AL West was still a very weak division relative to the East in 1984—the first five clubs in the Eastern Division all had better records than the Western Division–winning Royals, the only team in their division with a winning record—and the White Sox slipped out of contention and below .500 to stay by mid-August. For Chicago, the rest of the decade was a series of dispiriting years. Fisk had career highs in home runs (37) and RBIs (107) in 1985, and Tom Seaver got his 300th career win with the White Sox that year. Hemond was fired after the 1985 season and replaced as general manager by the team's opinionated broadcaster, Ken "Hawk" Harrelson. LaRussa thought Harrelson was in way over his head and was fired early in 1986. In 1988 talk of the franchise being moved to St. Petersburg, Florida, was enough to convince the Illinois legislature to approve funding for a new ballpark for Chicago's South-Side team.

* * *

The 1984 Royals won the AL West by three games, with only 84 wins, notwithstanding that the big headline going into the season was the year-long suspension handed down by Commissioner Bowie Kuhn to Willie Wilson and three other Kansas City players for pleading guilty to purchasing cocaine. Wilson, the catalyst at the top of the Royals' batting order, missed more than a month before Kuhn lifted his suspension after a successful appeal by the players' union. In sixth place, eight games below .500 in mid-May when Wilson returned to action, KC was 7½ games better than any other team in the AL West with him playing every game the rest of the way, clinching the division with two days to spare. They lost to Detroit in the ALCS.

Having revamped their pitching, the Royals won the West again in 1985 by a single game, knocking the Angels out of first place by winning three of four against them in the final week. Southpaws Charlie Leibrandt, Danny Jackson, and Bud Black and right-handers Mark Gubicza, 22 years old, and Bret Saberhagen, just 21, started all but four of their 162 games. Saberhagen won 13 of 15 decisions after July to finish the year with a 20–6 record and the AL's Cy Young Award. Employing a unique submarine delivery with exceptional control, Dan Quisenberry led the league in saves for the fourth consecutive year and the fifth time in six years, during which he walked just 1.2 batters every 9 innings. George Brett capped off his best year since 1980 by hitting .348 in the ALCS to help the Royals overcome a three-games-to-one deficit to advance to the World Series, and .370 in the World Series when KC again came from behind three-games-to-one to beat St. Louis, across state. Giving up just one run in two complete-game victories—with his first child born the day before he shut out the Cardinals on five hits in Game Seven—the telegenic Saberhagen became America's golden boy in the World Series.

As a small-market club with a relatively fallow farm system, the Royals were not financially able to compete for high-caliber free agents as their 1985 squad got older. The next six years the Royals fielded a quintessential middle-of-the-pack team. Manager Dick Howser, just 50 years old, was forced to step aside at the 1986 All-Star break after learning he had malignant brain tumors. Less than a year later, he was gone. Brett, having moved from third to first base in 1987 to account for age-related loss of quickness, won his third batting title in 1990. He retired three years later, having spent his entire career in small-market Kansas City, with 3,154 hits and a .305 lifetime batting average. Saberhagen went through a cycle of struggling in even-numbered years but excelling in the odd-numbered ones, including a 23–6 record in 1989 to win a second Cy Young Award. Three years later, his contract too much for a club that lost 90 games, Saberhagen was pitching for the New York Mets.

The biggest splash the Royals made in the second half of the eighties was signing 1985 Heisman Trophy winner Bo Jackson to play baseball. After four full seasons in the majors, 1987 to 1990, it all came to an end for Jackson—pro football and baseball—when he suffered a devastating hip injury during a January 1991 NFL playoff game. Every other major-league franchise, including all four 1990s expansion teams, played in the postseason at least once in the 29 years after the Royals brought a World Series trophy to Kansas City for the first time, in 1985.

* * *

The California Angels made it back to the top of the AL West in 1986, four years after winning the division and being upended by the Milwaukee Brewers in the 1982 ALCS. All but three of their core position regulars were at least 31 years old, including 40-year-old DH Reggie Jackson. Twenty-five-year-olds Mike Witt and Kirk McCaskill and 41-year-old veteran Don Sutton, signed as a free agent before the season, were a formidable top three in California's starting rotation. Sutton's 5th of 15 wins in 1986 was number 300 in his career. Gene Mauch, the Angels' manager when they won the division in 1982, was again in charge. Both the 1982 and '86 league championship series for the American League pennant ended badly for California as a result of controversial pitching decisions by Mauch that eerily echoed the fiasco of his 1964 Phillies' collapse in the final weeks of the season, when he virtually guaranteed failure by starting his top two pitchers, Jim Bunning and Chris Short, twice on short rest trying to stave off disaster.

In the 1982 ALCS, still a best-of-five affair, Mauch's Angels had a two-games-to-none lead with the series going to Milwaukee for its conclusion, needing to win one of the possible three games. No team in either league had ever come back from such a deficit in a league championship series to win the pennant. Milwaukee won the next two to even it up. In the seventh inning of Game Five, the Angels were up by a run when reliever Luis Sanchez walked Robin Yount—by far the best player in the American League that year—to load the bases with two outs. Coming to bat for the Brewers was Cecil Cooper, a dangerous left-handed hitter whose season totals included 32 homers, 121 RBIs, and a .313 batting average. Even though Cooper hit 49 percentage points better against righties than lefties that year, Mauch chose to stay with the right-handed Sanchez rather than bring in lefty Andy Hassler, against whom left-handed batters hit just .152 during the season. Cooper singled to drive home the tying and go-ahead runs. Six Angels outs later, the Brewers were American League champions, and Mauch was left to explain his decision. His answer—that Hassler got outs by enticing batters to go after pitches out of the strike zone, that Cooper had exceptional plate discipline, and that he was afraid Hassler would walk in the tying run—satisfied nobody. Not Hassler. Not Angels fans. Not General Manager Buzzie Bavasi. And not Gene Autry, the Angels' owner since their inception, now 75 years old and running out of patience. Mauch did not return as manager in 1983, but after two desultory seasons, he was brought back in 1985.

Facing the Red Sox in the 1986 ALCS, Mauch's division-winning Angels once again were on the cusp of going to their first World Series. Holding a three-games-to-one lead in Game Five—the league championship series had been extended to a seven-game format—California led 5–2 going into the ninth. Mike Witt, their ace, had retired 19 of Boston's previous 22 batters. A single and a home run made it 5–4. Witt got the second out. With the Angels needing just one more out to win the pennant, Mauch brought in lefty Gary Lucas to face the left-handed batter Rich Gedman, who had homered earlier against Witt. Lucas didn't get the last out; he hit Gedman with the pitch. Next up was Dave Henderson, a right-handed batter, so Mauch removed Lucas in favor of right-handed relief ace Donnie Moore. Henderson hit a two-run homer. Boston had the lead. California evened the score in their half of the ninth. The game went on. Still pitching in the 11th, Moore loaded the bases with nobody out. Next up once again was Dave Henderson. Mauch stayed with Moore. Henderson hit a sacrifice fly to score the go-ahead run. This time the Angels did not come back to tie. The ALCS returned to Boston. The Red Sox crushed the Angels in the final two games, and for the second time in four years Gene Mauch's Angels had blown a decisive series lead to lose the ALCS. It was the third time a Mauch-managed team seemingly had a pennant secured, only to lose it.

Despite the debacle of the ALCS, Mauch was back in 1987 to preside over a last-place finish. Unexpectedly, he retired from managing for good for health reasons before the 1988 season began. Donnie Moore, whose 52 saves in 1985 and 1986 made him one of the American League's top relievers, never recovered from giving up the home run to Henderson when the Angels were one out away from winning the pennant. Three years later, after being released by the Angels, he was dead—an apparent suicide.

* * *

After finishing next-to-last in the division in 1986 with the second-worst record in the American League, the Minnesota Twins were the AL West's surprise winner in 1987. It was their first division title since winning the first two in baseball's new divisional alignment in 1969 and '70. Once the 1965–1970 powerhouse Twins of Harmon Killebrew and Tony Oliva faded into history, Minnesota struggled to be competitive in the 1970s. Rod Carew, however, secured his future in Cooperstown with six batting titles in seven years between 1972 and 1978, during which he averaged 200 hits a year and hit .350. He flirted with .400 for much of the summer of '77 before his .304 batting average in July made that goal virtually unachievable. Hitting .439 in the final month brought Carew's season average up to .388—the highest since Ted Williams in 1957. Netherlands-born right-hander Bert Blyleven, called up as a 19-year-old in 1970, quickly became one of baseball's best pitchers before he and his 99–90 record were traded by Minnesota to Texas in June 1976. A devastating curve was Blyleven's signature pitch.

Undermining the franchise's prospects was the fact that the Twins were still Griffith family owned, and current owner Calvin adhered to Uncle Clark's family philosophy of frugality. Once free agency became a reality in 1976, that philosophy, grounded in the parallel realities of con-

sistently poor attendance at aging Metropolitan Stadium and no meaningful alternative revenue stream, made it all but certain the Twins could not
afford a competitive team. The Griffith family baseball business was
terribly undercapitalized relative to their fellow major-league owners,
most of whom made their fortunes outside of baseball. This might have
been less problematic before free agency. It was now untenable. Blyleven's trade was motivated in large part by his playing the season without
having signed a contract, meaning he would have been a free agent at
year's end. In 1978 the Twins lost two of their best young players—
outfielders Lyman Bostock and Larry Hisle—to free agency. Dan Ford,
another promising outfielder, and Carew were traded in the 1978–1979
off-season before they could become free agents.

Rod Carew's departure, however, became much more than about the
money. Irked by Carew's complaints about being underpaid, making it a
near certainty he would declare for free agency once his three-year
contract expired after the 1979 season, Calvin Griffith, speaking at a
private banquet in September 1978 and, first asking if blacks were
present, disparaged Carew and then said he had moved the club to Minnesota because "you've got good, hardworking, white people here." Even as
the 1978 schedule was winding down, a livid Carew said he had no
intention of being part of Griffith's "plantation" and would never sign
another contract with the Twins. Griffith's cringeworthy statements about
African Americans reinforced the perspective that a change in ownership
was needed.

Griffith was still there in 1982 when the Twins moved into a state-
funded indoor stadium that could accommodate both baseball and football. The new Metrodome, officially named after former vice president
Hubert Humphrey, who was from Minnesota, was considered by many a
travesty for baseball, however. Unlike Houston's Astrodome or Seattle's
Kingdome, the Metrodome had a fiberglass fabric roof that relied on
internal air pressure to stay inflated. That air flow had the unintended
effect of serving as a jet stream for long fly balls, giving the indoor
stadium the nickname "Homerdome." Outfielders looking upward at the
white-textured ceiling to make routine catches on fly balls often wondered, "Where the heck is it?" They also had to contend with artificial
turf so resilient that balls dropping in front of them might take a super-
ball-like hop high over their heads. And then there was the 23-foot-high

canvas wall in right field that looked remarkably like heavy-duty Hefty trash bags.

The long-awaited change in ownership finally occurred in August 1984 when American League owners approved Calvin Griffith's sale of the Twins to wealthy financier Carl Pohlad. Ironically, even as Griffith was in the process of selling, the Twins were unexpectedly competitive, especially for having lost 90 games the year before, but in a division where only the first-place Royals had a winning record. Minnesota bene-fited from the rules of baseball's amateur draft, now in its 19th year, that allowed teams to pick from high school and college players in reverse order of how they finished the year before, with the last choosing first. As a result of mediocre or very poor seasons in previous years, the Twins had assembled a rapidly improving ballclub by the time Pohlad bought the franchise—including southpaw Frank Viola, first baseman Kent Hrbek, third baseman Gary Gaetti, right fielder Tom Brunansky, and rookie center fielder Kirby Puckett. And in their minor-league pipeline was shortstop Greg Gagne. In first place nearly all of August, the Twins could have given Calvin Griffith a grand sendoff and Pohlad a rousing welcome had they won the division. There was still hope when they trailed KC by a half game as the season entered its final week. Then they lost six in a row to two teams with losing records to end up second, with 81 wins and 81 losses. After that teaser, Pohlad's Twins went backward the next two years.

Coming off 91 losses in 1986, nobody expected the Twins to do what they did in 1987—win the division, win the pennant, and win their first World Series since moving to Minnesota in 1961. Puckett, in the second of four straight 200-hit seasons in which he batted .339, was by now an elite player, and Viola a top-tier pitcher. The Twins had brought back Blyleven in 1985 and traded with Montreal before spring training for closer Jeff Reardon to bolster a bullpen that had been mediocre at best since the beginning of the decade. But their most consequential move was staying with interim manager Tom Kelly, elevated from the coaching staff for the final 23 games of their dismal 1986 season, to manage in 1987. The 1987 World Series was the first in which every game was a night game and the first to be played indoors, as it was for the four games at the Metrodome. The series went seven. The home team won every game. Beating St. Louis, Minnesota gave the franchise its first World Series triumph since the 1924 Washington Senators.

Four years later the Twins were back in the World Series, even more improbably than in 1987 because they finished last in the AL West in 1990. Rookie second baseman Chuck Knoblauch, batting second ahead of Puckett, was an inspired catalyst for the offense. Viola, after winning the Cy Young Award in 1988 with a 24–7 record, was traded to the Mets the next year, and Blyleven was also gone. In their stead stood Jack Morris, Detroit's venerable ace, signed by Minnesota as a free agent before the season. No team had ever gone from last place to winning the pennant in a single year. In 1991, two did—the Atlanta Braves, last in the NL West in 1990, and the Minnesota Twins.

The 1991 World Series between the Braves and the Twins was one of the most thrilling ever. It went the distance. The Twins won the first two in Minnesota. Puckett made a sensational over-the-fence catch of a would-be home run to save Game Two. The Braves took the next three in Atlanta. Back in Minnesota, Kirby Puckett, showing a flair for the dramatic, homered off reliever Charlie Leibrandt to lead off the last of the 11th inning, giving the Twins a 4–3 victory in Game Six. The seventh game, scoreless through nine, was an instant classic. Braves starter John Smoltz went 7⅓ innings without giving up a run. Jack Morris pitched a 10-inning complete-game shutout. He became the winning pitcher—and the Twins, once again, World Series champions—in the last of the 10th when little-known reserve Gene Larkin smacked a walk-off bases-loaded pinch-hit single to drive in the game's only run. The pivotal play, however, came in the eighth. The Braves had Lonnie Smith on first. No score. Nobody out. Terry Pendleton hit a double to left. Smith should have scored easily. Instead, either fooled into believing Pendleton's drive would be caught or losing track of the ball, he made it only as far as third. Morris still had to pitch out of a jam with runners on second and third and nobody out. That he did.

27

MUSICAL CHAIRS IN THE NL WEST

Four franchises won division titles in the National League West between 1983 and 1989, none consecutively. The Dodgers did so three times, the Giants twice, and the Padres and Astros once each. Only one of those clubs had a better record than the NL East club they met in the league championship series for the right to play in the World Series. That team was the 1983 Los Angeles Dodgers, and they were just one victory better than the Phillies, to whom they fell in the NLCS. By then, pitching aces Don Sutton and Tommy John had left LA as free agents. The Dodgers had also moved on from Steve Garvey, Davey Lopes, Bill Russell, and Ron Cey—together for nine years from 1973 to 1981—as their everyday infield. With Steve Sax ready, Lopes was traded in 1982. Garvey as a free agent and Cey in a trade were both gone in 1983. Along with Russell, catcher Steve Yeager and left fielder Dusty Baker remained from the core Dodgers team that won back-to-back pennants in 1977 and 1978. And of course, Tommy Lasorda, the Dodgers' Mr. Hollywood of the dugout, was still the man(ager) in charge.

The Dodgers had a new pair of high-profile stars. Alternating between third base and right field, Pedro Guerrero was the new power bat in Lasorda's lineup, hitting 32 homers in both 1982 and 1983. Mexican-born Fernando Valenzuela was the latest in a string of compelling Dodgers aces from Newcombe through Koufax and Drysdale to Sutton. He became such a phenomenon that "Fernando-mania" swept LA. The city's large Mexican American population was galvanized to show him and his team the love—especially on the days he pitched. A left-handed master of the screwball whose delivery featured a distinctive heavenward roll of his eyes, Valenzuela in 1981 became the first pitcher to win the Cy Young Award in his Rookie of the Year season. His first eight starts, all complete-game victories, included five shutouts. In his first 72 innings as a starting pitcher, Fernando gave up just 4 earned runs on 43 hits and 17 walks. Finishing the strike-interrupted season with a 13–7 record, Valenzuela won a key game in all three postseason series—the makeshift division series between the first and second half "winners" of the split season, the NLCS, and the World Series.

After the promise of 1983 gave way to fourth place in '84, the Dodgers were again the class of the NL West in 1985. Guerrero's 33 homers tied for third in the league, and his .320 batting average was second. Valenzuela was still the youngest member of a solid front four in the Dodgers starting rotation, which now included second-year right-hander Orel Hershiser, whose 19–3 record was the best in the majors. He ended

Mexican-born lefty Fernando Valenzuela was baseball's rookie sensation pitching for the Dodgers in 1981—a season otherwise sullied by a two-month players' strike that led to a split season. The 20-year-old was 13–7 and led the majors with eight shutouts. *National Baseball Hall of Fame Library, Cooperstown, NY.*

the season riding an 11-game winning streak. The Dodgers' season ended in the ninth inning of Game Six in the NLCS against St. Louis when they were unable to protect a 5–4 lead, needing one out to force a seventh game, despite having Tom Niedenfuer, their relief ace, on the mound. Two Cardinals were on base. Jack Clark, their only power threat, was coming to bat, hitting .350 against Dodgers pitching in the series. First base was open. Next up was Andy Van Slyke, a much less dangerous hitter with only one hit in 10 series at-bats. But the fact that he was also a left-handed batter apparently convinced Lasorda to let Niedenfuer, a right-hander, pitch to right-handed-batting Clark. Clark hit a three-run homer. The Dodgers began their winter vacation.

Their vacation turned into a two-year hibernation with exactly the same record, 73–89, in 1986 and '87. The most significant change to their roster in 1988 was signing Detroit free agent Kirk Gibson to add both a dangerous hitter to the lineup and a veteran no-nonsense leader in the clubhouse. Pedro Guerrero, for all his talent—including three 30-homer seasons—was a divisive presence on the club, undisciplined in his approach to the game, quick to lose his temper, and openly critical of both his teammates and the Dodgers organization. If Tommy Lasorda was unable to control Guerrero, Gibson made clear to his new teammates from the beginning that he would not tolerate his shenanigans, and neither should they. Guerrero's position became untenable, particularly after a neck injury sidelined him for virtually all of June and July. In mid-August he was traded.

Consistent all season and finishing with 25 home runs, Gibson was the NL's Most Valuable Player. The Dodgers also had the NL Cy Young Award winner—Orel Hershiser, whose 23–8 record included 15 complete games and 8 shutouts. Five of those shutouts came consecutively in September. He would have had six shutouts in a row were it not that the Dodgers didn't get him any runs in his final start of the regular season in San Diego; he pitched 10 innings of shutout ball before being relieved in the 11th inning of a game that went 16 innings before the Padres finally won. Hershiser's streak of 59 consecutive scoreless innings, dating back to the final four innings of his August 30 complete-game victory, broke the record of 58 set by another Dodgers pitcher—Don Drysdale—20 years before. It did not count in the record book of regular-season stats, but Hershiser extended his string of shutout innings by 8⅓ against the powerhouse Mets in the opening game of the NLCS before giving up a run. His five-hit shutout in Game Seven gave the Dodgers their 18th pennant of the twentieth century.

It was an improbable pennant against the overwhelmingly favored Mets. Now they were going into the World Series against the overwhelmingly favored Oakland Athletics—and they were doing so handicapped by an injury to Kirk Gibson, who hurt his knee so badly in a hard slide at second base in the NLCS finale that he could barely stand, let alone play baseball. The stage was set for quite likely the most theatrically dramatic home run in baseball history. Bobby Thomson's playoff pennant-winning and Bill Mazeroski's World Series–winning walk-off home runs were more dramatic in game context, and in the 1975 World Series Carlton Fisk demonstrated his own flair for the dramatic by ensuring his team forced a Game Seven (which they lost)—but for sheer drama of the circumstance, it's hard to beat Kirk Gibson's limping out of the dugout in the ninth inning of Game One in the 1988 World Series, the tying run on base and two outs, to pinch-hit against Dennis Eckersley, the best reliever in baseball, hitting a game-winning two-run home run on a 3–2 count and hobbling his way around the bases. Broadcasting the game for a national television audience, Vin Scully's extended moment of silence *after* exclaiming, "She is [pause] gone!" followed by his summation, "In a year that has been so improbable, the impossible has happened," is every bit as iconic as Russ Hodges on the radio exclaiming, "The Giants win the pennant! The Giants win the pennant! The Giants win the pennant!" after Thomson's "shot heard 'round the world." That was Kirk Gibson's only plate appearance in the World Series.

There could be no ending other than Gibson's heroics propelling the Dodgers to victory over the superior Oakland A's. Hershiser shut out the A's on three hits the next day and came back to allow the powerful A's only two runs on four hits in a complete-game victory in Game Five to win the World Series. He gave up only 5 earned runs in 42⅔ postseason innings. Including the regular season, those were the only earned runs scored against him in 97⅔ innings of pitching since the beginning of September—an ERA of 0.46. Hershiser's *official* consecutive scoreless innings streak ended two outs into the first inning of his opening day start in 1989. The 1989 Dodgers got off to a bad start and did not spent a single day in first place. Hershiser had another excellent year by advanced metrics, even though his record was only 15–15. It didn't help the Dodgers that the oft-injured Kirk Gibson played in only 71 games and hit just .213.

* * *

When the Dodgers faltered after their division title in 1983, San Diego's Padres were the team that stepped up to take the NL West, winning the division by 12 games. They then rallied from a two-games-to-none deficit against Chicago's Cubs in the still-best-of-five NLCS to win the next three and advance to the World Series, where they were summarily dispatched in five games by Detroit's Tigers. Not only was 1984 the first time the Padres finished first, it was the first time in franchise history they finished any higher than fourth. The 1969 expansion team had just one prior winning season, in 1978, and finished at exactly .500 in both 1982 and '83.

Perpetually in financial trouble, operating hand-to-mouth, and unable to build a credible player-development program or to acquire high-priced players, the Padres finished last each of their first six seasons, four times losing more than 100 games. The latest they were not in last place in any season was June 25, 1972. Power-hitting first baseman Nate Colbert, who hit 163 home runs in six years with the Padres from 1969 to 1974, was their most prominent player. The Padres began climbing out of their rut in 1975, the year after Ray Kroc, the man who turned McDonald's hamburgers into a fast-food empire, came to their rescue by buying the franchise, with a commitment to improving the team. In 1976 Randy Jones, a finesse pitcher garnering few strikeouts, became the first Padres player to win a major baseball award when his 22 wins and 25 complete games in 40 starts while striking out just 93 of the 1,251 batters he faced in his league-leading 315⅓ innings earned him Cy Young honors. By then, outfielder Dave Winfield was well on his way to being the first superstar to play for San Diego. Both were selected by the prior regime in baseball's annual draft. Winfield never played a day in the minor leagues.

Leveraging his fortune, the Kroc-owned Padres became active in the free agent market as soon as it opened for business with the first class of 1976 by signing Oakland A's ace reliever Rollie Fingers and first baseman/catcher Gene Tenace. They also aggressively pursued Reggie Jackson, for whom the bright lights of big city New York proved more alluring than San Diego. Fingers and Tenace both played four years in San Diego with significant success, even as their team never did better than fourth.

But as free agency giveth, so it taketh away—specifically Dave Winfield. After eight years with the Padres, 154 home runs, leading the league in RBIs in 1979, and twice hitting .308, Winfield was the most coveted free agent on the market. His decision to leave for New York was made easy by the Padres' falling back into last place in 1980, George Steinbrenner's largesse, and the Yankees' recent success. Winfield went to his first World Series with the Yankees in 1981. The Padres had the worst record in the NL West and the next year had both a new shortstop, trading Ozzie Smith to the Cardinals for Garry Templeton, and a new manager, Dick Williams, whose winning reputation included turning around losing clubs, as he did with the 1967 Red Sox and the 1979 Expos. He did so once again in San Diego.

The pennant-winning 1984 Padres had a mix of homegrown and traded-for talent in or entering their prime, leavened by veterans nearing the end of their careers with experience playing for pennant-winning clubs. Veteran leadership was provided by first baseman Steve Garvey, arriving as a free agent in 1983, and third baseman Graig Nettles and free-agent closer Goose Gossage, both former Yankees whose first year in San Diego was 1984. All three had extensive World Series experience. Catcher Terry Kennedy had come into his own as a consequential middle-of-the-order batter. The up-and-coming stars breaking through in 1984 were center fielder Kevin McReynolds in his first full season, whose 20 homers tied him with Nettles for the club lead, and right fielder Tony Gwynn, whose 213 hits and .351 batting average in his first full season were the best in baseball. In the 17 years still to come in his career, Gwynn never hit below .309 and won seven more batting titles—three in a row from 1987 to 1989 and four straight from 1994 to 1997.

Expectations that the Padres were on the threshold of being the team to beat in the NL West for the foreseeable future were unrealistic. Garvey, Nettles, and Gossage all had their best years behind them. Second baseman Alan Wiggins, a catalyst at the top of the lineup with 70 stolen bases in 1984, spent the beginning of the 1985 season in a drug rehab program. None of San Diego's starting pitchers in 1984 were then or ever would be top-tier in a contemporary context. Although he would remain their everyday shortstop until 1991, Templeton had regressed from the player he was in St. Louis. And Dick Williams, repeating his script from earlier managerial stints, had difficulty coping with what he divined as lack of effort and commitment as his team was out of the running by mid-August 1985. His criticisms alienating the entire team, first Williams said he would quit, then he was fired just as spring training for the 1986 season was about to begin. It would be another 10 years before the Padres were genuinely competitive again.

* * *

In 1986, the next time the Dodgers faltered in their defense of a division title, the Houston Astros were the NL West's team of destiny. Five consecutive walk-off wins against the Mets and the Expos in mid-July launched the Astros toward their second division title, which they won decisively by 10 games with 96 wins, then a franchise record. Their first came in 1980, when their 93 wins were one more than the Dodgers and two more than the Eastern Division–winning Phillies, to whom they lost in the NLCS. Not until 1979 did Houston even experience pennant fever, and it ended badly—blowing the entirety of a 10½-game lead on July Fourth by the end of August and ending up 1½ games behind Cincinnati. Before that, the 1970s Astros were the very definition of a slightly below-average team, typically around the .500 mark. Center fielder Cesar Cedeno was not only their best player in the decade, but from 1972 to 1977 one of the most impactful in the National League. He batted .295 and stole 337 bases, never fewer than 50 in any season. The totality of his "five-tool" abilities, however—specifically his power—was handicapped by his home stadium being the Astrodome, where he hit only 50 of his 118 home runs in those years. He was only 26. A severe knee injury in 1978, after which he was never the same, probably cost Cedeno a shot at the Hall of Fame.

Intending to improve their chances in 1980 following their 1979 implosion, the Astros signed Joe Morgan of Big Red Machine fame to play second base and Nolan Ryan to an already impressive pitching staff. Joe Niekro, a master of the knuckleball the same as his brother Phil, had tied his brother for the most wins in the National League, with 21, in 1979. The physically imposing 6-foot-8 J. R. Richard won 18 for the third year in a row (following 20 in 1976) and blew away 313 batters in 292⅓ innings. It was the second consecutive year Richard led the league, with more than 300 strikeouts and with more strikeouts than innings pitched. Richard's 4–1 record in September and 11 wins in his last 13 decisions since July 25 kept Houston relevant in the 1979 division race till the final weekend. For Ryan, going to the Astros was a homecoming; he had grown up and gone to high school in Alvin, Texas, about 45 minutes from downtown Houston. Morgan, from a small town north of Dallas, began his big-league career in Houston.

Astros manager Bill Virdon set up his rotation so that the intimidating Richard and Ryan bracketed both Joe Niekro and his slo-mo knuckleball and Ken Forsch and his slower sinking fastballs, maximizing the dissonance batters faced in any series against Houston. And the fear. Not only were Richard and Ryan nearly unhittable, but neither necessarily knew where his fastball was headed. In his eight prior years with the California Angels, Ryan had averaged 10 strikeouts and 5.4 bases on balls per 9 innings, never walking fewer than 114 batters in a single season and twice walking more than 200, while exceeding 300 strikeouts five times. Richard averaged 4.3 walks and 8.3 strikeouts per 9 innings in his five years as the ace of the Astros' staff before Ryan's arrival. The fewest walks he allowed in any of those seasons was 98 in 1979.

The 1980 NL West came down to the final four games of the season with the Astros in LA, holding a three-game lead over the second-place Dodgers and needing to win just one to clinch the division. Three Astros losses later, it was 161 games down and one to go; the division title would belong to whichever team won game 162. Niekro won his 20th, and Houston was in the postseason for the first time. The race would likely not have gone down to the wire had not tragedy befallen J. R. Richard. Dominating through his first 13 starts with an 8–3 record, a superb 1.50 ERA, and allowing just 55 hits while striking out 98 in 96 innings, J. R. took the mound on June 17 riding a string of three consecutive complete-game shutouts. Complaining of dizziness and blurred vision, he left the game after giving up a run on 2 hits with 8 strikeouts in 5 innings. J. R. sat for 10 days, made two starts before the All-Star break, pitched two shutout innings as the National League's starting pitcher in the All-Star Game (by virtue of his 10–4 record, 1.96 ERA, and 115 Ks in 110⅓ innings), took the mound six days later on July 14 against Atlanta, and walked off after 3⅓ scoreless innings saying his vision was too blurred to see his catcher's signs. It was J. R. Richard's last major-league game. Twelve days after that he collapsed from a stroke and required emergency surgery to save his life.

A series of agonizing departures from postseason baseball began in 1980, when the Astros could not hold a two-games-to-one advantage in the best-of-five-NLCS against the Phillies, then blew a three-run eighth-inning lead in Game Five. A similar scenario unfolded in the ad hoc division series between the first- and second-half winners of 1981's split season to determine which teams went to the league championship series—the Dodgers were in first place in the NL West when Major League Baseball came to a full stop because of the players' strike, and the Astros won the second half. Winning the first two games at home, then losing all three games when the series moved to Los Angeles, Houston became the first team in the divisional era to have a two-games-to-none advantage and not win a five-game playoff series.

The Astros did not get back to the postseason until 1986. Their core veterans left from 1980 and 1981, both closing in on 40, were left fielder Jose Cruz, one of the league's best outfielders since the mid-1970s and still a potent force in the middle of the lineup, and the redoubtable Nolan Ryan. First baseman Glenn Davis, in his first full season, was among the league leaders in homers (33) and runs batted in (101). Right-hander Mike Scott had transitioned from a run-of-the-mill pitcher to a bona fide ace by mastering the split-finger fastball as a new pitch in his repertoire. His 18 wins and league-leading ERA, strikeouts, and strikeout ratio earned him Cy Young honors. Arguably their division's best ballclub in the 1980s—their 96 wins were the most in the NL West between 1978 and 1992—the 1986 Astros had the misfortune of being a very good team in the same year the Mets were a great team. Undaunted by the Mets being by far the best team in baseball, with 108 wins, and the Mets' intimidating in-your-face posturing, the Astros nearly upended them in the NLCS. The Mets' relentless, refuse-to-lose swagger prevailed in one of the most exciting postseason series there ever was.

Beginning the very next year, the Astros reverted to being a slightly better than average major-league team for the rest of the decade. Scott's five-year stretch as one of the best pitchers in baseball ended with a 20–10 record for third-place, 86-win Houston in 1989. Davis was traded to Baltimore in 1991 for outfielder Steve Finley and right-hander Pete Harnisch, both of whom would star in Houston in the early 1990s. Also portending a more competitive future, first baseman Jeff Bagwell was the National League's Rookie of the Year in 1991 and 25-year-old catcher Craig Biggio shifted to second base in 1992.

After 106 wins in nine years pitching for Houston, Nolan Ryan left as a free agent at the end of the 1988 season to go pitch in Dallas for the Texas Rangers. He was by now part of Texas mythology. If his 11–10 record and 3.35 ERA in his first year in Houston in 1980 raised concerns that, approaching his mid-30s, the Ryan Express was worn out from having thrown so many pitches in 2,925 innings—what with 1,744 walks and 3,109 strikeouts behind him—he returned to being nearly unhittable and unbeatable in 1981, going 11–5. His 1.69 earned-run average was by far the best in the majors. Ryan's best pure-pitching season in Houston was 1987, when he had the distinction of having the league's best ERA despite an unworthy 8–16 record occasioned by his teammates scoring two runs or fewer in 16 of his 34 starts. Ryan also blew away a major-league-leading 270 batters in 211⅓ innings to post the highest strikeouts-to-innings ratio by a qualifying pitcher up to that point in major-league history. He was 40 years old.

Nolan Ryan rarely missed a start in his Astros years, but throwing as hard as he could for as long as he could, he was no longer an innings workhorse. After throwing 156 complete games in 288 starts in his eight years in California before coming to Houston, Ryan was in at the finish of only 38 of 282 games he started for the Astros, and only 19 of 191 after 1983. He had only one complete game in 1986 and none in 1987. While this reflected a trend in Major League Baseball toward earlier calls to the bullpen and fewer complete-game victories, it was primarily his managers' strategy not to overwork their must-see power pitcher.

* * *

Nearly 22 years went by at Candlestick Park between Willie Mays, at the end of his career, being traded in early May 1972 so he could finish his career in New York, where it all began, and the free agency arrival of his godson, Barry Bonds, in 1993. In the interim, San Francisco's Giants won division titles just twice—in 1987 and 1989—making it to the World Series the second time. Otherwise, they were a mostly mediocre team. The City by the Bay also nearly lost its major-league team in the mid-1970s because a steep drop in attendance and revenue that began the year after the Giants won the 1971 division title motivated Horace Stoneham, whose family had owned the franchise since 1919, to arrange the sale of his club to Labatt Brewing Company in Toronto. Not helping was the fact that sitting in the park on the bay, watching the Willie Mays–less and now noncompetitive Giants play was an often miserable experience because of the wind chill even in the middle of the summer. The impending move of the storied Giants to Canada provoked legal action by the city of San Francisco, giving Major League Baseball pause and prompting local financier Bob Lurie to step forward with an offer of his own. The City by the Bay kept its team; Toronto got a major-league franchise in the American League's 1977 expansion; and Mark Twain would have still been able to (allegedly) say that the coldest winter he spent was his summer watching the Giants play at the 'Stick.

Including the season of Mays's departure, the Giants had a losing record in 12 of those years. Of Willie's remaining teammates on a team that annually competed for the pennant in the 1960s, although winning just once, slugging first baseman Willie McCovey was traded to the Padres in 1974, returned as a free agent in 1977, and finished his career in 1980, with 469 of his career 521 homers coming as a Giant; pitching ace Juan Marichal left after the 1973 season with 238 victories—the third most in franchise history; and their other pitching ace, Gaylord Perry with 134 victories as a Giant, was traded after the 1971 season at the age of 33 but pitched another 12 years, winning an additional 180 games. Bobby Bonds, Mays's good friend and Barry's father, whose stellar 1971 season led the Giants to their last first-place finish for 16 years, was gone after 1974, traded to the Yankees for Bobby Murcer. Bobby Bonds was supposed to be the superstar heir apparent to Mays in San Francisco and Murcer to Mantle in New York—extraordinary expectations that were impossible for either, or anybody else, to live up to. Like his mentor Mays and son Barry, Bobby had an extraordinary combination of power and speed, three times hitting more than 30 homers in his seven years with the Giants and stealing at least 41 bases in all but two seasons. Between then and the mid-1980s, outfielder Jack Clark from 1978 to 1983 was the Giants' best player and primary long-ball threat.

Not until 1987 did the Giants return to the top of their division. Two years later they won the NL West again. In-season trades in 1987 for veteran right-hander Rick Reuschel, to give heft to a relatively mediocre pitching staff, and outfielder Kevin Mitchell, to bolster the offense, helped the Giants win the West that year and probably made the difference in the 1989 Giants beating out the Padres by three games. Reuschel led the team with 17 wins in 1989, and Mitchell had an MVP Award–winning year with his major-league-leading 47 homers and 125 RBIs. The Giants' best player, however, was first baseman Will Clark. He led the 1987 Giants with 35 homers as a second-year player, and his .333 batting average in 1989 was second in the NL. Averaging 27 homers, 104 runs batted in, and batting .304 between 1987 and 1991, Clark had the year-in, year-out consistency of Steve Garvey in his LA prime.

Two years after losing the 1987 NLCS in seven games to the Cardinals, the Giants handily dispatched the Cubs, one win better during the regular season, in the 1989 NLCS to return San Francisco to the World Series for the first time since 1962—only their second time since moving from New York. They squared off against the Oakland Athletics in baseball's first all–Bay Area World Series, which was more famous for being interrupted for 10 days by a major earthquake—6.9 on the Richter scale—that jolted the Bay Area just before the third game at Candlestick Park than for the far-superior A's sweeping the Giants with ease. As was the pattern in both NL divisions in the 1980s, the 1990 Giants did not successfully defend their division title.

The Dodgers, meanwhile, were retooling. Gone from their 1988 championship team by 1991 were Steve Sax, Kirk Gibson, and Fernando Valenzuela, and Orel Hershiser was battling shoulder problems. Replacing Sax at the top of the order was free agent center fielder Brett Butler, a get-on-base-and-run catalyst for the Giants from 1988 to 1990—reaching base 782 times, scoring 100 runs each year, and stealing 125 bases. Eddie Murray, acquired from Baltimore in a trade in 1989, had essentially replaced Gibson's power bat and no-nonsense leadership. Rail-thin Dominican right-hander Ramon Martinez, 20–6 in 1990, was the Dodgers' latest pitching star. Los Angeles came into San Francisco for their 1991 season-ending series tied for first with Atlanta. The Giants had the pleasure of eliminating their historical rival from the pennant race.

Two years later, Bob Lurie, having failed to get public funding for a new stadium in a more hospitable location than chilly windswept Candlestick Point, put the San Francisco Giants on the market. Sixteen years earlier he had saved the franchise from being moved to Toronto, but in August 1992 he accepted an offer that would have uprooted the Giants and sent them to St. Petersburg, Florida, where a domed stadium had already been built for the purpose of attracting one of the two expansion teams the National League planned for 1993. Once again city officials were up in arms, and once again a well-capitalized group of San Francisco investors, led by Safeway supermarket CEO Peter Magowan, stepped up with a late bid to keep the Giants in the City by the Bay.

Then Barry Bonds came to town as a free agent.

28

FAILURE TO LAUNCH

Where Winning Was a Losing Proposition

Once the Toronto Blue Jays cinched the American League's Eastern Division title on the next to last day of the 1985 season, 23 of Major League Baseball's 26 teams had been to the postseason since the first round of expansion 25 years before. They included three of the four franchises in the expansion class of 1961–1962, all four in the class of 1969, and one of the two teams added to the American League in 1977. By any measure, that was a remarkable number of clubs to make it beyond the regular season. The only three teams that failed to launch a pennant drive in the first quarter century of the expansion era were the long-established Cleveland Indians and two expansion clubs—the born-in-1961 Washington Senators–turned–Texas Rangers and the 1977-expansion Seattle Mariners.

It might be an exaggeration to say that Seattle got its team by resorting to extortion—but not too much of one. The Mariners becoming an expansion team in 1977 was the direct result of the American League's settling a breach of contract suit brought by King County, Washington, when the 1969-expansion Seattle Pilots were moved to Milwaukee the very next year, after voters had already approved public funding for a domed stadium—the Kingdome—suitable for major-league baseball for the Pilots. In a chronically weak financial position, the Mariners played 15 years before finally, in 1991, winning more often than they lost, which was still not better than fifth place in the AL West. Even after the franchise was sold to wealthy real estate magnate George Argyros in 1981, little was done to boost spending for a more competitive team. The Mariners' best players in the 1980s were first baseman Alvin Davis, the 1984 Rookie of the Year with 27 homers and 116 runs batted in, and left-hander Mark Langston, who led AL pitchers in strikeouts in 1984—also his rookie year—'86, and '87.

The transplanted Senators had a winning record in only eight of their first 20 years in Texas as the rechristened Rangers. They twice finished second in the West but were not in realistic contention either time. Texas had any number of one- or two-year wonders, like Jeff Burroughs, Bump Wills, and Pete Incaviglia; a number of good players who could not carry a club—including infielder Toby Harrah, catcher Jim Sundberg, and right-hander Charlie Hough; and a trio of Hall of Fame pitchers—Ferguson Jenkins, Gaylord Perry, and Bert Blyleven—whose Cooperstown credentials were earned elsewhere. Sundberg was overlooked as one of the league's best catchers because he was a direct contemporary of Carlton Fisk, Thurman Munson, and Lance Parrish. Acquired from Cleveland for Harrah in a trade of third basemen, Buddy Bell was one of the best position players in baseball in the first half of the 1980s. Jenkins's 93 wins in two stints with Texas were the most in franchise history until Hough passed him in 1987.

Whereas "small-marketitis" was a plausible excuse for Seattle's inability and unwillingness to improve a mediocre team, the same could not be said for the Texas Rangers. According to the 1980 US census, the Dallas–Fort Worth metropolitan area was the sixth-largest in the country, with a population of nearly 1.5 million to support the Rangers, compared to 652,000 in Washington State's Seattle-Tacoma region. And it would grow to 1.7 million by 1990, while the Mariners' core city feeds had barely reached 693,000. It was not that the Texas ballclub didn't spend money on players. Rather, they did so episodically, for the short term, and without any coherent long-term strategy to build for longer-term success. The Rangers dealt for established stars, including Bell; pitchers Jenkins (twice), Perry, Blyleven, and Jon Matlack; and outfielders Bobby Bonds, Al Oliver, and Larry Parrish. They also ventured into the free agent marketplace for the likes of shortstop Bert Campaneris, DH Richie Zisk, and pitchers Doc Medich and Frank Tanana.

Both Texas and Seattle hired—and fired, because it didn't end well— highly regarded managers with winning accomplishments to turn their losing franchises around. Following a pair of 100-loss seasons in their first two years in the Texas heat, the 1974 Rangers, driven by new manager Billy Martin, surged to 84 wins and second place in their division. Predictably, Martin's intensity and sometimes out-of-control, often alcohol-fueled personal behavior burned bridges with players and club executives. He did not survive the 1975 season. In Seattle, Dick Williams, in his second year there, led the 1987 Mariners to their best losing record so far in franchise history. Outspoken about Mariners players being lackadaisical in games and not really caring about winning, and complaining that the front office was complicit in undermining his authority and had no commitment to winning, Williams was gone from Seattle—and from baseball for good—early the following season. Believing that his 1987 Mariners had a potentially winning nucleus to build upon, the owner's unwillingness to spend money on players on the grounds that all that mattered was the financial balance sheet was particularly grating to Williams.

* * *

For both franchises, 1989 was the foundation year for better times ahead. In Seattle, first baseman/DH Ken Phelps and his 105 home runs since 1983 had been dispatched to the Yankees for inexperienced outfielder Jay Buhner the previous July; Mark Langston was the centerpiece of a May 1989 deal that sent him to Montreal for another southpaw—the frighteningly overpowering 6-foot-10 Randy Johnson—whose raw talent was undeniable but ability to harness it quite in question; Edgar Martinez, long before he came to define the designated hitter position, was a rookie third baseman trying to stick in the majors; and center fielder Ken Griffey Jr., an infectiously enthusiastic 19-year-old, made his rookie debut. Those four players would lead the 1995 Mariners to a stirring come-from-far-behind division title and dramatic division series victory over the Yankees in the Kingdome that ultimately saved baseball in Seattle.

In Texas, 1989 was the year power-hitting outfielder Juan Gonzalez made his big-league debut as a September callup. In the mid-1990s, "Juan Gone" would win two MVP Awards. It was the first year playing in their minor-league system for catcher Ivan Rodriguez, whose impressive throwing arm made him a must-sign priority as soon as Rangers scouts saw him at a tryout camp they hosted on his home island of Puerto Rico. And it was the year Nolan Ryan came to the Rangers. Ryan was both the least important and the most important of these players as the franchise looked to 1989 and beyond, yet to have ever contended for a division title. Gonzalez and Rodriguez, young and still unproven, were the future. They would be the face of the Texas Rangers team that finally made the postseason in 1996. Ryan was the present—one that was badly needed—while Rangers fans waited for the future to show first-place results.

Nolan Ryan was a Texas icon, embodying the state's indomitable cowboy myth. Before signing with the Rangers, Ryan pitched the previous nine years in Houston, where he led the National League twice in earned-run average and threw a record-setting fifth no-hitter in 1981. Ryan's 106 wins for the Astros brought him within 27 of the coveted 300 mark. He averaged more than a strikeout an inning. But despite having led the NL in strikeouts each of the two previous years, the Astros were not inclined to give a pitcher about to turn 42—not even Nolan Ryan—what he had just earned as he was about to enter the free agent market for the last time. The Rangers, coming off a 91-loss season in which their attendance ranked 11th of the 14 American League clubs, were only too happy to oblige by giving Ryan $1.8 million for 1989—the most he had yet earned in a single season.

He did not pitch long enough to help Texas win a division title, but the Ryan Express did not disappoint. He was everything the Rangers needed him to be. Fueled in large part by crowds coming to see him pitch, the Rangers drew more than 2 million for the first time in their history and would stay at that level, even playing in old Arlington Stadium until their new ballpark was completed in 1994. The crowds he drew helped make the case for public funding for the new ballpark. Ryan pitched his sixth and seventh no-hitters, led the American League in strikeouts in 1989 and 1990, led the league in strikeouts per 9 innings three years in a row, and finished his career in 1993, at the age of 46, with 324 major-league victories.

There was one other consequential development for Texas Rangers baseball in 1989 that set the stage for competitive ballclubs. Leading the consortium of Texas oil industry executives that bought the team in March 1989 was the son of President George Herbert Walker Bush, George W. Bush. All three previous owners of the Rangers seemed to care only about profiting as much as possible from their investment, and nothing about the ballclub being a community asset. To both Rangers players and Texas baseball fans, Bush the younger was a breath of fresh air. It was the first time they had a friendly and engaged owner to relate to, mostly because he so loved the game. The 41st president's son always said his dream job was to be commissioner of baseball. He ultimately had to settle for being the 43rd president of the United States.

* * *

In that same year of 1989, Charlie Sheen—son of Martin, who later played a president on TV in *The West Wing*—starred in a movie called *Major League*, which tells a fictional tale of the Cleveland Indians, a ragtag club of has-beens and wannabes, rising from super-inept losers to pennant winners, motivated by shared hatred for an owner wanting the team to tank so it could be sold for big bucks and moved to Miami. The movie took artistic license with the fact that the real Cleveland Indians had been in a noncompetitive funk even longer than the 1961-expansion Washington-to-Texas Rangers had been in existence. Until the 1960s, the Indians for the most part had not been a losing proposition for their fans. Even though they had just three pennants to show for their first 59 years, the Indians usually had good teams, many on the margins of pennant race competitiveness. Their problem, particularly after 1920, was the overwhelming dominance of the New York Yankees. If not for the Bronx Bombers, Cleveland might have won several pennants in the 1920s, would have been in contention for a few in the 1930s, and likely would have been the premier team in the American League in the first half of the 1950s.

It all began with the Indians trading fan-idol and reigning home run champ Rocky Colavito to the Tigers two days before the 1960 season for reigning AL batting champion Harvey Kuenn. Over the next five years Colavito added 173 home runs to the 129 he already had with Cleveland. Kuenn, batting .300 in 1960 for the eighth time in his nine big-league seasons, did not have Rocky's run-producing impact. He spent one year in Cleveland before being traded to San Francisco. "The Curse of Rocky Colavito," as Cleveland sportswriter Terry Pluto called it, was perhaps even more daunting than Boston's Curse of the Bambino or the Cubs' Billy Goat Curse as the century neared its end, because in the interim the Red Sox had won pennants and the Cubs had at least competed for them. The Indians went three and a half decades never competing for first place. Even had Cleveland shipbuilder George Steinbrenner's 1971 bid to buy the franchise been successful, it is unlikely the Indians' competitive trajectory would have been any different. The best they did was third place in 1965—one of only seven years between 1960 and 1993 they did not have a losing record.

What happened to Cleveland might perhaps better be called "The Curse of Trader Frank Lane." With an established reputation for deal-making that helped boost the White Sox into the top tier of American League clubs trailing in the Yankees' wake in the 1950s, Lane became Cleveland's general manager in the fall of 1957. His trading philosophy was less to build for the future than to win now. Some thought Lane liked brainstorming trades, with ideas he tossed out morphing into reality. Others thought he made trades simply for the sake of trades—as in, I trade, therefore I am. In August 1960, Lane went so far as to trade his manager, Joe Gordon, to the Tigers for their manager, Jimmy Dykes. Outraged by the Colavito trade and collectively scratching their heads about the Gordon-for-Dykes managers exchange, Cleveland's fans made their feelings known at the gate: Attendance declined precipitously in 1960. Lane resigned in January 1961.

The Lane-trading disease, however, proved contagious. In the fallow competitive decades that followed, Cleveland traded away the likes of Jim Perry, Mudcat Grant, Tommie Agee, Tommy John, Luis Tiant, Graig Nettles, Chris Chambliss, Dennis Eckersley, Buddy Bell, John Denny, and Julio Franco—all players whose best was yet to come for teams not named the Indians—for players who hardly measured up in return. Good or outstanding players passing through Cleveland for no more than a few years included Gaylord Perry, Bert Blyleven, Rick Sutcliffe, Brett Butler, and Joe Carter. Their one elite player over multiple seasons was hard-throwing lefty Sam McDowell, one of baseball's most intimidating and feared pitchers because he did not pitch with great control. In the eight years he was in his prime in Cleveland, 1964 to 1971, Sudden Sam averaged 4.4 walks along with 9.3 Ks per 9 innings. Pitching for a team that was mediocre at best, McDowell was a 20-game winner only once, in 1970.

It became increasingly apparent as the 1990s approached that Cleveland was a major-league wasteland. There were frequent changes in general manager and far more managerial changes. Since Al Lopez had left for Chicago in 1957 after six years managing in Cleveland, the Indians had gone through 21 managers, not including several interim placeholders, before Mike Hargrove took charge in 1991 to begin a tenure that would last nine years. Hampered by their persistent lack of promise and not helped by playing in cold and cavernous Municipal Stadium, Cleveland played before ever-smaller crowds; their attendance was consistently among the worst in the major leagues. Outfielder Joe Carter was the most vocal about the Indians having no prospect of signing attractive free agents until they played in a modern ballpark. In 1990, despite their team having another losing season, voters approved funding to build a new stadium for Cleveland's baseball team. The new stadium opened in 1994, and by the end of the 1990s, the Indians were one of baseball's powerhouse teams, having won five straight division titles and been to two World Series.

When *Major League* hit the theaters in 1989, all of that was in the future—an unforeseeable future. The Indians had yet to finish higher than fifth in the AL East since the American League expanded to seven-team divisions in 1977. There was still no commitment to a new ballpark. A movie plot premised on the Indians being so bad they could play themselves out of Cleveland was totally plausible. Unlike the good citizens in Boston and Chicago, for whom losing—or, more accurately, not winning a championship—had assumed epistemological importance as a metaphor for persistence and perseverance in a Sisyphean struggle to overcome seemingly everything being thrown in the way of their success, there was no moral high ground to continuous losing for the dwindling numbers still passing through the turnstiles of Municipal Stadium. Unlike the Red Sox and Cubs, the Indians had not been in contention for pennants and World Series since the 1950s. At least their fans could laugh along with the movie and take inspiration from its win-against-all-odds-even-when-the-owner-conspires-against-you plot.

No actual Cleveland Indians were harmed, or even used, in the making of the movie.

Part V

Baseball at the Brink

Mark McGwire greets Jose Canseco with a forearm bash following a home run. Unbeknownst to baseball's legions of fans, both sluggers were using steroids to enhance their offensive productivity—an issue the game would not grapple with until the late 1990s. *National Baseball Hall of Fame Library, Cooperstown, NY.*

29

THE PETE ROSE AFFAIR, THE A'S 'ROID AGE, AND THE INTEGRITY OF THE GAME

Major League Baseball faced a crisis that blew up in its face and a simultaneous revolutionary awakening about what got baseball fans excited in the immediate years after World War I. The crisis was the Black Sox scandal occasioned by eight Chicago White Sox players—two starting outfielders, three of the four regular infielders, two starting pitchers, and a bench player—conspiring with big-time gamblers to lose the 1919 World Series in exchange for a big-time payoff, most of which they didn't get. The revolutionary awakening was both the unprecedented frequency and the majestic distance of Babe Ruth's home runs. The crisis was resolved by the appointment of an all-powerful commissioner of baseball, a sitting federal judge and baseball enthusiast named Kenesaw Mountain Landis, whose first action was to remove any doubt concerning the integrity of baseball games by banning for life the players involved. The revolutionary awakening left mouths agape, brought astounded cheers, and introduced a new kind of celebrity to baseball—hero worship for the slugger.

Gambling on the outcome of baseball games dated back to the game's origins. To the extent players were involved, it was mostly *wagering about* the outcome rather than *affecting* the outcome of games. Landis's lifetime banishment of Chicago's Black Sox left it said in no uncertain terms that any player who conspired to fix the outcome of a game at any level of Organized Baseball would never again be allowed back into the ballpark. It was not until 1926, however, when Landis had to deal with a

1919 incident in which two of the game's greatest players—Ty Cobb and Tris Speaker—bet on the outcome of a game between their teams, but did not seek in any way to fix the game, that Major League Baseball specifically prohibited players, managers, and front office executives alike from placing wagers on baseball games. "No Betting on Baseball" became a posted sign in every clubhouse. Pete Rose knew all this.

* * *

It was the return that was expected and should have been, when the Cincinnati Reds in a mid-August 1984 deal with Montreal brought Rose back to be player-manager of the team for which he had been such a defining presence. An integral part of the Big Red Machine, Rose won legions of fans and admirers for his always hustling (in the baseball sense of the word, as opposed to the less savory activities to which the word also applies—which would eventually attach to him), aggressive style of play. He was an overachiever and showed, as it was then said, that even a singles hitter could buy a Cadillac, just like them home run guys. When Rose left Cincinnati as a free agent in 1979, he was closing in on Ty Cobb's record for total hits. He would now have the chance to make the record his own in the city where he was born, on the team for which he became famous. It also seemed the likely start of a promising long second career as a manager in the game he loved and played with such enthusiasm and disciplined abandon.

Almost exactly five years later, his second career as manager was over and, although his 4,256 career hits were the new record, his reputation was in ruins. Rose's pervasive gambling caught up with him when he got on the wrong side of his bookie, who not only laid out the breadth of his bets—not to mention the extent of his debts—but alleged that he took bets for the Reds' former star player and current manager on baseball games—including on his Cincinnati ballclub, although always to win. Commissioner Bart Giamatti had no choice but to investigate the allegations about his heavy gambling in general, and on baseball in particular. Giamatti's investigation concluded there was compelling evidence that Rose had indeed bet on baseball, which Rose steadfastly denied and tried to counter with a lawsuit to prevent the commissioner from acting on the evidence. That gambit failed. Cincinnati's 6–5, 10-inning win in Chicago on August 21, 1989, was the last game Rose managed. It was in fact his last-major league game in any capacity, because two days later Pete Rose signed an agreement that placed him on baseball's permanently ineligible list but allowed him to ask for reinstatement after one year. He continued to insist he never bet on baseball, both in his agreement with the commissioner and in public statements. Giamatti and his successors were not buying it. He was not reinstated.

The bitter irony for Rose was that the Cincinnati Reds under his guiding hand as manager were back to being a competitive ballclub. The Reds were in fifth place in mid-August 1984 when Rose took over as player-manager, after finishing last in the NL West each of the two previous years. The first of those last-place finishes, in 1982, was one of the most dramatic comedowns in baseball history—the worst record of all 12 National League clubs following the 1981 strike year in which they had the best record in Major League Baseball yet did not qualify for a postseason berth in either the first or the second half of the artificially split season. Riding a seven-game winning streak, Cincinnati was half a game behind Los Angeles when the 1981 season came to a screeching halt on June 11, and despite winning 11 of 13 games at the end of September, the Reds finished the second half 1½ games back of the Houston Astros.

By the time Rose returned to Cincinnati in 1984, the Big Red Machine was history. The only core regulars remaining from Rose's glory days with Bench and Morgan and Perez was shortstop Dave Concepcion, and he was 36 and very near the end of his playing days. The Reds' best players were right-hander Mario Soto and right fielder Dave Parker, signed as a free agent over the winter after 11 mostly stellar years in Pittsburgh. Although a switch-hitter, Rose the manager started Rose the player at first base only against right-handed pitchers. In September 1985 Pete Rose passed Ty Cobb on the all-time hits list. He was 44 years old, however, and batted just .264 in 119 games. When Rose retired as a player after hitting just .219 in 72 games in 1987, he had not only secured his legacy as the major leagues' new hit king, but also as the last player-manager in the history of Major League Baseball.

Pete Rose was now fully embarked on his second career as a manager, and all indications were that he would be successful. In his four full seasons as manager, the Reds finished each year as runner-up in the NL West. In 1987 they made a run for the division title before fading down the stretch. The promise of those years was shattered in 1989, beginning when Rose was confronted by Giamatti in spring training about the allegations he'd bet on baseball, which Rose assured him were not true. Despite that distraction, Rose's Reds got off to a good start and were in first place for most of May. Injuries to key players ultimately doomed the 1989 Reds, as did the tremendous distraction of the Pete Rose affair as it became increasingly clear it would not end well for their manager. The Reds were in fourth place, out of the running, when Rose agreed to his exile from Major League Baseball. They ended up fifth.

Banished from major-league ballparks, including Cincinnati's Riverfront Stadium, Rose was forced to watch on TV, listen on the radio, or read in the papers the extraordinary success of "his team" in 1990. The Reds finished every day of the regular season atop the NL's Western Division, beat the Pirates in a tough six-game NLCS to win the pennant, and capped off a near-perfect season with a sweep of the heavily favored Oakland Athletics in the World Series. Lou Piniella may have been the new manager, but there was no mistaking that the 1990 Cincinnati Reds were still Pete Rose's team.

Nearly all of the core players who won it all for Piniella proved their worth under Rose. After hitting .342 in an injury-curtailed 1989 season— his fourth in the big leagues—Barry Larkin was on the cusp of eclipsing Ozzie Smith as the most dynamic all-around shortstop in baseball. Taking over center field in 1986, Eric Davis was drawing comparisons to Willie Mays for his defense, speed, and aggressiveness on the basepath (130 stolen bases in 147 attempts in 1986 and 1987), and power (148 home runs between 1986 and 1990). While right fielder Paul O'Neill was hardly a star, his intense approach to the game since becoming a regular in 1988 reminded some of Pete Rose the player. Jose Rijo and southpaw Tom Browning emerged as the Reds' top starting pitchers during Rose's tenure, succeeding Soto when chronic shoulder problems derailed his career in 1986. Despite their dominance of Oakland's powerhouse team in the World Series, the 1990 Reds had too many weaknesses to be consistently competitive. As of today, they were the last Cincinnati team to play in the World Series.

* * *

The same is true for Oakland, even though in 1990, having just played in three consecutive World Series, the Athletics were the best team in baseball and a dynasty in the making. All three of their divisional titles were won by comfortable margins. They had the major leagues' best record all three years, with bookend seasons of 104 wins in 1988 and 103 in 1990 sandwiching 99 wins in 1989. And they did this in the American League's stronger division at the time. While none of the AL Eastern

Division winners those three years—Boston, Toronto, and Boston again—won as many as 90 games, four other teams in the AL West did. The A's were the first team since the 1976–1978 Yankees to win three consecutive league championship series, but baseball being baseball, they were beaten by the underdog National League club in two of the three World Series. Their legacy would soon enough be tarnished by how they got there.

Seeking an edge—any edge they think they can get away with, even if it skirts the rules and sometimes even if it's outright cheating—has always been a part of Major League Baseball. Several great careers were made in the 1910s by pitchers whose specialties were the spitball, the shine ball, and the emery ball. Hitters have long tried unleashing their inner Babe Ruth by using corked bats to drive the ball further. But notwithstanding the prevalent use of amphetamines beginning in the 1950s to help them get through long, hot summers, day games following night games, and the rigors of extensive long-distance travel, players competed as who they were without artificial enhancement of their basic skills and ability.

That began to change after free agency. Escalating salaries for average-performance major leaguers as well as the stars meant that those who had made it to the Big Time no longer needed off-season employment to make ends meet. They could focus instead on staying in shape. In fact, there was every incentive to do so, both to enhance their payday prospects should they take their club to salary arbitration or for when they became free agents, and to stay ahead of rising prospects fighting for their turn in the big leagues who would command less money. For those on the competitive free agent market, the widening salary gap between baseball's best players and everybody else provided strong incentive even for those with elite-level talent to do whatever it took to enhance their edge; the better their statistical numbers relative to their peers, the greater the odds they'd be rewarded with an outsized contract.

For position players, power numbers—home runs and runs batted in— were the ones that had the most impact. Upper-body strength especially was perceived as an essential attribute, along with eye-hand coordination, balance and timing, and bat speed, driving the baseball to the farthest reaches of the ballpark. Some past sluggers in the game—Ruth; Jimmie Foxx, nicknamed "The Beast" in part for his imposing muscles; and Ted Kluszewski, who showcased his bulging biceps by cutting the sleeves off his uniform jersey—looked as strong as they were. Others—like Williams, Mantle, Maris, Aaron, and Mays—were leaner, with more sinewy muscles. Weight lifting, however, was not a practiced regimen for most of the game's previous power hitters. There was a widespread perception that lifting weights was counterproductive in baseball because muscle mass would diminish the agility and speed required of ballplayers in the field and on the bases. That perception began changing in the 1980s as power hitters, and would-be power hitters, began strength-training programs—including lifting weights and taking muscle-enhancing supplements—in the hopes of boosting their home run and RBI totals—and their odds of cashing in on millions.

Jose Canseco was among those at the beginning of that trend. In his case, as it would be in the future for so many other prospects, it was to make it to the big leagues and take it from there. When he was drafted by the Oakland Athletics out of a Florida high school in 1982, the "scrawny" Canseco was hardly the physical specimen he would become. Reaching the Single-A minor-league level in 1983, he hit just .235 with 14 home runs. After another year in Single-A with 15 homers and a .276 batting average, Canseco decided his prospects for making the majors needed a significant boost. So he hit the gym. To get the most from his intensive weight-training routine, Canseco, by his own subsequent account, began using anabolic steroids. He belted 25 homers and drove in 80 runs in 58 games at the Double-A level in 1985, blasted another 11 for Oakland's Triple-A club, and was a September callup to the big club once the minor-league season was over. He started 25 of the Athletics' final 27 games, with 5 home runs, 13 RBIs, and a .302 batting average for the month. Canseco's workout routine, including the use of steroids, worked. And he intended for it to keep on working.

* * *

The Oakland Athletics were still recovering from three years of "Billy Ball" when the enhanced Canseco made it to the big leagues. Billy Ball came to town in 1980 in the person of Billy Martin, brought back to his original hometown by Charlie Finley after he was fired as Yankee manager by George Steinbrenner for getting into a barroom fight with a marshmallow salesman. As was typical under Martin, the A's improved dramatically in his first year as manager, ending baseball's 1981 split season with the American League's best record. And as in all his previous managerial stints, it all came undone in his third year. Martin, often coming unhinged in the clubhouse as his team plummeted to third worst in the AL, was fired after the season.

Exciting for the two years it lasted before flaming out in Martin's third year, Billy Ball emphasized aggressiveness and taking chances on the basepaths. He had the perfect catalyst in lead-off batter Rickey Henderson, whose 100 stolen bases in Martin's first year in Oakland set a new American League record. Two years later, in 1982, Henderson's 130 steals shattered Lou Brock's major-league record of 118 set in 1974. The power part of the Billy Ball equation came from center fielder Tony Armas, who belted 35 homers in 1980 and led the league with 22 in the strike-shortened 1981 season. Martin, however, wore out his starting staff with a pitching philosophy, enabled by the DH rule, that starting pitchers were expected to go the distance. Sandy Alderson's promotion to general manager after Billy Martin was fired signaled the end of Billy Ball days.

While Canseco was working out with weights and beginning his baseball marriage with steroids in December 1984, the Oakland A's were parting company with Henderson. Quite likely the best position player in baseball, Henderson expected to be paid as such. Having just played the 1984 season after losing his bid for a $1.2 million contract in salary arbitration, Rickey was clearly a player small-market Oakland could not afford, so Alderson traded him to the Yankees, with whom he agreed to a five-year $8.6 million contract. The next substantive move Alderson made was hiring Tony LaRussa to take the A's managerial reins three weeks after he was fired by the White Sox in June 1986. One of the game's most highly regarded young managers, LaRussa already had Chicago's 1983 Western Division title to his credit. Six weeks before hiring LaRussa, the A's signed right-hander Dave Stewart as a free agent.

But it was the power and potential of Jose Canseco that represented the future of the Oakland Athletics. His 33 home runs and 117 RBIs in 1986 earned him Rookie of the Year honors. The next year the A's had another slugger named Rookie of the Year—Mark McGwire, a physically imposing though still lean man whose 49 homers shattered the rookie record held jointly by Wally Berger and Frank Robinson and tied Cubs outfielder Andre Dawson for the major-league lead. McGwire's 49 home runs in his first year facing major-league pitching exceeded by one the number he had hit in two full minor-league seasons and 16 games of a third. They were the "Bash Brothers"—stars of the show when Oakland went to three straight World Series from 1988 to 1990. Both right-handed batters, usually hitting third and fourth, Canseco and McGwire were the most devastating one-two power punch in their generation of major-league ballplayers. Between them, they hit 200 home runs and drove in 584 runs during those 'hree years, and that was with Canseco playing only 65 games in 1989 because of a broken wrist. Canseco was a terrific player when he wasn't hurt, a lethal combination of power and speed seeming to be building the foundation for a Hall of Fame career. His 42 home runs and 124 RBIs in 1988 led the majors, and his 40 stolen bases made him the first player in history to hit 40 homers and steal 40 bases. He took all the first-place votes in the balloting for the American League MVP. McGwire was third in the league in homers in 1988 and '89, and second in 1990.

When Alderson reacquired dynamic attention magnet Rickey Hender-son from the Yankees in June 1989, the A's had a slim lead in the AL West but were without the injured Canseco. McGwire and Canseco may have been totally Bash, but Henderson was the most exceptional player of his generation. Already 30, he was hardly slowing down as the greatest leadoff hitter in history. Rickey was a master at getting on base by either a hit or a walk, and once on base he was always a threat to steal, at which his success rate was 85 percent since leaving Oakland for New York in 1985. After leading the league in stolen bases in 1989 for the ninth time in 10 years—it would have been 10 times in 10 years had he not missed 67 games in 1987 because of injury—Henderson was breathing down Ty Cobb's neck, his career 871 steals in his first 11 years just 26 shy of the Georgia Peach, and within 67 of Lou Brock's all-time record. His league-leading 65 base swipes in 1990 passed Cobb on the all-time list and brought him within two of Brock. Proving he was a multidimensional offensive threat, Henderson also smacked 28 homers in 1990—third on the club behind McGwire's 39 and Canseco's 37.

As imposing as the 1988–1990 A's offense was, their pitching was perhaps even more impressive. Cultivating a bone-chilling Darth Vade-resque death stare from beneath the brim of his cap, worn low over his brow, Dave Stewart was quite possibly the most intimidating starting pitcher of his time and the very model of consistency in his best years with the A's. In 1990 he became the first pitcher since Jim Palmer be-tween 1975 and 1978—and the last pitcher to date—to put together four straight 20-win seasons. In 1989 the Athletics just missed having three 20-game winners when Mike Moore and Storm Davis both won 19. In

1990 the relatively unheralded Bob Welch, a 17-game winner each of the two previous years, easily outpaced Roger Clemens to win the Cy Young Award with a 27–6 record. His 27 wins were the most in the major leagues since Steve Carlton in 1972. Only three pitchers have won as many as 24 since.

Except for Stewart, however, LaRussa rarely allowed his starting pitchers to go the distance. Even Welch in the year he won 27 games completed only two of his 35 starts. LaRussa could do so because he had an outstanding bullpen, closing with Dennis Eckersley. LaRussa had made Stewart a star by converting him from primarily a reliever; so too, he resurrected Eckersley's flagging career in 1987 after the veteran starting pitcher was picked up from the Cubs in exchange for three minor-league prospects (none of whom ever made it to the majors) by turning him into arguably the best reliever baseball had yet seen. A master of precision and virtually unhittable, the side-arm-throwing right-hander saved 126 of the A's 306 victories from 1988 to 1990, held opposing hitters to a .174 batting average, and allowed just 6.3 runners on base by hit or walk for every 9 innings of work. His control was so exquisite that in 1989 and 1990 he allowed only 7 walks to the 468 batters he faced while striking out 128. In 1990 Eckersley gave up just 5 earned runs in 73⅓ innings.

The A's stumbled trying for four pennants in a row in 1991. Canseco had another monster year with a career-high 44 homers. Henderson set the new career record for steals and once again led the league in stolen bases. But McGwire had a terrible season at the plate, possibly because of personal distractions, barely hitting .201 with only 22 home runs after four years with at least 32; Stewart went 11–11 with a horrific 5.18 ERA as age (he was 34) and having thrown more innings and faced more batters than any other pitcher during his four 20-win seasons caught up with him; and Eckersley's ERA jumped from 1.50 the three previous years to 2.96. Oakland finished fourth, well out of the running.

The last hurrah for LaRussa's Athletics came in 1992, when they returned to the top of the AL West for their fourth division title in five years, although this time they did not advance to the World Series. McGwire had an extraordinary comeback year, with 42 homers. Henderson had yet another outstanding season. Eckersley returned to form, his major-league-leading 51 saves and 1.91 earned-run average in 69 appearances earning him both the MVP and Cy Young Awards; no relief pitcher in either league has since been voted Most Valuable Player. Canseco finally wore out his welcome in Oakland and was exiled to the Texas Rangers on the last day of August for comparable slugger Ruben Sierra, whose rookie season also was 1986. He left Oakland with 254 home runs on his way to an ultimate career total of 462. The next year, the A's went from the best record in the American League (along with Toronto) to the worst. McGwire, the other Bash Brother, was mostly missing in action with foot injuries the next two years, playing in just 74 of his team's 276 games. Eckersley, now 38, was no longer untouchable. Tony LaRussa stepped down as manager after the A's finished fourth in 1995.

* * *

The accomplishments of the 1988–1990 Canseco-McGwire edition of the Oakland Athletics would soon be tarnished by allegations of steroid use by the Bash Brothers. Canseco's (and probably McGwire's) use was an open secret at the time. "I was the godfather of the steroid revolution in baseball," Canseco wrote in *Juiced*, his 2005 book about his baseball career, "but McGwire was . . . a thriving example of what steroids could do to make you a better player." Although baseball insiders knew or strongly suspected that major-league players were taking steroids since the mid-1980s, until 1990 there was nothing illegal about it. It was not until that year that congressional legislation made anabolic steroids a controlled substance, motivated in part by known widespread use in the NFL and by the steroid scandal in the 1988 Summer Olympics. In 1991 Commissioner Fay Vincent banned the use of steroids by major-league players. From 1989 to 1993, meanwhile, FBI investigations of steroid dealers uncovered the names of Canseco, McGwire, and several other Oakland A's as users. Since they were not the target of the investigation, none of them were charged.

According to Canseco, naming names in his 2005 tell-all, McGwire was not on any steroid regimen when he set the rookie record for home runs in 1987. He was, however, curious about what effect they would have on his baseball performance and, says Canseco, began using steroids in 1988. Despite bulking up impressively to be a mountain of a man, McGwire did not match his rookie record in any of his remaining seasons with the A's; 24 of his 58 home runs in 1997 came after he was traded in July to the Cardinals. The slugger remained under the radar of suspicion until 1998, when a bottle of androstenedione was discovered in his locker during his epic run in tandem with Sammy Sosa to break Maris's 37-year-old single-season-record 61 homers. Andro is said to enhance the effects of anabolic steroids but was not then on the federal controlled substance list or banned by Major League Baseball. By the end of the 1990s and well into this century, Major League Baseball was grappling with a steroid scandal that was threatening the integrity of the game.

Players using steroids or other performance-enhancing drugs were cheating the game in two very troublesome ways. The first and most obvious was that it potentially put those who did not use such drugs at a competitive disadvantage, particularly players whose natural talent was not top-tier or for whom a starting role, or even a reserve role, in the major leagues was not well established. Fighting for a position, and later for bigger paydays, gave them strong incentive to chemically cheat, especially if they believed those they were competing against were doing the same. It was this calculus that convinced Jose Canseco to take steroids. Even star players with exceptional accomplishments derived from their own natural talent, like Barry Bonds and Roger Clemens, fell prey to the allure of how much better they might be if they "juiced" their physical gifts, as McGwire was said by his Bash Brother to have wondered in his 49-homer rookie season. For Bonds and Clemens, whose Hall of Fame credentials were well established before they started using performance-enhancing drugs in the late 1990s, the allure was to set records.

And that raised a second troublesome issue about the credibility of record-breaking accomplishments being set by players whose natural skills may have been enhanced by steroids. This was particularly the case when baseball's most sacred records were the ones being broken, such as Maris's 61 homers being eclipsed in 1998 by McGwire and Sosa, both of whom were juiced. Baseball is, after all, a game where the history of achievements matters. The greatest players from the past are revered because of what they did, and what they did is invariably in the record books. When long-established records—some of which are part of American lore, not just baseball history—are broken, the expectation is that they are legitimately earned. That is in large part what contributed to the feel-good moment—a bonding moment for all Americans—when McGwire and Sosa both topped 61 home runs. Subsequently learning that they cheated to get there was a betrayal of the sanctity of the record.

McGwire's retirement in 2002 with 583 career home runs, more than half of them (306) in the last six of his 16-year career, followed two injury-plagued seasons that some experts on the subject attributed as quite likely caused by his use of steroids. Five years later, in his first year of eligibility, McGwire became the first test case of whether great players about whom there is compelling evidence or convincing allegations they used performance-enhancing drugs should be enshrined in baseball's Hall of Fame. Because McGwire was as well respected as a person as he was a player, because he was so gracious during his record-setting season— especially to the Maris family on the day he hit his 62nd homer, on his way to 70 for the year—and because his and Sosa's good-natured rivalry pursuing the record was so appealing, even unifying, to Americans, for a while there was an inclination to overlook his bottle of andro and protect him and his record by minimizing the implications. Tony LaRussa, his manager in both Oakland and St. Louis, tried to insist that Canseco's tale in *Juiced* about how and he and McGwire injected each other in the buttocks with steroids was not true. LaRussa also claimed he knew Canseco was juiced, but McGwire's burgeoning muscle mass in his Oakland years was legitimately earned in the weight room.

The credibility of Canseco's book was trashed around Major League Baseball. Dismissing his allegations, especially against McGwire, was made easier by Canseco's admitting resentment toward his teammate as a golden California boy and by the fact he lived his private life in the fast lane, was egotistical and self-destructive, and violated the sanctity of the clubhouse with his tell-all tale. By the time he left Oakland, Canseco was already a cautionary tale of talent squandered, even a menace to society— including illegal possession of firearms on a college campus and on a commercial flight, and charges of assaulting his wife. ("'Roid rage" would later become one of the defining characteristics of steroid use.) None of that made what he wrote untrue, even if some of it might be embellished. In any event, by the time Mark McGwire's name appeared on the Hall of Fame ballot for the first time in 2007, his accomplishments were burdened by a metaphorical asterisk. In his 10 years on the writers' ballot, McGwire never even got a quarter of the vote.

* * *

Pete Rose, on the other hand, because of his lifetime banishment by the commissioner of baseball from the game he loves, was never on any Hall of Fame ballot. Fifteen years after he agreed to accept his punishment without acknowledging he bet on baseball, Rose finally admitted in a book he entitled *My Prison without Bars* that he had indeed bet on ballgames while manager of the Cincinnati Reds—including games of the team he was managing, although never on any outcome other than that his team would win. It was a belated attempt to have his lifetime ban lifted so that he could at least be eligible for the Hall of Fame. But if he thought that might merit a pardon . . . Pete Rose is still banned from Organized Baseball in any capacity, and the Hall of Fame has not budged on his eligibility.

Yet there are a great many baseball fans, especially among those who saw him play, who believe that the Baseball Hall of Fame is diminished by his not being there and advocate that this wrong be corrected, if for no other reason than that his record 4,256 hits were legitimately earned (unlike, probably, McGwire's 70 homers in 1998). Besides, Rose's betting on ball games was when he was a manager, and he never bet against his team. Or so he said, and so they rationalize. It's a variation of the same argument made on behalf of Shoeless Joe Jackson, whose supporters for his belonging in the Hall of Fame point to his exemplary playing career and his statistical line in the 1919 World Series as evidence that, while he might have been in on the conspiracy, he played to win, not to throw the series.

Pete Rose is a sympathetic figure because of both his passion for the game and the fact that he was perceived, certainly during his playing career, as emblematic of the American dream. Like most of us, he was a little guy—which in baseball meant not a slugger and not preternaturally gifted—who worked very hard to make the most of his talent. He played for the love of the game. His enthusiasm for baseball was infectious. He loved every moment spent on the ball field. He was an overachiever who upended the conventional wisdom that only sluggers earned the big bucks to drive Cadillacs. More than that, Rose's human side—including his flaws, most notably gambling—have resonated with many Americans, particularly working-class Americans. Who among us isn't flawed? Culturally, America is a country quick to forgive those who seek redemption. He's asking for redemption, and many have come to believe that as grievous as his sins might be, Pete Rose was so good at what he did—and delighted us so much with how he did it—and never compromised the integrity of the game as a player that his time in purgatory should come to an end—in Cooperstown.

Ironically, there has been much less sentiment that Mark McGwire's exclusion from the Hall of Fame is a disservice to the game's history, even though his credentials—consecutive years in excess of 60 homers, nearly 600 career home runs—should have made him a first-ballot lock. Moreover, McGwire in virtually every other respect had a standout reputation as a person as well as a ballplayer, whereas Rose, when he wasn't on the ballfield, had more of a frat house lifestyle, not unlike a great many other stars. In an America that believes in second chances, there appears to be more of an inclination to give Rose a pass for his sins against the game than McGwire, perhaps because it cannot be shown that any of Rose's baseball bets affected the outcome of any game, whereas the use of performance-enhancing steroids by McGwire—and Barry Bonds, Sammy Sosa, Roger Clemens, Rafael Palmeiro, and others with Hall of Fame résumés—does call into question the integrity of their statistical accomplishments.

There is, however, a very big difference between the baseball sins of players like McGwire, who bolstered their game by using steroids, and those—and Rose appears to be the sole outlier—who bet on baseball games, and it does not work in Pete's favor. The distinction is that the use of performance-enhancing drugs is a *betrayal of sportsmanship*; betting on baseball, as Rose did, as a manager no less, is a *betrayal of trust*.

A betrayal of sportsmanship does not compromise the basic integrity of the games as played. In the intensely competitive world of professional sports, sportsmanship—loosely identified with the trite saying, "It doesn't matter whether you win or lose, it's how you play the game that counts"—is often cast aside by players, managers, and teams seeking an edge, any advantage they can get away with. The ethic of sportsmanship has *always* been compromised on the diamond by any number of what-can-we-get-away-with schemes, including corked bats, doctored pitches, and Herman Franks spying on opposing catchers' signs with a telescope from beyond the field of play for the 1951 Giants. Using performance-enhancing drugs undermines the credibility and integrity of *accomplishments* but does not necessarily undermine the integrity of the game itself. It is players seeking an unfair and illegal advantage, to be sure, but the games played on the field still unfold according to rules, strategies employed, and players' execution.

Moreover, the outsized accomplishments of any particular time— whether pitching in the Deadball Era, the proliferation of .300 hitters in the 1920s Lively Ball Era, or the power surge of the Steroids Era—are rightfully evaluated in that historical context. The keepers of baseball's historical flame ensure this because of their reverence for that history and for the statistical record. They will not delete the home run totals of those hitters who have surpassed Ruth's 60 in 1927 and Maris's 61 in 1961, but the fact that all three hitters who have done so—McGwire (twice), Sosa (three times), and Bonds with his record-setting 73 in 2001—have their names associated with steroids *diminishes* their accomplishments that will forever be in baseball's record book. If anything, they have enhanced the magnitude and the stature of the only player so far to have topped the Babe's 60 without pharmaceutical help—Roger Maris, a slugger with an unimposing physique.

A betrayal of trust—which is what betting on baseball certainly is—on the other hand, does compromise the integrity of the games, because the manager or players involved can deliberately affect the outcome by the decisions and actions they take or fail to take. We trust that the games are not fixed. The edict against anyone in Organized Baseball betting on baseball has been fiercely uncompromising because of the damage done to the integrity of the game by Chicago's Black Sox. It has to be, precisely because the integrity of the game depends on it. It does not matter that Rose did not conspire to fix games on behalf of gamblers the way Shoeless Joe and his fellow Black Sox did in the 1919 World Series. It also does not matter that Rose always bet on his own team; he could have done otherwise, especially if he felt he was too far in to his bookies.

An argument can be made that what Rose did was particularly insidious because he *was* the manager. Player performances certainly determine the outcome of games, but a manager controls the game. Every decision a manager makes, and there are countless decisions in every game, can affect the outcome. Never mind that Rose said he never bet against his own team, implicitly reassuring us that he was managing every game to win or that he was such a competitor that it's difficult to fathom he would ever manage to lose. But who could ever be sure that his betting on baseball did not affect his judgment as a manager, once a man—and manager—to whom is entrusted the integrity of the game betrays that trust? Once Rose decided to go down the path of betting on baseball, and especially betting on his own team, his integrity as a manager was hopelessly compromised and we can never be sure what impact that had on the games he managed. That's why Pete Rose's sin has been judged by every commissioner since Bart Giamatti as irredeemable and why none have pardoned him at least for the purpose of consideration for the Hall of Fame, even though there is no reason to believe he ever bet on baseball during his extraordinary playing career.

30

REDEFINING THE END GAME

Paradigm Shifts in the Role of Relief Ace

From 1988, when Oakland manager Tony LaRussa made him the A's closer, to 1992, when his closing excellence earned him both the American League's MVP and Cy Young Award, Dennis Eckersley pitched 310 games in relief with a 24–9 record and 220 saves. In 275 of those games—89 percent—the A's had the lead, 26 times the score was tied, and only nine times in the entire five years did LaRussa call upon Eckersley to pitch when his team was on the short end of the score, several times likely because his relief ace had not pitched in several days and needed the work. Not once did LaRussa call him into a game earlier than the eighth inning, and 80 of the 102 times there were runners on base or outs already on the scoreboard, and he wanted Eckersley to get a particular hitter out and take it from there to the end of the game. By contrast, LaRussa almost always had Eckersley start the ninth inning fresh. Eck rarely disappointed, blowing only nine games he came in to save in the ninth inning.

What LaRussa did with Eckersley was the logical conclusion to trends in the role of relief ace that had been accelerating since the beginning of the 1980s to this point of singularity—the ninth-inning closer to save victories. This was a fundamental change from the past, even the recent past. The traditional role of the relief ace dating back to after World War II was to finish close games in the late innings, regardless of the score, if the starting pitcher, or a long-relief man, was removed for a pinch hitter or for cause, and if "for cause," that usually meant the relief ace was expected to get his team out of a jam with runners on base, regardless of the inning. They even had a word for it—the relief ace was the "fireman" who doused the flames or smothered the embers of an opposition rally. The top relievers in baseball from the mid-1940s to the mid-1950s typically pitched between 55 and 65 games a year, averaging about two innings each time. Managers had workhorse expectations of their ace relievers, similar to the workhorse expectations they had of their best starting pitchers, which meant they might be called upon at any time in any game. In part this was because clubs continued to pay much greater attention to depth in their starting rotation than in their bullpen.

Even teams whose top reliever could truly be considered an ace generally had weak bullpens that typically did not have a pitcher the manager could rely on as a bridge to his relief ace at the end of the game. Consequently, ace relievers were often brought into games in high-stress situations with runners on base and several innings yet to play, and then pitched till the end of the game. They might get a decision—win or loss—as often as they would pick up a save, which was still not an official statistic and would later be defined for every generation of relievers before 1969 as being the game-finishing pitcher in a victory regardless of the final score. It was not uncommon for a team's relief ace to pitch four or five innings in a game several times a year. And unlike starting pitchers who were part of a (generally) set rotation, ace relievers, even after throwing multiple innings, had to be prepared to pitch in any game on any day. Unsurprisingly, ace relievers tended to burn out quickly and had relatively short careers. Such was the career path for both Joe Page, baseball's best reliever in the late 1940s, and Jim Konstanty, who in 1950 became the first relief pitcher to be voted Most Valuable Player.

The physically imposing, hard-throwing right-handed Page won 34, lost 23, and saved 60 games in 168 relief appearances for the Yankees between 1947 and 1949. Page came into half of those games on either one or no days of rest. Six times he pitched in both games of a doubleheader. Averaging about 2⅓ innings per relief appearance, he was called in from the bullpen 53 times when the Yankees were trailing and 27 times with the score tied. Page's role was that of fireman since the majority of times he entered the game there were runners already on base. Fifty of his relief appearances came in the middle third of the game. In 1947, when his unofficially counted 27 saves were the most so far in history, he twice pitched seven innings in relief; in 1948 there were five games in which he worked at least five innings, all in late August and September as the Yankees fought for the pennant until the last weekend; and in 1949 he pitched at least four innings nine times, including two when he was on the mound more than six innings.

Two signature moments in Page's career highlight the indispensable role he played in two Yankee championships. First was the seventh game of the 1947 World Series. Taking the mound in the fifth inning with the Yankees ahead, 3–2, Page shut out the Dodgers, facing the minimum number of batters the rest of the way to secure the Yankees' 11th World Series championship. The second was in the 153rd game of the 1949 season, when Boston arrived at Yankee Stadium for a season-ending two-game series holding a one-game lead. A Red Sox victory in either game would eliminate the Yankees. With his team behind, 2–0, and the bases loaded with one out in the third, Casey Stengel called upon Page to save the day. Page pitched the remaining 6⅔ innings without allowing a run of his own as the Yankees came from behind to win the game and pull even with the Red Sox, setting up their dramatic pennant-winning victory in their 154th game the next day. Page went on to pitch in three of the five games of the 1949 World Series, including 5⅔ innings in relief to beat the Dodgers in Game Three and 2⅓ innings in the finale to preserve the victory that brought the Yankees their 12th championship. After three years of the best run by a reliever to that point in history, but suffering hip and shoulder problems, Page pitched poorly in 1950 and was dumped by the Yankees the following spring.

Although Konstanty was hardly a kid at 33 in 1950, the Whiz Kid Phillies would not have won their first pennant in 35 years without him pitching out of the pen in nearly half their games. The 74 games he pitched were the most by a pitcher since the current distance between the pitching rubber and home plate was established in 1893. And he was a workhorse, averaging more than two innings an outing. Twenty-four of his appearances came the day after he had pitched, and he had just one day off between 21 others. He also pitched in both games of a double-header six times. Twice he pitched the equivalent of a complete game in relief—nine innings in a late-August game and 10 innings in a late-September game that lasted 19 innings. The price of Konstanty's work-load came at the expense of his effectiveness when the Phillies arguably needed him at his best. Pitching in eight of the Phillies' next 11 games, during which their 7½-game lead was reduced to just one with one game remaining, Konstanty gave up 16 hits, walked 9, and surrendered 10 runs in 17⅔ innings. He was not needed on the final day, thanks to Robin Roberts's 10-inning complete game to finish off the Dodgers. That was apparently time enough for him to recover for a new role in the 1950 World Series—that of starting pitcher.

With Roberts unavailable to pitch the opening game of the series and Curt Simmons, Philadelphia's number-two starter, called to the Korean War, Konstanty on three days of rest was the Whiz Kids' surprise starting pitcher against the Yankees. Having twice pitched complete-game equivalents and despite his recent struggles, Konstanty was up to the task, holding the Bronx Bombers to one run and four hits in eight innings. Unfortunately, the Yankees' Vic Raschi didn't give up any runs. He pitched twice more in the series—a Yankees sweep—in his actual role as a reliever, including 6⅔ innings after being called into Game Four in the very first inning to stymie a Yankees rally. Like Page, Konstanty was never the same again.

This pattern of using their bullpen ace, almost as though they were seconds for the starting pitcher, gave managers the option to reset any game at any point they wanted, resulting in workhorse ace relievers like Page, 14–8 and 13–8 in his two best seasons, and Konstanty, 16–7 in his best year, gaining as many decisions as some starters. In 1959 Pittsburgh's Roy Face took that to an unexpected level for a reliever by nearly winning 20 games—all in relief. In 57 games without a start, his 18–1 record gave Face a major-league-high .947 winning percentage. That remains the major-league record. Only four National League pitchers and two in the American League, all six with at least 32 starts, won more than 18 games. He worked just 93⅓ innings, averaging about 1⅔ innings an appearance, only twice worked more than three innings, and never entered a game earlier than the seventh inning. Ironically for a relief ace, Face was much more effective in games he entered with the score tied or his team behind than when he was called upon to protect a lead. Face got the win in eight of the 11 games he entered with the score tied and three of the 22 he came on to pitch with the Pirates behind, and his earned-run average in those nonsave situations was an excellent 1.80. In the 22 games he pitched where Pittsburgh was ahead, his nine blown saves being nearly as many as the 10 he saved was explained in part by his 4.45 ERA in save situations. Four of his 18 wins came after he could not hold the lead.

* * *

The 1960s and 1970s were the golden age of ace relievers as firemen. Until then, few who made their livelihood in the bullpen were considered exceptional pitchers by any standard. Exceptional pitchers, virtually by definition, were starting pitchers. The two most prominent relievers in the 1950s were in their role for specific reasons. Ellis Kinder, a 23-game winner for the Red Sox in 1949, was converted to ace reliever halfway through the 1950 season primarily because he was already in his mid-30s. From then until 1955, when he celebrated his 41st birthday, Kinder was unquestionably the best reliever in the game, with 89 saves and 37 wins in 257 relief appearances that averaged about 1⅔ innings. His impact was hardly as celebrated as it might have been because the Red Sox were a middle-of-the-pack team. Clem Labine, on the other hand, had widespread name recognition as the relief ace of the Brooklyn Dodgers. Given that relievers were brought in nearly as often in the middle of innings with runners on base, Labine got his calling because of his ability to routinely induce batters to hit the ball on the ground. Between 1953 and 1959, Labine entered 187 of the 350 games he pitched in relief with runners on base and induced 65 double plays.

By the 1960s, having a quality bullpen featuring a shutdown-the-rally ace reliever was a necessity for every team. Relief pitchers had never before been as prominent in either name recognition or their impact on the game. The need for such a specialty role on the pitching staff was both a product and a driver of the diminishing number of complete games in general, and complete-game victories in particular. The ace reliever's role was still not just to protect a lead; he was often called upon to pitch with his team losing or the score tied—whenever his manager felt the move was necessary to salvage a game, including hoping for a come-from-behind victory. Dodgers manager Walt Alston called on Ron Perranoski, his top reliever between 1962 and 1967, more often when his team was behind than in any other circumstance, which proved true for other ace relievers as well. As before, this approach suppressed the number of saves a pitcher earned while contributing to robust won-lost records. Along with 21 saves, Perranoski was 16–3 in 1963. Kansas City's John Wyatt was 9–8 with 20 saves in 1964 when he pitched in a record 81 games, all in relief, 38 of which he entered with the Athletics trailing and

15 with the score tied. Dick Radatz, Boston's overpowering bullpen ace from 1962 to 1965, had nearly as many decisions, with a 49–32 record, as his 98 saves.

Managers continued to bring their bullpen ace into stressful situations with runners on base in virtually any of the last three innings of a ball-game. Game exigencies often had greater priority for managers than when and how many innings their top reliever had last pitched. Regard-less of the circumstances of his entry into the game, whether he had to pitch out of a jam or not, managers expected their relief ace to pitch multiple innings if he entered the game before the ninth. The typical relief ace, including those above, averaged just below two innings an outing. Finally, not only had the demands on every club's relief ace not dimin-ished, they had grown greater, particularly in the number of games pitched. Before Wyatt's 81 relief appearances in 1964—accounting for exactly half of his club's scheduled games—only five pitchers in the twentieth century had pitched as many as 70 games in a season, the first being Giants' reliever Ace Adams in the war year of 1943. Seven pitchers came out of the pen at least 70 times in 1964; 30 relievers pitched in at least 70 games over the next seven years; and in 1969 Cincinnati's Wayne Granger became the first to be used out of the bullpen 90 times in a season.

To the extent ace relievers were overworked, the pinnacle of excess came in 1974, when Dodgers manager Walt Alston used Mike Marshall in an astonishing 106 games. That does not include Marshall's two ap-pearances in the NLCS, which went four games, and his pitching in all five games of the 1974 World Series. And this was a year after Marshall, then with the Expos, set a new record for appearances, with 92. He was 15–12 with 21 saves in 1974. Marshall may have brought some of this on himself, since he claimed he could pitch virtually every day because (he said) his mastery of body mechanics, kinetic motion especially, made him impervious to wearing out his arm or any other body parts.

Pitching virtually every day, Marshall's 208 innings were in the neigh-borhood of stalwart starting pitchers who lived for the complete game, except he was not pitching every four or five days. And unlike today's 80-game situational relievers or 50- to 60-game closers, Marshall wasn't in there for only a batter or two or one inning at a time. The Dodgers had 33 complete games in 1974, meaning Marshall appeared in all but 22 games in which LA's starting pitcher did not go the distance. And not only did he pitch in nearly two-thirds of the Dodgers' games, including 53 times on consecutive days, Marshall averaged nearly two innings an appearance. After the All-Star break, as Cincinnati started closing in, Alston never gave Marshall more than two days off. After appearing in 198 games and throwing 387⅓ innings in 1973 and '74, Marshall struggled the next several seasons before reprising his iron man act in 1979 with Minnesota, pitching 142⅔ innings in 90 relief appearances with a 10–15 record and 32 saves. He retired in 1981, having pitched 700 games in relief.

* * *

Dick Radatz was ahead of his time in presaging a future of intimidating, hard-throwing closers. Standing 6-foot-6 and weighing in at 230 pounds, not for nothing was Radatz nicknamed "The Monster." In his first three big-league seasons with Boston, 1962 to 1964, Radatz pitched in 43 percent of Boston's games, averaging exactly two innings an appearance; got the victory or the save in 116 games, accounting for over half of his team's 224 victories; and averaged 10.6 strikeouts per 9 innings. He was seventh in the league in strikeouts, with 181 (in 157 innings) in 1964—phenomenal for not being a starting pitcher. Having faced nearly 1,700 batters in three years, often entering games in stressful situations with runners on base and usually pitching on consecutive days or just a single day of rest, Radatz was never again remotely as good. But his menacing presence and overpowering arsenal of pitches set the template for 1970s relievers.

A parade of intimidating, overpowering relievers was at hand. While Rollie Fingers did not strike them out with the frequency of Radatz, he nonetheless averaged 8 Ks per 9 innings pitching for Oakland from 1972 to 1976, and his twirled-at-the-ends mustache gave him the aura of a swindling gambler-cum-gunslinger. The Cardinals' Al Hrabosky had fearsome facial hair himself, and stalked the mound in a display of anger, emphatically psyching himself up for the pitch—and presumably psyching out the batter—by adopting the persona of "The Mad Hungarian." Bruce Sutter was himself a scary proposition, striking out an average of 10 batters every 9 innings while going 21–19 with 95 saves for the Cubs between 1977 and 1979. The Mad Hungarian had one stellar season— 1975, when he was 13–3 with a league-leading 22 saves—before burning out and not being able to deliver on the menace of his antics. Fingers, with 341 career saves, and Sutter, with exactly 300, both made it into baseball's Hall of Fame. And then there was Goose Gossage, whose time as the Yankees' relief ace from 1978 to 1983—including scruffy appearance, posturing on the mound, and hard-driving delivery—made him a role model for the intimidating closer. In his six New York seasons, Gossage went 41–28, saved 150 games, and averaged just under 9 K's per 9 innings. Every year from 1980 to 1983, Gossage fanned more than a batter per inning.

In 2017, nine years after his election to the Hall of Fame, Gossage provoked controversy by insisting that the role of one-inning closers—even great ones like Mariano Rivera, who displaced the Goose as the best reliever in Yankees history—was comparatively easy compared to how he and his relief ace peers were used during his career. His point was that his role was to be as much a traditional fireman, snuffing out rallies to secure the victory, as it was getting the final three outs of the game. In 308 relief appearances in his six years as the Yankees' fireman-closer, Gossage entered the game most often (189 times) *before* the ninth inning, usually with runners on base (188 times), and pitched multiple innings more often than not (191 times). How he was used was not so different from ace relievers going back to the days of Joe Page, although Gossage rarely pitched more than three innings an outing.

The times were changing, however. Unlike Sparky Lyle, his predecessor as the Yankees' fireman-closer from 1972 to 1977, and the generation of ace relievers before him, Gossage was rarely brought into games with his team behind. The same was true of the ace relievers who flourished in the mid- to late 1980s, including Gossage's replacement on the Yankees, Dave Righetti; Kansas City's Dan Quisenberry; the Cardinals' Bruce Sutter; and Toronto's Tom Henke. St. Louis manager Whitey Herzog was ahead of the curve in hardly ever bringing Sutter into games his team was losing, doing so in only 18 of the 249 games Sutter pitched between 1981 and 1984. Moreover, while Gossage, Lyle, Fingers, and their peers in the 1970s came in more often than not to pitch out of jams with runners already on base, ace relievers in the 1980s were being asked to do that less often—a delta that widened as the 1990s approached. Managers were clearly increasingly inclined to call in their relief ace to protect leads in the late innings, emphasizing more the closer than the fireman role.

* * *

These trends were already pronounced by 1988—the year Dennis Eckersley assumed the ninth-inning role in the way that made his manager, Tony LaRussa, famous for "inventing" the modern-day closer. Eckersley was brought into a game with a lead to protect in all but three of his 60 relief appearances, and two of those were in extra innings with the score tied. His workload was such that in 60 games he threw only 72⅔ innings. Indicative, however, of the inevitability that, if not LaRussa with Eckersley, it would soon enough have been another manager with his ace reliever, is that in the same year Twins manager Tom Kelly used *his* relief ace—Jeff Reardon, whose 42 saves in 1988 were second most in the majors behind Eckersley—in almost exactly the same way. In 63 games, Kelly called upon Reardon 56 times to protect a lead, 37 of them in the ninth inning. Reardon pitched just 70 innings. LaRussa's more far-reaching innovation was establishing Rick Honeycutt as his eighth-inning reliever to set up Eckersley for the ninth. Honeycutt typically entered games where the A's had the lead, sometimes in the seventh inning if it was suddenly in jeopardy.

There were two mutually reinforcing factors that made the trend toward any team's best reliever becoming the ninth-inning closer inevitable. The first was that, however fraught with peril a game situation might be in an earlier inning, managers wanted to save their best for last to shut down their opponents' final-inning hopes, the more emphatically—three up, totally overmatched, three down—the better for both the victory at hand and psychological reasons. They wanted opponents to know that when Eckersley or any other elite closer entered the game, the watchwords in the dugout were, "Abandon hope, ye who have to bat against him."

Playing into that was Major League Baseball's officially adopting the save statistic for the first time in 1969 following a decade-long advocacy by influential baseball writer Jerome Holtzman that relief pitchers deserved a statistical measure that more accurately reflected their contributions to victories credited to other pitchers. Until then, with no specific statistical reference point to give relievers credit for what they did or when they did it, managers used their relief ace when the situation was most dire—in the 1940s and 1950s, often at any point in the game; in the 1960s, mostly in the last three innings. Relief pitchers were increasingly valued—as early as 1947, Yankees manager Bucky Harris routinely raised a beer to his relief ace after victories he had secured, "Here's to Joe Page!"—but were still measured by exactly the same games-pitched, wins-losses, and ERA stats as starting pitchers. Not only did those measures not capture the fireman dimension of the ace reliever's job, they could be misleading—particularly if a reliever gave up the lead and then got the win himself.

It was inevitable that the current definition of a save, in effect since 1975, would set the parameters on how managers would use their relief ace. Saves now were awarded to the final pitcher in a noncomplete-game victory who did not surrender the lead he was called upon to protect in any of three circumstances. A reliever could get a save in even a lopsided win if he pitched at least three complete innings. For a reliever entering the game in the eighth or ninth innings to be credited with a save, the lead could be no more than three runs and he must pitch a complete ninth inning. Finally, there was a fireman provision whereby a save would be awarded to a pitcher who entered the game with the tying run on base, at bat, or on deck even if there was just one out needed to end the game.

There was now a statistical measure to evaluate the performance of relief pitchers that served as a template for managers on when to use their ace in the bullpen. The unforeseen accident of timing, however—one year before the free agency era—reinforced those parameters by giving relief pitchers a specific statistical measure to use as leverage in contract negotiations. It was in everybody's interest for the ace reliever to be used in a manner that had the greatest effect based on a definition of "save" that gave increasing import to closing out the ninth inning.

31

THE CONSOLIDATION OF INTEGRATION AND THE IMPORTANCE OF CITO GASTON

History was made at Three Rivers Stadium, the new multipurpose stadium that replaced storied Forbes Field, on September 1, 1971. At 8:05 in the evening, all nine starting players taking the field for the hometown Pittsburgh Pirates against the Philadelphia Phillies were black. Less than 20 years before, major-league teams—even the Brooklyn Dodgers, the most enlightened when it came to integration—were debating how many black players in the starting lineup were too many. According to Roger Kahn, the elegant baseball writer who covered the Dodgers at the time and later wrote *The Boys of Summer*, it was understood in the beginning years of integration that teams should refrain from having a majority of players on the field at any one time be black. It wasn't until eight years into the Jackie Robinson era, on July 17, 1954, that the Dodgers became the first major-league team to start five black players in a game—Robinson, Roy Campanella, Jim Gilliam, Sandy Amoros, and Don Newcombe. Having a majority of players who were black in the starting lineup was a significant milestone in baseball's slow march toward consolidating integration because it meant a team's manager—the Dodgers' Walt Alston in 1954—was starting the best players he thought could win the game, without out regard to racial considerations.

That Pittsburgh was the team to do this was ironic given that the Pirates, along with the Phillies, were laggards in the National League when it came to integration. While it is true they had a black player—

indeed, a starting position player—on their big-league roster every year since 1954, whereas the Phillies did not integrate until 1957, the Pirates never had more than a single black player in a key role in any season during the 1950s or when they won the 1960 pennant, and Roberto Clemente was the only black player to be a regular for more than a single season until 1963. That changed dramatically in the 1960s. Power right-hander Bob Veale was their best pitcher and Al McBean, another right-hander, starred in the bullpen. A rookie in 1963, left-handed slugger Willie Stargell teamed with Clemente to give Pittsburgh a potent three-four punch in the batting order for as long as the two played together. Donn Clendenon was their starting first baseman from 1963 to 1968 and Dominican-born Matty Alou their center fielder for five years beginning in 1966. By 1971 the Pirates' everyday starting lineup featured Clemente, Stargell, Panamian-born catcher Manny Sanguillen, second baseman Dave Cash, and Al Oliver, an outfielder who minored in first base. In August, Cash moved to third so Panamian-born rookie Rennie Stennett could play second. Dock Ellis had replaced Veale as their best starting pitcher.

From Pittsburgh manager Danny Murtaugh's perspective, fielding an all-black starting lineup on September 1, 1971, with Ellis the starting pitcher, may have been a gimmick, but it also was a monumental talking point to the proposition that, in the 25th year since Jackie Robinson played his first game for the Dodgers, black players with major-league ability—not just those who were elite ballplayers—were every bit as capable and deserving of starting roles as white players of comparable skill and ability. The consolidation of integration would come only at such time that nobody in the baseball industry cared about or even noticed the skin color or ethnic origin of the players who took the field at the start of the game. All that should matter was that each team's starting lineup include the nine best players for that game, that each team's roster include the 25 best players providing the requisite balance the manager needed to make in-game changes, and that ability and performance be the only criteria that counted. Murtaugh and the Pirates may have been making the point in a way the baseball world—including fans—would need to understand it, but the consolidation of integration was for the most part complete, even if there were pockets where race was a fraught issue.

Four years later, 27 percent of the ballplayers on major-league rosters were black. That did not mean, however, that they didn't have to grapple with racial issues, particularly in certain cities. Boston and Philadelphia had especially noxious reputations when it came to race relations. In Boston the catalyst was busing to integrate public schools, overlaid by segregated neighborhoods. In Philadelphia it was the chasm of segregated neighborhoods, overlaid by white political fearmongering about black crime. The racial divisions born of public policies that promoted and enforced institutionalized segregation divided both cities well beyond the 1970s and did not go unnoticed by black ballplayers, even if they themselves—especially if they were star players on their teams, like the Red Sox' Jim Rice or the Phillies' Garry Maddox—were not necessarily mistreated. Neither city was a place that black players wanted to be.

* * *

Notwithstanding that more than a quarter of major-league players in 1975 were African American or black Hispanic, until that year not a single black man had ever managed in the major leagues. Twenty-five years earlier, before Game Two of the 1972 World Series (while being honored for breaking baseball's color barrier), Jackie Robinson expressed vexation that in all the intervening years he had yet to "see a black face managing in baseball." Young black players, both stars and those fighting to stay in the majors, had a generation of black stars to look up to and veteran black players to help guide them on their way. They did not, however, have black mentors on the coaching staff, let alone a black manager, to help them navigate through slumps, competition for playing time, and the various travails of life in the big leagues.

Major League Baseball at the time Jackie Robinson said this had no credible argument for why there were no black managers. It was disingenuous to say that blacks first needed to prove their managerial capability in the minor leagues or by coaching in the majors, since only two black men had ever been given the opportunity to manage a minor-league affiliate of a major-league club. Gene Baker, the mid-1950s Cubs second baseman alongside Ernie Banks, managed one of Pittsburgh's four Class-D clubs in 1961 and one of their four Single-A clubs in 1964, and 1960s Yankees outfielder Hector Lopez managed Washington's Triple-A team in 1969. Neither managed their minor-league team for more than one year. Only 10 black men had coached for a major-league team—former Negro League star Buck O'Neil, the majors' first black coach in 1962, and nine former major leaguers, including Jim Gilliam, who Robinson opined "would make an ideal manager," and Elston Howard. Black major leaguers nearing the ends of their careers in the 1960s were frustrated by their lack of opportunity to even coach in the major leagues, let alone get an opportunity to manage. Maury Wills was explicit in telling the *Phila-delphia Tribune* in 1969, "Darn right I want to manage a big-league club." *New York Times* sports columnist George Vecsey trenchantly ob-served that black players were not given the same opportunities to get into coaching and managing as white players at the end of their careers.

Jackie also thought Frank Robinson should be considered as a major-league manager because he had "managerial experience" in Puerto Rico's winter league. And it was indeed Frank Robinson who in 1975 finally broke through the major leagues' managerial color barrier when the Cleveland Indians, coincidentally the first American League team to inte-grate its roster in 1947, named him their next manager. Kept on the roster as a DH, Frank Robinson was also the first serious player-manager since Cleveland's Lou Boudreau from 1942 to 1950. F. Robby made history not only by being the first black man to manage a big-league team, but also for hitting a home run in his first at-bat in the first inning of the first game he managed. Cleveland won that day. It was mostly downhill from there. In part because of shoulder problems, Robinson started himself in only 37 games. He pinch-hit in 12 others and finished the year with 9 home runs. Although ending up fourth in the AL East, the Indians' 79–80 record was their best since 1968.

Cleveland had a winning record, finishing fourth again, in Robinson's second year as manager. He played in 36 games and hit 3 home runs to bring his career total to 586 before calling it quits as a player at the end of the year. In mid-June 1977, with his team struggling in fifth place, Robin-son suffered the inevitable fate of most managers. He was fired. The Indians were 186–189 during Robinson's tenure, which was probably a little better than they deserved for the talent they had. Third baseman Buddy Bell and right-hander Dennis Eckersley, a rookie in Robinson's first year at the helm, were the two players on the club with their best years still to come. Nearly all the others were former stars or players who would have modest careers.

A little more than a year later, Major League Baseball had its next black manager. He was Larry Doby, who made history following in Jack-ie's 1947 footsteps by integrating the American League that same year. Doby had long hoped for an opportunity to manage in the major leagues. The team he was handed 74 games into the 1978 schedule, however—the

Chicago White Sox—was already facing a lost-cause season, all the more disappointing since they had won 90 games the year before. Their team ERA was third worst in the league. They were outscored by nearly 100 runs. And their only position player to have a better-than-average season was center fielder Chet Lemon. The season ended with the White Sox having lost 90 games, after which Doby was told he would not return for a full season of his own. Already 54, Doby left embittered about not being given the opportunity to show what he could do managing a team he had shaped in spring training. He did not get another chance to manage.

Nearly two years after that, in early August 1980, Maury Wills finally got his much-wanted opportunity with the 1977-expansion Seattle Mariners. A game out of last place the day he took over, the Mariners lost that day to fall into AL West basement, from which they never escaped. They did worse under Wills than under his predecessor, ending up with 103 losses, then won only six of their first 24 games the next year before he was fired. While it is true his team was the worst in the American League, it was widely accepted that Wills was in way over his head as a manager. He paid little attention to the details he should have, made many questionable in-game decisions, and was not respected by his players.

Wills's getting the ax did not leave baseball without a black manager only because Frank Robinson was back in the dugout in 1981 with San Francisco. He managed the Giants for three full seasons and into August 1984 before he was fired a second time. In 1982, however, he came close to becoming the first black manager to lead his club into the postseason. Robinson's Giants made up a deficit of 13½ games on July 30 to enter the final weekend of the season tied with the Dodgers for second, one game behind the Braves. And Los Angeles was in San Francisco for the last three games. They took turns eliminating each other from contention. The 1982 Giants probably should not have been in the NL West race at all, given they surrendered more runs than they scored on their way to an improbable 87 wins.

In six years and 106 games of a seventh in Cleveland and San Francisco, Frank Robinson's record stood at 450 wins and 466 losses managing generally mediocre teams, one of which significantly overachieved to come close to a division title. But despite his availability and proven ability as a major-league manager, Robinson was not hired to manage another team the rest of the 1984 season, or in all of 1985, or '86, or '87.

Neither was any other managerial aspirant who happened to be black. It was not as though opportunities weren't there. Not including the vacancy made available by his being fired, there were 31 managerial changes between when the Giants bid adieu to Robinson and opening day in 1987, the 40th anniversary of Jackie Robinson's breaking the major-league color barrier.

* * *

If Jackie Robinson's 1972 World Series remarks about the absence of black managers were diplomatic to a fault, Dodgers general manager Al Campanis was anything but diplomatic in his cringe-inducing interview with veteran journalist Ted Koppel on the much-watched ABC news program *Nightline* on April 6, 1987. Asked by Koppel why there were no black managers or executives in Major League Baseball, Campanis suggested, first, that black major leaguers had not paid their dues by managing in the minor leagues—which was in fact true for Robinson, Doby, Wills, and any number of first-time managers throughout history—and then, explaining why "it's not prejudice," offered the opinion that black baseball professionals "may not have some of the necessities to be, let's say, a field manager." When Koppel asked for clarification, giving Campanis the opportunity to step back from what he had just said, the Dodgers executive doubled down by resorting to racist stereotypes, saying there were not many black quarterbacks, black pitchers, or black swimmers.

Al Campanis presumably would not have said what he said had the Frank Robinson–managed 1982 Giants won the pennant, or had any black manager led a major-league team to the World Series. The first tentative steps toward Major League Baseball's broad acceptance of black players on major-league rosters happened not only because trailblazers Jackie Robinson and Larry Doby were outstanding players clearly capable of playing with the best white players in baseball, but also because both helped already very good, pennant-competitive teams to the World Series in their first year as a regular—Robinson as a rookie with the 1947 Dodgers, and Doby as still officially a rookie with the 1948 Indians.

Had Robinson and Doby had the high-quality rookie seasons they did for clubs at the bottom of the standings—like the St. Louis Browns, for whom Hank Thompson and Negro League star Willard Brown played for five weeks in 1947—or even in the middle of the pack, their breakthroughs would more likely have been perceived as a sideshow and their excellence more easily dismissed. The pace of integration most likely would have proceeded much more slowly than it did. Remember that in 1952, already five years after Jackie's debut, 10 of the major leagues' 16 teams had yet to have a black player on their roster, and that was despite the Dodgers, Indians, and Giants all having won pennants they might not have without players named Robinson, Campanella, Newcombe, Doby, Paige, Irvin, Mays, and Thompson.

Just as the validation of black players was attributable in large part to trailblazers Robinson and Doby playing on pennant-winning teams in their rookie seasons, the pernicious stereotype trafficked by Campanis on *Nightline* that black baseball professionals "may not have some of the necessities to be, let's say, a field manager" suggested that the validation of black men as managers could only come from what a black manager did with a competitive team. None of baseball's first black managers— Frank Robinson, Doby, and Wills—were given teams with a realistic chance to contend, notwithstanding that Robinson nearly leading his relatively pedestrian 1982 Giants to a division title should have been validation enough. Apparently, it wasn't. Between Robinson becoming baseball's first black manager in 1975 and Campanis's *Nightline* interview, no front office making a managerial change on a club with a realistic chance to contend chose a black man to take charge.

* * *

The Montreal Expos were the one club that might have altered the script. After firing veteran manager Dick Williams in early September 1981 with the club still in contention for first place in the second half of the strike-split season, the Expos considered Felipe Alou as his replacement. A former star player for the Giants and Braves, Alou had both been involved in player development for the Expos and had three years of managerial experience in their minor-league system. He had also just managed Montreal's Triple-A affiliate in Denver to within three games of the American Association's 1981 West Division title. Instead, the Expos chose longtime front-office executive Jim Fanning, despite his never having managed in the majors and not even in the minor leagues since 1963. Alou was still managing for the Expos at the Triple-A level when they were looking to replace Fanning after the 1982 season. Once again he was considered, and once again bypassed—this time in favor of veteran manager Bill Virdon, fired by the Astros the previous summer. Featuring Gary Carter, Andre Dawson, Tim Raines, Tim Wallach, Warren Cromartie, and Steve Rogers among their core regulars, the early 1980s Montreal Expos were a bona fide contender. Many baseball experts considered them underachievers for *not* winning a division title with the talent they had.

Felipe Alou might not have led the Expos to the promised land of a pennant or World Series had he been given the chance, but he would have been the first black manager to have an outstanding team to work with. Like Frank Robinson, Alou sat on the sidelines, in his case continuing to manage Montreal affiliates and helping to develop players for the Expos, while none of the managers hired to take over major-league teams between the Giants firing Robinson in August 1984 and Campanis's remarks on opening day in 1987 were black. The outspoken F. Robby believed that Campanis was accurately reflecting the "ugly prejudice" of front-office executives about black men lacking the skills and ability to be managerial candidates.

The firestorm of criticism provoked by Campanis should have ensured that a black man would soon be managing again in the major leagues. Teams made six midseason managerial changes in 1987. None went to a black man. The 1988 season began with four new managers, including Billy Martin back in New York for a fifth round with George Steinbrenner. None were black. That soon changed when Frank Robinson was hired by the Baltimore Orioles, his old team, to take charge after Cal Ripken Sr. got them off to an 0–6 start. Robinson was unable to stop the losing. The Orioles lost 15 more games to run their season-opening losing streak to 21 before they finally were in the win column. Baltimore ended the season with 107 losses and the franchise's worst record since the St. Louis Browns lost 111 back in 1939. Robinson's Orioles tenure ended 27 games into the 1991 season.

The Orioles were a terrible team in 1988, mediocre at best in 1990, and pretty bad in 1991. In 1989, however, Frank Robinson was voted the American League's Manager of the Year for his club's improving by 33 wins to actually compete for the AL Eastern Division title the very year after they opened the season with just a single win in their first 24 games. The 1989 Orioles in fact held first place every day from the last week of May to the end of August and finished just two games behind the first-place Toronto Blue Jays, managed by a former outfielder who, except for 1970 when he hit 29 homers, drove in 93 runs, and batted .318 for the second-year San Diego Padres, was a marginal major-league player. His name was Clarence Gaston. He was called "Cito." He was also black.

* * *

Replacing Jimy Williams in mid-May 1989, Gaston was the first black manager to be given charge of a team with realistic potential to compete for a championship. Considered one of the premier teams in the AL East, Toronto's 12–24 funk to start the season, sealing Williams's fate, was quite the disappointment given that the Blue Jays had been arguably the best team in their division, if not the entire league, since 1985. The competitive turnaround for the Blue Jays began in 1982, when Bobby Cox became the third manager in the 1977-expansion club's history. Although the Jays had never finished anywhere but last the first five years of their existence, by the time Cox got to Toronto they had the foundation for significant improvement in players like outfielders George Bell, Lloyd Moseby, and Jesse Barfield (still developing in the minor leagues) and pitchers Dave Stieb and Jimmy Key (soon on the fast track to the major leagues).

Under Cox's guiding hand, the Jays worked their way up the standings until their league-best 99 wins put them atop the AL East in 1985. But it was not a runaway race. The Yankees had closed a 9½-game deficit at the beginning of August to 2½ games with 22 remaining when the Jays came into Yankee Stadium for a four-game series in mid-September. The Jays won three of four to leave town with a 4½-game lead and then held off the Yankees again on the final weekend to win the East by two games. The 1985 ALCS gave Cox his first taste of the postseason frustration he would endure so often with the Atlanta Braves. After taking a three-games-to-one lead over Kansas City, Toronto lost the next three and, with them, the chance to bring the World Series to Canada for the first time.

Despite every expectation he would lead the Jays to the World Series the next year, Bobby Cox left Toronto to return to Atlanta as general manager. Barfield led the majors in homers in 1986. The next year, Bell led the majors in total bases, the league in RBIs, and smacked 47 home runs to win the MVP Award. After a pair of subpar seasons, Stieb re-turned to form as one of baseball's elite pitchers in 1988, with a 16–8 record. Relief ace Tom Henke saved 86 games between 1986 and 1988, averaging 1.2 strikeouts an inning. But the Blue Jays did not win the AL East in any of those years, just missing out by two games in 1987 and '88. The Jays had the worst record in baseball when Cito Gaston took command in May 1989. They had the best record in baseball the rest of the way to win the AL East, making Gaston the first black manager whose team finished first. Being wiped out by Oakland in the ALCS kept him from being the first to manage in a World Series.

But not for long. A subsequent series of astute trades and free agent signings made the Toronto Blue Jays the most formidable team in the American League. After falling short by just two games in 1990, they traded Tony Fernandez, a terrific all-around shortstop, and first baseman Fred McGriff, whose 36 homers were tops in the AL in 1989, to San Diego for second baseman Roberto Alomar, a fast-rising star about to begin his fourth big-league season, and outfielder Joe Carter, a durable slugger with 175 home runs in seven years. They acquired speedy and defensively excellent center fielder Devon White from the Angels two years ahead of his free agency. The Jays won their third division title by seven games, but again lost in the ALCS. Being one of baseball's best-capitalized franchises because Toronto is in Canada's most lucrative media market, the Blue Jays were not allowing themselves to be constrained by salary considerations. Figuratively going for broke in 1992, Toronto pulled off major free agent coups by signing Minnesota's star of the 1991 World Series, Jack Morris, and former Yankees star Dave Winfield to be their designated hitter. The next year they replaced Winfield by signing free-agent DH Paul Molitor.

Toronto had the highest payroll in baseball in 1992 and 1993. It paid off handsomely. Alomar became a superstar and Carter a consistent power threat. Morris won 21 in 1992 and Winfield blasted 26 homers. Molitor hit .332 in 1993, second-year right-hander Pat Hentgen won 19, first baseman John Olerud hit .363 to win the batting title, and Duane Ward led the league with 45 saves, striking out 1.35 batters an inning. The Blue Jays won their division both years, went on to win the pennant both years, and won back-to-back World Series, beating Bobby Cox and the Braves in six games in 1992 and the Phillies in six games in 1993. The 1993 World Series was the second in baseball history to end with a walk-off home run. The Jays trailed the Phillies, 6–5, in the bottom of the ninth in Game Six in Toronto. They had two runners on base. Phillies closer Mitch Williams needed two outs to send the series to a Game Seven. Joe Carter blasted a three-run home run to end it all.

The importance of Cito Gaston in baseball history is that he was the first black man to manage a World Series championship team—and he did so in back-to-back seasons. His Blue Jays were the first team to win back-to-back championships since the 1977–1978 Yankees. The canard that black baseball professionals did not have "the necessities to be a field manager" was forever put to rest. What it took, however, was for a black manager to be given charge of a team with a competitive roster.

As the Blue Jays celebrated Carter's championship-winning home run on the infield of Toronto's SkyDome, there were now three other black managers in the major leagues undoubtedly sharing in Gaston's moment of triumph—Hal McRae, named manager of the Royals early in the 1991 season; Felipe Alou, finally given the manager's job in Montreal during the 1992 season; and Dusty Baker, a first-year manager in 1993 whose San Francisco Giants won 103 games only to come up short of Cox's 104-win Braves in the NL West. It would have been quite something had the Giants won the West, derailed the Phillies in the NLCS, and met in Toronto in the World Series. Two black managers matching wits for baseball's ultimate championship. That has yet to happen.

32

BASEBALL'S GREAT DIVIDE

There had always been a Great Divide in Major League Baseball when it came to building and keeping winning ballclubs intact. In the first half of the twentieth century, consistently competitive ballclubs—the Giants, the Yankees, the Cubs, and the Athletics for extended periods—were all very well capitalized. Franchises without their financial wherewithal were rarely competitive, and episodically so for short durations when they were. While the reserve clause bound players to their clubs in perpetuity, it was not uncommon for financially struggling small-market teams to make deals for their better players that included meaningful cash infusions. Branch Rickey's innovation of building a dedicated farm system for the St. Louis Cardinals in the 1920s was to compensate for teams like the Giants and Yankees being able to buy (or trade for) the best minor-league players at a time when minor-league franchises operated independently and made the best deals they could for their players.

But now the context was different. The economics of the industry called Major League Baseball had fundamentally changed, and not just because free agency had kicked off a self-reinforcing escalation of salaries. Franchise income distinguishing "rich" clubs from "poor" no longer relied on owners' individual wealth—inherited, as in the case of Boston's Tom Yawkey, or from profitable businesses such as those of the Yankees' Jacob Ruppert or the Cubs' William Wrigley back in the day—and ballpark revenues from attendance, concessions, and renting out the stadium for other events. Television, an increasingly lucrative revenue stream for baseball since the 1950s, became even more so by the mid-seventies with the advent of cable TV.

Baseball was the perfect programming for cable television, which in the 1970s and 1980s was still in its formative stages as a subscription-based medium trying to build market share against free over-the-air commercial television stations. Commercial networks prioritized news, entertainment, and scripted shows. Cable TV was a niche with vast potential for sports fans wanting to follow as many of their team's games as they could. Radio was nice, but television visuals were even better. And cable networks were willing to pay handsomely for the right to broadcast as many of their games as possible in a schedule that lasted half a year, from spring to fall. That made broadcasting rights for cable a far more lucrative proposition than commercial television for major-league teams. Even though cable TV was in far fewer households, meaning their games would be seen by a much smaller viewing audience, irresistible financial incentives caused teams to migrate an increasing number of their televised games in the 1980s from commercial stations that operated locally to for-pay cable networks. Between 1985 and 1990, local media revenues for major-league teams nearly tripled, from $117 to $342 million.

While revenue from mostly commercial-television contracts that Major League Baseball signed for national broadcasting rights was shared with the players' union and all major-league teams, local media revenue—an ever-increasing share from more lucrative cable television—was jealously guarded by individual teams, especially those in big media markets for whom sharing was not in their vocabulary. The significant difference in media-market size—New York compared to Pittsburgh, for example—resulted in huge broadcast income disparities in an increasingly important revenue stream for major-league clubs. The distinction between rich and poor franchises morphed into one between big-market—as in the size of local television, especially cable TV, audiences—and small-market teams. In the new baseball economy where the best players could command a bidding war for their services when they became free agents, the cable TV monies of big-market clubs provided a significant advantage. Having much less of that income stream in their coffers, small-market teams had a very tough time hanging onto their best players once they became free agents.

It was cable TV that placed the Yankees far ahead of the broadcast revenue pack among major-league franchises. In 1989 MSG Network, already televising New York Knicks basketball and New York Rangers hockey, offered the Yankees a staggering $493.5 million over 12 years for the right to broadcast nearly half their games initially and all but a handful of their games in two years. MSG executives were willing to pay such an exorbitant price because they correctly perceived that cornering the viewer market on Yankees baseball would be a gold mine to attract ever more customers to switch from broadcast to cable television. For George Steinbrenner, the deal was a financial windfall, never mind that very soon fans at home could watch his team only on cable television. Particularly at a time when it was obvious the Yankees were in decline—their victory total had decreased every year since 1985, and in 1989 they would finish 13 games below .500—Steinbrenner was counting on the revenue from the deal to bolster his ability to sign the best free agents in any given year to get the Yankees back to being the best team in baseball.

In January 1976 a new dynamic to baseball revenue streams was introduced when Ted Turner, the mid-30s owner of a fledgling cable network when cable TV was just getting off the ground, purchased the Atlanta Braves for the express purpose of having live original content to anchor his network's programming that would do nothing less than allow him to create and build TBS—Turner Broadcasting System—into a nationwide cable "superstation." It quickly became win-win-win for all parties concerned, two of which were now owned by Turner. It was a win for cable service companies carrying his network, which profited from the rapid and escalating increase in paid subscribers, many of whom did so for year-round sports programming, including hockey, basketball, and now baseball. It was a win for TBS for the increased subscription fees Turner was able to charge the cable companies because of his network's rising national audience share for programming that included a baseball game on any given night or day of the long season, broadcast by verbally deft and engaging announcers describing and commenting on the action viewers were seeing. And it was a win for the Braves because the ubiquity of their games on their owner's nationally distributed cable network soon allowed Turner to claim his Atlanta Braves were "America's Team"—or at least America's baseball team, since the NFL's Dallas Cowboys were the original "America's Team." Turner's boast seemed to bear out in 1991, when the Braves' rise from last place to first in the NL West substantially boosted the interest of fans across the country to follow their games, allowing Turner to raise subscription rates for cable providers carrying TBS. (He also entered celebrity marriage circles in 1991 by becoming Jane Fonda's husband.)

The profitability of Turner's cable superstation put the Braves on the same side of baseball's Great Divide as big media markets like New York, Boston, Chicago, and Los Angeles, even though the city of Atlanta was far smaller. As the owner of both the franchise and the cable network that had exclusive television broadcast rights to his team's games, Turner was in effect subsidizing both. His cable network paid below-market rates for the right to broadcast Braves' games while charging the highest possible price to cable companies in subscription fees to carry his network—money that Turner could then funnel as he saw fit into his baseball business while at the same time not declaring it as baseball income. TBS and the Braves soon had company. The Chicago-based Tribune Company, which had bought the Cubs in 1981, also had a nationwide superstation that broadcast their games on cable far and wide across the nation.

* * *

Ted Turner's dual ownership quite likely saved the Braves for Atlanta. The franchise relocation from Milwaukee that brought Major League Baseball to the Deep South also brought them to the second-least-populated urban area that was home to a big-league ballclub, according to the 1970 US census. Only Cincinnati was a smaller major-league market. (Both Minneapolis and St. Paul had lesser populations than Atlanta, but the Twin Cities combined gave Minnesota's Twins a population base nearly 50 percent larger than Atlanta's to draw from.) The only year the Braves had competed for the pennant was 1969, when they won the first NL West title in baseball's new division alignment, only to be swept by New York's Miracle Mets in the first NLCS. In the six years after that, the Braves were decidedly mediocre and consistently in the bottom tier of major-league teams in attendance. It wasn't as though they didn't have their moments. There was Hank Aaron's pursuit of the Babe's 714 career home runs. The 1973 Braves were baseball's first team with three players hitting 40 homers—second baseman Davey Johnson (43), third baseman Darrell Evans (41), and Aaron (40), who finished the season one short of Ruth and had to wait till the next year to set the new record. Left fielder Ralph Garr won a batting title in 1974 with his third 200-hit season in four years. And knuckleballer Phil Niekro was one of baseball's best pitchers, rarely missing a start.

By the mid-1970s the financially struggling franchise was being shopped for new owners. Amid well-founded rumors in the 1975–1976 off-season that the leading bidder was from Toronto and interested in bringing Major League Baseball there, and knowing that his new cable network, which had been broadcasting Braves games since 1974, could not succeed without summer-long Atlanta Braves baseball broadcasts, Turner wasted no time putting in the winning offer. Turner's acquisition of the Braves coincided with the beginning of free agency, which he quickly exploited by outbidding Steinbrenner for Dodgers ace Andy Messersmith in April 1976 after he won his case to be unleashed from the reserve clause. Later that year, when the first official class of free agents entered the market, Turner signed Giants outfielder Gary Matthews to a five-year deal worth nearly $2 million. Neither player helped lift the Braves out of their competitive funk, because most of the rest of the team was decidedly mediocre.

Neither, for the same reason, could long-established ace Phil Niekro, who clearly was not mediocre. It wasn't his fault he led the league in losses four straight years from 1977 to 1980, twice with 20. The Braves were that bad. In 1979, at 21–20, Niekro had the dubious distinction of being both a 20-game winner and a 20-game loser, a curse visited on only one other pitcher—the White Sox' Wilbur Wood, at 24–20 in 1973—since the Deadball Era. Released by the Braves at the age of 43 after the 1983 season, Niekro signed with the Yankees and won 16 games for them each of the next two years. The ease of throwing his knuckler allowed Phil Niekro to carry on until 1987, when he was 48. He won 318 games in his career, 268 of them with the Braves.

Even though the Braves finished last in each of Turner's first four years as their owner, things were changing for the better—and not just because of the enhanced revenues being brought in from TBS. In 1978 the franchise hired 37-year-old Bobby Cox to be their manager. Although failing to make the grade as a major leaguer in two stints as the Yankees' third baseman in the late 1960s, he had developed an outstanding reputation managing in their minor-league system and was even considered as Ralph Houk's replacement in 1974 before the Yankees decided on Bill Virdon. Cox managed four years in Atlanta before leaving for the challenge of trying to set the 1977-expansion Toronto Blue Jays on a path that didn't mean always finishing last. Only once under Cox did the Braves have a winning record—barely, at 81–80 in 1980—but they were a much better team when he left than when he arrived.

Former Braves catcher Joe Torre was hired to replace Cox in 1982, after five years managing the Mets. Indicative of how his first year would go, Torre's Braves began the season with 11 straight wins, then lost five straight. On July 29 they were the best team in baseball, with a 61–37 record and a comfortable nine-game lead in the NL West. Then they lost 19 of their next 21 games, five of them extra-inning walk-off losses, to lose their grip on first place and fall four games behind the Dodgers on August 18. Fourteen wins in 16 games had them back in first place in early September. They had a losing 13–15 record the rest of the way, just good enough to win the NL West by a game over LA. The Braves clinched the division title on the final day, despite losing, only because the Dodgers also lost their last game. That was the start of a four-game losing streak that included being swept by St. Louis in the NLCS. The Braves' extraordinary roller-coaster season, however, was compelling viewing for cable TV audiences on Turner's nationwide superstation. Within five years, TBS subscribers had doubled, from 20 to 40 million.

It was much the same in 1983, but without the extreme swings in winning and losing. The Braves led the Dodgers by as much as 6½ on August 11, only to go 17–28 the rest of the way, finishing second in the division. Torre's tenure came to an end in 1984, his reputation as a manager hardly enhanced by his team's failure to hold big midsummer leads in 1982 and '83. Five managerial changes over the next six years did not yield a winning record for the Braves. They finished last in the NL West four times. They had the worst record in the National League in 1988, '89, and '90. On cable television, however, the Braves did quite well—at least monetarily speaking for Ted Turner's other business enterprise. TBS helped ensure that Braves star-of-the-1980s center fielder Dale Murphy remained prominent in baseball's public eye no matter how badly his team fared. Murphy led the league twice in RBIs and homers, and was a two-time Most Valuable Player in 1982 and 1983.

* * *

After four years managing in Toronto and having just led the 1985 Blue Jays to their first division title in the AL East, Bobby Cox returned to Atlanta as general manager to take on the assignment of rebuilding a team that had just lost 96 games. The Braves got progressively worse while Cox set about improving their minor-league system, including player development, to build a strong foundation for the future. After successive last-place seasons, with 106 losses in 1988 and 97 in 1989, and with his club on a pace to lose 110 games in mid-June 1990, GM Cox chose to replace Russ Nixon as manager with himself. Although the Braves were a much better club the rest of the year, they still finished with 97 losses and the worst record in Major League Baseball—which made it quite the surprise when he led the Atlanta Braves to the Western Division title—and, moreover, into the World Series—the very next year.

The Braves' winning ways might have come more quickly than he expected, but Bobby Cox knew what he had from having spent the five previous years as general manager—a position he vacated in 1991 to John Schuerholz, formerly GM of the Kansas City Royals. What he knew was that the Braves had a strong group of young players already in Atlanta or soon to be there. When Cox took over as manager in June 1990, the Braves had on their major-league roster right-hander John Smoltz and southpaws Tom Glavine and Steve Avery; middle-infielders Mark Lemke, Jeff Treadway, and Jeff Blauser; and power-hitting outfielders Ron Gant and David Justice. Cox had wrested Smoltz, a top minor-league prospect, from Detroit in August 1987, when the Tigers wanted veteran pitcher Doyle Alexander to help them on their pennant push. The others were signed by the Braves and promoted through their system. Cox had also signed veteran outfielder Lonnie Smith as a free agent in 1988 and traded with the Royals for veteran left-hander Charlie Leibrandt for the 1990 season.

In preparation to set the Braves on an upward trajectory in 1991, new GM Schuerholz was active on the free agent market, signing veterans Rafael Belliard and Terry Pendleton to solidify the left side of the infield; Sid Bream, a left-handed batter, to platoon at first base; and 36-year-old Juan Berenguer to be their ace reliever. Pendleton, Bream, and Berenguer had established big-league pedigrees. Belliard, a throwback to the great-field, no-hit shortstops a generation earlier, had been primarily a role player in Pittsburgh since his rookie year in 1986. Just as the season was about to get underway, Schuerholz traded for Expos outfield reserve Otis Nixon, which proved fortuitous when Justice missed nearly two months because of injury.

It turned out the 1991 Braves' future was right then and there. Historically, major-league teams rising to the top from the bottom or near bottom of the standings spent some number of years getting their footing in the middle of the pack, which is what Cox and Schuerholz likely expected. From 1903, when the first World Series was played, to 1990, only 23 of the 174 pennant-winning teams facing off in the Fall Classic had a losing record the year before. Five times that happened during a war year or the first postwar season because rosters had been depleted by players serving in World Wars I or II. Although the 1967 Red Sox and 1969 Mets famously won pennants after finishing no more than one game out of the cellar the previous year, no team had ever gone from last place to the World Series. In 1991 both the AL-champion Minnesota Twins and NL-champion Atlanta Braves did exactly that. The Braves were unique in being the first club to go from the worst record in their league—in the major leagues, in fact—to the pennant; the 1990 Twins finished last in the AL West, but over in the East, the Yankees—Steinbrenner's Yankees, one of the "rich" teams—were seven games worse than Minnesota.

At the All-Star break in July, the Braves were third in the NL West, 9½ games behind the Dodgers and one game below .500. Their 55–28 record the rest of the way—the best in baseball—was capped by an eight-game winning streak at the end of the season that brought them from two games behind to clinch the pennant with a game remaining. Gant smacked 32 homers and Justice had 21, notwithstanding playing in only 109 games. Nixon swiped 72 bases, second in the league to Montreal's Marquis Grissom, whose 76 steals came in 24 more games than Nixon played. Free agent acquisition Terry Pendleton did more than provide mature leadership on the field and in the clubhouse. Coming in with a .259 batting average and 44 home runs in seven years with St. Louis, where he was more a dependable everyday player than a star, Pendleton's .319 average in 1991 led the league, and he hit 22 home runs. Pendleton was voted the National League MVP.

The blossoming of Atlanta's young pitching staff ultimately made the difference in the pennant race. Glavine, now in his fifth year, had the first of three consecutive 20-win seasons. Avery, in his second year, went from 3–11 and a 5.64 ERA in 1990 to 18–8 and 3.38. Leibrandt won 15 and Smoltz 14. Avery and Smoltz shut down the Pirates—the NL Eastern Division winner with the best record in the majors—without allowing a run in Games Six and Seven in the NLCS to send the Braves to the World Series for the first time since 1958, when they were still in Milwaukee. In one of baseball's most exciting World Series, Smoltz and Twins ace Jack

Morris hooked up in a classic Game Seven, which Minnesota won, 1–0, in 10 innings.

The Braves' repeat performance winning the NL West in 1992 was anticlimactic since their margin of victory was a comfortable eight games. Pendleton and Glavine again had outstanding years. And again Atlanta, this time with the best record in the majors, matched up with Pittsburgh in the NLCS. The battle for the National League pennant again came down to the seventh game. And again, the Braves won—this time by scoring three runs in the bottom of the ninth to overcome a 2–0 Pirates lead. The winning run scored on backup catcher Francisco Cabrera's pinch-hit two-out single to left field with bases loaded, when slow-speed former Pirate Sid Bream, starting from second base, just barely scored ahead of Barry Bonds's throw from the outfield. Also again, they lost in the World Series.

* * *

The Atlanta Braves went on to become a dynasty with one of the most successful—and longest—runs in baseball history. Not so the arguably better Pittsburgh Pirates, whom they beat in both the 1991 and 1992 National League Championship Series. The Braves won 12 more consecutive division titles, including after they were transferred to the NL East in 1994 in a move that made the utmost geographic sense. The Pirates endured a dispiriting two decades-plus of losing seasons. The reason? The Turner-run Braves, with their tie-in to the Turner-run cable superstation TBS, was on one side of baseball's Great Divide—the same side as Steinbrenner's Yankees and their enormously lucrative cable TV contracts. The Pirates were on the other.

When Sid Bream rumbled home with the winning run in the bottom of the ninth of Game Seven in the 1992 NLCS, giving the Atlanta Braves their second straight pennant, it was widely understood also to be the end of an era that never was for Pittsburgh's Pirates. Despite having won three consecutive NL East titles and the talent to plausibly extend that run into the mid-1990s, everyone knew that their best player, Barry Bonds—one of the premier players in all of baseball and just entering the prime of his career—and their best pitcher, right-hander Doug Drabek, were playing their last year in Pittsburgh because they were about to hit the free agent market. Free agency is all about putting a price on talent, skills, and track record, and Bonds's price was definitely not in the Pirates' league.

Notwithstanding Pittsburgh's long, proud, and generally very success-ful baseball history, the Steel City was now the face of major-league cities on the wrong side of the Great Divide that separated those with and those without the financial resources necessary to compete in a free agen-cy market that was made even more expensive by the owners' failed collusion fiasco in the mid-1980s to subvert free agents' leverage on the market. All but one of the 28 major-league teams played in a larger metropolitan area than Pittsburgh; the Pirates did not have the money to pay what the best, most expensive free agents wanted. Right fielder/third baseman Bobby Bonilla, their dangerous clean-up hitter in 1990 and 1991, had already abandoned the Steel City for free-agent money that New York's Mets, but not the Pirates, could afford.

Even worse, teams in lesser-revenue markets, knowing they could not afford the talented players they developed, were becoming more aggres-sive in trading them for players of much less ability in the year before their free agency rather than lose them for nothing. Before the 1992 season started, the Pirates traded John Smiley, their left-handed ace on the cusp of free agency, whose 20–8 record tied for the best in the majors in 1991, to the Twins for pitching prospect Denny Neagle. Various teams have been a poster child for notable achievement prematurely denied because their best players' free agency, or impending free agency, took them away just when the team was on the threshold of potentially signifi-cant accomplishments. The 1990–1992 Pirates, however, were perhaps the best to have been undone by baseball's Great Divide.

The beginning of their promising future came in the wake of two abysmal seasons when the Pirates hired Jim Leyland off Tony LaRussa's White Sox coaching staff to take command at Three Rivers Stadium in 1986. At the end of May they called up top prospect Bonds and in July traded for Bonilla, also a rookie. The next year, Andy Van Slyke was acquired from the Cardinals to play center field and Drabek from the Yankees to improve the pitching, and Smiley was auditioned as a reliev-er. In 1988 Leyland moved Smiley and veteran right-hander Bob Walk from the bullpen to the starting rotation. All the while, the Pirates were getting better. Dealing for Cleveland shortstop Jay Bell in spring training 1989 was final piece of the championship-caliber team being built in Pittsburgh. It all came together in 1990. The Pirates claimed the NL East title with a National League–best 95 wins. Bonds's 33 homers, 114 runs batted in, 52 stolen bases, and .301 batting average and Bonilla's 32 homers and 120 RBIs earned them first and second place in the MVP voting. Drabek led the league with a 22–6 record. In what would become a sad repetition in their Leyland-Bonds era, however, the Pirates lost the NLCS to Cincinnati in six games. Bonds was just 3-for-18, with no extra-base hits.

On the eve of spring training in 1991, team president Carl Barger gave a fiscal realities brief that dampened the afterglow of Pittsburgh's first division title since winning the World Series in 1979. Despite Pittsburgh's setting a new franchise attendance record two years running and becoming the team to beat in the NL East, Barger claimed operating losses in excess of $7 million. Various factors went into those losses, he said, most noteworthy of which was the significant increase in player salaries. Barger identified this as a serious and sobering dilemma for small-market franchises like his. "We have to be realistic," the *Pittsburgh Post-Gazette* quoted him as saying. "There comes a point where economically we might have to reassess our players' salaries."

Barger was speaking as Bonds, Bonilla, and Drabek were going to salary arbitration for the year ahead. Whatever the outcome, all three would be paid substantially more. They were not shy in saying they were underpaid for their level of performance and might reassess their commitment to Pittsburgh once they were eligible for free agency. Drabek was the only one to win his case, but the three of them alone ended up with more than a third of the Pirates' $23,635,000 player payroll in 1991—a 52 percent increase in player salaries from the previous year. Pittsburgh's was now the fifth-highest payroll in the league. This trend, Barger made clear, would be unsustainable in the years ahead. "I think there is an awakening throughout the industry," he said; "the salary escalation will kill the golden goose."

Perhaps the money wasn't worth it from Barger's perspective, but the 1991 Pirates ended up with 98 wins and a 14-game margin of victory in the NL East. Bonds, Bonilla, and Drabek were all worth the money, although Barry again struggled in the NLCS, with just 4 hits in 27 at-bats as Atlanta outlasted Pittsburgh in seven games. Not surprisingly, Bonilla exercised his right to free agency after the season, and Smiley was traded a year before he became eligible. Pittsburgh's 1992 payroll nonetheless rose by 44 percent, to fourth-highest in the league with Bonds, Drabek, and Van Slyke alone accounting for 38 percent of Pittsburgh's $33.9 million in player salaries. Without Bonilla and Smiley, the 1992 Pirates lost hardly a beat in becoming the first National League team since the 1976–1978 Phillies to win three division titles in a row. They did so convincingly, nine games ahead of second-place Montreal, with 96 victories. Bonds had another exceptional year, winning his second MVP Award in three years, but for the third year in a row was a major disappointment in Pittsburgh's NLCS loss, with 6 hits in 23 at-bats.

* * *

Predictably, once the 1992 season was over, both Bonds and Drabek became free agents whose asking price was beyond what the Pirates were willing to pay. The very next year Pittsburgh began a string of 20 years in a row without a winning record that would not end until 2013, an unmatched record of losing futility. Jim Leyland's remaining years as Pirates manager must have seemed like the trials of Job. Without Bonds and Bonilla, Pittsburgh's offense immediately went from one of the most prolific to the least effective in the National League. In the absence of Smiley and Drabek, the Pirates' pitching staff went from one of the best to one of baseball's worst. Indicative of the impact of free agent losses and player trades to cut payroll, the collective player value for the Pirates' roster dropped from an average of 39.8 combined pitching and position player wins above replacement from 1990 to 1992, to 19.8 in 1993, 9.2 in 1994, and 13.5 in 1995. Leyland departed after the 1996 season with a .445 winning percentage in the four years since Bonds and Drabek left.

With a core group of players in their prime the likes of Bonds and Bonilla, Van Slyke and Bell, and Drabek and Smiley, Pittsburgh had been poised to be a power in the National League for some number of years beyond 1992. Only twice before in the twentieth century had any franchise abruptly terminated a run as successful as that of the 1990–1992 Pirates by a deliberate decision to cut payroll. In 1915 Connie Mack dismantled a great team that had won four pennants and three World Series in five years by letting go of his best players as well as numerous prospects soon to be stars. That plunged the Philadelphia Athletics into nearly a decade of terrible last-place ballclubs. He did the same thing beginning in 1933, dismantling a team that had won three straight pennants between 1929 and 1931, whose best players were still in their prime. The Athletics were a mostly very bad team for the rest of their years in Philadelphia. Both times Mack acted because the price of keeping his great team intact was too high. It was strictly about the money.

Mack did so the first time against the backdrop of a biting economic recession and the second time in the midst of the Great Depression.

What happened to the Pirates was Exhibit A, giving credibility to team president Carl Barger's 1991 predictive complaint that escalating salaries resulting from salary arbitration hearings and free agency was making it very difficult, if not impossible, for franchises on Pittsburgh's side of the Great Divide to sustain competitive teams against far better capitalized franchises, like both New York teams and Atlanta, on the other side. According to the *Post-Gazette* article in which Barger said his club could not afford star players like Bonds, Bonilla, Drabek, and Smiley, the Pirates in 1990 were in the bottom third of major-league teams in broadcast revenue, earning just 12 percent of the $50 million the Yankees brought in.

Barger preceded his warning about free agency killing "the golden goose" by saying, "I think there is an awakening throughout the industry" about that judgment. His sentiment was indeed shared by his fellow owners, big and small market alike. But it was disingenuous at best, because there was a Great Divide between clubs like his and franchises owned by the likes of Steinbrenner and Turner, which owed far more to their relative riches than they did to players exercising their hard-won right to ask fair market value for their talent, skills, and—especially since free agency was not granted until they had six years in the big leagues—experience.

The "awakening" Barger was talking about was not an awakening at all as much as the owners' party line dating back to Marvin Miller's negotiating the parameters of free agency after the Messersmith decision, reinforced by the costly two-month 1981 players' strike that ended with the owners' unconditional surrender to the basic principle. Even though small-market teams wanted to restructure the business of Major League Baseball so that franchises with lucrative broadcasting deals would share some of their bounty, the industry's emphasis was on constraining player salaries. All franchises, rich and poor alike, were in lockstep on that, although Steinbrenner was reluctantly so because he viewed being able to outbid every other club for star free agent players to be a tremendous competitive advantage.

In the mid-1980s the owners tried to do something about it, and were humiliated—and paid a heavy monetary price. They were still licking their wounds from "collusion" when Barger so explicitly resurrected the owners' party line that free agency was an existential threat to Major

League Baseball. The game was heading toward a showdown of apoca-
lyptic proportions.

33

FROM COLLUSION TO BUD SELIG'S COUP (AND THE EVE OF DESTRUCTION)

Major League Baseball headed into the 1990s beset by an owner-instigated catalytic event that ultimately precipitated the game's greatest existential crisis since the Black Sox scandal. That event was the owners' conspiracy in two acts to neuter free agency by not signing other teams' star players, the embarrassment and financial consequences of which, when rooted out, opened an even wider chasm of trust than before between them and the players' union.

It all began in vengeance over the outcome of the 1985 negotiations on a new collective bargaining agreement with the players' union. The owners went into the negotiations claiming that the economic health of their industry was very precarious and that escalating salaries were the reason why. Major League Baseball had not turned a profit in six years, they claimed, and in the 1984 season just past all but five of the 26 franchises lost money. It was up to the players to accept that payroll expenses needed to be reined in. The players' union was having none of that, particularly after an in-depth analysis of the owners' financial ledgers revealed that their "losses" were mostly explained by accounting methods covering up their gains and that the baseball industry had in fact made a profit in 1984. That did not stop the owners from demanding the new CBA must include limits on how much clubs above the average major-league payroll could offer free agents—a nonstarter for the union. By now the 1985 season was well underway, and the players were prepared to stage a repeat of the 1981 strike that cost two months of the season.

They were not bluffing. While the owners were quick to back down when the players did indeed go on strike in early August, the players' union, also wanting a quick settlement, agreed to raising the eligibility for salary arbitration from two years to three and to reducing its share of television revenue for pensions. The 1985 players' strike cost just two days of games before the new CBA was reached, with none of the damage from four years earlier.

Ironically, it was baseball's new commissioner, Peter Ueberroth, who ordered the owners to open their books for analysis. A California businessman whose entrepreneurial and public relations savvy made the 1984 Los Angeles Summer Olympics such a financial success despite the absence of the boycotting Soviet Bloc, Ueberroth had just replaced Bowie Kuhn. Ueberroth told the owners it was not up to the players to fix their financial problems. In October 1985, for owners' ears only, he laid out an alternate vision—an ultimatum, really—for how to control payroll without engaging the union. Drawing on conclusions from a report prepared by former American League president Lee MacPhail, son of Larry, whose 1946 MacPhail Report warned that any viable players' union would be a significant threat to Major League Baseball, Ueberroth took the owners to task for the expensive long-term contracts being offered to star players. He told them not to overpay free agents. Ueberroth also said that he wanted, as commissioner, for clubs to justify their free agent spending relative to their teams' financial situation.

With those marching orders, and mistakenly concluding that the players' willingness to give ground on salary arbitration and the pension plan indicated the union's solidarity was broken and that they now had the upper hand, the owners spent the off-season subverting the premise of free agency. They did so in a way that violated a key provision of the 1985 collective bargaining agreement, which explicitly stated that neither side—not the players, not the owners—could act collectively in the free agent market.

None of the top players in the free agent class of 1985 got offers from any but the team they played for that year. Detroit's Kirk Gibson should have been the most coveted player on the market, having just had the best year of his career, with 29 homers, 97 runs batted in, and a .287 batting average. The Tigers were the only club to make him an offer—$4.1 million for three years. Veteran catcher Carlton Fisk, although turning 38 in December, had just set career highs with 37 homers and 107 RBIs for the White Sox—and also received no offer other than from his own club. Both waited in vain for an offer commensurate with their performance and, in 28-year-old Gibson's case, future potential before signing the deal offered by their former club at the last possible moment. Had either waited longer, he would have been ineligible to re-sign with his old team before May if there were still no suitors. The big-name free agents who did change teams—Tommy John, Phil Niekro, and Cesar Cedeno—were all aging veterans whose former teams didn't want them back. It was obvious what was going on. The Major League Baseball Players Association filed a grievance alleging collusion.

It was the same story for the free agent class of 1986. The three most attractive free agents on the market were Detroit right-hander Jack Morris, 21–8 with a 3.27 earned-run average in the year just passed, and Expos outfielders Andre Dawson and Tim Raines. Morris thought he had an agreement to pitch for Minnesota in 1987, only to have the deal nixed by GM Andy MacPhail, the third generation of MacPhail family executives dating back to granddaddy Larry, whose loyalties to the brotherhood of ownership were never in doubt. He re-signed with the Tigers. Raines, the reigning National League batting champion, with a .334 average and (for the second year in a row) 70 steals in 79 attempts, kept waiting for offers. There were none for a 27-year-old very much in his prime with a .306 batting average and 454 stolen bases the last six years. He kept waiting before being forced to re-sign with Montreal in May 1987, having missed the first 21 games of the season because he was not eligible to return to the Expos till then. Dawson took a different—and revealing—tack. Receiving no offers, Dawson proposed signing a blank contract to be filled in by whatever team was interested. The Cubs filled in the blank for $500,000—less than half what he was paid by Montreal in any of the three previous seasons—with up to $200,000 in bonuses. It turned out to be quite the bargain for the Cubs; Dawson blasted 49 homers, drove in 137 runs, and was voted the National League's Most Valuable Player. The MLBPA filed a second collusion grievance.

According to Andrew Zimbalist in his book on baseball economics and policy titled *May the Best Team Win*, free agents' salaries for the class of 1986 grew by only 5 percent and the overwhelming majority received just one-year contracts, all of which was consistent with Ueberroth's October 1985 admonition to the owners. The average salary for the free agent class of 1987 declined 16 percent, again with most contracts

good for no more than one year. In September 1987 baseball's independent arbitrator ruled that the owners had in fact colluded against the
players in the free agent market two years earlier. That put an end to Act
One.

Having been called out on their unwillingness to offer free agent
contracts to another team's players as a way to force them to return to
their former club at much less than they would have commanded on a free
market, the owners responded with a new gambit. Free agents in the
winter of 1987–1988 *did* receive offers from other clubs. What they
didn't know was that the owners were keeping each other informed about
which free agents they wanted to keep or go after and what salaries and
terms they were offering. That was Act Two. This too had the effect of
limiting player movement and suppressing free agent salaries. The top
free agents changing teams—including the Cardinals' Jack Clark signing
with the Yankees, the Indians' Brett Butler signing with the Giants, and
the Giants' Chili Davis signing with the Angels—did so mostly for very
modest increases in salary. Most of the others stayed with the same team.
The players' union filed its third grievance in three years alleging owner
collusion.

In 1988 baseball's arbitrator sided with the players in the second grievance alleging collusion, and in July 1990 ruled the same on the third.
The third ruling called the sharing of information on offers to free agents
"to track just how far they would have to go with particular players" akin
to a "secret buyers' auction." Soon after the 1990 World Series ended, the
owners and the players union reached agreement on the overall financial
penalty for collusion in the three cases. Totaling the damage on estimated
lost salary to the free agents, as well as the cascading effects on their
contracts—including that so many were one-year deals, contrary to the
multiyear contracts free agents had earned in earlier years—the arbitrator
assessed $280 million in damages to be paid by Major League Baseball to
the MLBPA.

In the meantime, baseball had changed commissioners twice. In April
1989 Ueberroth was replaced by National League President Bart Giamatti, a career academician. Getting out before the financial fallout of collusion hit, Ueberroth left with the game more profitable than ever and with
a positive legacy of accomplishments—credit for averting a damaging
players' strike in 1985 and spearheading negotiations for baseball's most
lucrative national television contract yet. In September 1989, just days

after rendering his verdict on Pete Rose and the day after learning that Major League Baseball was ordered to pay $10.5 million in damages to the players harmed in the first round of collusion, the 51-year-old Giamatti died unexpectedly of a heart attack. He was succeeded by his deputy, Fay Vincent, whom Giamatti had hired for his business acumen.

* * *

Slapped down hard and chastened by the arbitrator's ruling on collusion and the assessment of an exorbitant financial penalty, the owners became stronger in their resolve to undo as much of free agency as possible. Half a year after that decision, during spring training 1991, Pirates president Carl Barger underlined the sentiment of most of them by talking about salary escalation because of free agency killing "the golden goose." From the owners' perspective, Vincent wasn't helping by trying to interject himself into the never-ending drama of negotiations between the owners and the players' union. He had in fact become a significant part of the problem.

In 1990 the owners voted to lock players out of spring training to gain leverage in negotiations for a new collective bargaining agreement, the previous one having expired at the beginning of the calendar year. This time they were pushing the players to accept not only a salary cap, which would inherently limit free agents' bargaining power, but a pay-for-performance regime based on a statistical ranking of players *not* eligible for free agency. Once it quickly became clear the union was not budging, and with the owners divided between those wanting to force the players to capitulate and those concerned about the consequences of losing a significant portion of the season, Vincent waded into the morass. He did so at first with the blessing of Milwaukee Brewers owner Bud Selig, whose understated but laser-focused approach made him an ideal congressional-like "whip" to keep his fellow owners on the same page. Much to the chagrin of the majority of the owners, Vincent offered his own set of proposals that became the basis for negotiations. Undercut by their commissioner, the owners ended their spring training lockout after 32 days. Free agency was left mostly unfettered, allowing player salaries to not just continue upward, but skyrocket upward.

Fay Vincent, perhaps basking in the glory of having played a decisive role in averting a baseball shutdown for some period of time in 1990, if not for the entire season, had sown the seeds of his own undoing. He projected himself as a commissioner who stood above the game—an honest broker between players and owners—almost akin to medieval kings ruling by divine right, whose decisions were infallible. His imperious and egocentric approach to being commissioner also led Vincent to missteps on other issues that alienated owners in both leagues. In the summer of 1991, American League owners were outraged about his decision mandating the 14 clubs in their league contribute 42 players, and the existing 12 clubs in the National League only 36, for the expansion draft by two new National League franchises that would begin play in 1993, while receiving just $42 million of the $190 million the new NL franchises would pay Major League Baseball in expansion fees, compared to the $148 million NL clubs would get. Less than a year later, in the winter of 1992, Vincent further upset American League owners by involving himself in the sale of the Seattle Mariners to a group led by the Japanese video game conglomerate Nintendo because he was concerned about bad press should the AL derail its bid because it was a foreign entity.

The next year, Vincent took matters into his own hands after the Cubs, who were within their rights to do so, vetoed a National League realignment plan, to take effect in 1993 with the addition of the new franchises in Miami and Denver, that would have moved Chicago and St. Louis from the East to the Western Division and Atlanta and Cincinnati from the West to the Eastern Division. Using his "in the best interests of baseball" authority, Vincent decreed there would be realignment and the Cubs had no choice. They did have a choice. They sued the commissioner in federal court to block the move. Among those outraged by his decision was Dodgers owner Peter O'Malley, a power broker in the National League, who in fact supported the NL's realignment plan but declared that Vincent's usurping the authority of franchise owners in a league matter—and this *was* a National League matter—was a "dangerous precedent."

And then there was the public embarrassment of his treatment, both dictatorial and demeaning, of Yankees manager Buck Showalter, general manager Gene Michael, and senior team executive Jack Lawn over testimony they gave as character witnesses at the commissioner's hearing in July 1992 on Steve Howe's appeal of a lifetime ban imposed by Vincent for pleading guilty after being arrested in the act of buying illegal drugs. Howe had already been suspended six times for drug abuse in his star-crossed, cocaine-addled career that began as the Dodgers' relief ace in the early 1980s. In 1991, after three years away from the game, the Yankees with Vincent's blessing gave him another chance to make good, and he responded with his best season since 1983, the year before his first drug suspension.

Showalter, Michael, and Lawn, testifying at his hearing before the commissioner, said that in their opinion a lifetime suspension was too harsh for a circumstance like Howe's. Vincent called each of them in separately to tell them they had kissed their baseball careers goodbye by offering an opinion opposed to his at Howe's hearing. Because they were part of Major League Baseball's management structure, and not players, Vincent's view was that they were obligated to support all of Major League Baseball's policies. As such, their testimony, even as character witnesses for Howe, should have been, "Of course the commissioner was right to give a lifetime suspension to Steve Howe, because the commissioner is always right." Vincent was skewered in the press. The union filed a complaint with the National Labor Relations Board charging the commissioner with witness tampering. Baseball's arbitrator warned Vincent that he'd best back off on his threats to Showalter, Michael, and Lawn—which Vincent did. Howe's seventh suspension turned out to be for the rest of the year, not forever. He pitched four more years for the Yankees.

* * *

The damage to Vincent's reputation, already sour inside ownership circles, from the Steve Howe case was severe in the public realm. The commissioner was made to seem to like a tin-pot dictator. And with the next round of negotiations with the players' union due in 1994, there was a groundswell of support among the owners for the proposition that Fay Vincent must not be involved. As perhaps the most influential power broker among owners that belied his franchise—the Milwaukee Brewers—being a small-market team, Bud Selig had a plan. Working assiduously behind the scenes to skillfully build a supermajority of owners to have his back, Selig intended to force Vincent out as commissioner. With the requisite humblebrag that he did not want to be the commissioner of baseball, Selig also intended to take control of the game himself if necessary—and he believed it was—to save the game.

From Selig's perspective, drawn from his experience as an owner and from keeping abreast of what his fellow owners were thinking, saving the game required not only that the players' union be taken on so that free agency would be redefined in terms more acceptable to ownership, but that all of baseball's owners agree on the necessity of a revenue-sharing plan that would help small-market franchises like his. Revenue sharing was a fraught issue for the owners. Those on the "poor" side of Baseball's Great Divide insisted that those on the "rich" side share a portion of their annual riches so that they could better compete. The clubs with impressive annual revenue streams—principally from broadcasting rights in their big-market cities—were not inclined to do so. Selig threaded the needle by arguing that agreeing to a revenue-sharing plan would give the owners much-needed leverage to force the union into accepting a salary cap, which by definition would neuter free agency and stop the escalation of player salaries.

With all pretense of modesty, Selig knew he would be more effective than any commissioner—and certainly more effective than Fay Vincent—in nudging the owners toward a compromise on meaningful revenue sharing and standing fast against the players' union in the upcoming negotiations for the next collective bargaining agreement. Based on his pulling the rug out from under them in the 1990 CBA negotiations, neither Selig nor any other owner wanted Vincent involved this time. White Sox owner Jerry Reinsdorf put it bluntly, saying the owners were going "to war with the union" and wanted a commissioner whose "obligation" would be "only to the owners." He left unsaid that the owners this time had no intention of compromising with the union and did not want a commissioner to force their hand "in the best interests of baseball." Vincent had already proven he was not that commissioner, and he continued to insist that, as commissioner, he must necessarily be involved. Even when he said he would stand firm with the owners, they had no reason to believe he would not double-cross them to prevent a players' strike. Nor were the owners about to trust him in the matter of revenue sharing. Both sides of the Great Divide worried he would impose an agreement that gave either too much or too little to baseball's financially struggling franchises.

To achieve both his ends, Selig needed to control the process, and he needed the powers of the commissioner to do that, even if not explicitly as commissioner. He mounted his coup at an owners' meeting he convened for that very purpose in early September 1992. Vincent threatened to fight the owners in court if they tried to oust him. By then, however, his alienating approach had left him with few owner-allies, although one who was—Texas Rangers principal owner George W. Bush—happened to be son of the president of the United States and had ambitions of being commissioner himself someday. Made to realize his cause was hopeless, Vincent resigned—but not without issuing a knifing statement saying he could not in good conscience, as commissioner of baseball, represent *only* the owners. Selig became acting commissioner. Although there was consensus that Bud Selig could be "acting" for as long as he wanted, the owners formed a committee for the pretense of identifying candidates to assume the office. Rangers owner George Bush gave up on any hopes for his dream job of commissioner of baseball. He began preparing to run for governor of Texas in 1994.

* * *

The National League expanded to 14 teams in 1993, placing the Florida Marlins in the NL East and the Colorado Rockies at altitude in the NL West. Although the American League had been operating with two seven-team divisions since 1977, the NL expansion allowed Major League Baseball to reconsider the now-traditional alignment of two divisions in each league with an eye to involving more teams in pennant races, which would surely benefit the game's bottom line in fan interest and, especially important, television revenues. Beginning in 1994, baseball fans across America would be treated to eight pennant races instead of just four. The new alignment would include three divisions—East, Central, and West—hence, three pennant races for first place in each league, plus a fourth "wild card" race for the best record among the three second-place clubs. Each league's wild card team and the three division champs would pair off in a pair of five-game division series, the winners of which would advance to the seven-game league championship series to decide who played in the World Series.

Something indelible would surely be lost, however—the excitement of two outstanding ball teams with the best records in the league battling to the end of the 162-game schedule to determine which, if they happened to be in the same division, would have the opportunity to play for the pennant and a World Series championship, and which would have to wait till next year to try again. There would not have been the drama of Bucky "F-word" Dent's home run being the capstone of the 1978 Yankees' extraordinary drive to force a playoff in Boston for the AL's Eastern Division title had the wild card been in effect that year, because both would have been assured a role in the postseason regardless of which won the division title. With no incentive for either to fight for first place, their priorities would have been resting core players as needed and lining up the pitching staff to maximize the odds of success in the first five-game round of playoffs. While the wild card team would not have had home-field advantage, they would have gone to a best-of-five division series with the same theoretical chance of winning as any other team making it to the postseason.

If baseball needed any reminder of what was being lost with three divisions and a wild card team, they need have looked only to the 1993 season just ended, when the Atlanta Braves and the San Francisco Giants battled it out for first place in the NL West. It was shades of 1962, when the Dodgers and Giants both finished the regular season with 101 wins, requiring a three-game playoff to decide the pennant winner. With no wild card to fall back on, the Braves engineered one of the great come-backs in baseball history to win Major League Baseball's last traditional pennant race in which the only way to reach the postseason was to finish first, whether in unitary league standings that prevailed until 1969 or in their division since then. Trailing the Giants by nine games on August 11, with 47 remaining, Atlanta stormed to a 36–11 record the rest of the way, beating out San Francisco by a single game. They won 104, the Giants won 103. Philadelphia had the third-best record, with 97 wins. Perhaps weary from their exertion to make it that far, the Braves lost the NLCS to the Phillies in six games.

The Braves had grabbed the best pitcher and Giants the best position player on the free agent market to fortify themselves before the season began. The position player was Barry Bonds, who had just won his sec-ond MVP Award with the Pirates. He signed with the Giants for six years and $43 million. The Yankees, having just endured their fourth consecu-tive losing season for the first time since 1915 and desperate to get back to forever dynasty status, tried to entice him to New York, but not only was Bonds's heart in San Francisco, his demand to be the highest paid player in baseball was too much even for George Steinbrenner. But it was not too much for new Giants owner Peter Magowan, for whom signing a great player having family ties to San Francisco icon Willie Mays was just the thing to reenergize the team he had just saved from being moved to Florida. Barry Bonds did not disappoint. His 46 homers tied for the major-league lead, his 123 runs batted in led the National League, and he batted .336 and got on base in 46 percent of his plate appearances. The Giants went from 90 losses in 1992 to 103 wins the next year. Despite still playing in Candlestick Park, where fans had to endure many cold nights even in the summertime with winds coming off the Bay, attendance soared from 1.5 to 2.6 million.

The pitcher was Greg Maddux, who had just won 20 games and the Cy Young Award for the Cubs. Maddux turned down a better offer from the Yankees to sign for five years and $28 million in Atlanta. He strengthened an already excellent pitching staff that included left-hander Tom Glavine, whose 20 wins in 1991 and '92 helped Atlanta capture the NL West both years; right-hander John Smoltz; and Steve Avery, another lefty. Glavine won 22, Maddux 20, Avery 18, and Smoltz 15 for the 1993 Braves. The pivotal point in Atlanta's season, however, was trading with sixth-place San Diego on July 18 for power-hitting first baseman Fred McGriff, already with 18 home runs. Two days later, batting cleanup in his first game with the Braves, McGriff's two-run homer capped a five-run sixth to erase a 5–0 deficit and help propel his new team to a victory. Paced by his nine homers and 20 RBIs, the Braves won 21 of their first 27 games with McGriff in the lineup. He hit 19 home runs in 68 games for the Braves, of which Atlanta won 51 to win the division. With right fielder David Justice belting 40 homers, second in the league to Bonds, and left fielder Ron Gant hitting 36, the Braves also finished one home run ahead of the Bonds-powered Giants for the team lead in the National League, 169 to 168.

The contract Bonds signed as a free agent with the Giants in December 1992 was the largest ever. Maddux's free agency contract, signed a day later, was the largest ever given to a pitcher. In the very first off-season after Bud Selig's coup ousted Commissioner Vincent, free agents cashed in on contracts totaling more than $365 million. In an equally disturbing development on the escalating-salaries front, the Seattle Mariners signed young superstar outfielder Ken Griffey Jr. to a four-year, $24 million deal. Notwithstanding that his career was off to a terrific start—a .301 batting average, 87 homers, and 344 RBIs in his first four seasons— "The Kid" had only just turned 23. Since Griffey was still two years removed from free agency, the Mariners did not need to give him $6 million a year so early in his career. He was obviously an exceptional player. His new contract was fair market value given his level of performance. If Seattle was willing to pay him that much now—years before free agency—what would The Kid command when he became a free agent at the end of his contract? Reinforcing the point, Griffey celebrated

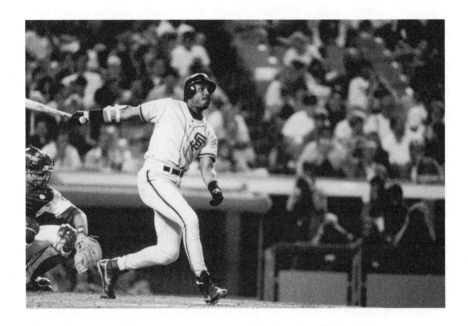

Outfielder Barry Bonds signed a record-setting free-agent contract with San Francisco in 1993, following four extraordinary seasons with Pittsburgh in which he won three Gold Glove Awards and two Most Valuable Player Awards. That small-market teams like the Pirates could not afford a player of his caliber reinforced the determination of baseball's owners to rein in free agency, leading to the 1994 players' strike that shut down a major-league season. © *Photofest.*

his new contract in 1993 by smashing 45 home runs—18 more than his career high from the year before—driving in 109 runs, and batting .309. It was his best year yet—and he was only going to get better.

Selig himself had to swallow his bile when Paul Molitor, the best player on his small-market team and a Milwaukee Brewer for life since his rookie year in 1978, left town as a free agent for the defending World Series–champion Blue Jays with a new three-year, $13 million contract he signed on the same day Bonds became the best-paid player in history. Also leaving as free agents in December were pitching ace Chris Bosio and shortstop Scott Fletcher. Selig's Brewers went from second place and 92 wins with them in 1992 to last place and 93 losses without them in 1993. Selig surely didn't need that to happen to be convinced small-market franchises like his could not compete in an environment without revenue sharing and a cap on player salaries—he had unceremoniously orchestrated the owners' Dump Vincent movement just three just months earlier so he could have a free hand in building an ownership consensus for going to war with the players' union—but it reinforced his point.

The groundwork for that war was laid by baseball's owners in January 1994, after a year of desultory talks with the union that went nowhere. The owners agreed on specifics for revenue sharing. They gave full negotiating authority to the Office of the Commissioner, Bud Selig, Acting. Selig locked them into a game plan of no compromise on a salary cap— his nonnegotiable demand—even if, as expected, the union took its players out on strike. Should negotiations collapse or even just stall, the owners would unilaterally impose their salary cap and revenue-sharing plan on the players. If necessary, they would lock out their players and replace them with minor leaguers. To head off the possibility that rich clubs like the Yankees might be willing to compromise because they could afford to, Selig also secured agreement that any new CBA must be approved by 21 of baseball's 28 owners—a supermajority that meant he would need just eight votes to block any deal not including a salary cap, and there were enough hardliners that eight votes were easy to be had.

Falling into line behind Selig, even those owners most inclined to back down if the players went on an extended strike were persuaded by the acting commissioner's calculation that players, especially those yet to cash in on free agency, had so much to lose in salary—the major-league average was now $1.2 million—they would not stay on strike for long. But that would happen only if ownership ranks stood firm. It would likely be a waiting game. The owners had to call the union's bluff. Predictably, the players' union rejected the owners' proposal. In late July the union set a strike date. Bud Selig was prepared, if necessary, to get his way with the Major League Baseball Players Association by sacrificing a baseball season—if it came to that.

On August 12, 1994, it did.

34

THE DAY THE MUSIC STOPPED

When America (and Canada) awoke on Friday, August 12, 1994, the best record in baseball, at 74–40, belonged to Montreal's Expos, one of the small-market clubs Selig and Major League Baseball singled out as being at a severe financial and, hence, competitive disadvantage in a baseball economy driven by escalating player salaries. Their loss the previous night ended a six-game winning streak and was only their third loss in 23 games. All three of their 27-year-old outfielders—Moises Alou, Marquis Grissom, and Larry Walker—and their 27-year-old closer, John Wetteland, were having outstanding seasons. Pedro Martinez, used almost exclusively in relief by the Dodgers the previous year, was 11–5 as a starting pitcher with the Expos, including 142 strikeouts in 144⅔ innings, and had not given up a run in two starts so far in August. Ken Hill was tied with the Braves' Greg Maddux for the league lead in wins, with 16.

After years of practiced frugality, and with the major leagues' second smallest payroll, the Expos had already made clear they could not afford to keep together their exceptionally talented young team—one that might have been a power in the NL East for years to come—without a fundamental change in the baseball industry's business model and more of baseball's revenue going to Montreal. Walker would be a free agent after the season, and three other core players with salaries already in excess of $1.4 million were contractually due the next year for big increases in pay that the club could ill afford. Having extended their lead to six games over presumptive overwhelming favorite Atlanta, for Montreal it was going to be 1994 with these guys, or never.

Now in the more geographically sensible NL East rather than the NL West, Atlanta was hoping for a fourth consecutive division title. The Braves did not have the financial viability concerns of sustaining a competitive team for the long term. They had an outstanding starting rotation—Maddux, Glavine, Smoltz, and Avery; they had a hearty trio of power bats in the middle of the order—Gant, McGriff, and Justice; they had fresh talent from down on the farm—catcher Javy Lopez and outfielder Ryan Klesko made the Opening Day roster, third baseman Chipper Jones was waiting in the wings, and 17-year-old outfielder Andruw Jones, signed out of the Caribbean island of Curaçao, was beginning his first season at the rookie level in Atlanta's minor-league system; and, as signing Greg Maddux showed, they were prepared to spend liberally on the free agent market if necessary.

Even if, with 114 games down and 48 to go on the 1994 schedule, Atlanta was unable to make up the six games they trailed Montreal, they had the second-best record in the National League and every reason to expect they would still win a postseason slot, courtesy of the wild card, to try for a third pennant in four years. Maddux, already with 16 wins and a superb 1.56 earned-run average that was well more than a run lower than any other qualifying major-league pitcher, seemed destined for a third straight 20-win season. Glavine, with 13 wins, had an outside shot at 20 for a fourth straight year. McGriff, picking up where he left off in 1993, already had 34 home runs—his seventh consecutive year with more than 30—and 94 RBIs in 113 games.

In the AL East, New York's Yankees looked well on their way to returning to the postseason for the first time since 1981. Although stumbling at the moment, having lost five of their last six games and seeing their 10-game lead in the AL East a week ago reduced to 6½ over second-place Baltimore, they had the best record in the American League, at 70–43. A 19–3 run just before their recent struggles put the Yankees in command of the division race. Buck Showalter, in his third year as manager, was surely under few illusions that should the Yankees not hang on to their lead, George Steinbrenner might force him to find alternate employment.

Never really having a shot at Bonds and spurned by Maddux in the free agent class of 1992, the Yankees nonetheless scored big by signing

Boston third baseman Wade Boggs, undeterred by his batting below .300 for the first time in his career at .259 in 1992, and Toronto lefty Jimmy Key, fresh off two wins in the 1992 World Series against Atlanta. The Yankees that winter also traded with Cincinnati for right fielder Paul O'Neill. All three were having outstanding seasons. O'Neill was leading the league in batting, with a .359 average, and Boggs, batting .342, had returned to form. Key's 17 wins (he had only four losses) were the most in the majors. Bernie Williams was in his second year as the Yankees' center fielder, and the Yankees had a future outstanding shortstop (Derek Jeter), catcher (Jorge Posada), left-handed starter (Andy Pettitte), and closing gem in the making (Mariano Rivera) in the minors preparing to join Williams as the foundation for the next iteration of their forever dynasty.

In the American League's new Central Division, Chicago's first-place White Sox were playing their fourth year in a new ballpark, named after franchise founding father Charles Comiskey. While they had won the AL West handily in 1993 on the strength of excellent starting pitching and first baseman Frank Thomas's 41 homers and 128 RBIs, the White Sox could not expect the same for what remained of the 1994 season—assuming the schedule was to be played out—because, after finishing sixth and losing 86 games the previous year in the AL East, Cleveland's Indians were 66–47, just a game behind, and intent on winning it all to celebrate their first year in brand-new Jacobs Field, named after their owner who provided more than half the funding to have it built. Cleveland had arguably the most imposing offense in the major leagues, batting .290 as a team and leading both leagues in runs, hits, doubles, and home runs. Their leadoff batter, Kenny Lofton, was batting .349, and his 60 stolen bases in 72 attempts were the most in the league for the third straight year. Cleanup hitter Albert Belle was playing like a superstar. His .357 batting average was second in the league, and with 36 home runs and 101 RBIs, Belle was well on the way to surpassing his career highs of 38 and 129 the previous year.

Notwithstanding that the 1994 season had shaped up to promise competitive races in September for first place in four of baseball's six divisions, and that the Braves and Orioles might just have what it took to close the gap with the first-place Expos and Yankees in the two other divisions, Major League Baseball in the very first year of the three-

division-plus-wild-card alignment was also facing the likely embarrassment of a ballclub's winning its division with a losing record.

On the morning of August 12, 1994, with 114 games done, the Texas
Rangers, in the midst of a seven-game losing streak, were in first place by
one game over Oakland's Athletics despite being 10 games under .500 at
52–62. They had not been above .500 since they were 31–30 on June 13.
Neither had any other team in the AL West. Oakland last had a winning
record on April 19; third-place Seattle spent six days in first place at the
end of April and four during the month of May but never once had a
winning record; and last-place California had a winning record the first
seven days of the season and again on April 15 before losing became
contagious. With 44 games yet to play, it seemed unlikely the Rangers, or
any other team in the division, would win at least 27 and lose only 17 just
to break even at the top of the AL West. Baseball faced the near-certainty
that the AL West would be won by a team with a losing record and the
possibility, however unlikely, that *that* team might get hot in the postseason, win the division series, win the league championship series, and
(dare we say?) win the World Series. That would have been a catastrophic
beginning to the new wild-card era.

It was player performances, however, that were most riveting as the
1994 season gained momentum. When baseball fans across America
picked up the sports page on Friday, August 12, 1994, and looked at the
leaderboards, they could see Tony Gwynn batting .394—not only far
ahead of everyone else but flirting with a .400 average. The Padres,
however, still had 45 games on their schedule, over which Gwynn would
have to do even better than that to become the first player since Ted
Williams in 1941 to hit .400.

The year 1994 was already very much a hitters' year. Four NL players
and seven in the American League were batting .333 or better. Ten
players—six in the National League—already had 30 homers and were
aiming for 50. Five major leaguers had already driven in at least 100 runs,
four in the American League. Frank Thomas was having a Ted
Williams–like season, with 38 home runs, 101 RBIs, a .353 batting average, and a .487 on-base average. Williams five times and Mantle in 1957
were the only players since World War II to exceed where Thomas was
113 games into 1994 in on-base percentage.

But most compelling was the run that Giants third baseman Matt
Williams was making at the record 61 home runs Roger Maris set 33

years earlier. Williams came into the season having hit at least 33 homers in three of the four years since he became an everyday player for San Francisco in 1990. His 43 through the Giants' first 115 games was exactly the number Maris had through the Yankees' first 115 games in 1961. Like Maris, he was well ahead of Ruth's 38 in 115 games when the Babe hit his 60 in 1927, which became the gold standard for which power hitters aimed. Ken Griffey Jr., with 40 home runs in Seattle's first 112 games, and Jeff Bagwell, with 39 in Houston's first 115, were also ahead of the Babe's 1927 pace, although neither was projected at this time to quite reach 60.

And then there was Cal Ripken's consecutive games streak. Baltimore's shortstop had not only played in every Orioles game since May 30, 1982, he had started all 2,009 of them. He had in fact played every day the Orioles had a game since May 7 of that year, missing only the second game of a doubleheader on May 29. Closing in rapidly on Lou Gehrig's 2,130 consecutive games and fully expecting to reach 2,059 by the end of the year by playing in each of Baltimore's 50 remaining games, Ripken was set to break the record in the 71st game of the 1995 season, barring injury—or the owners deciding, baseball heaven forbid, to replace major leaguers with minor-league replacement players. That was exactly what Acting Commissioner Selig was advocating should the impasse in collective bargaining negotiations lead to a players' strike and, in turn, an owners' lockout. The immortals on baseball's Mount Olympus be damned, the owners were demanding the unconditional surrender of the players when it came to free agency and revenue sharing. The players were united in opposition, even at the cost of Tony Gwynn's aiming for .400 and Matt Williams's having a good shot at 61 and 62.

And so, to borrow from Ernest Thayer's legendary baseball ballad of 1888 (and modernized for a century later), as Americans went about their day on Friday, August 12, 1994:

> Somewhere in this favored land the sun is shining bright,
> Movies are playing somewhere, and somewhere hearts are light;
> And somewhere adults are shouting, and somewhere children laugh,
> But there is no joy in Baseball—*The Mighty Game's on Strike.*

BIBLIOGRAPHY

STATISTICAL SOURCES

This book would not have been possible without the indispensable website baseball-reference.com, which buttresses the traditional record of annual player and team statistics with multiple data aggregations, including batter and pitcher splits. Baseball-reference.com includes game logs featuring the starting lineups, box score, and complete play-by-play for nearly every game played in the years covered by this book, as well as day-to-day standings, teams' minor-league affiliates and their rosters, player transactions, attendance, and (for the years available) player payroll. This book uses the baseball-reference.com version of wins above replacement, an advanced metric developed to measure the totality of a player's performance in terms of how many additional wins that player contributed to his team over what a replacement player from the highest minor-league level would have contributed instead.

RECOMMENDED READING

Books

Adelman, Tom. *Black and Blue: Sandy Koufax, the Robinson Boys, and the World Series That Stunned America*. New York: Back Bay Books, 2006.
———. *The Long Ball: The Summer of '75—Spaceman, Catfish, Charlie Hustle, and the Greatest World Series Ever Played*. New York: Back Bay Books, 2003.

Allen, Dick, with Tim Whitaker. *Crash! The Life and Times of Dick Allen*. New York: Houghton Mifflin, 1988.

Appel, Marty. *Casey Stengel: Baseball's Greatest Character*. New York: Anchor Sports, 2017.

———. *Pinstripe Empire: The New York Yankees from before the Babe to after the Boss*. New York: Bloomsbury, 2012.

Armour, Mark L., and Daniel R. Levitt. *Paths to Glory: How Great Baseball Teams Got That Way*. Washington, DC: Brassey's, 2003.

Barber, Red. *1947: When All Hell Broke Loose in Baseball*. New York: Da Capo Press, 1982.

Barra, Alan. *Mickey and Willie: Mantle and Mays, the Parallel Lives of Baseball's Golden Age*. New York: Three Rivers Press, 2013.

———. *Yogi Berra: Eternal Yankee*. New York: Norton, 2009.

Bjarkman, Peter C. *Cuba's Baseball Defectors: The Inside Story*. Lanham, MD: Rowman & Littlefield, 2016.

Bjarkman, Peter C., ed. *Encyclopedia of Major League Baseball Team Histories: American League*. Westport, CT: Meckler, 1991.

———. *Encyclopedia of Major League Baseball Team Histories: National League*. Westport, CT: Meckler, 1991.

Bondy, Filip. *The Pine Tar Game: The Kansas City Royals, The New York Yankees, and Baseball's Most Absurd and Entertaining Controversy*. New York: Scribner, 2015.

Bouton, Jim, with Leonard Shecter. *Ball Four: My Life and Hard Times Throwing the Knuckleball in the Big Leagues*. New York: World Publishing, 1970.

Bradley, Ben Jr. *The Kid: The Immortal Life of Ted Williams*. New York: Little, Brown, 2013.

Bradley, Richard. *The Greatest Game: The Yankees, the Red Sox, and the Playoff of '78*. New York: Free Press, 2008.

Breton, Marcos, and Jose Luis Villegas. *Away Games: The Life and Times of a Latin Ball Player*. New York: Simon & Schuster, 1999.

Brioso, Cesar. *Havana Hardball: Spring Training, Jackie Robinson, and the Cuban League*. Gainesville: University Press of Florida, 2015.

Bryant, Howard. *Juicing the Game: Drugs, Power, and the Fight for the Soul of Major League Baseball*. New York: Plume, 2006.

———. *The Last Hero: A Life of Henry Aaron*. New York: Anchor Books, 2011.

———. *Shut Out: A Story of Race and Baseball in Boston*. Boston: Beacon Press, 2002.

Burk, Robert F. *Marvin Miller: Baseball Revolutionary*. Urbana: University of Illinois Press, 2015.

Caruso, Gary. *The Braves Encyclopedia*. Philadelphia: Temple University Press, 1995.

Cohen, Stanley. *Dodgers! The First 100 Years*. New York: Birch Lane, 1990.

Cramer, Richard Ben. *Joe DiMaggio: The Hero's Life*. New York: Simon & Schuster, 2000.

Creamer, Robert W. *Stengel: His Life and Times*. New York: Simon & Schuster, 1984.

D'Antonio, Michael. *Forever Blue: The True Story of Walter O'Malley, Baseball's Most Controversial Owner, and the Dodgers of Brooklyn and Los Angeles*. New York: Riverhead Books, 2009.

Dickson, Paul. *Bill Veeck: Baseball's Greatest Maverick*. New York: Walker Publishing, 2012.

Durocher, Leo. *Nice Guys Finish Last*. New York: Pocket Books, 1976.

Eisenberg, John. *From 33rd Street to Camden Yards: An Oral History of the Baltimore Orioles*. Chicago: Contemporary Books, 2001.

Fetter, Henry D. *Taking on the Yankees: Winning and Losing in the Business of Baseball*. New York: Norton, 2003.

Florio, John, and Ouisie Shapiro. *One Nation under Baseball: How the 1960s Collided with the National Pastime*. Lincoln: University of Nebraska Press, 2017.

Frommer, Harvey. *New York City Baseball: The Last Golden Age, 1947–1957*. Lanham, MD: Taylor Trade, 2013.

Frost, Mark. *Game Six: Cincinnati, Boston, and the 1975 World Series—The Triumph of America's Pastime*. New York: Hyperion, 2009.

Fussman, Cal. *After Jackie: Pride, Prejudice, and Baseball's Forgotten Heroes*. New York: ESPN Books, 2007.

Goldman, Steven, ed. *It Ain't Over 'Til It's Over: The Baseball Prospectus Pennant Race Book*. New York: Basic Books, 2007.

Golenbock, Peter. *Wild, High and Tight: The Life and Death of Billy Martin*. New York: St. Martin's Press, 1994.

Green, G. Michael, and Roger Launius. *Charlie Finley: The Outrageous Story of Baseball's Super Showman*. New York: Walker, 2010.

Halberstam, David. *October 1964*. New York: Villard Books, 1994.

———. *Summer of '49*. New York: HarperCollins, 1989.

———. *The Teammates: A Portrait of a Friendship*. New York: Hyperion, 2003.

Helyar, John. *The Lords of the Realm: The Real History of Baseball*. Rev. Ed. New York: Ballantine Books, 1994.

Hensler, Paul. *The New Boys of Summer: Baseball's Radical Transformation in the Late Sixties*. Lanham, MD: Rowman & Littlefield, 2017.

Hirsch, James S. *Willie Mays: The Life, The Legend*. New York: Scribner, 2010.

Humphreys, Michael A. *Wizardry: Baseball's All-Time Greatest Fielders Revealed*. New York: Oxford University Press, 2011.

Jaffe, Chris. *Evaluating Baseball's Managers: A History and Analysis of Performance in the Major Leagues, 1876–2008*. Jefferson, NC: McFarland, 2010.

James, Bill. *The Bill James Guide to Baseball Managers from 1870 to Today*. New York: Scribner, 1997.

———. *The New Bill James Historical Baseball Abstract*. New York: Free Press, 2001.

———. *Whatever Happened to the Hall of Fame? Baseball, Cooperstown, and the Politics of Glory*. New York: Fireside, 1995.

Jordan, David M. *The Athletics of Philadelphia: Connie Mack's White Elephants, 1901–1954*. Jefferson, NC: McFarland, 1999.

———. *Occasional Glory: The History of the Philadelphia Phillies*. Jefferson, NC: McFarland, 2002.

Kaese, Harold. *The Boston Braves, 1871–1953*. Boston: Northeastern University Press, 2004.

Kahn, Roger. *The Boys of Summer*. New York: Harper & Row, 1971.

———. *The Era, 1947–1957: When the Yankees, the Giants, and the Dodgers Ruled the World*. Lincoln: University of Nebraska Press, 1993.

———. *Memories of Summer: When Baseball Was an Art, and Writing about It a Game*. New York: Hyperion, 1997.

Kashutus, William C. *Almost a Dynasty: The Rise and Fall of the 1980 Phillies*. Philadelphia: University of Pennsylvania Press, 2008.

———. *September Swoon: Richie Allen, the '64 Phillies, and Integration*. University Park: Pennsylvania State University Press, 2004.

Keri, Jonah. *Up, Up & Away: The Kid, The Hawk, Rock, Vladi, Pedro, Le Grand Orange, Youppi!, the Crazy Business of Baseball, & the Ill-Fated but Unforgettable Montreal Expos*. Toronto: Vintage Canada, 2015.

Koppett, Leonard. *Koppett's Concise History of Major League Baseball*. Philadelphia: Temple University Press, 1998.

Leavengood, Ted. *Clark Griffith: The Old Fox of Washington Baseball*. Jefferson, NC: McFarland, 2011.

Leavy, Jane. *The Last Boy: Mickey Mantle and the End of America's Childhood*. New York: HarperCollins, 2010.

Levy, Alan H. *Joe McCarthy: Architect of the Yankee Dynasty*. Jefferson, NC: McFarland, 2005.

Lowenfish, Lee. *Branch Rickey: Baseball's Ferocious Gentleman*. Lincoln: University of Nebraska Press, 2007.

Macht, Norman L. *Connie Mack and the Early Days of Baseball*. Lincoln: University of Nebraska Press, 2007.

———. *The Grand Old Man of Baseball: Connie Mack in His Final Years, 1932–1956*. Lincoln: University of Nebraska Press, 2015.

Madden, Bill. *1954: The Year Willie Mays and the First Generation of Black Superstars Changed Major League Baseball Forever*. Boston: Da Capo Press, 2014.

———. *Steinbrenner: The Last Lion in Baseball*. New York: Harper, 2010.

Madden, Bill, and Moss Klein. *Damned Yankees: A No-Holds-Barred Account of Life with "Boss" Steinbrenner*. New York: Warner Books, 1990.

Maraniss, David. *Clemente: The Passion and Grace of Baseball's Last Hero*. New York: Simon & Schuster, 2006.

Marshall, William. *Baseball's Pivotal Era, 1945–1951*. Lexington: University Press of Kentucky, 1999.

Miller, Marvin. *A Whole Different Ball Game: The Inside Story of Baseball's New Deal*. New York: Fireside, 1991.

Montville, Leigh. *Ted Williams: The Biography of an American Hero*. New York: Anchor Books, 2004.

Nathanson, Mitchell. *The Fall of the 1977 Phillies: How a Baseball Team's Collapse Sank a City's Spirit*. Jefferson, NC: McFarland, 2008.

Neyer, Rob, and Eddie Epstein. *Baseball Dynasties: The Greatest Teams of All Time*. New York: Norton, 2000.

Nowlin, Bill. *Tom Yawkey: Patriarch of the Boston Red Sox*. Lincoln: University of Nebraska Press, 2018.

Okrent, Daniel. *Nine Innings: The Anatomy of a Baseball Game*. New York: Houghton Mifflin, 1994.

Paper, Lew. *Perfect: Don Larsen's Miraculous World Series Game and the Men Who Made It Happen*. New York: New American Library, 2009.

Pappu, Sridhar. *The Year of the Pitcher: Bob Gibson, Denny McLain, and the End of Baseball's Golden Age*. New York: Houghton Mifflin Harcourt, 2017.

Pearlman, Jeff. *The Bad Guys Won: A Season of Brawling, Boozing, Bimbo Chasing, and Championship Baseball with Straw, Doc, Mookie, Nails, the Kid, and the Rest of the 1986 Mets, the Rowdiest Team Ever to Put on a New York Uniform, and Maybe the Best*. New York: HarperCollins, 2004.

Pennington, Bill. *Billy Martin: Baseball's Flawed Genius*. New York: Houghton Mifflin Harcourt, 2015.

Pessah, Jon. *The Game: Inside the Secret World of Major League Baseball's Power Brokers*. New York: Back Bay Books, 2015.

Pluto, Terry. *The Curse of Rocky Colavito: A Loving Look at a Thirty-Year Slump*. New York: Simon & Schuster, 1994.

Prager, Joshua. *The Echoing Green: The Untold Story of Bobby Thomson, Ralph Branca, and the Shot Heard Round the World*. New York: Vintage Books, 2006.

Proctor, Mel. *The Little General: Gene Mauch—A Baseball Life*. Indianapolis: Blue River Press, 2015.

Rains, Rob. *The St. Louis Cardinals: The 100th Anniversary History, 1892–1992*. New York: St. Martin's Press, 1992.

Rampersad, Arnold. *Jackie Robinson: A Biography*. New York: Ballantine Books, 1997.

Reisler, Jim. *The Best Game Ever: Pirates vs. Yankees, October 13, 1960*. Cambridge, MA: Da Capo Press, 2007.

Rhoden, William C. *$40 Million Slaves: The Rise, Fall, and Redemption of the Black Athlete*. New York: Three Rivers Press, 2006.

Ruck, Rob. *Raceball: How the Major Leagues Colorized the Black and Latin Game*. Boston: Beacon Press, 2011.

Shapiro, Michael. *Bottom of the Ninth: Branch Rickey, Casey Stengel, and the Daring Scheme to Save Baseball from Itself*. New York: Times Books, 2009.

———. *The Last Good Season: Brooklyn, the Dodgers, and Their Last Good Season Together*. New York: Doubleday, 2003.

Skirboll, Aaron. *The Pittsburgh Cocaine Seven: How a Ragtag Group of Fans Took the Fall for Major League Baseball*. Chicago: Chicago Review Press, 2010.

Snyder, Brad. *A Well-Paid Slave: Curt Flood's Fight for Free Agency in Professional Sports*. New York: Viking, 2006.

Soderholm-Difatte, Bryan. *The Golden Era of Major League Baseball: A Time of Transition and Integration*. Lanham, MD: Rowman & Littlefield, 2015.

Swaine, Rick. *The Black Stars Who Made Baseball Whole: The Jackie Robinson Generation in the Major Leagues*. Jefferson, NC: McFarland, 2006.

———. *The Integration of Major League Baseball: A Team by Team History*. Jefferson, NC: McFarland, 2009.

Thorn, John, and John Holway. *The Pitcher: The Ultimate Compendium of Pitching Lore*. New York: Prentice Hall, 1987.

Tygiel, Jules. *Baseball's Great Experiment: Jackie Robinson and His Legacy*. New York: Oxford University Press, 1983.

Vecsey, George. *Baseball: A History of America's Favorite Game*. New York: Modern Library, 2000.

———. *Stan Musial: An American Life*. New York: Ballantine Books, 2011.

Weaver, Earl, with Terry Pluto. *Weaver on Strategy: A Guide for Armchair Managers by Baseball's Master Tactician*. Rev. Ed. Dulles, VA: Potomac Books, 2002.

Wendel, Tim. *Down to the Last Pitch: How the Minnesota Twins and the Atlanta Braves Gave Us the Best World Series of All Time*. Boston: Da Capo Press, 2014.

White, Bill, with Gordon Dillow. *Uppity: My Untold Story about the Games People Play*. New York: Grand Central, 2011.

Zimbalist, Andrew. *May the Best Team Win: Baseball Economics and Public Policy*. Washington, DC: Brookings Institution, 2003.

Articles from Society for American Baseball Research Publications

Abrams, Roger I. "Arbitrator Seitz Sets the Players Free." *Baseball Research Journal* (fall 2009).

Alito, Samuel A. Jr. "The Origin of the Baseball Antitrust Exemption." *Baseball Research Journal* (fall 2009).

Bonnes, John. "The Minnesota Twins Story." *National Pastime (Baseball in the North Star State)* (summer 2012).

Boren, Stephen D., and Eric Thompson. "The Colt .45's and the 1961 Expansion Draft." *National Pastime (Houston Since 1961)* (summer 2014).

Cronin, John. "The Historical Evolution of the Designated Hitter Rule." *Baseball Research Journal* (fall 2016).

Haupert, Michael. "Marvin Miller and the Birth of the MLBPA." *Baseball Research Journal* (spring 2017).

Hennessy, Kevin. "Calvin Griffith: The Ups and Downs of the Last Family-Owned Baseball Team." *National Pastime (Baseball in the North Star State)* (summer 2012).

Hirsch, Paul. "Walter O'Malley Was Right." *National Pastime (Baseball in Southern California)* (summer 2011).

Kinlaw, Francis. "The Franchise Transfer That Fostered a Broadcasting Revolution." *National Pastime (Baseball in the Peach State)* (2010).

McCue, Andy, and Eric Thompson. "Mis-Management 101: The American League Expansion for 1961." *National Pastime (Baseball in Southern California)* (summer 2011).

Soderholm-Difatte, Bryan. "The '67 White Sox: 'Hitless' Destiny's Grandchild?" *National Pastime (Baseball in Chicago)* (summer 2015).

———. "1977: When Earl Weaver Became Earl Weaver," *Baseball Research Journal* (fall 2011).

———. "Beyond Bunning and Short Rest: An Analysis of Managerial Decisions That Led to the Phillies' Epic Collapse of 1964." *Baseball Research Journal* (fall 2010).

Thornley, Stew. "Twin City Ballparks of the 20th Century and Beyond. *National Pastime (Baseball in the North Star State)* (summer 2012).

Warrington, Robert D. "Departure without Dignity: The Athletics Leave Philadelphia." *Baseball Research Journal* (fall 2010).

Selected Articles from Other Publications

Jaffe, Jay. "The Hall of Fame is Incomplete without Marvin Miller." *Sports Illustrated*, November 16, 2017.

Keith, Larry. "After the Free-for-All was Over." *Sports Illustrated*, December 13, 1976.

Wulf, Steve. "All My Padres." *Sports Illustrated*, April 5, 1989.

Zirin, Dave. "25 Years Since Al Campanis Shocked Baseball: What's Changed and What Hasn't." *Nation*, April 16, 2012.

Sports Illustrated's annual preseason previews were a valuable source of information.

Websites

Bedingfield, Gary. Baseball's Greatest Sacrifice ("dedicated to all baseball players who lost their lives while serving with the armed forces."), baseballsgreatestsacrifice.com.

Clem, Andrew. Clem's Baseball: Our National Pastime and Its Green Cathedrals, andrewclem.com/Baseball.php.

Major League Baseball Players Association, mlbplayers.com.

Selected Posts of Note in Baseball and Sports Blogs

Baseball Almanac. "The Strike Zone: A History of Official Strike Zone Rules," baseball-almanac.com/articles/strike_zone_rules_history.shtml.

Blickenstaff, Brian. "Baseball's Forgotten Brotherhood, The First Athlete Union in American Pro Sports," October 20, 2016, sports.vice.com/en_us/article/d7mdxm/baseballs-forgotten-brotherhood-the-first-athlete-union-in-american-pro-sports.

Caple, Jim. "The Night Wrigley Field Lit Up." ESPN, August 8, 2013, espn.com/mlb/story/_/id/9547756/wrigley-field-first-night-game-25-years-ago.

Friend, Harold. "Keith Hernandez Used Cocaine and Was Forced to Name Others." *Bleacher Report*, February 17, 2010, bleacherreport.com/articles/1070283-keith-hernandez-used-cocaine-and-was-forced-to-name-others.

Heuer, Ben. "The Boys of Winter: How Marvin Miller, Andy Messersmith and Dave McNally Brought Down Baseball's Historic Reserve System." Berkeley Law, University of California/Sports Stories, 2018, law.berkeley.edu/sugarman/Sports_Stories_Messersmith_McNally_Arbitration.pdf.

Markusen, Bruce. "Cooperstown Confidential: Baseball and Vietnam." *Hardball Times*, September 17, 2010, tht.fangraphs.com/cooperstown-confidential-baseball-and-vietnam/.

Posnanski, Joe. "Save Evolves from Stat to Game-Changer." MLB.com, April 13, 2017, mlb.com/news/how-save-rule-has-changed-baseball/c-223677902.

Resar, George. "The Height of the Hill." *Hardball Times*, June 27, 2014, tht.fangraphs.com/the-height-of-the-hill/.

Spence, Blaine. "From Unhittable to Homeless: The J.R. Richard Story." *Bleacher Report*, June 14, 2009, bleacherreport.com/articles/217945-from-unhittable-to-homeless-the-jr-richard-story.

Thorn, John. "Baseball and the Armed Services, Part 3." *Our Game*, July 3, 2016, ourgame.mlblogs.com/baseball-and-the-armed-services-part-three-1276ec524c89.

Walker, Rhiannon. "Jackie Robinson's Last Stand: To See Blacks Break into the MLB Managerial Ranks." *Undefeated*, April 13, 2018, theundefeated.com/features/jackie-robinson-last-stand-to-see-blacks-break-into-the-mlb-managerial-ranks/.

Other Important Sources

Curt Flood's letter of December 24, 1969, to Commissioner Bowie Kuhn and Kuhn's reply to Flood on December 30, 1969, are on the National Archives website, catalogue.archives.gov/id/278312 and catalogue.archives.gov/id/278313.

The MacPhail Report, formally *The Report for Submission to National and American Leagues on 27 August 1946*, is archived at the University of Kentucky Libraries, Box 162, A.B. Chandler Papers, Special Collections Research Center.

United States Supreme Court. *Federal Club v National League, 1922*. No. 204. Decided May 29, 1922. Complete text in caselaw.findlaw.com/us-supreme-court.

United States Supreme Court. *Flood v Kuhn (1972)*. No. 71-32. Decided June 19, 1972. Complete text in caselaw.findlaw.com/us-supreme-court.

United States Supreme Court. *Toolson v New York Yankees, 1953*. No. 18. Decided November 9, 1953. Complete text in caselaw.findlaw.com/us-supreme-court.

Population data is drawn from US Census Bureau statistics on the 100 largest urban places in America by decade, which can be found on the website census.gov/population. Official Selective Service System (SSS) information on the number of draftees by year is from the website sss.gov/about/history-and-records/induction-statistics.

INDEX

ABOUT THE AUTHOR

Bryan Soderholm-Difatte is the author of *America's Game: A History of Major League Baseball through World War II* (Rowman & Littlefield, 2018) and *The Golden Era of Major League Baseball: A Time of Transition and Integration* (Rowman & Littlefield, 2015). He is a former senior analyst for the Central Intelligence Agency and the National Counterterrorism Center and lives in Arlington, Virginia.